G000092541

A History of Women's

A *History of Women's Writing in Italy* offers a comprehensive
historical account of writing by women in Italy. Covering
writing from the Middle Ages to the present day, it moves away
from narrow definitions of literature, and brings to the reader's
attention other forms of expression such as letter writing,
religious and devotional writing, scholarly and philosophical
essays, travel writing and journalism. Contributors point to the
considerable practical, social and ideological difficulties faced by
women in writing and presenting their work to a wider reading
public, but also highlight the resourcefulness and
determination of women through the centuries in making their
voices heard. Extensive guides to further reading and a detailed
guide to more than two hundred writers form an integral part of
the volume. The international team of contributors have
produced a striking work of new scholarship and research,
which will be invaluable for students and scholars alike.

LETIZIA PANIZZA is currently Research Fellow in Italian at
Royal Holloway College, University of London. She is a
contributor to *The Cambridge History of Italian Literature* (1996). She
has published widely on Italian humanism and intellectual
history of the fifteenth century, and in Women's Studies she has
published a critical edition of Arcangela Tarabotti's *Che le donne
siano della spezie degli uomini* (*Women are no less rational than men*)
(1994). She is also the translator and editor of Tarabotti's *Paternal
Tyranny* (2001), and the editor of *Women in Italian Renaissance
Culture and Society* (2000).

SHARON WOOD is Professor of Italian at Leicester University.
She has specialised in the study of modern and contemporary
narrative, with particular reference to women's writing. She is
the author of *Woman as Object: Language and Gender In the Work of
Alberto Moravia* (1990) and *Italian Women's Writing 1860–1994* (1995).
In 1993 she published a critical anthology of short stories called
Italian Women Writers.

A History of
Women's Writing in
Italy

Edited by
LETIZIA PANIZZA
Royal Holloway College, University of London

and

SHARON WOOD
University of Strathclyde

CAMBRIDGE UNIVERSITY PRESS
Cambridge, New York, Melbourne, Madrid, Cape Town,
Singapore, São Paulo, Delhi, Tokyo, Mexico City

Cambridge University Press
The Edinburgh Building, Cambridge CB2 8RU, UK

Published in the United States of America by Cambridge University Press, New York

www.cambridge.org
Information on this title: www.cambridge.org/9780521578134

© Cambridge University Press 2000

This publication is in copyright. Subject to statutory exception
and to the provisions of relevant collective licensing agreements,
no reproduction of any part may take place without the written
permission of Cambridge University Press.

First published 2000

A catalogue record for this publication is available from the British Library

Library of Congress Cataloguing in Publication data

The Cambridge history of women's writing in Italy / edited by Letizia Panizza and
Sharon Wood
    p. cm.
    Includes bibliographical references.
    ISBN 0 521 57088 3 (hardback) ISBN 0 521 57813 2 (paperback)
    1. Italian literature – Women authors – History and criticism. 2. Women and
literature – Italy – History. 3. Women – Italy – Intellectual life. I. Panizza, Letizia. II.
Wood, Sharon

PQ4055.W6C36 2000
850.9'9287–dc21   00-037914

ISBN 978-0-521-57088-6 Hardback
ISBN 978-0-521-57813-4 Paperback

Cambridge University Press has no responsibility for the persistence or
accuracy of URLs for external or third-party internet websites referred to in
this publication, and does not guarantee that any content on such websites is,
or will remain, accurate or appropriate. Information regarding prices, travel
timetables, and other factual information given in this work is correct at
the time of first printing but Cambridge University Press does not guarantee
the accuracy of such information thereafter.

Contents

Notes on contributors

JUDITH BRYCE

Professor of Italian at the University of Bristol. Author of *Cosimo Bartoli (1503–1572): The Career of a Florentine Polymath* (Geneva, 1983). Articles on Italian writers from Ariosto and Verga to Calvino and Maraini, and principally on Renaissance Florence. Currently working on women's literacy and women's writing in later fifteenth-century Florence.

ANN HALLAMORE CAESAR

Professor of Italian at the University of Warwick. Co-editor with M. Caesar of *The Quality of Light: Modern Italian Short Stories* (London, 1993). Author of *Characters and Authors in Luigi Pirandello* (Oxford, 1998), and articles on women's writing. Currently working on the evolution of the novel and its relationship to conduct literature in nineteenth-century Italy.

ADRIANA CHEMELLO

Teaches at the Institute of Italian Philology and Letters, University of Padua. Critical edition of Moderata Fonte, *Il merito delle donne* (Mirano–Venice, 1988). Joint editor with Marina Zancan of *Nel cerchio della luna* (Venice, 1983); and with A. Arslan and G. Pizzamiglio of *Le stanze ritrovate. Antologia di scrittrici venete* (Mirano–Venice, 1991). Editor of *Alla lettera: Teorie e pratiche epistolari dai Greci al Novecento* (Milan, 1998).

VIRGINIA COX

Lecturer in Italian at the University of Cambridge and Fellow of Christ's College. Author of *The Renaissance Dialogue in its Social and Political Contexts, Castiglione to Galileo* (Cambridge, 1992), and of articles on women's writings in the Renaissance. Translator and editor of Moderata Fonte, *The Worth of Women* (Chicago, 1997).

MARIA LUISA DOGLIO

Professor of Italian, University of Turin. Critical editions of Galeazzo Flavio Capra, *Della eccellenza e dignità delle donne* (Rome, 1988); Torquato Tasso, *Discorso della virtù feminile e donnesca* (Palermo, 1997) and Enea Silvio Piccolomini, Virgilio Malvezzi and Lorenzo Magalotti. Author of *Lettera e Donna. Scrittura epistolare al femminile tra Quattro e Cinquecento* (Rome, 1993), and *Il segretario e il principe* (Rome, 1993).

ADALGISA GIORGIO

Senior Lecturer in Italian in the Department of European Studies and Modern Languages, University of Bath. Articles on Annie Vivanti, Elsa Morante, Natalia Ginzburg, Fabrizia Ramondino, Edith Bruck, and Italian feminist theory. Joint editor with Anna Cento Bull of *Culture and Society in Southern Italy: Past and Present* (Supplement to *The Italianist,*1994); and currently editing a volume on the mother–daughter relationship in Western European narrative by women.

VERINA R. JONES

Senior Lecturer in Italian, University of Reading, where she set up the Centre for Italian Women's Studies in 1996. Author of *Le 'Dark Ladies' manzoniane* (Rome, 1998). Joint editor with C. Honess of *Le donne delle minoranze. Le ebree e le protestanti d'Italia* (Turin, 1999); and with A. L. Lepschy of *With a Pen in her Hand. Women and Writing in Nineteenth-Century Italy* (Leeds: Society for Italian Studies, forthcoming).

LUCIENNE KROHA

Associate Professor of Italian Studies, McGill University, Montreal. Studies on nineteenth- and twentieth-century authors such as Giorgio Bassani, Maria Messina, G. A. Borgese and Luigi Pirandello. Author of *The woman writer in late nineteenth-century Italy. Gender and the formation of literary identity* (Lewiston, Queenstown, 1990).

ANNA LAURA LEPSCHY

Professor of Italian, University College, University of London. Joint author with G. Lepschy of *The Italian Language Today* (London, 1977; new edition, 1991), and of *L'amanuense analfabeta e altri saggi* (Florence, 1999). Author of *Tintoretto Observed. A Documentary Survey of Critical Reactions from the 16th to the 20th Century* (Ravenna, 1983; Italian version Venice, 1998); *Narrativa e teatro fra due secoli: Verga, Invernizzo, Svevo, Pirandello* (Florence, 1994). Joint editor with V. Jones, *With a Pen in Her Hand* (see Jones).

PENNY MORRIS

Lecturer in Italian at the University of Glasgow. Author of *Giovanna Zangrandi: Una vita in romanzo* (Verona, 2000, forthcoming). Currently working on a study of Alba de Céspedes.

CATHERINE O'BRIEN

Professor of Italian, National University of Ireland, Galway. Articles on Cesarotti and Ossianic poetry and on modern Italian poetry. Joint editor with Alessandro Gentili of an anthology on modern Italian poetry,*The Green Flame* (Dublin, 1987). Editor of *Italian Women Poets of the Twentieth Century* (Dublin, 1996).

ÁINE O'HEALY

Professor of Modern Languages and Literatures, Loyola Marymount University, Los Angeles. Articles and book chapters on Italian cinema, cultural studies and Irish cinema. She is currently co-editing a collection of essays on cinematic constructions of the Balkans.

SILVANA PATRIARCA

Teaches in the Department of History, Columbia University, New York. Author of *Numbers and Nationhood. Writing Statistics in Nineteenth-Centuy Italy* (Cambridge, 1996), and of several studies on the social and cultural history of modern Italy. Author of *Remaking Italians: the Question of Character from the Risorgimento to the Second Republic* (forthcoming).

GIOVANNA RABITTI

Teaches in the Dipartimento di Italianistica, University of Florence. Critical editions of *Lettere e rime di Chiara Matraini* (Bologna, 1989), and of *Giacomo Zane, Rime* (Padua, 1997). Author of several articles on Italian Renaissance lyric poets including Laura Battiferri Ammannati, Vittoria Colonna and Chiara Matraini. Contributing editor (G. Leopardi) to *Antologia della poesia italiana* (Turin, 1999).

LUCIA RE

Teaches in the Department of Italian Studies, University of California Los Angeles. Author of *Calvino and the Age of Neorealism: Fables of Estrangement* (Stanford, 1990) and *Women and the Avant-Garde: Experimentalism, Gender and Politics in Modern Italian Culture* (forthcoming). Translator with Paul Vangelisti of Amelia Rosselli's *War Variations (1964)*, forthcoming in a bilingual translation.

Luisa Ricaldone

Teaches modern Italian literature at the University of Turin. Editor of eighteenth-century texts concerned with women, and author of *La scrittura nascosta. Donne di lettere e loro immagini tra Arcadia e Restaurazione* (Paris–Fiesole, 1996). Joint editor with Adriana Chemello of *Erudite e letterate tra Sette e Ottocento* (Padua, 1999).

Ricciarda Ricorda

Teaches modern Italian literature in the Faculty of Literature and Philosophy at the University of Venice. Author of *La 'Nuova Antologia' 1866–1915. Letteratura e ideologia tra Ottocento e Novecento* (Padua, 1980); *Dalle parte di Ariele. Angelo Conti nella cultura di fine secolo* (Rome, 1993); *Pagine vissute. Studi di letteratura italiana del Novecento* (Naples, 1995); and articles on eighteenth-century women travellers in Italy.

Gabriella Zarri

Professor of History at the University of Florence. Editor of *Donna disciplina creanza cristiano tra xv e xvii secolo. Studi e testi a stampa* (Rome, 1996); with L. Scaraffia, *Donna e fede. Santità e vita religiosa in Italia* (Rome–Bari, 1994), translated as *Women and Faith. Catholic Religious Life in Italy from Late Antiquity to the Present* (Cambridge MA, 1999); and *Per lettera. La scrittura epistolare femminile secoli xv–xvii* (Rome, 1999).

Acknowledgements

As the editor who has seen this book through from its inception up to publication, the pleasant task falls on me to thank everybody else, beginning with Katherina Brett of Cambridge University Press, with whom I first discussed a book on the history of women's writing in Italy that would form part of a series, and continuing with Linda Bree, who has guided the project from submission to production.

A book of this size and complexity is of its very nature a team effort; and has benefited from the collaboration of colleagues. I am grateful to Verina Jones, who agreed to be joint editor during the early stages of planning the book, contacting possible contributors, and preparing initial proposals for Cambridge University Press. Sharon Wood has shared the editorial burdens for the greater part of the journey, always managing to make the most demanding tasks appear light and easy. We have shared all policy decisions, and final planning lists of contributors and chapters; read and discussed all the submissions, including our own, from first versions through all revisions, and all the translations. Penny Morris has performed the invaluable task of co-ordinating the bibliographical guide to women writers and their work, from setting up the database and continually adding to and amending it over a long period. All of us who sent in material for our chapters owe her a great debt.

The contributors, without whom there would be no book, represent a truly representative band of Italianists from Great Britain, Ireland, Italy, the United States and Canada. We appreciate their patience in considering revisions, even when this meant repeated trimming of text and notes to meet the strict word-length of chapters, and in the completion of the bibliographical guide. We hope that when they see their own chapters set into the larger framework of the complete volume, they will be as pleased and impressed as we are by the final result.

We have also been fortunate in finding translators who believe that translations should read as if they were written in English, and have been willing to take the time to achieve that result. Our deepest thanks go to Peter Brand, Abigail Brundin, Susan Haskins and Jennifer Lorch for their labours of love. (Sharon Wood also translated a chapter.) The Department of Modern Languages at Strathclyde, and the Department of Italian, Royal Holloway, have both made generous contributions towards the translations; the Department of Italian at the University of Cambridge assisted Abigail Brundin. Ann Caesar suggested the cover illustration of *Woman Reading* by Faruffini.

Letizia Panizza

Abbreviations

Aricò	S. Aricò, *Contemporary Women Writers in Italy: A Modern Renaissance*. Amherst, 1990.
Asor Rosa	A. Asor Rosa, *Letteratura italiana del novecento*. Rome, 1992.
Blelloch	P. Blelloch, *Quel mondo dei guanti e delle stoffe . . . Profili di scrittrici italiane del '900*. Verona, 1987.
Bondanella	P. Bondanella and J. Conaway Bondanella, eds., *Dictionary of Italian Literature* (revised). Westport, 1996.
CHIT	P. Brand and L. Pertile (eds.), *Cambridge History of Italian Literature*. Cambridge, 1996, revised 1999.
Costa-Zalessow (Cos-Zal)	N. Costa-Zalessow, *Scrittici italiane dal XIII al XX secolo. Testi e critica*. Ravenna, 1982.
Cutrufelli	M. R. Cutrufelli, *Scritture, scrittrici*. Milan, 1987.
DBI	*Dizionario biografico degli italiani*. Rome, 1960–
DS	*Dictionnaire de spiritualité*, ed. M. Viller, Paris, 1937.
De Giovanni	N. De Giovanni, *Artemide sulla soglia. Donne e letteratura in Italia*. Teramo, 1994.
Della Fazia Amoia	A. Della Fazia Amoia, *Women on the Italian Literary Scene*. New York, 1992.
GLdS	*Il grande libro dei santi, dizionario enciclopedico*, 3 vols., Cinisello Balsamo, 1998.
Lazzaro-Weiss	C. Lazzaro-Weiss, *From Margins to Mainstream: Feminism and Fictional Modes in Italian Women's Writing*. Philadelphia, 1993.
Morandini	G. Morandini, *La voce che è in lei. Antologia della narrativa femminile italiana tra '800 e '900*. Milan, 1980.
Nozzoli	A. Nozzoli, *Tabù e coscienza. La condizione femminile nella letteratura italiana del novecento*. Florence, 1978.

Petrignani	S. Petrignani, *Una donna, un secolo*. Rome, 1986.
Rasy	E. Rasy, *Ritratti di signora*. Milan, 1995.
Russell	R. Russell, *Italian Women Writers*. Westport, 1994.
Stanze	A. Arslan, A. Chemello, G. Pizzamiglio, *Le stanze ritrovate. Antologia di scrittrici venete*. Mirano–Venice, 1991.
Testaferri	A. Testaferri, *Donna. Women in Italian Culture*. Toronto, 1989.
Wilson	K. Wilson (ed.), *Women Writers of the Renaissance and Reformation*. Athens, GA, 1987.
Wilson	K. Wilson (ed.), *An Encyclopedia of Continental Women Writers*. 2 vols., New York, 1991.
Wood	S. Wood, *Italian Women's Writing, 1860–1994*. London, 1995.

GSLI	*Giornale storico della letteratura italiana*
IT	*Italian Studies*
MLN	*Modern Language Notes*
RBLI	*Rassegna bibliografica della letteratura italiana*
RCLI	*Rassegna critica della letteratura italiana*
RQ	*Renaissance Quarterly*
RS	*Renaissance Studies*

Note on the text

This book is meant for the interested general reader, as well as for the university student coming to the subject for the first time, and the more advanced student and researcher, able to read texts and studies in Italian. It also presupposes a minimal acquaintance with Italian culture, although it does not take for granted any knowledge of the Italian language.

Prose quotations are rendered in English, while poetry quotations are given in the original Italian followed by a prose English translation. The titles of books and poems referred to within the body of the chapters have also been translated. If there is a published translation, the title is given in italics within parentheses: *Il merito delle donne (The Worth of Women)*; if there is not, a translation of the title within single quotation marks is provided: *I misteri di Napoli* ('The mysteries of Naples').

The bibliographical guide to women writers and their work is a special feature of this book, and writers in the guide are indicated in the chapters by an asterisk (*) before a name. The guide contains basic biographical facts, a list of the author's main works (with dates of first editions, and translations into English), some major studies, and a list of (a) reference works with entries about the author in question and (b) anthologies. Do not, therefore, expect to find a 'life and works' for an asterisked author in the body of the chapter itself or in the notes.

The bibliographical guide has allowed us to keep notes in chapters to a minimum. Where sufficient, shortened titles will be found in the notes. Complete bibliographical entries for all studies mentioned, and main works of authors discussed in chapters, but not asterisked and therefore not found in the bio-bibliographies, will be found in the general bibliography, comprising reference works, primary texts and studies.

If you wish to know more about Italian literature, we recommend *The Cambridge History of Italian Literature*, edited by Peter Brand and Lino Pertile (Cambridge University Press, 1996, revised and in paperback, 1999). If you would like to pursue historical and cultural contexts, we recommend the various paperback volumes of the Longman History of Italy, General Editor, Denys Hay.

Introduction

The title of this book, *A History of Women's Writing in Italy*, has been carefully chosen: first, 'women's *writing*' rather than 'women's *literature*' is meant to indicate that where women are concerned, one has to look beyond the conventional genres classed as literature. In Italy, in particular, which has only recently broken its ties with its classical Latin heritage, and where authors have been rebelling right up to the present against models of style and genre in vernacular prose and poetry imposed for centuries, writing *literature* has assumed both a classical education, and an education in a fixed canon of vernacular authors, beginning with Dante, Petrarch and Boccaccio. *Writing* on the other hand does not assume such a formal preparation, nor adhesion to fixed models. Women's writing does not fit easily into a literary tradition or a canon, and very talented women writers were of necessity self-taught.

Second, the phrase *in Italy* rather than 'Italian' indicates on the one hand that all the writers were and are geographically based in the Italian peninsula. We are not dealing with Italian writing outside Italy or by writers of Italian descent. On the other hand, it indicates that these women do not always write in what is now called 'standard Italian', but in Latin, French and a variety of dialects – a natural enough condition if one realises that Italy as a nation state did not exist before 1870.

The third point concerns 'a history of *women's* writing'. What criteria justify separating women's writing in Italy from a history of Italian literature? Is this not another way to 'ghettoise' women and what they do? We would not subscribe to the notion of *écriture féminine*, advanced by some feminist theorists, that the very act of writing is gender-determined, as if there were an essentialist distinction between the way women and men use language. On the other hand, we do accept that gender is, in fact, a social construction shaped by historical circumstances. In the Western world, and in Italy in particular, women have led very different lives, have taken on very different roles and have not enjoyed the same levels of literacy and access to cultural and intellectual circles that men have. Furthermore, women have not been granted full citizenship in the existing histories of literature. They have often been passed over, or dealt with haphazardly rather than systematically, simply because their writings fall outside what is thought to be the best style, the best genres or the best scholarship.

The constraints under which women writers in Italy have had to labour may need recalling to modern readers. Women's general lack of education has been mentioned. This alone has led to at least two problems: illiterate women – religious authors above all, even St Catherine of Siena, come into this category – need a scribe to write down what is being said. This mediation may alter the spoken words, make them more respectable or at least more 'correct', leave things out, or add glosses here and there. One confessor actually put his own name to the visions he recorded. On the other hand, women who have struggled to acquire learning in order to write and publish, find themselves stripped of authorship by men who cannot believe that women have written what they have written; even worse, men appropriate women's compositions – a practice that happened as late as the twentieth century.

Women's enforced domesticity, resulting above all from their status as wives and mothers, goes hand in hand with their low levels of literacy. The brute facts of so many women's lives – early marriage, frequent child-bearing and child-rearing, and lack of effective birth-control – left little or no time for reading and writing. The institution of marriage itself, with its emphasis on woman's subjection to her husband, and his dominion over her, hallowed whatever double-standards already existed in social practice. Intelligent, learned women threatened the sexual hierarchy asserted by Church and state, and enshrined in civil and canon law. Widows and nuns, provided they could afford books, or at least have access to them, sometimes fared better. An added obstacle to equality and to entrance into the public world of letters mentioned by women themselves was not just the lack of education that followed from their isolation, but being actively denied it by men. Women did not and could not take part in the social processes of learning and literacy: university lectures and debates, discussions in academies, participation in group efforts of research and writing, contacts with publishers and invitations to travel abroad. That women accomplished all they did in such a harsh climate is truly astonishing. Up to World War II, women needed heroic determination first to learn, then to write and then to persist. This Cambridge *History of Women's Writing in Italy* illustrates their multi-faceted ingenuity in making themselves heard.

The Renaissance and early modern periods: 1350–1850

What were the principal historical and cultural features of the periods this book addresses that impinged the most on what and how women wrote? In Italy, the legacy of Latin as the language of literature, learning and authoritative institutions like the Church and the law acted as a barrier to most men and all women, except a handful. The blossoming of the vernacular in the Middle Ages, with Dante, Petrarch and Boccaccio – the 'three crowns' of Italian literature – and its growing use for all kinds of expression, on the other hand, gave women brought up in a dominantly oral culture the chance to participate. The first great collection of letters in the vernacular was dictated by Catherine of Siena to a scribe; she herself could not write. Letters are the dominant genre for women in the period: whether highly polished and erudite ones written in Latin, by women who long to belong to a 'republic of letters' where they would be on equal terms with men, or intimate family ones of a mother to her sons in exile.

The second principal feature of the period, which goes hand in hand with the respectability of the vernacular, is the emergence of the printing press. Printing arrived in Italy from Germany in the second half of the fifteenth century; by the end of the century, Italy and above all Venice had become the European centre for publishing. The desire of an ever-widening public to buy printed books, and of publishers to look for material, provided favourable conditions for women. They specialised, as it were, in two areas, poetry, and religious and devotional writing. Petrarch's collection of sonnets and other metrical forms in his *Canzoniere* fired a band of imitators, creating Petrarchism that lasted a good two centuries after his death in 1374. While preserving the vocabulary and imagery of Petrarch, women redirected his poetry of morally tormented love for an unattainable (married) object of desire into diverse channels, sometimes more spiritual, other times less so, to suit their own voice. Vittoria Colonna's *Rime spirituali* of 1538 used the verse forms to express a devoted wife's grief for a noble dead husband, and then for Christ. In the middle of the sixteenth century, an anthology composed entirely of women poets was printed.

Women found expression and publication in the most popular genre of writing, devotional prose and poetry. Here they gained respect for their moral and spiritual example and advice, whether they were composing mystery plays in poetry in the Medici circle, promoting religious renewal through devotional writings based on Scripture, or charismatics dictating their revelations and ecstasies with messages for the renewal of society.

It is hard to point to any one institution promoting women's literacy. Women's education remained haphazard, dependent within the family on obliging fathers, brothers and far-sighted mothers, who were themselves educated. The northern Italian courts of the fifteenth and sixteenth centuries – Milan, Mantua, Ferrara and Urbino (the setting of Castiglione's *Book of the Courtier*, with its pioneering promotion of women's intellectual and moral equality with men) can be singled out. There women could enjoy the company of a political and cultural elite, and take on roles beyond the domestic. They were often patrons in their own right. Discussions in the vernacular by women about their own status took root at the courts, although they reach a climax at the end of the sixteenth and beginning of the seventeenth centuries in Venice, among professional groups. At court, women also promoted fiction, put on spectacles, encouraged translations into the vernacular, and found in the short story or *novella* deriving from Boccaccio's *Decameron* a source of continual entertainment, yet they themselves remained aloof from writing it until much later in the sixteenth century. Their reputation as chaste and virtuous wives and mothers was paramount, and would all too be easily be compromised by the very act of writing lascivious dialogue about erotic, usually adulterous, adventures. Religious orders, too, usually provided women with the basics of literacy and some Latin for participation in divine services; and judging from accounts of ecstasies and revelations, God seems to privilege communication with them.

Nevertheless, at the time of maximum cultural creativity in literature of all kinds and the arts, political and religious turmoil dominated the entire Italian peninsula. The French King Charles VIII invaded Italy in 1494, Louis XII in 1499, the German Charles VI in 1515, all this culminating in the Sack of Rome by the same Holy Roman Emperor in 1527. The states of the Italian peninsula, with the exception of Venice, lost their political independence and became virtually colonies of the Spanish–Austrian Hapsburg monarchy; the thriving Italian mercantile economy also declined with growing competition from France, Spain, the Netherlands and England, while debilitating wars with the Turks drained Venice's economy, too.

Impinging more directly on women were the events of the Protestant Reformation in the north, beginning with Luther posting his challenge to Rome on the doors of Wittenburg cathedral in 1517, continuing with Calvin and the burgeoning of other sects in disagreement with Rome. The reaction in Italy was at first favourable – several reforming groups, like Vittoria Colonna's, also wished to renew the spiritual and moral life of the Church – but later became hostile, even persecutory. The Catholic Church responded with the Council of Trent, which opened in 1545, and continued fitfully until 1563, producing a massive programme of institutional, theological and moral reform, including an Index of Forbidden Books and legislation for enforcing censorship. For women, it meant stricter control over their sexuality, and greater emphasis on the 'rightness' of their subjection. The wave of enthusiasm for Neoplatonism, starting with new translations into Latin of Plato throughout the fifteenth century, and culminating with Marsilio Ficino's publication of Plato's works, with commentaries at the end, had offered new interpretations of Plato's inspired love, *furor*, that some poets adapted for women as well. The possibilities of sexual equality this offered were soon dampened with Trent and ensuing Counter-Reformation propaganda that put women firmly back in the home, with, ideally, only the literacy required to teach their children.

Economic and political decline went hand in hand with the loss of relative freedom of expression in Italy, and led to stagnation in Italian culture up to the middle and late 1700s. (It should be mentioned, however, that the very first university degree was granted to Elena Cornaro Piscopia in theology and philosophy from the University of Padua in 1678, and her works were published in Parma, 1688.)

From about this time to 1850, the period we have called 'Enlightenment and Restoration' ('Restoration' referring to attempts to restore the monarchy after the French Revolution, the Napoleonic Wars and subsequent revolts in Italy), French culture dominated Italy. It is significant that our chapters on early women's writing leave a gap from 1650 to roughly the French Revolution at the end of the next century. The kind of writing then employed shows a distinct break from the Renaissance. There is an almost total oblivion of earlier Italian writers, accompanied by a slow beginning to recover them, as if they were ancient monuments of a for-gotten civilisation.

As in the early seventeenth century, Venice is at the centre of this revival of women's writing. Scholars like Luisa Bergalli pioneer the recovery of a genealogy of women poets and intellectuals. There is the occasional woman academic: Laura Bassi taught science at the University of Bologna from 1732 to 1778; and Maria Agnesi taught mathematics at Bologna from 1750 to 1799. Of fundamental importance is the establishment of the literary salon, also imported from France, and also centred in Venice, of which women were the chief protagonists. The salon enabled women – admittedly an elite, but an influential elite – to expand their literary and cultural horizons, to find the stimulus and support needed for writing and publishing, and to participate in and shape political and social events. Women like Giustina Renier, with her massive social history of the origins and significance of Venetian festivals, engaged in serious scholarship. Other new directions open up. For the first time, women become journalists and pamphleteers, more often than not in favour of revolution, or at least social reform. Other women write for journals that provide practical advice unobtainable elsewhere. Women travellers, another new and daring phenomenon, write their diaries and publish accounts of trips as far abroad as the Orient; and they now begin to take up the historical and philosophical novel.

Unification and after: 1850–2000

With the achievement of a united Italy in 1860, the declared task of successive governments, in D'Azeglio's notorious phrase, was to 'make Italians', and the role and function of women within the new nation state were seen to be fundamental to the new order. While many women, particularly those from the north and the north-east, forfeited social and economic power under the new centralised Civil Code, they were nonetheless required by nationalist rhetoric to serve as mothers to the new nation, the repository of virtues prized alike by right-wing and Catholic groups and barely dissented to on the fledgling left.

In reality, women's lives differed almost as much as the regions which had hastily come together to form the new nation. If domestic life was not necessarily cast in the rigid mould of Verga's Sicilian novels, nonetheless throughout the peninsula the family retained its central importance as bearer of tradition and as a means of economic survival. Other options were limited. Most professional life was still barred to women and there were very few alternative ways of making a living outside the family home, while their rights within marriage remained minimal.

Despite these obstacles, there were some remarkable shifts in the relation of women to reading and writing. A large-scale literacy programme – largely carried out by poorly paid women teachers – led to a substantial growth in a reading public no longer exclusively identifiable with a cultural and social elite. The most popular genre was no longer poetry but the novel, frequently serialised, which was much more adaptable to the requirements of the new reading public. Women wrote poetry and drama too, however, much of it in dialect, and still to be fully explored. Many women writers, given the limited access they still had to formal patterns of education, were self-taught and relatively unskilled in the traditional canon of literature; their models were contemporary French rather than classical. It can be argued that the lack of formal education of these women led them, on the one hand, to be particularly responsive to the desires and requirements of their market and to adapt accordingly, and, on the other, freed them to experiment in form and style, in that they were not bound by the constraints of canonical expectations.

Involvement in the Risorgimento, together with the impetus of a fledgling feminist movement, led to a heightened awareness amongst women of social issues, and broadened considerably the scope of their writing; essayists and political activists dealt with such contentious issues as the vote, the role of the Church and divorce, as well as more philanthropic matters such as hygiene and child welfare. Middle-class women, rather than just the aristocracy, began to make a living from contributing to the burgeoning number of periodicals, many of them dedicated to women. Journalism, essays and novels with a social, political and polemical intent began to appear, along with the first feminist novels.

The First World War (1915–18 for Italy), followed by two decades of Fascism (1922–43), left women confronted with an ideologically hostile barrage from Church and state alike. Fascism and Catholicism both allowed little space for women outside their traditional domestic and reproductive functions. Mussolini was supported by both the traditional elite and the Vatican, which formally ratified their acceptance of Fascism through the Lateran Pacts of 1929: this move effectively made Catholicism the religion of the state, with a powerful say in family and social matters.

Fascist propaganda required women to be mothers to soldiers, and promoted the archetype of the rural earth-mother in preference to the subversive cosmopolitan chic imported from abroad.

Women were required to conform to a traditional and regressive ideology of gender, to be wives and mothers, to produce soldiers for the nation. Women writers, in accordance with increasingly threadbare models, were regarded as sexually dissolute, unfeminine, emasculating and sterile. Literary histories have been rather too eager to concur with the view that women achieved little of merit during the years of Fascist dictatorship. Yet writing by women during this period, generally dismissed as mediocre and low-brow, limited to the popular or romantic novel, reveals itself to be rich in avant-garde and formal experimentation, with women exploring new genres and very modern modes of writing, experimenting with symbolism and expressionism, as well as realism. Women writers were engaged in a range of literary activity, from the hugely successful popular novel nonetheless despised by a critical elite, to works of high modernism. During these middle decades of the twentieth century, writing by women became increasingly attentive to alternative cultural forms within an international context, and this remained largely true after the Second World War.

Italy changed swiftly and dramatically in the post-war period. Women had been active in the Italian Resistance, a movement celebrated in the immediate post-war period in literature and cinema alike, earning themselves the vote and, for many of them, a first taste of political and militant activity. Population shifts – whether out of Italy or from the south to the north – loosened the ties of the traditional family, while surging industries led to rapid industrialisation and urbanisation. Increasingly secular, with a level of prosperity undreamt of a generation before, Italy was experiencing seismic and sometimes violent change. None were more affected by the social and cultural change than women, who in the two decades between the end of the war and the beginning of the new feminist movement had the vote, access to wider areas of employment, much better levels of education and increased freedom from domestic drudgery. Their aspirations, and their expectations, were bound to change. The issue of divorce was one of the first rallying points for the new feminism. A divorce law was finally approved in 1974, a clear sign that Italians were no longer subservient to traditional authority. Abortion was the second issue which drew women in their hundreds of thousands in a campaign of information and civil disobedience, and was finally legalised in 1978, thus largely ending a hidden but widely felt scandal. The 1970s saw a considerable amount of legislation which put women's legal and civil status on a firmer footing.

Women, urban and literate, demanded a great deal more from Italian society than their mothers had done. Writing from the 1960s and 1970s challenges the dominance of a traditional elite, male culture, seen as an arm of repressive social and ideological thinking, and women wrote of their own experience with a new raw directness which eschewed attempts to conform to standard literary models. With the end of the period of social and feminist militance, too, women began to explore new ways of writing. Their work displays increasing confidence and sophistication at a formal level, while they also increase the scope of their work to address previously neglected or hidden areas of female experience, such as the relationship between mothers and daughters or the expression of female sexuality. While they have made the greatest gains within the fields of poetry and the novel, at the same time, women have also moved into more areas of cultural and literary production than ever before, becoming active as critics and academics as well as dramatists and film-makers. They have also addressed traditional discourses of philosophy, producing theory, as well as fiction, which explores and challenges the construction of female identity within dominant and age-old traditions.

'Giving a voice' provides a cogent motivation for writing this history, and distinguishes it from conventional histories of national literatures mentioned above. We believe this book to be the first of its kind to be published either in Italy or in the English-speaking world. While there are other, more specific, histories of women's writing, especially for the modern period, this is comprehensive in its attempt to map out the main features of women as writers, and the genres of writing they engaged in from the Middle Ages to the present. Just as important, it brings to maturation a process that has been going on in earnest since World War II: that of women discovering their own past. Writing of whatever kind and genre by women in previous generations has begun to be recovered and rediscovered, and the question of women's relationship to the written word over the centuries to be reassessed. By this process, we are bringing back to life, as it were, and giving voice to whole groups of women writers in Italy who even when they were published, often sank into early oblivion. They were often hardly aware that they had an ancestry, and could never have hoped for descendants who cared as much as we do about what they achieved.

Part I

The Renaissance, Counter-Reformation and seventeenth century

MARIA LUISA DOGLIO

Translated by Jennifer Lorch

1
_____

Letter writing, 1350–1650

In ancient Greece the invention of the epistolary genre was attributed to a woman, a queen from the East with the name of Atossa. She was
the daughter of Cyrus the Great, the wife of Darius (who organised the
first Imperial mail system), and the mother of Xerxes; and she also figured
prominently as a character in Aeschylus's play, *The Persians*. This attribution can seem ingenuous today, for it is well established that the letter has
no historical beginnings and originated with writing itself. However, it is
not without significance, particularly if we bear in mind not only the feminine gender of the Greek word *epistolé*, but also the testimony of Cicero,
the greatest Latin letter writer of all antiquity. He affirmed that one of the
most illustrious women of the Roman Republic, Cornelia, daughter of
Scipio Africanus, who conquered Hannibal at Zama, and mother of the
Gracchi, was a model letter writer: 'We have read the letters of Cornelia . . .
they make it plain that her sons were nursed not less by their mother's
speech than at her breast' (*Brutus*, 211). Her letters to her son Caius were
the first to be collected among the Romans. With the subtle aphorism,
originating with Cicero, 'a letter does not blush' (*Ep.* v.12.1), Cicero
implied that the letter, written *in absentia,* was especially important for a
woman. It granted her emotional detachment, thus enabling her to write
freely what dared not be uttered face to face. At the same time, he denies
to letter writing the emotionalism, involvement in feelings and the 'right
to blush' traditionally associated with the 'weaker sex'.

If Cicero drew attention to the fact that the first letters to be collected in
Rome were a woman's, Ovid in the *Heroides* first established the image of the
woman as letter writer. In a splendid gallery of imposing heroines telling
their famous love stories, the *Heroides* offers a complete spectrum of the love
experience in a 'woman's heart'. But Ovid's outstanding innovation lies in

the model of the woman who entrusts to writing, in the form of the letter, her concern about her distant loved one, the frustration of waiting, the gnawing distress of jealousy, the regret for the loss of love, the desperation of being abandoned. Penelope, Phyllis, Briseis, Phaedra, Oenone, Hypsipyle, Dido, Hermione, Dejanira, Ariadne, Canace, Medea, Laodomia, Hypermnestra, Sappho, Helen, Hero, Cydippe, in addition to making present a distant past, realise an autonomous intellectual dignity. By the very act of writing, awareness of the power of writing is linked to these heroines. The letter, then, becomes the sign of the determination and the 'modernity' of woman, a sign and a topos which remains unaltered until the nineteenth century, when it moves from poetry to the short story, to drama and the epistolary novel itself.

After Ovid, the image of the woman as letter writer is consolidated during the Middle Ages in two different ways. On the one hand, *epistolae* are written by well-educated women enclosed within monastery walls. In her letters to Abelard, Héloise not only tells the story of an exemplary love and conversion, but also asks her former lover to guide her along the path of 'monastica perfectio', by giving his teachings and his rules to the monastery she founded, called the Paraclete because devoted to the Holy Spirit. Supported by the certainty that her 'grieving mind' can 'obey as does the hand as it writes', Héloise shows herself ready to dedicate herself entirely to divine love. In the same century, Hildegard of Bingen, musician, philosopher and saint, one of the most enigmatic and fascinating figures of the Middle Ages, wrote letters to St Bernard, to Elizabeth of Shönau and the prelates of Magonza, revealing an original epistolary style imbued with scholastic philosophy. Her letters display a strong didactic intent, but with their own distinctive touches and particular rhythms, and they rise at times to intuitions and theorisations on the love of God, the problems of the inner life and the mission of the nun.

In addition to *epistolae* written by real women, the literary model of woman as letter writer also began to establish itself. In this regard Boccaccio's *Elegia di Madonna Fiammetta* (composed 1343–4) is definitive.[1] Within the fiction of the lived story, Boccaccio revives the great Ovidian topos of the self-aware woman determined to confide her experience of suffering to the letter. Fiammetta narrates 'very true things', associating her writing with the urge of a fiery and passionate love which changed her from a 'free soul' into the 'most wretched servant', an extreme example both of the happy wife caught unawares and struck down by sudden passion, and of the abandoned mistress. Fiammetta is certain not only of the power, but also of the lasting value of her letters. Through her and the fifteenth-century figure of Lucrece in the Latin *Tale of Two Lovers* by Aeneas Sylvius Piccolomini,[2] this genre is transmitted to the epistolography of the sixteenth and seventeenth centuries.

*St Catherine of Siena was born at the time when the *Elegia di Madonna Fiammetta* was gaining recognition. Although her letters, dictated between 1365 and 1380, entail a series of very intricate textual and historical problems concerning the oral nature of dictation and the interventions of scribes, they are still the first great collection of letters in the vernacular. Undoubtedly, they are one of the finest examples of Italian epistolary writing of any period, both for the perfect match of the human and spiritual message and their linguistic innovations and stylistic characteristics. Catherine of Siena's writing carried an exceptional weight and was widely read. It bore witness to an authority and importance not yet attained by any woman in Italian society, and which she claimed not only in mystical and religious spheres but also in political, social and cultural ones as well. Catherine's starting point was mysticism, but far from absorbing herself in the mystical experience and in solitary contemplation, Catherine turned her mysticism outwards in an intense and fruitful determination to spread the word in a community of the faithful, identified with the mystical body of the Church. All the letters begin with the formula 'I, Catherine, servant and slave to the servants of Jesus Christ, write in His precious blood', a formula which expresses not the inferior condition of woman but a considered choice and firm commitment to service. It confirms the intention to 'bathe' and to 'drown' in the blood of the Divine and to offer her own blood, by taking upon herself the ills of the world and transforming violence and evil.

The distinctive expressive strength of her letters combines with a complex variety of tone. St Catherine employs both the language of the Holy Scriptures and contemporary idiom. Metaphors drawn from Biblical language and the Epistles of St Paul mingle with simple expressions about domestic matters and the minutiae of daily life, mystical terminology with popular Sienese dialect. The collection includes an address to the Pope, reminding him of the responsibilities of his office, and of the need to reform the Church and to bear himself 'in a virile manner as a virile man'. Other letters express maternal care for her disciples and townsfolk, and focus on the presentation of her inner life centred on love. Long before the impressive 1500 edition, by the scholar-printer

Aldus Manutius, containing 353 of her letters, which heralded the great century of letters and letter collections, she exerted a strong influence on epistolary writing, and continued to do so in the Renaissance and Baroque periods.

While in the fourteenth century St Catherine's letters were an exceptional phenomenon on all counts, in the fifteenth the image of woman as letter writer was no longer restricted to queens and saints, and began to figure in the literary scene of the whole peninsula, from *Alessandra Macinghi Strozzi in Florence, to Ceccarella Minutolo in Naples. Women letter-writers make their appearance not only in the secret register of strictly private family or love letters but also in an official register, the 'high' register of written Latin (see the next chapter). When the leading Florentine humanist and poet, Angelo Poliziano, met Cassandra Fedele in Venice in June 1491, he recorded his admiration for her in a letter to Lorenzo de' Medici: she was an exceptionally accomplished woman, whether in Latin or the vernacular, and beautiful as well.[3]

In the vernacular, the most remarkable case is undoubtedly Alessandra Macinghi Strozzi, whose letters, written between 1447 and 1470, constitute the first real collection of letters by a lay woman.[4] Macinghi Strozzi found in writing to her distant sons, who had been banished from Florence, the only possible form of family life and the only comfort in her loneliness and difficulties, intensified by the mass of problems encountered by a woman widowed young with five children to rear. The seventy-two letters which have come down to us are responses to an immediate and urgent need to communicate. They have no literary concern or aim, no character or mark of being 'public' works. They are absolutely private texts in which the very grammar belongs to the spoken word: opinions, maxims, memories, news and reports of events, sometimes with parts in cipher or code, and decisions relating to the family and to the intimacy of the house. These letters form a secret correspondence to be seen only by the sender and receiver, according to strict instructions, repeated many times, to consign the letters to a 'trustworthy person', and to check, when they are received, that they have not been opened. Carefully kept for centuries amongst the family papers, and published at the end of the nineteenth century, these letters form a collection which reflects an internal order and measure revealing their author as participant in the cultural conditions of her time. But they also reveal an external order. Their structure, invariably articulated according to traditional rules – *salutatio, exordium, narratio, petitio, conclusio* (greetings, opening, narrative, requests and conclusion), indicates the continuation of the rigidly codified formulae of letter writing, even in the context of a form of communication bound to secrecy, and therefore devoid of literary intentions. This structure remained unchanged over the years.

Far more than notes dictated spontaneously from the heart, the letters comprise a continuous educative process articulated in three categories: ethical-religious, economic and political. Exhortation to virtue, such as the practice of imparting good rules of conduct – the first duty of parents in relation to their children – is firmly anchored in the premise of encouraging young people in self-knowledge, so as to give a good account of themselves, and of educating them in patience, temperance, justice and honesty. Within this traditional viewpoint, broadened by the impulse of maternal love, come recommendations to her first born, Filippo, on affectionate and responsible behaviour towards his younger brother. Alessandra's words mingle with those of the Holy Scriptures, paraphrased and freely adapted. Each letter reveals an intimate familiarity with both sacred texts and vernacular sermons in the mould of St Catherine of Siena and St Bernardine. This is not the familiarity of someone who has meditated upon them with speculative intent, but of one who has found in them nourishment and models for living. Scriptural echoes linked with frequent allusions to secular literature permeate the rules about running the house, household economy, duties of hospitality, appropriate conduct with servants and procedures governing the choice of a wife.

The whole cycle, from the choice of a wife to the formation and presentation of the good mother, follows the path laid down in learned treatises. In Alessandra Macinghi Strozzi's family letters, however, we see a radical difference. For the first time, woman becomes subject rather than object. Clearly conscious of everything she describes, formulates and institutes, Macinghi Strozzi is present and active, maker of her own image. In corresponding with her sons she does not only assume awareness of herself and her condition, of her responsibilities and her competencies; she coherently imparts her advice according to an educative design analogous to that theoretically proposed by Leon Battista Alberti (1404–72) in Book II of *Della famiglia (The Family in Renaissance Florence)* and entrusted, in Book III, to the merchant householder, Giannozzo. The paradigm is the education of the prince, seen as the exclusive task of men of letters. Macinghi Strozzi, like Giannozzo, does nothing but remind her children of everything that 'è di nicistà', that is necessary for them to do. And in so doing she links an ethical/religious and economic education with a political one in a unified organic programme, clearly deviating from the feminine sphere by crossing over into an area distinctly marked as masculine and, in the historical context, not pertinent to women. She recounts no anecdote about the life of the city to her distant sons, but offers maxims and political memories reflecting a precise ideological position and a mature personal reflection.

After the long-desired return of her sons in 1466, there is a significant change of register. The advice now links the family with the Medicean court, countering domestic traditions with courtly rules of behaviour. Between the two poles of 'doing everything for a good end' and 'being prepared', Macinghi Strozzi's intention is always clear: to provide a private education, with no literary pretensions, but in tune with the supreme credo of the humanists, who promoted education as sign of a good upbringing, the peak of personal development and proof of excellence and dignity. These ideals are reaffirmed in the same period by the Florentine humanist who also wrote in the vernacular, Giannozzo Manetti (1396–1459), whose words are directly evoked in her letters.

Through her letter writing Strozzi achieved and broadened that gender equality which Leon Battista Alberti had given some recognition to. But Alberti limited that equality to the running of the house, postulating the superiority of man as agent/maker ('my wife', says the merchant Gianozzo, 'was certainly an excellent mother on account of her native intelligence and behaviour, but much more so because of my advice'). She was 'excellent' because her husband, like a god, instructed her both to 'seem to be, and be, very honest and happy'.[5] As a woman who committed to paper the good teachings of a complete education, however, Alessandra Macinghi Strozzi attained equality with those who wrote to transmit ideas and to mould minds, albeit in the restricted sphere of private communication.

*Vittoria Colonna's Litere also share the distinction of being first in a special field. A celebrated poet who was admired by the best writers and artists of her time, Colonna was revered as 'divine', as were Petrarch, Ariosto and a little later, Tasso. Addressed to Costanza d'Avalos, duchess of Amalfi, the Litere appeared in Venice in 1544, in the early stage of the flowering of the epistolary genre (Pietro Aretino's acclaimed collections of letters had appeared between 1538 and 1542). In addition to the date, the long title ('Letters of the Divine Vittoria Colonna, Marchioness of Pescara to the Duchess of Amalfi, on the Contemplative Life of St Catherine and on the Active Life of St Magdalen') clearly links the relationship between author and addressee not only with the spiritual connotation of the collection but also with the figures of the two exemplary saints, Catherine of Alexandria and Mary Magdalen, themselves emblematic of the period between the Renaissance and Counter-Reformation. The collection, which comprised three letters with neither date nor indication of place, is remarkable for a number of editorial, biographical and historical/documentary reasons. The letters are also of particular significance within the context of a deep religious and intellectual experience. These issues have been explored with reference to Colonna's poetry (see chapter 3, by Giovanna Rabitti), but have received little attention with reference to the letters; for example, the relationship between letter writing and the expression of her inner life, or the relationship between letter writing and the search for Christian spiritual perfection, mirrored in the 'works' and in the imitation of the 'thoughts' of the two saints. Here is not the place to return to the complex editorial issues, nor to emphasise the changes in her life, mind and spirit caused by the events of the years between 1541 and 1544, with her residence in the convent of St Caterina of Viterbo, her links with Reginald Pole and the circle of the Spirituals, her return to Rome in the summer of 1544 and her subsequent seclusion in the Benedictine convent of Sant' Anna – events well-researched by historians from the nineteenth century to the present day. But it is important to highlight one detail: this small but significant collection by Vittoria Colonna is undoubtedly the first of what is to become a genre of spiritual letters, preceding not only the massive volume of *Lettere spirituali* by Bonsignore Cacciaguerra, reprinted many times between 1563 and 1584, but also the intense *Lettere spirituali* by Angelica Paola Antonia de' Negri, which were published in Milan in 1564, and the self-defined 'instructive' and 'preceptive' *Lettere spirituali sopra alcune feste e sacri tempi dell' anno* ('Spiritual letters on some feast days and holy seasons') by Giovan Pietro Besozzi, published in 1578.

Furthermore, Colonna's volume heralds the clearly defined series of letters composed by women. Emblematically, the *Litere* of Vittoria Colonna precede not only the *Lettere a gloria del sesso femminile* ('Letters in praise of women') of Lucrezia Gonzaga da Gazuolo (1552), but also the *Lettere amorose* of Celia Romana (1563), the *Lettere familiari* of *Veronica Franco, and the *Lettere,* gathered together with the poetry, of *Chiara Matraini (1595). Vittoria Colonna's letters constituted, as did her poetry in

1538, a first, a major milestone of a printed correspondence of letters by a woman, with her own first name and surname, just forty years after that fundamental Aldine edition of the *Epistole* of St Catherine of Siena. Colonna's letters mark the eruption of the figure of woman as letter writer, woman poet and intellectual, into the official ranks of a tradition-ally masculine literary society, a phenomenon which Carlo Dionisotti highlighted in the development of Italian culture, along with the opening up of linguistic horizons, as characteristic of the period around 1530.[6]

In terms of style, her use of rhetorical tropes is most striking: sequences of antithesis, oxymoron, metaphor and allegory; play with amplification and repetition; and a continuous use of superlatives, drawn from that type of figurative language characteristic of the mystical tradition, but adapted to Colonna's very individual, intimate, fleeting and ineffable religious experience. Frequent quotations from or allusions to the Gospels, St Paul's Epistles, the Acts of the Apostles and lives of the saints are added to the typical modes of figurative language and to specific allusions to the letters of Catherine of Siena, a model which had a very strong influence and bearing on the epistolary writing of Colonna. By expressing in letter form 'what Christ writes in my heart', the letters are intended to transmit a need which is the structural and determining principle factor in the whole sty-listic process. This original didactic element united with an aspiration towards the sublime (not only towards the desire for God, but also to the ideal of linking 'the perfections of the will with those of the intellect'), is a determining and marked feature of the exemplary and normative charac-ter of her writing.

In their outward form the three letters present a structural scheme articulated in three parts: the pure initial address, the final subscription and, between these, the spiritual nucleus. This identical tripartite struc-ture, with its first and last part reduced to a minimum, concentrates the attention, even visually, on the central nucleus. This communicates both the edifying discourse of encouragement, in the dialogue between the 'I who write' and the 'you who read', separated by time and space (but indis-solubly brought together, united, bound in the common contemplative practice) and the ways and levels of the process of ascent and revelation, of reading and illumination. The recurrent metaphors of inner vision, of the inner eye and of the table which eases hunger and thirst, document a precise understanding of the spiritual letter as an instrument and model through which to teach and to learn the 'way of perfection', the 'ladder', the journey upwards to the union of the soul with God which is achieved through meditation on sacred texts and, within the privacy of her study, readings commented on by members of Colonna's circle at Viterbo.

The *Lettere familiari* of the poet and courtesan Veronica Franco, published in 1580 (and a complimentary copy of which was sent to Michel de Montaigne on his way to Venice), also mark a first. Again they are the first example of a collection composed by a woman, this time with the word 'familiar' included in the title, which hitherto had been used exclusively by 'illustrious authors', from Pietro Bembo to Annibale Caro. This is a book of letters, fifty to be precise, with no date, no indication of addressee, except for the first addressed to Henry III of France (thanking him for having paid her a visit in her 'humble dwelling', bearing with him a portrait of Veronica), but also doubling up as a supporting feature for two celebratory sonnets. The relationship *à deux,* between writer and addressee, becomes triangular: the writer engages both with the private addressee of the letter and then with the reading public, present and future. In the process, every reference to the first addressee is omitted, and every element of possible identification is carefully removed, cancelled and rendered vain by formulae like 'signor H', 'signor A', 'signor N'. With no names and places, and no temporal and spatial references, Franco's collection aims to put forward, not only an exemplary anthology and a new epistolary model, but also her own individual image of a woman writing letters: letters of introduction; thank-you letters; letters of information, supplication, recommendation and invitation; letters of blame as well as good cheer; model love letters and letters discussing a particular issue. All of them present an image of a woman who deliberately uses the letter to exercise what she sees as 'l'ufficio di parole', the function and duty of words themselves.

It is in this term *ufficio* that we find the key to Veronica Franco's letter writing. It surfaces regularly, and particularly in an instructional letter sent to a mother to dissuade her from the 'evil intention' of planning to ruin her daughter by advising her to become a 'woman of the world'. The fact that this letter is the most extended of the whole collection, and placed almost exactly at the centre, exemplifies best this notion of 'the duty of the written word'. The letter assumes an emblematic character with its interweavings of admonishments, exhortations and warnings typical of educational treatises. Exercising her 'duty of the written word', Veronica Franco assumes, with full ideological and rhetorical awareness,

a traditionally male role, employed for millennia by men in their genea-
logical, historical and cultural prerogative of educator and teacher. The
letter – a 'familiar' one in the humanistic sense of 'care of the family', of
'civic obligation', of reminding parents of their responsibilities towards
their children – transcends the character of private communication. It
becomes a document and model not only of epistolary writing in general,
but (to adapt Cicero's formulation) of that 'proper role and function of the
letter' to instruct the person addressed, and to ensure that they become
aware of things which on their own they would not know.

   If by exercising this 'duty of the written word' women express their
intellectual autonomy and attain equal dignity with men, by writing to
instruct, women demolish the barrier of submission founded on the age-
old ban forbidding women to teach. This ban was sanctioned by the
Apostle Paul in his Epistles (II Timothy, 2. 11–15; I Corinthians, 14. 34), and
became part of the Statutes of the early Church, of the laws of Gratian, and
of social custom. Veronica Franco knew how to exercise an activity as a
man would have exercised it, an exercise which afforded her equal dignity
in the difference, both repeated and emphasised, of her nature and condition. For Franco, moreover, instruction is not directed only at women; she
turns to men as well, as she weaves into her increasingly impressive
pattern of her image of herself as a woman writing, not only poems and
letters but compositions which reach the heights of poetry. From the first
to the last piece of the collection, Franco gradually crystallises her idea of
letter as a 'duty of the written word' and her sense of the permanence of
her art form, with the image of woman as letter writer.

The picture of woman as letter writer is further developed by *Isabella
Andreini. As a famous actress, well known on both the Italian and
French stage, a star who not only reaped success but who, at the age of
sixteen, had already indelibly linked her name to the theatre in her role
of the 'first female lover' in the Gelosi company, Isabella appears as a
fully realised individual both in her professional and her personal life as
woman, wife and mother. With her husband Francesco, an actor celebrated for his role of Captain Spavento, they formed an impressive
couple, both on the stage and in their domestic reality of a family
abounding in fame and children. She makes clear-sighted plans with
her husband for the up-bringing of their children, and carefully watches
over their joint ascent to the peak of their acting career. All this is not
enough, however. Isabella has pronounced cultural interests, not only

relating to reading but also to literary writing. With complete self-awareness, she confirms the image of herself in the introductory poem to her *Rime* as a woman who writes 'a good thousand sheets in a variety of styles'; and composes not only *La Mirtilla* (1588), a pastoral fable in drama, but a variety of genres, from poetry to letters to dramatic dialogues. Beyond her total but ephemeral fascination with the stage, beyond the magic of gesture and voice, beyond the ever-new 'captivation' of acting, Isabella wants to live on, not just in the eyes and impassioned memory of all those who applauded her on the stage – princes, cardinals and poets – but through writing, through the very pages of her compositions.

In this regard, her *Lettere* are extremely revealing. Printed in Venice in 1607, three years after her death and edited by her husband (a fact which involves still unsolved problems concerning his possible interventions, additions and modifications), they are preceded by an important dedication to Charles Emanuel I of Savoy. After defining herself 'citizen of the world' who is marked by an extraordinary 'desire to know', Isabella Andreini gives an account of the phases of her writing career: *La Mirtilla,* the poems, the pressing need to 'snatch time' from her work 'to give to the light of day' a collection of her letters, the desire to distinguish herself from the majority of women only interested in 'the needle, the distaff and the wool-winder', but, above all, to gain through writing 'if not everlasting life, at least a very long one'. The collection comprises 151 letters, unnumbered, without date or indication of place, or even, in the majority of cases, of the addressee. All lack references to biographical detail and day-to-day events, with the exception of one letter, expressing deep feeling on the death of Torquato Tasso 'who will never die because oblivion will never have power over him'.

Each letter is nevertheless distinguished by a summary which indicates its theme. Mentioned are debates concerning love on the one hand and moral and social issues on the other. In the first category she considers beauty, falling in love, the ineffable quality of love, fear, pain, illusion, disillusion, jealousy, suspicions, unfaithfulness, and constancy; in the second, honour, virtue, marriage and living at court. Just as on the stage, 'now woman and now / man I created, representing in various style / what nature and art required', so in her letters, Andreini impersonates feminine and masculine roles with equal ease, achieving a work of instruction through a catalogue of teachings on how to choose a lover, on how to keep and increase love, and through the revaluation, in the area of love, of the primary role of woman. It is her duty to safeguard honour and virtue, which will ensure life after death and gain her immortal fame.

Thus at the turn of the sixteenth century, aspirations of enduring life link the configuration of the image of woman as letter writer with the commitment of the woman who entrusts to the written page her vision, her life's work and her engagement with culture.

NOTES

1. In C. Segre (ed.), *Opere di Giovanni Boccaccio* (Milan, 1963); *The Elegy of Lady Fiammetta*, trans. and ed. M. Causa-Steidler and T. Mauch (Chicago, 1990).

2. 'Historia duobus amantibus', Latin and facing Italian in M. L. Doglio, *L'exemplum nella novella latina del '400* (Turin, 1975).

3. For the Italian text of this letter, see Angelo Poliziano, *Prose volgari inedite, poesie latine e greche edite e inedite*, ed. I. Del Lungo (Florence, 1867), pp. 78–82.

4. For the letters of Macinghi Strozzi, Colonna and Franco, see M. L. Doglio, *Lettera e donna. Scrittura epistolare al femminile tra Quattro e Cinquecento* (Rome, 1993).

5. Leon Battista Alberti, *I Libri della Famiglia,* in *Opere volgari*, ed. C. Grayson, 3 vols. (Bari, 1960–73), vol. I, pp. 221, 222, 218, 233. *The Family in Renaissance Florence*, trans. R. Watkins (Columbia, SC, 1969); also trans. by G. Guarino as, *The Albertis of Florence: L. B. Alberti's 'Della Famiglia'* (Lewisburg, NJ, 1971).

6. Carlo Dionisotti, *Geografia e storia della letteratura italiana* (Turin, 1967), pp. 191–4.

2

The fifteenth century

(i) Humanism

In the last chapter, we saw how women from the fourteenth to the sixteenth centuries excelled above all as letter writers. This is particularly true when it comes to women humanists, or women writing in Latin according to models derived from classical Latin literature, a phenomenon limited almost exclusively to the fifteenth century.[1] Within the formal conventions of the letter (which includes the oration, a letter meant to be delivered orally), women expressed their point of view in dialogues, eulogies and invectives, and what we would call essays, on a wide variety of subjects: personal, social, philosophical and theological.

Women's presence in the humanist movement was bound to be circumscribed. They did not, and could not, play a part travelling all over Europe in the search for manuscripts, amassing libraries, emending texts, running schools and learned academies, negotiating in chanceries and acting as secretaries for rulers. The main hurdle was getting an education beyond the elementary 'vernacular' school, as beginning with puberty young girls were not allowed to leave the home and attend a public school with boys, where Latin and sometimes Greek would be taught. Their classical studies had to take place at home, with a private tutor (often the case in a court setting), or under the guidance of educated brothers and fathers. Women found themselves discouraged from mastering the skills of rhetoric, with its emphasis on public speaking and disputation. Furthermore, women who strove after intellectual excellence ran the risk of being labelled 'unnatural', and had to defend their studies as morally improving on, not undoing, their 'female nature'. Finally, writing in Latin was itself suspect: a striving to be superior and a public advertisement of the self –

which for women was inexorably associated with immodesty. Women humanists continually justified the act of writing, assuring disapproving male (but also female) readers that their learning had not put vain or immoral thoughts into their heads, nor caused them to question or disobey (male) authority. They needed heroic strength of will not to be deterred by such a hostile cultural climate.

In the late fourteenth and early fifteenth centuries, learned women were found most often in the northern courts, members of the ruling dynasties, and often patrons of learning and the arts as well. Battista da Montefeltro Malatesta (1383–1450) was encouraged in an educational treatise written for her by Leonardo Bruni Aretino to study authentic Latin classics and even Latin Fathers of the Church. As the widow of an assassinated despot, she delivered an oration pleading for the restoration of the small town of Pesaro to herself and family. She also tutored her own granddaughter, Costanza Varano, who composed Latin letters, orations and poems as a young woman. Once married, Varano's studies ceased, and she died at nineteen in 1447, shortly after giving birth to her second child.[2]

Outstanding in this first half of the century was *Isotta Nogarola, proficient in Latin and Greek, taught by humanists of Guarino Veronese's circle along with her two sisters, Ginevra and Angela. Isotta corresponded with educated men in Latin, but when she wrote to Guarino himself, he snubbed her by first not answering, and then anwering only at others' insistence. In 1438, a defamatory pamphlet circulated, accusing her, without a shred of evidence, of incest with her brother. Her learning was to blame, for 'an eloquent woman is never chaste'.[3] Isotta became a recluse, refusing both marriage and life in the convent.

Nevertheless, Isotta did engage in a formal debate with a Venetian lawyer-humanist, Lodovico Foscarini, between 1451 and 1453, where she showed herself a theologian, a Scholastic dialectician and the possessor of a fine legal mind. The issue was whether Adam or Eve sinned the most, and was more to blame for the consequent fall of humankind in the Garden of Eden (see Genesis, 2:7–25, and 3:1–24). Isotta had read the Bible carefully, and Augustine's authoritative commentaries among others, as well as Aristotle; she knew that theologians and philosophers agreed in declaring woman morally infirm and less rational than men. Her chosen debating tactic was therefore to point out contradictions, where she could and did succeed. Isotta used Eve's inferiority to point the finger at Adam: for if Eve (and therefore all women) was so much more ignorant and more lacking in reason than Adam (and therefore all men), why did theologians maintain that her sin and her guilt were greater, and her punishment (pain in childbirth and subjection to her husband) 'justly' harsher than Adam's? 'Where there is less intellect and less constancy there is less sin', Isotta shrewdly pointed out.[4] Since Adam's excellence was greater, he was the greater sinner. Quoting Genesis correctly, she reminds Foscarini that Adam had been forbidden to eat the apple, not Eve; it was through Adam, the Church agreed, that the human race 'fell'; indeed, if only Eve had eaten, nothing would have happened! These first steps in deconstructing the Adam and Eve story would be taken much further, well into the mid-seventeenth century, with *Arcangela Tarabotti's *La tirannia paterna* (see chapter 5).[5]

In the second half of the Quattrocento, women humanists often belonged to professional upper-middle-class families in an urban milieu. *Cassandra Fedele and *Laura Cereta of Brescia came from Verona and Brescia respectively, where their fathers encouraged and even directed their Latin and Greek studies. Fedele was the most renowned woman scholar of the last decades of the Quattrocento, appearing regularly in later collections of famous women.[6] She achieved instant fame for delivering an oration at the University of Padua, where she praised the philosophical studies of a male relative, Bertuccio Lamberto (the only work of hers printed in her lifetime, 1487 and 1488), even though no woman was permitted to study or obtain a degree from a university at the time. She also delivered public addresses before the Venetian Doge, and citizens. Her correspondence was the most extensive of all women humanists, and embraced famous women like Queen Isabella of Spain, Eleonora of Aragon (Duchess of Ferrara) and Beatrice Sforza – yet for some unfathomed reason, she would not reply to letters from Laura Cereta, who longed to hear from her. The leading Florentine humanists Angelo Poliziano and Pico della Mirandola admired her. 'She is a miraculous phenomenon', reported Poliziano to Lorenzo de' Medici in 1491, comparing her to the most learned woman in Florence, Alessandra Scala (1475–1506), fluent in Latin and Greek.[7]

While not in touch with as wide or distinguished a circle as Fedele, Cereta was arguably the most outspoken women humanist of the Quattrocento, especially on women's education and equal dignity with men. In her *Epistolae familiares,* she wrote on personal and public matters to family, friends and other women, entering the male preserves of astrology, education and advice on marriage, and composing pastoral eclogues, even a satirical dialogue on the death of an ass. Some of her orations may have been delivered at informal gatherings in Brescia. Yet she, too, encountered hostility, and had to defend herself both from carping women resentful of her 'unwomanly' attainments, and from men who denied she could have written such polished Latin.

In a letter-essay of 1488 answering a misogynist who doubted women's capacity for education, Cereta became the first woman writer to lay down a canon of intellectual women from antiquity to the present; placing three women of her own century, Isotta Nogarola, Cassandra Fedele and Nicolosa of Bologna (see below) alongside classical models. Rewriting in effect Boccaccio's collection of biographies, *Concerning Famous Women,* in which he had ranked heroic preservation of chastity above all virtues,[8] Cereta names the same names, but gives pride of place to the learned qualities of these women prophets, orators, poets, philosophers and historians. She refers to these women as a 'republic', *respublica mulierum,* and so recalls the frequently alluded to phrase used by humanists about a republic of letters, *respublica litterarum,* where all freely share in and contribute to the banquet of knowledge as equals. 'Nature has granted to all enough of her bounty; she opens to all the gates of choice'.[9] The main distinction between the sexes is consequently a social and political one.

Cereta also rewrote another traditional genre, indulged in only by men since classical antiquity, 'Whether a man should take a wife', which arrived at the sour conclusion that the disadvantages of marriage outweighed the advantages because wives of their very nature would never keep faith.[10] Cereta takes the opposite view, urging Pietro Zecchi to take a wife because marriage is meant to make a couple joyful, *hilares,* above all in their common desire to beget and raise children. She even lets slip a vein of sarcasm: 'Surely the great and unshakeable faith of wives in their husbands is excessive', for wives 'remain constant through all fortune's changes', while husbands rarely behave according to the same standards.[11] A short letter to a woman dated 1486[12] affirms the radical ideal of friendship, *amicitia,* between women, again counter to accepted doctrines going back to classical antiquity, which saw friendship as a rare bond existing primarily between men who shared similar moral and intellectual activities.[13] With her thoughts on a *respublica mulierum* and friendship – whether between women or between men and women – Cereta anticipated yet again issues that would be central to later women writers.

Nicolosa Castellani Sanuti of Bologna, one of the three outstanding learned women of her age according to Cereta, actually brought about a change in the law. From a distinguished family herself, she married into a wealthy high-ranking Bolognese family, and is famous for an oration challenging an edict issued in 1453 by no less an ecclesiastical authority than the learned Greek Cardinal Legate to Bologna, Bessarion. The over-zealous Cardinal had imposed strict sumptuary laws on the city, limiting the jewellery and textiles as well as the number of garments to be worn by the three main social classes of women. Those who disobeyed were excommunicated. Sanuti took on the role of a lawyer, and pleaded (in Latin) against these intolerable measures on behalf of all women of Bologna. She argued that dress was part of a socially accepted code, conveying distinctions of rank, public office, social status and even personal merit recognisable by all.[14] Interestingly, Sanuti thought that the dignity of women who were both scholars and rulers – like Bianca Maria Visconti, Battista Montefeltro, and Costanza Varano – was especially deserving of the finest, costliest garments. Her oration was so effective that the ruler of Bologna, Sante Bentivoglio, granted her case, and reported that Bessarion, too, would revoke the unpopular edict. She became famous all over northern Italy.

It is hard to trace a continuity between these women humanists writing in Latin and their successors writing in Italian in the next and later centuries. The very qualities that made them so exceptional – classical learning and writing in Latin – ensured that later women, able to gain literary recognition by writing solely in Italian, did not read them. At the same time, the issues they raised – women's education, the inequalities between the sexes and the reform of marriage – never went away. Lists of famous women kept their memory alive, and there is the faintest of possibilities that the Latin orations and letters of Cassandra Fedele and Laura Cereta, edited by Cardinal Filippo Tomasini in 1636 and 1640 respectively, were known to the Venetian poet, polemicist and defender of women, Lucrezia Marinella (see chapter 5).

NOTES

1. This section draws on King and Rabil (eds.), *Her Immaculate Hand* (Binghampton, NY, 1983; Albert Rabil, Jr., *Laura Cereta: Quattrocento Humanist* (Binghampton, NY, 1981); Diana Robin, 'Humanism and feminism in Laura Cereta's Public Letters', in L. Panizza (ed.), *Women in Italian Renaissance Culture and Society* (Oxford, 2000), pp. 368–84 and P. O. Kristeller, 'Learned Women of Early Modern Italy: Humanists and University Scholars', in P. Labalme (ed.), *Beyond Their Sex* (New York, 1980), pp. 91–116. Translations of Laura Cereta from her *Collected Letters*, translated, edited and with introduction by Diana Robin (Chicago, 1997).

Important women humanists of the sixteenth century include Olimpia Fulvia Morata (1526–55), and Tarquinia Molza (1542–1617). Morata, educated at the court of Ferrara, was forced to leave Italy after marrying a Lutheran physician. Her *Opera Omnia* (Basel, 1562) comprise orations, poems and letters in Greek and Latin and in particular dialogues dealing with moral, social and religious issues. Molza, taught by Francesco Patrizi, translated from Greek into Italian a Plutarch treatise, Aristotle's *Rhetoric* and versions of two dialogues by Plato, *Charmides*, and *Crito*. Some of her works were published only in 1750.

2. For more examples, see King and Rabil, *Her Immaculate Hand*, pp. 16–17. On the close family ties between ruling women of the northern courts, see Cecil Clough, 'Daughters and Wives of the Montefeltro: Outstanding Bluestockings of the Quattrocento', *RS* 10.1 (1996), pp. 31–55.

3. King and Rabil, *Her Immaculate Hand*, p. 17. Also, L. Jardine, 'Women Humanists: Education for What?' in A. Grafton and L. Jardine, eds., *From Humanism to the Humanities: Education and the Liberal Arts in Fifteenth- and Sixteenth-Century Europe* (London, 1986), pp. 29–57. For Isotta, see pp. 29–45.

4. King and Rabil, *Her Immaculate Hand*, p. 59.

5. For the European context, see E. Pagels, *Adam, Eve and the Serpent* (New York, 1988).

6. On Fedele, King and Rabil, *Her Immaculate Hand*, pp. 48–50, 69–77; Jardine, 'Women Humanists', pp. 45–57.

7. Jardine, 'Women Humanists', p. 47; see also A. Brown, *Bartolomeo Scala (1430–1497) Chancellor of Florence* (Princeton, NJ, 1979), pp. 226–9.

8. Cereta, ed. Tomasini, Letter 18; Robin, 'Humanism and Feminism', pp. 74–80.

9. Robin, 'Humanism and Feminism', p. 79.

10. Cereta, ed. Tomasini, Letter 64, pp. 178–87; Robin, 'Humanism and Feminism', pp. 65–72.

11. Robin, 'Humanism and Feminism', p. 71.

12. Cereta, ed. Tomasini, Letter 47, pp. 105–7; Robin, 'Humanism and Feminism', pp. 136–8.

13. For the history of friendship, see Ulrich Langer, *Perfect Friendship: Studies in Literature and Philosophy* (Geneva, 1994).

14. On Sanuti, see Jane Bridgeman, '"Pagare le pompe": Why Quattrocento Sumptuary Laws Did Not Work', in L. Panizza (ed.), *Women in Italian Renaissance Culture and Society* (Oxford, 2000), pp. *209–26*.

(ii) Vernacular poetry and mystery plays

Past narratives relating to the history of fifteenth-century Florentine literature have traditionally foregrounded the work of two poets active in the last quarter of the century, Angelo Poliziano and Lorenzo de' Medici, deemed to mark a resurgence of the vernacular as a vehicle for serious literary activity after the so-called 'secolo senza poesia' ('century without poetry'), 1375–1475. As we now know, this scenario tended to downplay or to obscure the existence throughout the century of an admittedly more modest but nonetheless vibrant vernacular culture in the city, dominated on the one hand by poetry, both secular and religious, and on the other by religious drama. It is perhaps scarcely surprising then, that awareness of two Florentine women as creative writers, *Lucrezia Tornabuoni de' Medici and *Antonia Tanini Pulci, has been fitful.[1]

Both women belonged to the Florentine mercantile elite, although Lucrezia had special status as wife and mother of successive leading citizens of the Republic, Piero and Lorenzo de' Medici. Both lived in a family environment in which male writers operated in the vernacular – in the case of Lucrezia, her son, Lorenzo, and his circle, and in the case of Antonia, her husband, Bernardo Pulci, and his brothers, Luca and Luigi. Both women drew on familiar religious material for their subject matter, thereby helping to deflect censure for their entry into the male territory of authorship. Something of the transgressive nature of that activity, from the male point of view, emerges from Niccolò Valori's early biography of Lorenzo, where he praises Lucrezia as not inferior to her husband, given her sex. She also demonstrates in her verse translation of sacred Scripture an eloquence very rare in a woman, for she composed without having neglected either her spiritual or her domestic duties!

Lucrezia Tornabuoni's surviving works comprise one sonnet, eight *laudi* (hymns), and five substantial narrative poems on sacred subjects, not all of which are in print. These are the stories of St John the Baptist and Judith in *ottava rima* (a verse form associated traditionally with narrative poetry), and of Esther, Susanna and Tobit in *terza rima* (the form famously used by Dante in the *Divine Comedy*).[2] The sonnet, the only secular composition of hers which survives (undermining, incidentally, the notion of a purely religious output), is a playful, occasional piece, part of an exchange with Medici poet, Bernardo Bellincioni. The hymns, of which the most famous, 'Ecco il Messia' ('Behold the Messiah') was once attributed to Savonarola who transcribed it, were the first compositions by her to appear in print in a seventeenth-century collection of *laudi* by both mother and son. The indication that four of them are to be sung to the music of the poem 'Ben venga maggio' ('Welcome May') by Angelo Poliziano, her grandchildren's private tutor in the 1470s, provides an insight into complex contemporary relations between sacred and secular.

The five long narrative poems are her most ambitious works. St John the Baptist was perhaps an obvious authorial choice as the patron saint of Florence, but more striking is her selection of Biblical heroines, Judith, Susanna and Esther. All would be familiar to her from written sources and sermons, as the subject of contemporary plays, and as depicted on domestic furniture such as wedding chests and in works of art. Donatello's bronze statue, *Judith and Holofernes*, might have been seen in the courtyard of the Medici Palace during the festivities for Lorenzo's wedding in 1469, while after Lucrezia's death Ghirlandaio was to paint scenes from the life of the Baptist in the Tornabuoni family chapel in Santa Maria Novella, including a possible portrait of her attending the birth of the saint.

Lucrezia's written source is the Vulgate Bible, read either in Latin or in one of the vernacular translations which proliferated in fifteenth-century Florence. The extent of her education remains unclear. We can cite a letter to her in which a priest quotes Biblical passages in Latin and another in which reference is made to her personal library containing books in both Latin and Greek, but the interpretation of these details is not unproblematic. While following the Biblical text closely, she demonstrates a penchant for descriptive amplification where female beauty, banquets and gardens are concerned. It is the Biblical world seen through the lens of the popular narrative poems on both sacred and secular topics called *cantari*, accessible to women and men of a range of cultural sophistication through a thriving tradition both oral and written. The admonition of Archbishop (later St) Antonino, Lucrezia's spiritual adviser until his death in 1459, that women should read about God rather than knights and their amorous exploits, is neatly circumvented in some, at least, of her subject choices. Judith, Susanna and Tobit belong to the Apocrypha with an ambivalent status in the Biblical tradition. Although they were never excluded from the Vulgate Bible (unlike, for example, the English

Authorised Version) and were frequently cited by the Church Fathers as well as by Renaissance preachers such as Archbishop Antonino, they were regarded as morally edifying rather than as having scriptural status. Modern scholarship views them as Hebrew 'romances' or folktales, hence perhaps their particular attraction for a fifteenth-century Florentine woman imbued with the popular culture of her day.

A line near the conclusion of *La ystoria della devota Susanna* suggests that Lucrezia envisaged her poem being either read or read aloud (line 400). Her primary intended readership was probably limited to the family circle and intimate friends, and a handsome manuscript with fine calligraphy and miniatures survives. A letter from Poliziano in 1479 reports one of her granddaughters (also Lucrezia) learning some of her poetry by heart, but how did Lucrezia and her granddaughter read the story of Judith? As well as its pious messages, this was also undoubtedly entertainment, an adventure story featuring a female protagonist. Judith, indeed, may have been the author's favourite as she introduces a rare personal comment: 'tanto m'è piaciuto il suo ardire' (III, 2; 'I liked her daring so much'), linking that special grace accorded by God to a weak widow with her own situation as a woman writer about to embark on her own narrative. Inspirational, then, but also potentially transgressive if we remember Florentine doubts a few years later about the proposed relocation of Donatello's *Judith and Holofernes*, removed from the Medici Palace after the family's exile – a statue of a woman killing a man on public display! The clearly negative female exempla, Salome and her mother Herodias, guilty of the death of John the Baptist, are of course condemned, and in *Ester*, having described Vashti's wifely disobedience, the narrator warns her audience: 'Donne, non apparate da costei!' (3,10, 'Women, don't follow her lead!'). Lucrezia, on the other hand, had no doubts about the heroic status of the young widow, Judith, or of Esther, liberators of their people.

Lucrezia Tornabuoni was neither an ascetic nor a mystic but rather an intensely practical individual, as appears from her correspondence (for she, with Alessandra Strozzi, is also one of the two well-publicised women letter writers of late fifteenth-century Florence). As the manager of a household, an astute businesswoman with a keen political sense, with a robust sense of humour which could appreciate Luigi Pulci's earthy, irreverent, mock-epic poem *Morgante*, and a capacity to enjoy life in spite of frequent illnesses, she contrasts with Luigi's sister-in-law, Antonia Pulci, a rather different personality. While there is no apparent tension between Lucrezia's domestic and other roles and her personal piety, Antonia, married at eighteen and childless, became a member of the Augustinian third order after being widowed in 1488. (The third order, or tertiaries, were lay people, not formally bound by vows but following a life of restraint and poverty, usually within their own houses.) She eventually founded a lay community, the sisters of Santa Maria della Misericordia, in February 1500 (still 1499 according to the Florentine calendar and therefore in time for the crucial half millennium).[3] Despite their geographical proximity, we have no evidence of direct contact between Lucrezia Tornabuoni and Antonia Pulci. It may be only coincidence that in two of Pulci's plays she refers briefly to Susanna, Esther and Tobit. They shared much the same religious and secular culture but Antonia's creative bent was towards the Florentine theatrical tradition of the *sacra rappresentazione*, that is, the scripted sacred play in *ottava rima* which emerged in mid-century, performed by companies of boys in churches, convents and even in the garden of Lorenzo de' Medici.[4]

Antonia Pulci's choice of religious material involves no overlap with that of Lucrezia. Of her three securely identified plays, two are based not on Biblical heroines but on female saints and martyrs, Guglielma and Domitilla. The third play celebrates the life of St Francis. Other attributions are less certain: plays on the Prodigal Son (her name was attached to it in the mid-sixteenth century), St Anthony Abbot, St Theodora and a *Festa di Rosana*.[5] Her sources are less obvious than Lucrezia Tornabuoni's and remain to be researched in detail. Guglielma, perhaps drawn from a Ferrarese Franciscan source, is an English princess, obliged by her parents to marry the recently converted King of Hungary. He promptly goes on a pilgrimage to the Holy Land during which his brother tries and fails to seduce Guglielma and takes his revenge by accusing her of adultery (the chaste wife falsely accused is a traditional theme exemplified not least by the Biblical Susanna). Escaping execution, she lives for many years in a desert nunnery, and after reunion with her husband and his leprous brother, persuades them to go off to live a holy and chaste life in desert solitude. Guglielma remains an obedient wife – she will return home with her husband if he so wishes – but she is also presented as superior, a medium of male salvation. Perhaps this play, like *Domitilla*, which is dated 1483, was written while her husband Bernardo Pulci was still alive, for Antonia seems anxious to show that marriage is no impediment to sanctity.

St Flavia Domitilla, on the other hand, is a virgin martyr of the late first century who resists or converts all those who would force her to marry. Antonia's source, also used by her husband for his single play, *Barlaam and Josaphat*, is that late thirteenth-century medieval Latin classic widely available in translation, Jacopo da Voragine's *Golden Legend*, where the story is briefly recounted in the chapter devoted to Sts Nereus and Achilleus. Antonia, however, turns Domitilla into the central figure. She repeats her source's anti-marriage message with its picture of domestic violence, infidelity, and the dangers of childbirth; and contrasts the Christian state of perfection, virginity, which offers the least problematic route to sanctity.

Antonia's version of the story of St Francis is interesting for its concluding section which features the Lady Jacopa di Settesoli, a Roman widow of the Frangipane family and friend of the saint, who was miraculously forewarned of his approaching death and witnessed his stigmata. Even in a play celebrating a male saint, it would seem that the author has a particular interest in the relation of women to sacred history and to the divine, but it is also surely not coincidental that Antonia's mother appears in the records as Jacopa da Roma.

Antonia Pulci is the first Italian woman vernacular playwright, a fact which renders her relative obscurity in the canon of Italian writers all the more extraordinary. We do not know whether her plays were performed by the boys' companies associated with those of her male contemporaries (Feo Belcari, Bernardo Pulci, Lorenzo de' Medici, Castellano Castellani) or whether, like Lucrezia Tornabuoni's sacred poems, their performance was limited to being read aloud at home or in some Florentine religious community such as the Benedictine convent of Le Murate where she had a close relative, Annalena Tanini.[6] Unlike Lucrezia, however, Antonia had the satisfaction of seeing her work appear in the new medium of print in her lifetime. She was to be extensively reprinted in the following century, the market undoubtedly stimulated by a contemporary flowering of Tuscan convent or spiritual drama with plays written by nuns for in-house performance by their comrades. The name of Beatrice del Sera (1515–85) has recently been brought to our attention.[7]

Our two fifteenth-century examples, however, give the impression of only a tiny minority of literate Florentine women actually advancing into creative authorship, using the protective device of employing unimpeachable material, whether Biblical or hagiographic. In this they are subject to the dictates of prevailing cultural and social norms but also clearly use that authorship for their own purposes as women. Only tantalising fragments exist to suggest that younger Florentine contemporaries aspired to

express themselves in other territories: a Greek epigram by Alessandra
Scala (1475?–1506), and a poem by Ginevra de' Benci (1457–1520), known to
posterity only through her portrait by Leonardo da Vinci. Only the first
line remains – a fragile link with that flowering of women's lyric poetry
which would take place in the following century.[8]

NOTES

1. Compare Peter Marinelli, 'Pulci and the Narrative Tradition', in Peter Brand and Lino
Pertile (eds.), *The Cambridge History of Italian Literature* (Cambridge, 1997, revised edn
1999), where Tornabuoni is mentioned as a patron rather than as a writer (p. 168).
Antonia Pulci's name is absent. On the other hand, the volume provides an excellent
overview of the wider cultural context in which the two women operated.

2. In *ottava rima* the stanzas are composed of eight lines, ending in a couplet: ab ab ab cc.
In *terza rima,* rhyme words in the three-line stanzas intertwine: aba bcb cdc.

3. For important new information on Pulci's life, see James Wyatt Cook and Barbara
Collier Cook (eds.), Antonia Pulci, *Florentine Drama for Convent and Festival. Seven Sacred
Plays*, annotated and trans. James Wyatt Cook (Chicago and London, 1996).

4. See Nerida Newbigin, *Nuovo corpus di sacre rappresentazioni fiorentine del Quattrocento*
(Bologna, 1983) and Paola Ventrone, 'Per una morfologia della sacra rappresentazione
fiorentina', in Raimondo Guarino (ed.), *Teatro e culture della rappresentazione. Lo spettacolo
in Italia nel Quattrocento* (Bologna, 1988), pp. 195–225.

5. For arguments in favour of a positive attribution of these plays to Antonia Pulci, see
Cook and Collier Cook, *Florentine Drama*, pp. 27–32.

6. The nuns of Le Murate were not only consumers of the written word (Antonia's
husband, Bernardo, dedicated a religious poem to Suor Annalena) but also active as
copyists and eventually as historians in the person of Giustina Niccolini (1597). See Kate
Lowe, 'History Writing from Within the Convent in Cinquecento Italy: the Nuns'
Version', in L. Panizza (ed.), *Women in Italian Renaissance Culture and Society* (Oxford,
2000), pp. 105–21.

7. See Elissa Weaver (ed.), Beatrice del Sera, *Amor di virtù: commedia in cinque atti, 1548*
(Ravenna, 1990).

8. See John Walker, '*Ginevra de' Benci* by Leonardo da Vinci', *National Gallery of Art: Report
and Studies in the History of Art, 1967* (Washington DC, 1968).

3
———————

Lyric poetry, 1500–1650

A regrettable tendency of sixteenth-century literary historiography has been to concentrate attention on a few exemplary figures, without considering women's literary production as a whole. There is little doubt, however, that the literary environment of the sixteenth and early seventeenth centuries derived its vitality from the encounter between, on the one hand, strong and authoritative literary models, and, on the other, a public capable of assimilating these and fostering in its turn a thriving, if derivative, literary production. This is true of writing by women in general, but particularly of poetry.

The poet who made the most remarkable impact in this period was *Vittoria Colonna, an exemplary figure, possessed to an unusual degree of the qualities that would equip her for the role she came to assume in the panorama of Italian literature. Born into the powerful Roman Colonna clan, she married Ferrante d'Avalos in 1509. It was a brief marriage, as in 1525 d'Avalos died in battle in Milan, leaving Vittoria widowed at the age of thirty-five. The intense anguish Colonna suffered brought the poet into being; at the same time, the development of Colonna's literary career takes on the features of a masterly balancing act act between self-promotion, an authentic spirituality and an unusual poetic gift. By 1530 she was widely acclaimed, despite the fact that not one of her poems had as yet been published; and she conducted an exchange of letters with Paolo Giovio (1483–1552) and Pietro Bembo (1470–1547), in which they exchanged sonnets and she competently discussed questions of metre and style. In the 1532 edition of the *Orlando furioso*, Ariosto was able to bequeath to her the role of high priestess of poetry and of conjugal faithfulness:

> Quest'una ha non pur sé fatta immortale
> Col dolce stil di che il miglior non odo
>
> (canto 37, stanza 16)
>
> (This one woman has not only immortalised herself / Through her
> sweet style, of which I have heard none better)

Colonna's first appearance in print was managed with extreme care. In
1535 – ten years after her husband's death, and the end of Colonna's self-
imposed period of mourning – a single sonnet appeared in the second
edition of Bembo's collected poetry, sanctioning the beginning of a steady
ascent to the literary elite of the age. Three years later, in 1538, the
complex editorial and publishing history of the poems began with
Pirogallo's edition in Parma.[1] The *Rime* would remain a constant presence
on the Italian literary scene for the remainder of the century, both in print
and through a limited manuscript circulation. During the last decade of
her life, Colonna's legendary status was enriched by her deepening spiritual involvement. Since 1530 she had been drawn to the teachings of Juan
de Valdés (1498?–1541), and developing an increasingly close relationship
with evangelical groups in Italy. She became a leading light in the reforming Viterbo circle together with Cardinal Reginald Pole (1500–58), and in
the last years of her life her failing health allowed her finally to achieve
her strong desire for the contemplative life, through her withdrawal into
the convent of Saint Anna. The quality of her friendships (one only need
mention Michelangelo) and of her reading prompted Colonna to devote
herself with ever greater intensity to the composition of religious poetry.
In 1546, one year before her death, a first edition of her *Rime spirituali*
('Spiritual poems') was published.

Although Colonna's literary activity spanned over twenty years, her
lyrics are clearly marked by a uniform maturity of style. She achieved a
highly successful balance between, on the one hand, 'correct' poetic language (in which she imitated Petrarch rigorously) and content (unblem-
ished devotion to the memory of her husband); and on the other hand a
perfect harmony between stylistic tension (always in search of a 'high' linguistic register both in vocabulary and syntax) and an exploration of feelings (from the mourning of her husband to divine love and the
contemplation of Christ), which excludes any trace of light-heartedness
or lover's playfulness.

Justifiably famous as an example of Colonna's style is the opening
sonnet of Pirogallo's 1538 edition of her *Rime* (number A1:1 in Bullock's
edition):

Scrivo sol per sfogar l'interna doglia
ch'al cor mandar le luci al mondo sole,
e non per giunger lume al mio bel Sole,
al chiaro spirito e a l'onorata spoglia.

Giusta cagion a lamentar m'invoglia;
ch'io scemi la sua gloria assai mi dole;
per altra tromba e più sagge parole
convien ch'a morte il gran nome si toglia.

La pura fe', l'ardor, l'intensa pena
mi scusi appo ciascun; ché 'l grave pianto
è tal che tempo né ragion l'affrena.

Amaro lacrimar, non dolce canto,
foschi sospiri e non voce serena,
di stil no ma di duol mi danno vanto.

(I write solely to relieve the inner anguish / which the only lights in the world send to my heart / and not to add glory to my radiant Sun, / to his splendid spirit and venerated remains. / I have good reason to lament; / for it grieves me greatly that I might diminish his glory; / another trumpet, and far wiser words than these / would be suited to deprive death of his great name. / My pure faith, passion, intense sorrow, / excuse me before all; for my heavy weeping / is such that neither time nor reason can contain it. / Bitter lamentation, not sweet songs, / heavy sighs, and not a steady voice, / enable me to boast not of my style, but of my suffering. /)

Nothing is lacking from the perfect expression of conjugal love, celebrated through the memory of the honour and great spirituality of the dead lover (defined as 'splendid spirit' and 'venerated remains'), rather than through mourning her beloved. In fact, the only trace of regret here regards the poet's sense of inferiority which prevents her from doing justice to the exceptional qualities of the one she celebrates (see lines 5–8). The co-ordinates are already in place which will determine the representation of the more qualified and mystical bond with Christ, as in the *Rime spirituali*, number S1:60 (Bullock's edition). Here, the poet consoles the suffering Christ by testifying to her love and devotion:

Fido pensier, se intrar non pòi sovente
entro 'l cor di Gesù, basciaLi fore
il sacro lembo, o pur senti il Su' odore;
volaLi intorno ognor vivo ed ardente.

(Faithful thought, if you cannot often enter / within the heart of Jesus, then kiss from without / the sacred hem [of his garment], or else inhale His fragrance; / fly near Him at all times full of life and fervour. /)

The poet *Veronica Gambara was a contemporary on the literary scene and the same age as Vittoria Colonna. Despite her role, together with Colonna and Gaspara Stampa, as protagonist in the small group traditionally labelled as the standard bearers of female Petrarchism, she has not achieved the same recognition, and has always remained a somewhat distant figure.[2] Of the same aristocratic rank as Colonna, Gambara became Lady of Correggio in 1508 when she married Count Giberto X. She, too, was widowed quite young, in 1518, but in contrast to Vittoria, Veronica continued to be involved in the responsibilities of family and property. This fact helps to highlight the difference in their lives and their poetic choices. Gambara's verse, for example, seldom betrays a tendency to spiritual reflection. Neither before nor after her husband's death does she show herself drawn to a religious or mystical life. In fact, if one compares her with Colonna, it is perhaps in this tension between her literary activity and her active life in the world that we can occasionally glimpse the frustration and dissatisfaction which cloud Veronica's polished image. Since we find in her verses serious, measured emotions which adhere to a pessimistic, Petrarchan understanding of the temporality of all things, it could be maintained that Veronica, and not Vittoria, deserves to be acclaimed as the role model, for her ability to control a language which was easily imitable, and more neutral than Colonna's own intensely expressive tone. The difference between the two can be seen by comparing sonnets of the two poets published in the 1535 edition of Bembo's *Rime*. Veronica's literary baptism is a harmonious and delicate eulogy to her teacher Bembo:

> A l'ardente desio ch'ognor m'accende
> di seguir nel camin ch'al Ciel conduce
> sol voi mancava, o mia serena luce,
> per discacciar la nebbia che m'offende.
>
> (sonnet 36, in Bullock's edition)

(The burning desire which inflames me at every moment / to follow that path which leads to Heaven / is lacking only you, oh my calm light, / to chase away the fog which impedes my way. /)

Colonna's sonnet on the other hand (A1:71 in Bullock's edition) is a bitter reflection on the missed opportunity of an encounter between d'Avalos and Bembo, her worthy master:

Ahi quanto fu al mio Sol contrario il fato!
Chè con l'alta virtù de' raggi suoi
pria non v'accese, ché mill'anni poi
voi sareste più chiaro e più lodato?

(Alas, how the fates conspired against my beloved Sun! / Why did he not
inflame you sooner with the noble virtue / of his rays, so that for a
thousand years to come / you would be still more honoured and
esteemed?)

Regrettably, Gambara's poems had to wait until the 1759 edition printed
in Brescia by Rizzardi to be collected and arranged thematically, and until
the twentieth century to see the first complete edition (by Bullock) to remain
faithful to their fragmentary nature. We can now appreciate that there are
similarities between her poems and those in Pietro Bembo's dialogue, the
Asolani (1505), as well as in his first collection of *Poems* of 1530, republished in
1535. Like these early poems, Gambara's verse moves with more or less equal
elegance along various thematic paths: love for her homeland ('Poichè, per
mia ventura, a veder torno' – 'Since, to my good fortune, I return to see', 'In
praise of Brescia' no.37), the accomplishment of some public duty, and in
general various kinds of eulogy and relationships with public figures. All of
these are expressed with a fluency that has consistently been underrated.
But above all the poetry displays an unusual sensitivity towards nature,
filtered and arranged with consummate skill according to the model of the
locus amoenus (the idyllic setting) used by Petrarch and Bembo:

Ride la terra e d'ogni parte rende
mille soavi e dilettosi odori;
coperta di leggiadri e vaghi fiori
a guisa d'un bel ciel tutta risplende.

(sonnet 26, in Bullock's edition)

(The earth laughs, and from everywhere emits / a thousand sweet and
delicious fragrances; / covered with graceful and beautiful flowers / it
is as resplendent as a clear sky. /)

Gambara never found a passionate poetic voice able to eulogise a lover,
nor even a husband, in flesh and blood; and likewise never could (or never
wanted to) find the words fully to celebrate his manly qualities. She does,
paradoxically, manage to find a more original voice when she occasionally
confronts two pressing questions of early sixteenth-century Catholic
orthodoxy: the Virgin's motherhood ('Oh gran misterio, e sol per fede
inteso' – 'Oh great mystery, understood by faith alone'), and the theme of

predestination (the very famous and widely circulated 'Scelse da tutta la futura gente' – 'He chose from amongst all future peoples').

In contrast to Gambara, *Gaspara Stampa has received perhaps an excess of critical attention.[3] From a titillating emphasis on her presumed courtesan status, we move on to a reading which pays excessive attention to the exaltation of passionate instincts as the expression of an extreme and self-conscious femininity.[4] The fundamental distortion is the same in both cases: the 'woman' is privileged to the partial detriment of the writer, largely obscuring the level of cultured awareness which made Stampa one of the most interesting literary figures in Padua. A member of the 'Accademia dei Dubbiosi' ('Academy of the Doubtful') in Padua under the name of Anassilla, and well established in the Paduan-Venetian circle which included amongst its leaders Trifone Gabriele (1470–1549) and Sperone Speroni (1500–88), Gaspara participated in discussions and developed relations with other writers. But she published only three sonnets during her lifetime, found in Ruscelli's anthology of 1553, *Il sesto libro delle rime di diversi eccellenti autori* ('The sixth book of verse by various excellent authors'). She became famous above all for the freedom and brilliance of her life, and no less for the passionate love story which for a number of years connected her to Count Collaltino di Collalto. The numerous poems which make up her *canzoniere* (certainly one of the most evocative of her century) are for the most part inspired by this experience and dedicated to the man who remained her 'Beloved', even when their relationship was over and the poet had embarked upon another amorous adventure with the Venetian patrician, Bartolomeo Zen. As Gaspara's *canzoniere* was compiled and published posthumously in 1554, a year after her death, thanks to Cassandra Stampa, Gaspara's sister, we will never know what the author's original intentions were.[5] The publication of the three sonnets in 1553 makes one think that Stampa did have in mind an appearance on the publishing scene. Here is a quatrain, packed with Petrarchan antitheses on 'life' and 'death', from one of her widely-known poems:

> Così, senza aver vita, vivo in pene,
> e vivendo ov'è gioia, non son lieta;
> così fra viva e morta Amor mi tiene,
> e vita e morte ad un tempo mi vieta.

> (CXXXIII, 1–4, in Salza's edition)

(Thus, robbed of all life, I live in anguish, / and living where there is joy, I cannot be glad; / thus Love holds me suspended between life and death,/ and yet at once forbids me from both living and dying. /)

Gaspara Stampa studiously controlled her strategy of self-representation. For example, as the female lover who speaks in the first person (and not through a male voice) of her own erotic impulses ('vivere ardendo e non sentire il male' – 'to live on fire and never feel the pain'), she operates at the limits of what was acceptable, and contributes substantially to the creation of a *topos* that has been so successful it stills exists today. Stampa's dexterity in manipulating poetic language is striking. She chose an approach, far from obvious, which in Venice owed much to the contribution of Domenico Venier (1517–82). In the process she also acquired a little-known but interesting disciple in Olimpia Malipiero, whose verse was published in anthologies of *Rime* in 1559 and 1565, edited by Lodovico Domenichi and Dionigi Atanagi respectively.

In 1555, one year after the publication of Stampa's verses, *Chiara Matraini's *Rime e prose* ('Verse and prose') was published, the work of a poet from Lucca who had modelled her life and poetry on Vittoria Colonna. She, too, was widowed; and up to 1555 had remained quite unknown, apart from the liveliness and worldliness of her social life, as well as a 'scandalous' affair with a married man, Bartolomeo Graziani. In 1560 she probably met Cesare Coccapani of Carpi, sent to Lucca to work as a judge, and a new love was born, or at least a long-lasting intense spiritual and intellectual bond, while her relationship with Ludovico Domenichi (1515–64), her teacher and admirer during the 1550s, seems to have been abandoned. From 1576, however, at last protected by her age from potential gossip or the traces of old scandals, she began to rebuild her self-image according to a painstakingly constructed model which she studied carefully and supported through rigorously spiritual prose writings. Significantly, the three publications of her *Canzoniere* (1555, 1595, 1597) are in fact three different books, with the material substantially rearranged and rewritten. These changes reflect a shifting extra-textual scenario: the poetic collections are inspired by two separate lovers (Bartolomeo Graziani and Cesare Coccapani) and in some cases lyrics referring to her first lover are replaced. The 1555 edition of the poems included various prose writings, but in 1595 Matraini prepared a volume of *Lettere e rime* ('Letters and verse') and kept to this format in the last edition as well.

Laura Battiferri (1523–89) from Urbino adopted Florence as her home and took as her second husband the famous sculptor Bartolomeo Ammannati.[6] Unlike the other poets, Battiferri has left no complete *canzoniere*, nor any unified edition of her work; in fact, her first and principal lyric undertaking remains the 1560 collection, *Il primo libro delle opere toscane* ('The first book of works in Tuscan'), entitled thus on the advice of Benedetto Varchi (1503–65). Battiferri's use of the word 'opere' is significant because it sheds light on the author's understanding both of the importance of a precise definition of her work and of the very nature of the book, and her uncertainty about what to call a combination of mixed lyrical genres alternating between traditional compositions (sonnets and madrigals), free translations from Latin into the vernacular ('Inno alla gloria' –'Hymn to glory') by St Augustine in blank verse; 'Orazione a Geremia profeta' ('Oration to the Prophet Jeremiah') in *terza rima* and also an eclogue 'Europa'.

The figure of Laura's husband occupies a central position in her poetry. We find him celebrated in verse as a lifetime companion, with no attempt to present him as the Eternal Lover, nor any desire to pass him over in favour of extra-marital experiences, even if only abstract or purely literary. What is more, he is celebrated during his lifetime, a hitherto unheard-of role in the production of poetry by women in the sixteenth century. Battiferri calls attention to this new departure in her prefatory address to her readers. The book, she says, is a response to encouragement from friends (as we know, primarily from Benedetto Varchi); above all it enjoys the approval of her husband, who thus indirectly assumes the role of patron. The reasons for this somewhat unusual treatment can be ascribed to Ammannati's professional status as a renowned artist, and personal prestige – of which Laura was distinctly aware. Thus we are confronted with an authentic (and in some poems highly modern) companionship in both life and art. Battiferri's religious verse acts almost as a prelude to her other important work, *I sette salmi penitenziali tradotti in lingua toscana* ('The seven penitential psalms translated into the Tuscan tongue'), published in 1564 and dedicated to Vittoria Farnese della Rovere, Duchess of Urbino. This genre was so popular at the time (specifically the Penitential Psalms), that in 1568 Giolito was able to publish a proper anthology of these vernacular translations.

Another poet with ideas similar to those which inform Battiferri's works is the Florentine Maddalena Salvetti Acciaioli (d.1610), the interesting but little-known author of *Rime toscane* ('Tuscan rhymes') dedicated to the Grand Dukes Cristina di Lorena and Ferdinando de' Medici.[7] The atmosphere evoked in this collection is by now markedly *fin-de-siècle*: every trace of narrative ambition has disappeared, and with it all attempts to construct a persona following an exemplary model. The writing of poetry, by both women and men, explores new linguistic registers and genres. In many cases the importance of a social network is emphasised, and the eulogies and occasional verses, always in any poet's portfolio, assume a privileged position in these late sixteenth-century works. As far as the women writers are concerned, we should remember that even earlier *Tullia d'Aragona and Laura Terracina (c.1519–c.77) published books containing primarily encomiastic verses within a year of each other. D'Aragona, a writer of Roman origins and a courtesan by profession, published her poems in 1547 with a dedication to the dukes of Florence. It is clear enough that what inspires her is the desire to manipulate a middle-range poetic register into the desired form, employing a single lyric genre, primarily the sonnet. Though not a negligible poet, d'Aragona's range is limited. She is more important as a prose writer and achieves much higher ends in the writing of dialogues such as *Dell'infinità d'amore* ('On the infinity of love', 1547), a nuanced treatise on Platonic love (see chapter 5).

The other poet mentioned, Laura Terracina, expanded the potential of occasional verse by fashioning volumes intended solely as flattering decoration to honour influential individuals. The illustrious contemporaries addressed included Colonna, Gambara and Michelangelo Buonarroti. It would seem that this writer of nine books of poetry, two of which were ambitiously based on the *Orlando furioso* (published in 1549 and 1567), was brought into being through the skilful and determined Marc'Antonio Passero, book collector and a leading figure in a large Neapolitan literary circle. Certainly no one else in this century was so prolific and so fluent, nor did the publishing industry smile upon anyone else with such kindness (the total number of editions, including reprints, is remarkable, as are the short intervals between editions).[8] Particularly interesting, and illustrative of the techniques used by the poet, was the virtuoso exercise based on Ariosto. Terracina composed the same number of cantos as there are in the *Orlando furioso*, each one with a different dedicatee. In addition, each line of Ariosto's opening octave makes up the final line of Terracina's first six octaves, and the rhyming couplet from Ariosto is used as the rhyming couplet for Terracina's seventh and last octave of her each and every canto. She also attempts thematic parallels. Just as Ariosto's Canto 1 speaks of the wars of the Emperor Charlemagne against the Moors, so Terracina dedicates her Canto 1 to Emperor Charles V, also engaged in wars against contemporary infidels, the Turks. In her opening octave, she says she will not sing of ancient heroes of antiquity, 'ma dirò quel che fer, con vari ardori / *Le donne, i cavalier, l'arme, e gli amori*' ('But I shall speak of the deeds that, with diverse passions, /Ladies, knights, arms and love performed.') Her last line (in italics) is the first of Ariosto's opening octave.[9]

It seems apt to close a study of the sixteenth century with the Venetian *Veronica Franco, famed during her lifetime principally as a high-class courtesan. Her poems were published in 1575 (some critics say in 1576), in an almost clandestine edition bearing no date. Very few copies are recorded. The collection constitutes a poetic exchange. There are some poems addressed to Franco herself, seemingly by other hands, but their affinity with poems undoubtedly her own has posed serious critical problems of attribution. It has at least been verified that these *capitoli* (used largely in the sixteenth century for satirical verse) must have been written by a member of the Venier family, with whom Veronica was deeply involved. She was the lover of Marco Venier (1537–1602), the target of attacks by Maffio (1550–86), and a close friend of the learned Domenico. For her own poetic style, the contact with Maffio is especially significant, as he is now increasingly recognised as a fine poet capable of controlling diverse linguistic registers, and certainly the only poet to have exploited the highly expressive potential of *capitoli* in dialect. Franco, too, shares a great deal with this approach to poetry. Her choice of *capitoli* is highly original when compared to the output of other women writers, although less unusual if one looks further afield. Sexuality, which is generally repressed or else sublimated into sentimental eroticism in poetry by women, is explicitly addressed in these well-known lines of Franco's:

> Così dolce e gustevole divento,
> quando mi trovo con persona in letto,
> da cui amata e gradita mi sento,
>
> che quel mio piacer vince ogni diletto,
> sì che quel, che strettissimo parea,
> nodo de l'altrui amor divien più stretto.

('Terze rime', II, lines 154–9, in Salza's edition)

(So sweet and delicious do I become / when I find myself in bed with a man / who, I feel, loves and enjoys me, / that the pleasure I bring excels all delight, / so the knot of love, however tight / it seemed before, is tied tighter still. /)

(Tanslation from Jones and Rosenthal, *Selected Poems*, p. 69)

Even the more conventional poems are strongly tinted with sensuality: sighs for her lover's departure ('Le sue lettere mandatemi ognor leggo' – 'I read the letters he sent me over and over again', 'Terze rime', xv, line 7), the desire to touch and kiss, which are infiltrated even into poetic situations clearly of Petrarchan stamp.

Sexuality can therefore be viewed as a cornerstone of Franco's poetic self-imaging, both as the 'mistress of the art of love' (we recognise the numerous autobiographical allusions) and also as the 'Lover' legitimated by poetry. The poet dominates her material with great skill, and 'enacts' sexual union with the aid of metaphor. Thus military metaphors substitute explicit sexual references, which only a male speaker could articulate without loss of dignity: and what is unspeakable is spoken.

> Non più parole: ai fatti, in campo, a l'armi,
> ch'io voglio, risoluta di morire,
> da sì grave molestia liberarmi.
>
> . . .
>
> Forse nel letto ancor ti seguirei,
> e quivi teco guerreggiando stesa,
> in alcun modo non ti cederei:
>
> per soverchiar la tua sì degna offesa
> ti verrei sopra, e nel contrasto ardita,
> scaldandoti ancor tu ne la difesa,
>
> teco morrei d'egual colpo ferita.

('Terze rime', XIII, lines 1–3, 79–85)

(No more words! To deeds, to the battlefield, to arms! / for, resolved to die, I wish to free myself / from such merciless mistreatment. / . . . Perhaps I would even follow you to bed, / and, stretched out there in skirmishes with you / I would yield to you in no way at all: / To take revenge for your unfair attack, / I'd fall upon you, and in daring combat, / as you too caught fire defending yourself, / I would die with you, felled by the same blow.)

(Translation from Jones and Rosenthal, *Selected Poems*, pp. 133, 137)

The anti-Petrarchism and the pornographic, Rabelaisian and erotic experiences expressed by Pietro Aretino (1492–1556) and other Venetian writers, together with her knowledge of Latin poets (especially Ovid and Horace), allowed Franco to find a literary formula capable of expressing the desires of the female body on a basis of cultural and literary parity.

As the sixteenth century drew to a close, a number of minor figures appeared on the scene, linked to specific projects (one thinks of Matraini's third edition of 1597) or else conforming to the standard so well established by Terracina. With the arrival of the seventeenth century, however, the great actress Isabella Canali, better known as *Isabella Andreini, achieved celebrity status in poetic as well as dramatic circles. A renowned director and interpreter of pastoral dramas and tragedies, Andreini followed in the wake of Torquato Tasso (1544–95), who remained not only the undoubted principal literary protagonist of the second half of the sixteenth century, but also Andreini's personal role model. She eloquently interpreted the male lead role in Tasso's pastoral, *Aminta*, a choice which says a great deal about Andreini's expressive powers and psychological complexity. Such richness is also evident in her writings, above all her letters (see chapter 1), and helps to challenge the rigid boundaries of gender representation. Her book of poetry, too, published only once in 1601, draws upon the variety of Isabella's artistic experiences. The opening stanzas of the first sonnet are exemplary:

> S'alcun fia mai che i versi miei negletti
> legge, non creda a questi finti ardori;
> chi ne le scene imaginati amori
> usa a trattar con non leali affetti,
>
> con bugiardi, non men con finti detti,
> de le Muse spiegar gli alti furori,
> talor piangendo i falsi miei dolori,
> talor cantando i falsi miei diletti.

(Rime)

(If anyone should ever read my forgotten verses, / let them not believe in this feigned ardour; / I am the one who on stage is used to act out / imaginary loves and faithless affections, / and so with fictive and invented speeches, / I now describe the noble furies of the Muses, / sometimes grieving over my false pain, / and sometimes praising my pretended delights. /)

A reading of this poem is a sufficient measure of the enormous gulf which separates it from the Petrarchan experience of the mid- and late-sixteenth century, for the art of impersonation reigns supreme. The situation described by the sonnet, in which the poet, like the actor, enacts the various types of love experiences, is entirely new. The author's candid and openly autobiographical declarations are equally unusual, not because such elements have been lacking in all the cases examined thus far (one thinks of Colonna, for example), but because normally personal details are absorbed into the codified structure of a model that is nearly always removed from everyday realities. Andreini overturns this assumption by presenting her professional credentials (hence the significance of make-believe), to the detriment of any presumed 'confession' of thoughts and feelings which was the basis of the sixteenth-century lyric.

Explicit references to the various artistic environments in which she moved, also evoked through the mention of other artists with whom she worked (a technique used frequently by Tasso), led Andreini to commemorate in her poetry the figure of Laura Guidiccioni Lucchesini (1550–99), a writer from Lucca better known for her plays than for her poetry. The poems dedicated to Guidiccioni's memory appear to be written in the voices of the people evoked, as if mimicking the dynamics of the relationship daily set up between the playwright and the actor on stage. Andreini becomes her characters, and even takes on the voice of Petrarch (with a change of gender not new to her), singing in praise of this new Laura.

> Tra questi duri sassi,
> Laura che tanto amai,
> Laura mia, ch'amo ancor, rinchiusa stassi;
> tu, Viator che passi,
> le più degne Dee veder potrai
> che tutte insieme accolte
> piangono l'onorate ossa sepolte.
> Sol la diva beltà mirar non puoi,
> che seco Laura mia la tolse a noi.
>
> (Madrigal LV, *Rime*)

(Beneath these hard stones, / Laura whom I loved so much, / my Laura, whom I still love, is imprisoned; / you, traveller passing by, / you may see the noblest goddesses / all gathered together / who are mourning the venerated remains buried here. / Only you cannot see her divine beauty, / because my Laura took it away from us with her. /)

Andreini can be interpreted as a figure emblematic of a new sensibility, while Guidiccioni Lucchesini brings attention to a general move towards the theatrical, clearly demarcating an area which will come to be increasingly occupied by women. Such a trend is beautifully exemplified by Margherita Costa Ronaca, probably a Roman courtesan, certainly a singer and 'virtuosa' (the seventeenth-century version of an eighteenth-century extemporary poet). Active in Rome, Florence and Paris, where she enjoyed the protection of Cardinal Mazarin, Costa Ronaca wrote dramas, works in various genres (letters, treatises), and also poetry collections which, independently of their artistic merit, provide us with valuable insights into the change in the conception of poetry, beginning with the titles. Between 1638 and 1639 Costa Ronaca published three collections entitled *La chitarra* ('The guitar'), *Il violino* ('The violin') – both published in 1638 – and *Lo stipo* ('The cabinet', 1639). Nothing could be further from the generic sameness of the *Rime*: it is clear that the sixteenth-century conception of the lyric is dead.

Even the use of poetic forms (sonnet, canzone, etc.) and metre changed irreversibly, leaving more and more space for free composition. Sonnets still abounded, as did complete collections of poems, but increasingly women participated in the writing of longer poems with narrative aspirations. *Lucrezia Marinella is a fine example of this tendency. If in recent times critical attention has been focused exclusively on her treatise of 1600 in defence of women (see chapter 5), in the past Marinella was primarily celebrated for her imposing heroic poem 'L'Enrico overo Bisantio acquistato' ('The Henriad, or Byzantium gained'), dealing with the struggles of Christian Venice against Moors and (here) Greeks. After 1570, the victory of European forces against the Turks at Lepanto, the subject matter grew ever more appealing. The narrative poem of another writer, *Margherita Sarrocchi, also dwelt on the same events (see chapter 4). But Marinella also offers valuable evidence of the way in which the new literary boundaries were shifting. A glance at the titles of her verse compositions – predominantly in octaves – reveals a subject that is hagiographic or didactic, typical of this period of a triumphant Catholic Counter-Reformation, even for a writer who adopts audacious social views, as in her learned defence of women, for example. The time is no longer right for an effusive expression of heart and mind in a love which encompasses all internal drives, nor for a lyric voice capable of conveying the whole of existence. Marinella's lyric poems are uniformly spiritual.

In this context, the editorial work of the Neapolitan Antonio Bulifon (1649–1707), carried out at the end of the seventeenth century, deserves attention. A publisher fundamentally important for the diffusion of women's poetry, Bulifon was responsible for a posthumous collection of Marinella (1693) where he placed her lyrics together with a selection by the earlier poets Gambara and Morra, as well as his contemporary, Maria Selvaggia Borghini (1654–1731). This collection of sixteenth- and seventeenth-century poets, however, created a false sense of continuity which did little justice to the evolution of the lyric over a hundred and fifty years. Thus, at the very moment Bulifon rightly brought to the attention of a new public the splendours of sixteenth-century Petrarchism by women, he also formalised a poetry that no longer had any vitality. For all writing, by women and men alike, had by now abandoned the shared experience which had characterised the sixteenth century, and lyric poetry had lost its status as the queen of poetic form, as is illustrated by the most innovative female poet of the seventeenth century, the Venetian *Arcangela Tarabotti. She was without doubt the most acute, brilliant, keen-edged writer (in her style and even more in her subject matter) that her century had to offer, but she wrote almost entirely in prose (see chapter 5).

NOTES

1. For the diffusion of Colonna's poems, see A. Bullock's edition of her *Rime*. Colonna quotations are from Bullock, following his numbering. For additions and corrections to his 1982 edition, see Bullock, 'Vittoria Colonna: note e aggiunte alla edizione critica del 1982', *Giornale storico della letteratura italiana* 162 (1985), 407–13.

2. Quotations from A. Bullock's edition of Veronica Gambara's *Rime*.

3. Quotations from A. Salza's 1913 edition of Gaspara Stampa, *Rime*.

4. See M. Zancan, 'Gaspara Stampa. La differenza: questioni di scrittura e di lettura', in M. Pecoraro (ed.), *Studi in onore di Vittorio Zaccaria* (Milan, 1987), pp. 263–73.

5. See chapter 10 for the eighteenth-century edition by Luisa Bergalli and Apostolo Zeno (Venice, 1738).

6. See entry by G. Rabitti in Russell. In the Biblioteca Nazionale Centrale, Florence, Victoria Kirkham has discovered the manuscript prepared by Battiferri for the press. See her article 'Laura Battiferra degli Ammannati's "First Book" of poetry', *Rinascimento* (1996), pp. 1–40.

7. Hardly anything has been written about her; see G. M. Mazzuchelli, *Gli scrittori d'Italia* (Brescia, 1753–63), vol. III, p. 549; and entry in G. Negri, *Istoria degli scrittori fiorentini* (Ferrara, 1722).

8. See B. Croce, 'La casa di una poetessa (1901)' in *Storie e leggende napoletane* (Bari, 1948); L. Montella, *Una poetessa del Rinascimento: Laura Terracina* (Salerno, 1993); Russell; Cos-Zal, pp. 79–84.

9. The anthologies mentioned are a vast reservoir of the collective phenomenon of women writing poetry in the mid- and late-sixteenth century, some known for a handful of poems, others for only one or two. See F. Piéjus, 'La première anthologie de poèmes féminins', in *Le pouvoir et la plume* (Paris, 1982), pp. 193–213.

4
_____

Fiction, 1560–1650

Introduction

The history of women's writing – or of published women's writing –
in early modern Italy may be seen as falling into two main phases, with
the dividing-line falling around 1580. In the first of these, the great
majority of published writings by Italian women tend to adhere to the
relatively narrow formula for feminine literary practice established by
*Vittoria Colonna, consisting of the Petrarchist lyric, in its amatory and
spiritual variants, and the *lettera familiare*. Published fiction by Italian
women barely exists from this period, the only significant exceptions
being the *sacre rappresentazioni* of *Antonia Pulci, discussed in chapter 2,
part ii, and two works by the Roman courtesan *Tullia d'Aragona, both of
disputed authorship, the quasi-autobiographical *Dialogo d'amore* (1547)
and the romance *Il Meschino* (1560). From the 1580s, by contrast, the range
of women's published production broadened significantly, quickly
coming to encompass practically every polite literary genre of the day.
Thus the works of the Venetian *Moderata Fonte, published between 1581
and 1600, comprise a romance, a prose dialogue, a libretto and two religious narratives in *ottava rima*; while the more substantial output of her
long-lived compatriot *Lucrezia Marinella, published between 1595 and
1650, includes a polemical treatise and an epic poem, as well as an assort-
ment of narrative poems on mythological, religious and pastoral themes.
Fonte and Marinella were admittedly exceptional in the ambitiousness of
their literary output, but a glance at the careers of less prolific women
writers in this period confirms the trend. To remain in the Veneto,
between 1585 and 1591, the Vicentine *Maddalena Campiglia published a
pastoral eclogue, a pastoral drama and a discourse on the Annunciation,

while the Paduan Valeria Miani Negri was the author of another pastoral drama (1604) and, most unusually, a tragedy, *Celinda*, (1611).[1]

What reasons may be adduced for this dramatic expansion in the range of women's writing from the ninth decade of the Cinquecento onwards? The most obvious is simply precedent: writing over a century after women humanists had first caught the eye of the Italian literary public, and with a substantial tradition of published women's writing behind them, writers of Fonte's and Campiglia's generation were better poised than their mothers or grandmothers to venture an incursion into traditionally 'masculine' genres. Another reason, however, is likely to have been the change in the Italian literary climate that took place in the wake of the Counter-Reformation, and whose effects were felt increasingly from the 1560s onwards. A very significant barrier to the authorship of fiction on the part of women in the first half of the sixteenth century was undoubtedly sexual decorum. The dominant secular fictional forms in this period – the *novella*, the comedy and the chivalric romance – all tended to adopt a predominantly 'realist' erotic language reminiscent of Boccaccio, and more precisely his *Decameron*, in sharp contrast to the sublimated erotic codes derived from Petrarch and Neoplatonism that dominated lyric production. This placed the aforementioned genres, to differing degrees, beyond the reach of aspiring women writers, Boccaccian eroticism being disapproved of as reading matter for respectable women, let alone as a model for literary imitation. No early modern Italian woman writer published a *novella* collection, and only one a secular comedy (the Roman courtesan Margherita Costa, in 1641), while the first chivalric romance to be published under a woman's name, Tullia d'Aragona's *Meschino*, mentioned above, was prefaced by a denunciation of the 'obscenities' of the genre as generally practised, and an announcement of the author's intention to produce a chivalric poem so 'utterly chaste, pure, and Christian' in content and language that it might be safely read by any woman, whether 'matron, virgin, widow or nun'.

The moral rigour informing the preface to the *Meschino* may be related to its putative author's status as a former courtesan anxious to redeem her reputation; at the same time, however, it locates the poem within the literary vanguard of the day. The second half of the sixteenth century saw a significant moral reorientation of Italian literature, prompted by the social and spiritual concerns of the Counter-Reformation. A major indicator of this shift was the displacement of the 'realist' erotic language that had characterised much Italian narrative and drama in the first half of the century by more elevated idioms with their roots in Petrarch, the *stilnovo*, early Boccaccio and the Renaissance Neoplatonic tradition. One result of this development was a modification in the tacit gender boundaries of polite literary culture; as standards of sexual decorum in male-authored literature shifted closer to those that had traditionally circumscribed 'feminine' literary practice, so women found a diminishing area of literary culture closed off to them on grounds of their sex. The most innovative and distinctive fictional forms of later sixteenth- and early seventeenth-century Italy were the pious historical *poema eroico* and the courtly pastoral drama, the latter hailed by one theorist as a moral advance on comedy in that it allowed 'chaste virgins and decent women' on to the stage.[2] Both genres, as we shall see, proved amenable to adoption by women writers, whose new freedom to experiment with fictional forms may thus be seen, rather paradoxically, as a by-product of Counter-Reformational moral repression. The works that resulted, though often applauded by contemporaries, have left barely a trace in subsequent literary history. This neglect is unfortunate, given the interest of this production as evidence of women's place in early modern literary culture, and, in particular, of the dynamics of early women writers' appropriation of 'masculine' literary codes.

Pastoral drama

Pastoral drama in Italy is generally acknowledged to have emerged as a self-conscious and autonomous literary genre in mid-Cinquecento Ferrara, evolving out of the vibrant but amorphous courtly traditions of mythological spectacle, with some input from the humanistic form of the pastoral eclogue.[3] Spreading out from Ferrara through the courts of Italy and Europe, especially after Tasso's *Aminta* (1573) had demonstrated the literary sophistication of which the genre was capable, pastoral drama established a hold on the aristocratic imagination that it would retain throughout the following century. Its appeal was a complex one, combining a tacit reaffirmation of social hierarchies with a strain of anarchic hedonism, its amorous nymphs and faithful shepherds offering up a flattering mirror to its courtly readers and spectators, while at the same time acting as repositories for psychological yearnings to which courtly society could offer little release. Romantic in its portrayal of love where comedy was lewd, and psychologically rather than socially oriented, pastoral drama proved a notably congenial genre for women writers. Perhaps the earliest recorded essay in the form by a woman, completed by 1587, was the *Partenia* of Barbara Torelli Benedetti of Parma, whose warm reception may have encouraged emulation by others; soon afterwards, in 1588, there appeared the first two published pastorals by women, both natives of the Veneto, *Isabella Canali Andreini's *Mirtilla* and Maddalena Campiglia's *Flori*, the latter of which echoes the *Partenia* in a number of narrative motifs.[4] Also from the Veneto was Valeria Miani (*Amorosa speranza*, 1604), while a further small group of women writers of pastoral were from Lucca: Isabetta Coreglia (*Dori*, 1634; *Erindo*, 1650), Eleonora Bernardi Bellati (b. 1559), author of a lost pastoral drama perhaps entitled *Clorindo*, and, most intriguingly, Laura Guidiccioni Lucchesini, whose three pastoral dramas, also lost, were performed at the Florentine court in the 1590s, set to music by Emilio de' Cavalieri.[5] Geographically – aside from the oddity of this cluster of Lucchesi – the distribution of recorded women writers of pastoral dramas corresponds more or less with that of the genre as a whole; socially too, in that, true to the pastoral's class allegiances, these writers were for the most part from the major or minor nobility of their cities. The exception, Isabella Andreini, is less anomalous in this company than she might at first appear, in that her exceptional celebrity as an actress gave her access to aristocratic circles to which her birth would not have entitled her.

As is unsurprising in such a powerfully stereotypical genre, the surviving early modern pastorals by women have many features in common: all share the basic cast-list of languishing nymphs and shepherds, lustful satyrs and wise elders; all open on an intricate knot of unreciprocal loves, later disentangled through a series of variously improbable changes of heart; certain episodes – the lover's dialogue with Echo, the misreported or misfired suicide, the climactic scene in which characters' true identities are revealed – occur so frequently as to be almost obligatory. Nonetheless, there are significant differences in character between the various plays. One formal distinction may be made on the grounds of the inclusion or otherwise of comic and farcical material: of the earlier plays, for example, Torelli's *Partenia* and Campiglia's *Flori* are unusual in taking their cue from the consistently elevated, 'tragic' tone of Tasso's *Aminta*, while Andreini's *Mirtilla* and Miani's *Amorosa speranza* abound in comic elements, introducing goat-herds to parody the 'noble' shepherds' amorous passsions with their baser gluttonous appetites, and developing with relish the stock farcical episode in which a satyr is outwitted and humilated by nymphs.[6] A further discrimination might be made on the grounds of the relation established between the fictions of these plays and their ambient realities: here one might distinguish between plays such as Andreini's and Miani's, set in generic Arcadian groves, and those of Torelli and Coreglia, which are located in recognisable, if poetically transfigured, local settings, or that of Campiglia, which hints with sufficient insistence at the historical permeability of its fiction to have tempted critics to autobiographical readings.[7] Finally, these plays might be distinguished on grounds of literary quality and ambition: while the works of Coreglia and Miani are no more than workaday genre exercises – in the case of Miani, a rather inept one – those of Andreini and Campiglia have sufficient literary interest to merit more serious attention than they have hitherto received. Campiglia's *Flori*, in particular, recombines its largely traditional elements in a notably original manner, using the conventional device of an amorously inspired madness as a poignant metaphor for the alienated state of its eponymous heroine, possessed by a yearning for transcendence that expresses itself variously in her ambitions for literary immortality (i, 1), in the obsession with her dead fellow-nymph Amaranta which is the ostensible cause of her madness and in the equally extreme and solipsistic platonic passion for the grieving shepherd Alessi, aroused when she catches sight of him during the sacrifice organised to exorcise her of her previous doomed love (iii, 5).

The *Flori*'s reworking, in its central character, of the pastoral stereotype of the recalcitrant nymph is perhaps the single most striking feature of Campiglia's play. The success of this innovation, however, owes much to its dramatic context: the sublimity of Flori's passion is effectively offset by the more earthbound, though still elevated, love of her faithful companion Licori for the aptly named Androgeo, while a third, less distinguished love, between Urania and the fickle Serrano, provides an ironic counterpoint to these two. This calibration of differing modes of love suggests the presence of a Neoplatonic conceptual framework: a suggestion confirmed in passages such as the set-pieces in i, 5 and iii, 5 in which Licori and Flori rapturously describe, respectively, the mouth and the eyes of their beloveds, the two zones of the body whose relative 'nobility' qualified them, to differing degrees, as appropriate focuses of a spiritualised love. A further point of interest in such passages is their inversion of the gender relations conventionally obtaining in Neoplatonic literature, in which female beauty tends to be configured as the object of the desiring male gaze. This tendency to privilege women's experience is a distinctive and interesting feature of the *Flori*; not only does female desire tend to be consistently foregrounded in its heterosexual love narratives, but the play also brings centre-stage, in Flori's relationships with, respectively, Licori and Amaranta, a friendship and an erotic attachment between women, both phenomena relatively little touched on within male-authored literature in this period.

As was noted above, the only pastoral by a woman at all comparable with the *Flori* on the grounds of literary quality is Isabella Andreini's *Mirtilla* – in terms of publishing success, by far the most successful of all the works surveyed in this chapter. Published in the same year and in similar cultural contexts, the two plays differ radically in their character: where the *Flori* is remarkable for its psychological depth and troubled lyricism, the *Mirtilla* is breezily superficial in its tone, and sufficiently unconcerned with psychological realism to dish up no fewer than three instant changes of heart in its last act with no more explanation than a casual aside about the miraculous powers of love and an allusion to Ariosto's ironic praise for women's remarkable capacities for spontaneous decision.[8] The *Mirtilla*'s energies are directed elsewhere – to fulfilling the didactic task it light-heartedly sets itself, of demonstrating the benignity of love when directed at matrimony; more obliquely, to promoting the author's carefully stage-managed social identity as an actress whose culture and virtue elevated her from the questionable morality associated with the profession; finally, to providing a showcase for Andreini's fluent and seemingly effortless powers of poetic invention, well displayed in the series of virtuosistic monologues and elaborately patterned dialogic exchanges that are such a prominent feature of the play's dramatic texture. The element of 'modularity' in the structure of the *Mirtilla* is of interest, given Andreini's background in the improvisatory theatre of the *commedia dell'arte*, which appears from the surviving evidence to have constructed its spectacles around precisely the kind of generic and recyclable set-piece speeches and exchanges that feature so large in the play.

Chivalric romance and epic

Despite their well-documented popularity with women readers of this period, the chivalric romance and the historical *poema eroico* which displaced it in great part from the 1580s onwards, are, on several grounds, more improbable candidates for adoption by women writers than pastoral drama. One disqualifying feature was such poems' vast scale, contrasting sharply with the decorous confines of more 'feminine' genres; another, the nature of their subject matter – public and political, in the case of the epic, and, in both genres, centrally concerned with what Ariosto called 'le armi e gli amori', both of which were, for different reasons and to differing extents, considered inappropriate topics for women. As was suggested at the beginning of this chapter, the moralising inflections that increasingly characterised the treatment of love in chivalric fiction from around the 1560s onwards must have mitigated this inappropriateness to a certain degree. It is unlikely, however, to have dispelled entirely the sense that for women to venture on to such quintessentially masculine literary territory constituted a notable transgression. The gendered language with which Tasso characterises the austere magnificence of epic style, by contrast with the refined and delicate charms of the lyric, is revealing in this respect, as are male commentators' remarks on women's rare essays in the genre, whether sympathic (Giovanni Niccolò Doglioni's admiring wonder in his prefatory sonnet to Moderata Fonte's *Floridoro* that a 'little maid confined to her chamber' could range with her imagination over battles and distant voyages), or hostile (Giambattista Marino's snort of contempt that the 'chattering magpie' Margherita Sarrocchi should dare to turn her 'unpolished rhymes' to the suject of arms and love).[9]

Notwithstanding these prejudices, as the examples just cited indicate, a handful of chivalric works by women do exist from this period. The first of these, already mentioned, is *Il Meschino*, attributed to the Roman courtesan and poet, Tullia d'Aragona, though the work's authenticity may reasonably be doubted, given its posthumous publication and dissimilarity to Tullia's other writings. *Il Meschino* narrates the odyssey in search of his parents and identity of the eponymous hero, a scion of a minor Carolingian dynasty, following in the tracks of the popular prose romance of the same name by Andrea da Barberino (*c.* 1380–1432). Unappealing in many respects, the poem has a certain historical interest as a good example of the mid-century drive to correct the deviancies of the traditional chivalric romance with a dose of the structural unity and moral gravity prescribed by contemporary neo-Aristotelian criticism. Moral correctness is particularly stressed, especially, as has been noted, in the interesting preface, which sternly censures the laxness in this respect of Pulci, Boiardo and even Ariosto. A further respect in which *Il Meschino* typifies Counter-Reformation literary trends is in its suspicious and often hostile treatment of its female characters: within a genre of literature famously ambiguous in its treatment of women, reproducing many traditional patriarchal or misogynistic stereotypes (the helpless damsel, the heartless seductress), but also experimenting with more transgressive types (notably the female warrior), *Il Meschino* is distinctive for the rigour with which it eliminates the latter class of figure from its cast-list, while enthusiastically embracing the former. The poem's relatively few women characters fall neatly into the two categories of the colourlessly good and the luridly bad. Typical of the former is Antinisca, who waits meekly for a decade to marry the hero, rapidly produces a son and heir and then dies. The latter category is best represented by the classical figure of the Cumaean Sybil, who appears in the poem incongruously conscripted into the role of the fatal enchantress who attempts to impede the hero's mission, and is portrayed without half-tones as a squalid epitome of feminine perfidy and carnality.[10]

A sharp contrast with *Il Meschino*, under all the aspects just discussed, is presented by the next chivalric work by a woman to be published, Moderata Fonte's *Tredici canti del Floridoro* (1581), the object of the fondly admiring characterisation by Doglioni quoted above. Although written two decades later than Tullia's *Meschino*, and published in the same year as Tasso's *Gerusalemme Liberata*, Fonte's poem shows a blissful indifference to the neo-Aristotelian literary trends of which the former is an anticipation and the latter the culmination, adhering instead unabashedly to an earlier, Ariostan model of romance. The *Floridoro*'s air of dreamy unconnectedness, no doubt fostered by Fonte's relative social isolation, is compounded by its being one of the only romances of the century to invent its narrative matter, rather than, as was conventional, embroidering traditional French or Spanish material. The poem, dedicated to Francesco de' Medici, and his Venetian wife Bianca Cappello, is set in a fantastical ancient Greece, and appears set to follow the adventures of the young prince Floridoro, putative founder of the Medici dynasty. In the thirteen cantos that are all that was published, however, the protagonist's story is scarcely initiated; rather, these cantos present us, in true romance mode, with an anarchic proliferation of loosely interconnected plotlines, whose outcome, given the loss of the remainder of the poem, can only be a matter for conjecture.

It is not only in structural respects that Fonte's *Floridoro* has something of the air of a throwback; in its tone, as well, the work is closer to the careless and irrepressible fantasising of early Cinquecento romance than to the moral and religious earnestness of more nearly contemporary works. Moreover, in its representation of women, the *Floridoro* is notably lacking in the misogynistic tendencies often found in later Cinquecento chivalric literature; on the contrary, the future author of *Il merito delle donne* portrays her female protagonists with an almost unvarying sympathy. A comparison with *Il Meschino* is illuminating here: where the earlier work converts the traditionally revered figure of the Cumaean Sybil into an object of loathing and ridicule, *Il Floridoro*, in the structurally equivalent scene, attempts by contrast to redeem the traditionally equivocal figure of the classical siren Circe by portraying her notorious abuses of her magical powers as motivated by a legitimate desire for revenge.[11] A similarly polemical edge is apparent in the episode which contrasts the character and fate of the identical twin sisters Biondaura and Risamante, the first of whom, the product of conventional feminine upbringing, we encounter in the form of a painted portrait, inspiring her male champions to valour, while the second, kidnapped at birth by a wizard and schooled in the military arts, embodies 'masculine' prowess herself.[12] The authorial aside in the proem to Canto 4 in which Fonte proposes Risamante as an emblem of women's potential in the fields of arms and letters became something of a cult among subsequent Venetian women writers, being cited by Lucrezia Marinella, Arcangela Tarabotti and, much later, by Luisa Bergalli.[13] Beyond this passage, however, much else in Fonte's treatment of the episode is worthy of scrutiny: the striking scene in Canto 2 juxtaposing the 'mirror images' of feminine identity represented by the painted Biondaura and the living Risamante offers rich material for feminist analysis, as does the complex scene in Canto 3 in which Risamante rescues the adulterous Queen of Phrygia and learns of her dynastic dynasty.

The life-span of the chivalric romance was not entirely over in Italy by the time of the *Floridoro*; as a late and rather hybrid example of this never particularly well-defined genre, one might cite Barbara degli Albizzi Tagliamocchi's slack reworking of Virgilian material, *Ascanio errante* (1640).[14] As the impact of the *Gerusalemme Liberata* was absorbed, however, the historically based *poema eroico* began to assert itself ever more surely as the dominant genre of chivalric fiction; and it is unsurprising that the other two chivalric works by women published in the Seicento both took this form. The poems in question are Margherita Sarrocchi's *Scanderbeide* (1623), which takes as its subject the campaigns against the Turk of the Albanian hero Scanderbeg (Giorgio Castriota (*c.* 1414–68)), and Lucrezia Marinella's *L'Enrico, overo Bisanzio acquistato* (1635), which celebrates the opportunistic 'conquest' of Byzantium by Venetian forces under the leadership of Doge Enrico Dandolo in the course of the fourth crusade

(1202–4).[15] Stylistically, both poems are conservative in character, Marinella's *L'Enrico* in particular looking back beyond Tasso's rich proto-Baroque idiom to the relative clarity and simplicity of Ariosto. In structural and ideological respects, however, both *L'Enrico* and *Scanderbeide* adhere more or less to Tasso's prototype, despite Marinella's hubristic claim in the preface to her poem to owe nothing to 'i moderni Poeti', and to have drawn her inspiration entirely from Aristotle's theory and the model of Homer.

Of the two poems, Marinella's *L'Enrico* is likely to be of interest to modern readers primarily for its reworkings of gender conventions, which show a self-consciousness perhaps not surprising in the author of *The Nobility and Excellence of Women* (1600). It is notable, for example, that Marinella is one of the few imitators of Tasso to resist the temptation to dispatch her 'enemy' heroine in a sexually charged duel with a male admirer from the opposing camp, having her Byzantine Meandra instead succumb, in a mutually fatal encounter, to her Venetian counterpart, Claudia. Sarrocchi's *Scanderbeide*, revised meticulously over a long period, offers a broader literary interest than *L'Enrico*, and is a work that would certainly repay a closer study than is possible here. Two versions of the text survive: an early, incomplete draft published seemingly without the author's consent in 1609, and a more finished redaction which appeared posthumously in 1623. The later version is more successful stylistically, abandoning the tortuous syntax and intricate wordplay which the earlier draft had adopted in deference to current literary fashion. It is also characterised by a more rigorous and consistent ideological control, apparent most obviously in its treatment of religious and sexual 'deviancy': neutral references to the Islamic faith in the first version tend to be qualified by adjectives such as 'false' or 'lying' in the second, while a sympathetic account of a Turkish warrior's despair at the murder of his catamite in a Christian ambush is modified in the revised version by the substitution for the boy of a devoted, camp-following wife.[16] Similar moral scruples may have motivated the most substantial narrative change made by Sarrocchi in her revision: her omission, in its entirety, of the interesting sub-plot featuring the pagan sorceress Calidora and her love for the calculating Christian agent Serano.[17] Structural considerations may also have been in play here, given the stress within the genre tradition on unity of plot. Whatever its motives, the omission of this psychologically complex and morally ambiguous episode is likely to strike the modern reader as a loss.

Writing in other genres

In the interests of concision and coherence, the present discussion has concentrated on the two fictional forms in which women wrote in sufficient numbers for comparative analysis to be feasible, pastoral drama and chivalric narrative. Other fictional genres, such as tragedy, comedy and dialogue, were practised only exceptionally by women, though brief mention should be made here of Moderata Fonte's dialogue *Il merito delle donne* (1600), one of the very few Italian dialogues of the entire early modern period to represent a discussion exclusively among women, and a work of considerable literary interest.[18] Two heroic poems by women on non-chivalric subjects deserve notice in connection with the chivalric works discussed above: Lucrezia Marinella's *Colomba sacra* (1595), an epic of martyrdom set in ancient Rome, and the unfinished *Davide perseguitato* of the Florentine Maddalena Salvetti Accaiuoli, whose first three canti were published posthumously in 1611, along with a quietly revisionary essay by the same author in the eminently patriarchal Florentine genre of family history.[19] Finally, mention might be made of a group of religious narratives in *ottava rima* by Moderata Fonte and Lucrezia Marinella: Fonte's interesting *La passione di Christo* (1582) and *La resurretione di Christo* (1592), and Marinella's lives of the Virgin and Sts Francis, Justina and Catherine of Siena.

Conclusion

Of the dozen or so writers mentioned in this chapter, a comfortable majority was born in the 1550s or 1560s. All were dead by 1620, with the exceptions of the later-born and marginal Coreglia and Degli Albizzi, and the exceptionally long-lived Marinella. The phenomenon surveyed in this chapter was thus a relatively contained one, concentrated mainly in the last two decades of the Cinquecento and the first of the following century. Rather than the opening of a new era in writing by Italian women, it is perhaps best seen as the closing phase of a 'long sixteenth century' whose privileged literary idiom of Petrarchism had proved unusually amenable to assimilation by women. It is noteworthy that no Italian woman writer successfully mastered the showy, brilliant and erudite poetic language of the Italian Baroque: an idiom, for Croce, whose 'extravagances appeared to demand a certain virility'.[20] The Seicento, which had opened with women writers seemingly poised to move into the centre of Italian literary culture, was in fact to witness their remarginalisation.

NOTES

1. On Miani Negri (b. 1560), see Maria Bandini Buti (ed.), *Donne d'Italia. Poetesse e scrittrici*, 2 vols. (Rome, 1942), vol. II, pp. 25–6.

2. Angelo Ingegneri, *Della poesia rappresentativa, e del modo di rappresentare le favole sceniche* (Ferrara, 1598), p. 9.

3. On the origins and diffusion of pastoral drama in Italy, see Louise George Clubb, *Italian Drama in the Age of Shakespeare* (New Haven–London, 1989), ch. 4; Marzia Pieri, *La scena boschereccia nel Rinascimento italiano* (Padua, 1983), esp. pp. 151–80.

4. Torelli's work survives in manuscript (Cremona, Biblioteca Comunale, sixteenth-century MSS, a, a, 1, 33). For a summary, see Giuseppe Zonta, 'La *Partenia* di Barbara Torelli Benedetti', *RBLI* 14 (1906), pp. 206– 10; also, on the author (1546–post 1598), Buti, *Poetesse e scrittrici*, vol. II, pp. 305–6.

5. On Bellati (b. 1559) and Coreglia, see Buti, *Poetesse e scrittrici*, vol. I, p. 75 and vol. I, p. 174; on Guidiccioni (1550–*c.* 1597), Warren Kirkendale, 'L'opera in musica prima del Peri', in *Firenze e la Toscana de' Medici nell'Europa del '500*, 3 vols. (Florence, 1982–3), vol. II, pp. 365–95.

6. On the prevalence of the 'comic' model within the pastoral production of the period, see Clubb, *Italian Drama*, pp. 104–5.

7. See, for example, Bernardo Morsolin, *Maddalena Campiglia. Episodio biografico* (Vicenza, 1882).

8. *La Mirtilla*, ed. M. L. Doglio, p. 146 (v, 5, 2911–16); compare Ariosto, *Orlando Furioso*, XXVII, 1, 1–2.

9. Doglioni's comment is in his prefatory sonnet to Fonte, *Tredici canti del Floridoro* (Venice, 1581); for Marino's, Giambattista Marino, *Adone*, ed. M. Pieri (Bari, 1975), 2 vols., vol. I, p. 531 (Canto 9, 187–9). For Tasso, see *Discourses on the Heroic Poem*, trans. M. Cavalcanti and I. Samuel (Oxford, 1973), pp. 165–70.

10. Tullia d'Aragona, *Il Meschino, altramente detto il Guerrino*, fos. 124v–132v (Cantos 25–6). For a survey of representations of women in Italian chivalric romance and epic, see Margaret Tomalin, *The Fortunes of the Warrior Woman in Renaissance Literature* (Ravenna, 1982).

11. Moderata Fonte, *Tredici canti del Floridoro*, ed. V. Finucci, pp. 124–7 (Cantos 8, 12–25). For a discussion of the episode, see V. Cox, 'Women as Readers and Writers of Chivalric Poetry in Early Modern Italy', in Gino Bedani et al. (eds.), *Sguardi sull'Italia* (Leeds, 1997), pp. 142–3.

12. Fonte, *Floridoro*, p. 30 (Canto 2, 30–2); discussed in Finucci's introduction, pp. xxvii–xxxiv.

13. For references, see Moderata Fonte, *The Worth of Women*, trans. and ed. V. Cox, pp. 21–2; for the text of the passage in question, pp. 261–3.

14. Buti, *Poetesse e scrittrici*, vol. I, p. 27.

15. Lucrezia Marinella, *L'Enrico, overo Bisanzio Acquistato*, Canto 24, 35–49 (pp. 563–6). On Marinella's representation of the enchantress-figure Erina in this poem, see Cox, 'Women as Readers', pp. 142–3.

16. The episode is at Canto 7, 25–34 of the earlier version (Naples, 1701 edition, pp. 185–8), and Canto 5, 16– 33 in the revised version (Rome, 1623 edition, pp. 43–4).

17. The episode, in the first version, begins at Canto 3, 36, and extends, with interruptions, over the following four canti. It is discussed briefly in Cox, 'Women as Readers', pp. 143–4.

18. For a discussion of this work, see chapter 5.

19. On the author (d. 1610), see Buti, *Poetesse e scrittrici*, vol. I, p. 14; on the work's literary context, A. Belloni, *Gli Epigoni della Gerusalemme Liberata* (Padua, 1893), pp. 141–7, and 394–8.

20. Benedetto Croce, 'Donne letterate del Seicento', in *Nuovi saggi sulla letteratura italiana del Seicento* (Bari: Laterza, 1949), pp. 159–77 (p. 169).

5

Polemical prose writing, 1500–1650

In the sixteenth century, the Italian vernacular triumphed over Latin as the perfectly appropriate language for handling a wide variety of moral, historical, political and cultural issues in prose – the key text being Pietro Bembo's *Prose della volgar lingua* of 1525. This was accompanied by the rapid spread of the printed text, which displaced forever the labour-intensive manuscript, and stimulated public appetite for reading matter – resulting in the dissemination of more prose writing like the essay, treatise and dialogue than ever before. Women, too, for the first time shared in book production as readers, patrons and writers: the letter, lyric poetry and devotional religious literature were their strong points (see chapters 1, 3 and 6). On the other hand, if writing fiction posed moral problems (see chapter 4), writing treatises or dialogues proved daunting. It presupposed immersion into an erudite literary tradition familiar with the classics, as well as practice in debating skills learned by the study of rhetoric and dialectic in which women had little training.

As objects of debate, women themselves – their 'nature' and their very soul, their rationality or irrationality, their status and roles in marriage and the family as wives, mothers and daughters, and in society – nevertheless occupied a central place in polemical prose writings by men from roughly 1450 to 1650. Women writing in the vernacular about themselves did not become a force until the end of the sixteenth and first half of the seventeenth century, and then under provocation.

This chapter will consider first a dialogue by the courtesan *Tullia d'Aragona exploring the desirability of friendship with men outside marriage, *Della infinità d' amore (Dialogue on the Infinity of Love)*, of 1547; and then the dazzling prose dialogues and treatises affirming women's dignity and equality with men by *Moderata Fonte, *Lucrezia Marinella and *Arcangela

Tarabotti, all three Venetians living at the end of the sixteenth and the first half of the seventeenth century. Attention will also be given to a Venetian prose writer searching for religious equality and liberty, *Sara Copio Sullam. What loosely unites these writings thematically, apart from Sullam's, is a direct and indirect questioning, engagement with and over-turning, of doctrines about woman's subjection in marriage, where it is the main feature of a wife's relation to her husband. In the Book of Genesis of the Bible, seen as the most irrefutable of all authoritative texts because uni-versally accepted as the Word of God, subjection is women's condition from the very beginning. It is not good for Adam to be alone, God opines: 'let us make him a help like unto himself' (Genesis 2.18) – not, women were admonished, someone independent, equal and free. She was drawn from Adam's side, symbolising her creation *from* Adam and *for* Adam. As punish-ment for Eve's disobedience, God decreed that Eve should be under her husband's power, and that he should have dominion over her (Genesis 3.16). St Paul sacralised this relationship: 'Let women be subject to their hus-bands as to the Lord: Because the husband is the head of the wife as Christ is the head of the Church ... Therefore, as the Church is subject to Christ, so also let wives be to their husbands in all things' (Ephesians 5.22–4).[1] Equality was often declared 'unnatural', against God's law. Both civil and canon law took subjection for granted, a concomitant of woman's greater feebleness, *infirmitas*, in body and mind.[2]

The search for friendship

In Castiglione's *Libro del cortegiano* (*Book of the Courtier*, 1528, but composed much earlier and set in Urbino in 1507), the debonair Giuliano de' Medici in Book III sets about refuting dominant commonplaces deriving from the Greek philosopher Aristotle, in order to favour women's moral and intellectual equality with men. He also has Pietro Bembo crown these arguments (in Book IV) by a radical adaptation of Neoplatonic love theo-ries already popularised by Marsilio Ficino.[3] Castiglione's breakthrough lay in extending the divinely inspired *furor* of love to women, whether married or not. He thus paved the way for the growth of genuine friend-ship between men and women in which conversation, and displays of affection up to a kiss (representing symbolically the exchange of souls) were not only allowed, but declared honourable.

It is important to remember that in the abundance of love dialogues and treatises that are particularly prolific up to the end of the Council of

Trent, friendship and freely elected love take place *outside* marriage, never between husband and wife.[4] These works often introduce a number of historical women into the dialogues who actively participate in the debates about their condition.[5] Extra-marital friendships are seen as alleviating the plight of women married to incompatible or cruel husbands. In the second half of the century, however, the Neoplatonic love dialogue suffered a decline as clerical moralists, writing during and after the Council of Trent, fretted about these liaisons providing a breeding ground for adultery. It was replaced by a rise of dialogues and treatises on marriage, seeking to bring some weak elements of Neoplatonic love into marriage itself.[6] None of these authors renounced subjection; rather, they examined ways of making it attractive by setting limits to the husband's dominion. When Eve was called Adam's 'help', this did not mean 'servant'; neither did it mean that husbands had the right to behave like tyrants. Instead, a wife was a 'companion' to whom a husband gave good example and showed affection. But sexual double standards still prevailed. If a wife was disobedient, it was a husband's duty to discipline her. A wife, on the other hand, should tolerate a husband's adultery.

Tullia d'Aragona's dialogue belongs in particular to a group of three dialogues – by herself, by Sperone Speroni and by Giuseppe Betussi – all written in the wake of Leone Ebreo (born between 1460 and 1463; died after 1523), whose masterpiece, *Dialoghi d'amore* (1535),[7] was published only seven years after Castiglione, and just before the Council of Trent was convened.[8] The most philosophical of all the love dialogues, to some extent responsible for eclipsing Castiglione and the earlier works of Ficino, and Bembo's *Gli asolani* of 1505 (on which Castiglione had drawn), Ebreo's work affirmed more unequivocally than the Neoplatonists the goodness of natural sexual attraction between men and women, while placing the various levels of love within a religious interpretation of love as a cosmic force infusing all creation. All three make rapturous statements about Ebreo – Tullia's interlocutor Benedetto Varchi (1503–65), a philosopher himself, judges his dialogue the supreme philosophical work on love, better even than Plato and Ficino.[9]

What is paradoxical is that in all three the professional courtesan is held up as the model for a woman with literary aspirations, who wishes to enjoy a relationship of equality with men. Such a friendship had never before been advanced before in Italian literature. In Sperone Speroni's (1500–88)

Dialogo d' amore ('Dialogue on love', published in 1542 but composed by 1537, just after Leone Ebreo), Tullia d'Aragona herself is a speaker, and portrayed in a partnership of mutual tenderness and respect with the married poet Bernardo Tasso.[10] She approves of the views of another lover, the poet and satirist Francesco Maria Molza, who praises the goodness of a sexual union governed not by egotistical lust but by mutual love. The interlocutor Nicolò Grasso (Il Grazia) even delivers an unreserved praise – tongue-in-cheek? – of courtesans as the highest form of female excellence: if that classical Roman paragon of chastity, Lucretia, came back to life, and heard about them, he quips, she'd have joined them! They are the descendents of the philosopher Diotima and the poet Sappho. (Speroni would also write a separate oration in praise of courtesans, yet in his dialogue *Della dignità della donna* ('On woman's dignity'), attacked by Lucrezia Marinella, would have a woman speaker recommend servitude for the married woman.)[11] In Giuseppe Betussi's *Raverta* (1544), the courtesan Francesca Baffa, lover of Betussi, speaks in favour of a platonising ascent to a spiritual love, while Ottaviano Raverta, later a cleric at the Council of Trent, clearly endorses Baffa's independence, and delivers a fulsome summary of Ebreo's teaching. He defines 'honest love' – not marriage – as a 'free affection of the will to take part in or to be made part of the known object, esteemed beautiful'.[12]

These two dialogues, like heralds, prepare the way for the triumphant arrival on stage of the diva, Tullia d'Aragona herself, both author and interlocutor, whose house, like a prestigious academy, is frequented by the most distinguished men of Florence. She portrays herself as equal in disputation to the greatest Florentine poet and intellectual of the day, Benedetto Varchi. Primarily an Aristotelian philosopher, he was also steeped in the Florentine tradition of predominantly Neoplatonic commentaries on love poems going back to Dante.[13]

The theme of the dialogue, whether love can go on for ever, or must come to an end, would seem to pick up from Tullia's role in Speroni's dialogue, where her lover, Bernardo Tasso, must depart for Salerno. Tullia knows that love *does* end, but not by giving 'reasons' as Varchi demands: 'I want you to bow to experience, which I trust by itself far more than all the reasons produced by the whole class of philosophers', she explains (*Dialogue on the Infinity of Love*, p. 71). But then, following his Neoplatonic leanings filtered by Leone Ebreo, Varchi shows that love can be infinite in its desire: a point taken up by Tullia, who explains that poets like Dante, above all Petrarch, and even Bembo, illustrate the inner workings of desire better than philosophers. Poets understand the role of the 'spiritual'

senses, sight and hearing, and above all, the imagination (*fantasia*), in nurturing a noble love (p. 90).

Tullia occasionally mocks Varchi's casuistry: for example, she impa-
tiently cuts through his arguments defending Plato's praise of the love
of older men for young boys as merely metaphorical. When Varchi
applies 'honest and virtuous' love between souls primarily to men, the
Neoplatonic line, Tullia objects to the exclusion of women (pp. 96–7): 'I
should like to know why a woman cannot be loved with this same type
of love. For I am certain that you don't wish to imply that women lack
the intellectual soul that men have and that consequently they do not
belong to the same species as males.' She thus brings Varchi to confess
that 'not only is it possible for a man to love women with an honest and
virtuous love, but . . . one ought to' (p. 97). A third interlocutor,
Lattanzio Benucci, abolishes further any hint of inequality between
lover and beloved by clarifying that 'in the case of a perfect love relationship, when it is reciprocal, each partner is both lover and beloved inter-
changeably' (p. 107). This point corrects attitudes in traditional love
poetry where the woman is all too often a silent and passive object of
adoration.

The search for liberty and equality

In 1549 there appeared a short, anonymous oration, translated into
Italian (most probably) by Alessandro Piccolomini (1508–79), which more
than any other single writing turned upside-down the theological and
legal case for the subjection of women: *Della nobiltà et eccellenza delle donne
(Declaration on the Nobility and Pre-eminence of the Female Sex)*, written originally in Latin by Henricus Cornelius Agrippa.[14] Anonymity allowed the
little work to be plundered freely. For the rest of the century and beyond,
it was an arsenal of weapons with which to fight for women being not
merely equal in nature to men, but in many respects more excellent. In
rousing words, echoed by Lodovico Domenichi in his long *Della nobiltà
delle donne* of 1549, by Tommaso Garzoni, *La nobiltà delle donne*, and then by
all three Venetian polemicists – Fonte, Marinella and Tarabotti – Agrippa
shifted the focus of debate away from woman's good, bad or weak nature.
Patriarchy was to blame for women's subjection: 'But since the excessive
tyranny of men prevails over divine right and natural laws, the freedom
that was once accorded to women is in our day obstructed by unjust laws,
suppressed by custom and usage, reduced to nothing by education'

(*Declaration*, pp. 94–5). In the following three works, the possibility of friendship with men takes the back seat, and women turn their attention to demonstrating their own equality and excellence in spite of men and even against them.

Completed just before her death in childbirth in 1592, Moderata Fonte's dialogue *Il merito delle donne (The Worth of Women)* was published only in 1600, the same year as Lucrezia Marinella's more blatantly polemical answer to Giuseppe Passi's diatribe, *I donneschi difetti* ('The defects of women', 1599). In the early seventeenth century, both works were confusedly seen as answers to Passi, an opinion which cannot be true given the dates. Fonte's dialogue is remarkable: for the very first time in literary history, a gathering of seven all-women speakers, whom we know only by their first names, in an idyllic garden somewhere in Venice, lifts the lid off marriage and gives us the woman's point of view.

After centuries of prescriptive treatises and dialogues by men discussing 'Whether a man should take a wife?' – a genre which even had a Latin name, *An uxor ducenda*, Fonte turns the tables and inverts the question to, 'Whether a woman should take a husband?' Typical of these male debates was the commonplace that men would lose their liberty along with other advantages of the single life in taking a wife, seen at best as a nuisance and at worst as a spiteful enemy. Fonte turns the tables here, too: the lead speaker, Corinna, after announcing her desire to remain single in the world pursuing learning and letters, delivers the first poem whose leitmotiv is none other than the priceless freedom belonging *to women* in the single state: 'Libero cor nel mio petto soggiorna / Non servo alcun, né d'altri son che mia.' ('The heart that dwells within my breast is free: / I serve no one and belong to no one but myself.')[15] There is no doubt that marriage means servitude, as the older married woman, Lucretia, makes clear: 'We are only ever really happy when we are alone with other women; and the best thing that can happen to any woman is to be able to live alone, without the company of men' (*The Worth of Women*, p. 47).

The other single, married and widowed women are just as forthcoming about their experiences of the domestic scene. The young widow Leonora in whose garden they meet is resolutely opposed to remarriage. The commonplace of misogynistic literature that women do not love their husbands is trounced by Cornelia, a married woman, who reveals that men are the ones incapable of loving. They drive their wives to seek revenge with their possessiveness. Many are compulsive gamblers; in addition, they squander money on prostitutes, seduce their servants and then require their wives to bring up any resulting offspring 'so that the poor wives see themselves turned from the mistress of a household into the prioress of an orphanage' (*The Worth of Women*, p. 69). Helena's hopes for a happier marriage can be forgiven as she is young, and newly wed.

A large part of the book is devoted to the women teaching one another on a range of matters, including natural science. For Lucretia, self-help is fundamental: 'It would be a good thing if there were women who knew about medicine as well as men, so men couldn't boast about their superiority in this field and we didn't have to be dependent on them' (p. 181). Fonte's garden discussions realise the utopian dream of the *respublica mulierum,* a 'republic of learned women' longed for by Laura Cereta over a century ago (see chapter 2(i)), where a community of like-minded women share their knowledge, and provide an audience for one another's poems, songs and points of view.

Corinna lays down the conditions of true marriage: a friendship built on the principles derived from the authoritative text on the matter since antiquity, Cicero's *De amicitia,* in which friendship was described as a rare relationship founded on absolute equality of virtue and noble purpose. 'When a friendship is genuine', comments Adriana, the elder widow, 'the two friends should be united in their desires and their dislikes, and should share everything' (*The Worth of Women*, p. 127). Fonte does not follow the Neoplatonic and 'courtesan' solution of friendship and love *outside* marriage, nor the weak kind of affection *within* marriage of the clerical treatises that nevertheless preserve a mitigated form of dominion and subjection. By substituting Cicero for the Neoplatonic *furor*, and expanding what had been a relationship exclusively between men to between men and women, Fonte is original, and reconciles the unreconcilable: marriage and equality. Unfortunately, explains Leonora, it is unrealisable, not because women are weak or irrational but because men do not see that 'this sacred virtue of friendship is utterly pure and unaffected; it rejects all falsity, cares nothing for honour, scorns all boasting, pretense and simulation, and is never idle, but is always eager to show itself concretely in demonstrations of affection' (p. 124).

Like Agrippa, Fonte blames men for women's subordinate place in the family and society. Like Agrippa, Corinna does not shrink from interpreting the creation story to favour woman's superiority, and renders the Latin word for 'help', *adiutorium,* from Genesis by a number of additional synonyms that emphasise women's dignity: *onor, allegrezza e compagnia* – 'honour, joy and companion'. But 'men, though they know how much women are worth and how great the benefits we bring them, nonetheless seek to destroy us out of envy for our merits' (p. 60).[16]

The most prolific woman writer of her age in lyric, narrative and epic poetry (see chapters 3 and 4), Lucrezia Marinella also entered an arena that no woman had ever entered before, the formal disputation, for which one needed skills in rhetoric and dialectic, philosophical training and immense erudition. Marinella was goaded into polemic by a particularly virulent invective, even by Renaissance standards, *I donneschi difetti* ('Women's defects'), published in Venice in 1599 by Giuseppe Passi of Ravenna. He attacked women's alleged depraved nature, perverse emotions and especially their incapacity – 'proved' by countless authorities, arguments and examples – to behave in civilised social and benevolent relationships with men; and skirted close to denying that women were human beings. Marinella responded a year later with *La nobilità et l'eccellenza delle donne, co' difetti et mancamenti de gli uomini (The nobility and excellence of women, and the defects and vices of men)*, published first in 1600, then in an enlarged definitive form in 1601.[17] There was a reprint in 1620. 'My desire,' she claims boldly, 'is to make this truth shine forth to everybody, that the female sex is nobler and more excellent than the male. I hope to demonstrate this with arguments and examples, so that every man, no matter how stubborn, will be compelled to confirm it with his own mouth' (*Nobility and Excellence*, pp. 39–40).

Where Passi attacked, Marinella answered with a double counterattack. She not only praised women in Part I for the virtues contrary to the vices Passi condemned, but in Part II, condemned men for nearly all the same vices – and many more – that Passi had accused women of. Marinella also matches Passi's method of argument: for each chapter, there is a definition of the virtue or vice under consideration, followed by reasons for it being good or bad supported by quotations from 'authorities', and finally examples, or illustrations of women or men who have been noted for the virtue or vice. Marinella steers clear of theology and legal jargon, drawing instead on literature, especially poetry, history and some Neoplatonic love doctrines drawn from Ficino and Leone Ebreo. She is implacably opposed to the Aristotelian commonplaces that Passi used profusely to declare woman imperfect, a 'mutilated male', and 'a mistake of nature'.

While nowhere endorsing the kind of Neoplatonic love relationships between men and women expounded by Tullia d'Aragona, Marinella does appropriate some aspects of Neoplatonic doctrines. Woman is the manifestation of a perfect Idea or form existing in the mind of God, and since excellent causes give rise to excellent effects, woman must herself be excellent. In this context, she deals with Passi's central chapters about the vileness of woman's body and mere superficial beauty artifically enhanced by cunning women to bring about men's moral ruin. Visible beauty in creation reflects spiritual beauty, argues Marinella, drawing on philosophers and the canon of Italian lyric poetry from Dante down to her contemporaries who extolled the ennobling effects of woman's beauty. 'The greatest poets teach us clearly that the soul shines out of the body as the rays of sun shine through transparent glass. The more beautiful the woman, the more they affirm that it is her soul that renders grace and loveliness to her body. Petrarch demonstrates this a thousand times' (p. 57).

Marinella's long defence of woman's body and soul, her whole person, is part of her defeat of Passi and Aristotelians, whose insults about woman's defective nature turn them into 'slanderers', motivated not by reason, but by 'anger, self-love, envy and insufficient intelligence' (p. 119). Nurture and not nature have caused woman's apparent backwardness. 'Would to God that in our times it were permitted for women to be skilled at arms and letters!' If they were, they would outstrip men in every field, an opinion upheld by long quotations from Ariosto and Moderata Fonte among others (p. 80). In proof of women's learning and virtue, there are long chapters with examples of learned women, and women illustrious for the full range of the cardinal virtues: prudence, justice, temperance and fortitude. (Temperance, or chastity, was usually the only virtue deemed proper for women, and even then, Passi did not believe they were capable of it.) By Marinella's time, there existed a long tradition of modern women writers to add to the ancients, constituting a genealogy. Marinella includes Laura Cereta, Cassandra Fedele, Vittoria Colonna, Veronica Gambara, Isotta Nogarola, Laura Terracina and Catherine of Siena. Moderata Fonte's poetry is quoted several times. Marinella locates the fundamental reasoning error committed by misogynists like Passi: that of generalising from the example of *one* woman or *some* women to *all* women indiscriminately. If there are some bad women, rebuts Marinella, there are not only many more good ones, but also many more bad men!

In the 1601 edition, Marinella added chapters constituting the first examples of feminist literary criticism. She deconstructs the works of respected literary figures who either vituperated women (Boccaccio's

Corbaccio, composed in 1355 but printed in the sixteenth century), or who belonged to the revival of Aristotelianism at Padua that included making subjection within marriage 'reasonable': Sperone Speroni's *Dialogo della dignità della donna* of 1542; Torquato Tasso's oration, *Della virtù feminile e donnesca* of 1585; and Ercole Tasso's *Dello ammogliarsi* of 1595 – the last two within Marinella's lifetime.

Unencumbered by examples and quotations from authorities, Marinella's sharp wit scintillates in these chapters. Speroni's dialogue, for example, introduces a respectable, aristocratic married woman, Signora Beatrice Obiza, who refuses equality, gladly embracing servitude as the 'natural' condition of a wife, especially a Christian one. Like Christ's yoke, her husband's rule is sweet and light, so much so that she does not even wish liberty! 'And so the wife should serve', declares Beatrice, 'for she is born for that purpose' (Speroni, *Della dignità della donna*, p. 583). Marinella is not impressed by this 'pretty fiction'. Aristotle and Christ have not inspired Speroni, but 'the tyrannical insolence of those many men who make not only their wives serve them but also their mothers and sisters, showing greater obedience and fear than that with which humble servants and slaves serve their lords and masters' (Marinella, *Nobility and Excellence*, p. 138). Tasso continues along the same alarming lines to develop a separate moral code for men and women, Marinella's analysis reveals, based on the supposition that the female soul is naturally more deficient than the male, and not suited for the exercise of intellectual virtues like philosophical speculation. But if women have given proof of their rationality, she counters, how can they be deprived of a soul equal to men's?

What distinguishes Arcangela Tarabotti from her Venetian compatriots is her intense anguish at women's oppression, driving an equally intense demand for liberty. Tarabotti's indignation sprang from being pressured into taking religious vows that bound her for life when a mere girl. She grasped more than most to what extent social and political interests favoured the concentration of a family's wealth on to a male child, with the resulting relegation of daughters into convents against their will. Significantly, Tarabotti did not refer to herself as a nun (*suora*), but as a laywoman (*signora*) unjustly sentenced to life-imprisonment in a monastery, whose mission it is to reveal to the world the duplicity and injustice of the patriarchs – fathers, and civil and religious authorities. All her works are prose polemics that defy literary categories. In *Tirannia paterna* (*Paternal Tyranny*), toned down posthumously to *La semplicità ingannata* ('Innocence betrayed', 1654),[18] she speaks of liberty as a natural and God-given right that cannot be taken away by society. It was placed on the Index of Forbidden Books. *L'Inferno monacale* ('Monastic life as hell') was never published until this century. In her most brilliant philosophical work, *Che le donne siano della spezie degli uomini* (*Women are No Less Rational than Men*, 1652), she acts the part of a prosecuting attorney destroying paragraph by paragraph an outrageous tract which claimed that women lack a rational soul, and are therefore, like animals, incapable of good or evil.

In *Paternal Tyranny*, Tarabotti rewrites the Old and New Testament from a feminist perspective that condemns subjection: 'Divine Providence, no less, has granted free will to his creatures, male and female, and bestowed on both sexes intellect, memory and will', she affirms. Women are as fully human as men not just for their rationality but for their ethical capabilities, since 'both sexes were endowed with this precious treasure of free will without distinction'. Tarabotti quotes her favorite poet-theologian, Dante, to confirm her argument: 'God's greatest gift . . . / . . . conforming best to His goodness / The one He Himself most treasures / Was freedom of the will' (*Paradiso*, 5:19–22) (*Paternal Tyranny*, pp. 3–4). Moreover, God did not give Eve to Adam as an *adiutorium* in the sense of a help inferior to himself, but *simile sibi*, 'like unto himself' (Genesis 2.18). 'Woman's creation was one of parity – indeed, its circumstances were marked by greater excellence – in which both were made similar in knowledge and with equal claims to eternal glory' (*Paternal Tyranny*, p. 20). Tarabotti is also incensed by men who hold the view that woman is man's *adiutorium* only when it comes to reproduction; and in other things is a slave 'as you keep on maintaining in your specious arguments in your own favour' (p. 23). She reminds them that 'God established both sexes as rulers of the world, without discrimination'; and therefore 'woman is not deserving of less respect than you, unless you have reduced her so by your proud stratagems'(p. 23). Meditating on the Gospels, she shows that Christ treated women with respect, and that they in turn remained faithful to him up to his crucifixion.

If woman's lack of liberty and equality are contraventions of God's law and nature, their lack of education, or rather, denial of it by 'paternal tyranny', is equally unjust. Men have become great thinkers, leaders and lawgivers only because they were taught by other men, individually or at schools or universities. Tarabotti wants books, schooling, university for women, for then their alleged irrationality would vanish. But men go about 'scribbling their specious reasonings to the detriment of women, whom they struggle to keep at arm's length from schooling'.[19] As a result,

Tarabotti observes bitterly, 'illiteracy is our proper condition. We are brought up in it, thanks to your decisions which want us to remain in ignorance as far as possible' (*Paternal Tyranny*, p. 153). Women are the victims of male hypocrisy, too: 'You forbid women to learn in order for them to become incapable of defending themselves against your schemes, and then you proclaim how stupid they are, and how you defeat them' (p. 170).

Tarabotti depicts family life in sombre tones, unmasking pretexts used by fathers to break a daughter's resistence to taking vows. She is blackmailed with the argument that 'it is much better for one woman to be encloistered to serve God than for a whole family to go to rack and ruin' (p. 246). Brothers are encouraged from an early age to gang up against their sisters, and boast that they alone will inherit (p. 301). Mothers are utterly silent, with no say in the destiny of their own offspring. Religious superiors, eager to boost their intake of young girls with dowries (much less than the ones needed for marriage), collude with fathers and the state policy to limit marriages. Tarabotti's own rejection scarred her so that she could not even imagine a family where a father showed affection for a daughter. She accuses them all of inhumane avarice, fraud and violence: 'Woe to you [fathers] for whom political interest has removed the righteousness of feelings!'[20] One has to wait until Sibilla Aleramo's *Una donna* (1906, see chapter 12) to hear such anger against family and society again.

Sara Copio Sullam, a Venetian contemporary of Marinella and Tarabotti, belonged to a distinguished Jewish family living in the Ghetto. Like Marinella, she received a thorough education in languages and literature, including Hebrew and Biblical studies. A close family friend, the learned rabbi Leone Modena, was probably her most important tutor; he dedicated a tragedy, *Esther*, to her. After marriage in 1613, she was encouraged by her father and husband to launch a literary salon in her home, frequented by both Jews and Christians. But like Tarabotti, she was marginalised because of her suspect opinions on philosophical and religious issues. Sullam defiantly resisted pressures to convert to Christianity; she wanted Jews to be equal to Christians, friends sharing common cultural interests.

From 1619 to 1622, she carried on a correspondence with the Genovese writer Ansaldo Cebà, initiated by Sullam herself on reading his epic poem, *La reina Ester* ('Queen Esther', 1618). In 1623, only his letters with Sara's sonnets, but not her side of the correspondence, were published. In a far more acrimonius exchange with the poet, priest and jurist Baldassare

Bonifaccio of Venice, she was accused in print of denying the immortality of the soul – a serious charge that tarred her with the same brush as Epicureans, materialists, heretics and atheists.[21] This time her spirited reply has been preserved, entitled a *manifesto* – in the sense of a public declaration or proof – although her authorship was denied by Bonifaccio himself, and by a malicious contemporary Angelico Aprosio, who also attacked Tarabotti.

Sara Copio Sullam understood perfectly that the issue of the immortality of the soul was a pretext for ruining the reputation of a Jewish woman who had dared to stand up to a Christian ecclesiastic, and had refused to be won over to the 'true faith'. Since both Jews and Christians believe in 'an incorruptible, immortal and divine soul, infused by God' while the child is 'in the womb' (fol. B1 ro), there is no genuine dispute between them. She then scornfully reduces Bonifaccio's charge to one of spiteful vanity: 'the mercy of my own Law fills me with compassion for your simplicity, which has led you to believe that you could make yourself immortal with fame by treating the immortality of the soul' (fol. B2 ro). She denies that he is a philosopher or a theologian, or even skilled in the basic art of argument, because his statements are 'full of erroneous use of terminology, of twisted interpretations and forced meanings of the Scriptures, of false syllogisms, wrong causal connections, and *nihil sequitur* from one subject to another; of mistaken quotations from Authors, and finally mistakes in your use of language' (fol. C2 vo).

The women in this chapter discuss their nature and condition with the utmost lucidity. Time and again, they overturn the arguments against their equality in dignity with men and for their subjection and above all for their supposed rational 'infirmity', showing that the fault does not lie with their 'nature', but rather with social and legal injustices. What one also senses, however, is an increasing exasperation, bordering in Tarabotti on despair, that although right was on their side, might was not; that however irrefutable their reasoning, patriarchal institutions were to all extents and purposes immutable. It would take the seismic revolutionary movements of the late eighteenth century, and the creation of a secular Italian state in the nineteenth, to raise hopes that women's lot in Italy could change.

NOTES

1. English from the Douay Bible, translated from the Latin Vulgate in the sixteenth century.

2. See I. Maclean, *The Renaissance Notion of Women* (Cambridge, 1980); and M. Graziosi, 'Women and criminal law . . . in Renaissance jurists', in L. Panizza (ed.), *Women in Italian Renaissance Culture and Society* (Oxford, 2000), pp. 166–81.

3. See Marsilio Ficino, *Commentary on Plato's Symposium on Love* (first published in Latin in 1484, and in Italian only in 1544), trans. Sears Jayne (Dallas, 1985) with introduction. Also, J. Kraye, 'The Transformation of Plato in the Renaissance', in A. Baldwin and S. Hutton (eds.), *Platonism and the English Imagination* (Cambridge, 1994), pp. 76–85.

4. For these treatises, see B. Richardson, 'The Cinquecento: Prose', Brand and Pertile, *CHIT*, esp. pp. 212–20; for love literature, J. C. Nelson, *Renaissance Theory of Love* (New York, 1958).

5. See V. Cox, 'Seen but not Heard', in L. Panizza (ed.), *Women in Italian Renaissance*, pp. 385–400.

6. See B. Richardson, ' "Amore maritale": advice on love and marriage', in L. Panizza (ed.), *Women in Italian Renaissance*, pp. 194–208.

7. Ed. by S. Caramella (Bari, 1929); trans. *The Philosophy of Love* by F. Friedeberg-Sieley and J. H. Barnes, with introduction by C. Roth (London, 1937).

8. See E. Cochrane, *Italy: 1530–1630* (London, 1988), pp. 106–64.

9. R. Russell and B. Merry, trans., *Dialogue on the Infinity of Love*.

10. See J. L. Smarr, 'A Dialogue of Dialogues: Tullia d'Aragona and Sperone Speroni', *MLN* 113 (1998), pp. 204–12.

11. Both Speroni dialogues in *Trattatisti del Cinquecento*, Mario Pozzi (ed.), (Milan–Naples, 1978).

12. *Il Raverta*, in M. Pozzi (ed.), *Trattati d'amore del Cinquecento* (Rome–Bari, 1975), pp. 1–145; this quotation p. 8.

13. For the Florentine tradition of the philosophical commentary on love poems, see intro. by J. Colaneri (ed.), Francesco de' Vieri, *Lezioni d'amore* (Munich, 1973), pp. 7–72.

14. *Declaration on the Nobility and Pre-eminence of the Female Sex*, trans. and ed. A. Rabil, Jr. (Chicago, 1996). Latin original printed in 1529.

15. *The Worth of Women*, trans. and ed. V. Cox; this quotation p. 49.

16. For the dowry problem in Venice, see V. Cox, 'The Single Self: Feminist Thought and the Marriage Market in Early Modern Venice', *RQ* 48 (1995), pp. 513–81.

17. *The Nobility and Excellence of Women*, trans. and ed. A. Dunhill, intro. by L. Panizza.

18. Pages refer to *La semplicità ingannata* (Leiden: Gio. Sambix [=Elzevir], 1654); see my forthcoming trans., *Paternal Tyranny*.

19. Tarabotti, *Antisatira*, ed. Elissa Weaver, pp. 100–1.

20. *L'Inferno monacale di Arcangela Tarabotti*, ed. Francesca Medioli.

21. *Manifesto*. Translations my own.

GABRIELLA ZARRI

Translated by Susan Haskins

6
_____

Religious and devotional writing, 1400–1600

The foundations for a profound change in women's status and forms of commitment in the Church were developed between the mid-fifteenth and mid-seventeenth centuries. Religious orders were restructured into a striking number of new foundations, patronised by rulers and cities, and observing a rigid discipline.[1] While the traditional monastic model of the state of perfection was encouraged by the growing number of those taking vows, humanistic culture and religious currents of the fifteenth century influenced a model of the active life that rejected the cloister, privileging instead charitable work with the poor, the sick and orphans. The most significant example of the renewal of religious life in the fifteenth century was the *devotio moderna*, begun by Geert Groote (1340–84) in the Low Countries. It spread across France and Germany in particular, fuelled by an intense production of spiritual texts and the foundation of religious institutions observing the customs of the sisters and brothers of the Common Life begun by Groote in Deventer (the diocese of Utrecht) in 1379 and 1383 respectively. Groote's main purpose was to promote a renewal of religious life based on meditation on the Holy Scriptures (which depended on their translation into the vernacular), on study of the Church Fathers and mental prayer. In contrast to current trends, he gave impulse to a less theological and intellectual spirituality, one that was, rather, more affective, Christ-centred and directed essentially to religious practice.[2]

The sisters of the Common Life, who became widespread above all in Holland and north-west Germany, where at the beginning of the fifteenth century there were ninety communities, came mostly from aristocratic-bourgeois circles. There were, however, no restrictions to acceptance either with regard to social condition or to age. The sisters did not have to take vows, and they were able to maintain their rights to property. Their days were divided between prayer and work.

The institution's way of life and the aspirations that inspired it met the social and religious needs of many women in the Renaissance in several ways. To this day there is no documentary evidence of a direct relationship between the *devotio moderna*, which started in northern Europe, and Italy; but it has been increasingly suggested that the *devotio*'s influence on fifteenth-century spirituality came through religious orders such as the Gesuati, Benedictines and Lateran canons regular. In fact, it was principally through these orders that the method of mental prayer was disseminated, as well as texts of Flemish and German mystical theology.

Ferrara has been particularly singled out with regard to the influence of the *devotio* in fifteenth-century Italy, as well as its female Augustinian community without monastic vows where *Caterina Vegri lived before entering the cloister.[3] The group of religious women that formed round one Lucia Mascheroni during the first half of the fifteenth century did not last long, though some of the young women decided to take their vows and helped to found the monastery of the Poor Clares of Corpus Domini. Caterina Vegri had an important role in the monastery, although she had no administrative responsibility. She was, in fact, for a long period mistress of novices, by virtue of the education she received at court which enabled her to write in prose and verse, to play the viola, paint and illuminate. While at Ferrara, she wrote her *Libro devoto,* which became one of the best-known spiritual treatises written by a woman. The book remained unknown until after her death in Bologna in 1463. Vegri had been sent to Bologna seven years previously, together with some of her companions, to found a monastery of Observant Poor Clares similar to the foundation in Ferrara. This monastery, too, was known as the Corpus Domini, and Vegri became its abbess.

The *Libro devoto*, which came to be known as *Le sette armi spirituali* ('The seven spiritual weapons') in reference to its contents and structure, devoted an all-important section to the 'weapon' of the Holy Scriptures, which reveals a knowledge of the Bible thought to be typical at that time of the circles of the *devotio*. Although the most recent commentator has traced the principal source of inspiration of Caterina's spirituality to the Franciscan and Italian environment, the prominence given to prayer and frequent communion in the treatise is very marked.[4]

Written in about 1438 and later reworked, Caterina Vegri's principal work is directed at the mothers and sisters of the Corpus Domini in

Ferrara, but particularly at those novices who, having entered the religious life, believed themselves to have lost merit through being continually tempted to resist their monastic obedience. The monastery is not conceived as a refuge but rather as the terrain on which a battle takes place necessary for the attainment of virtue, of which Christ is the main model.

The work consists of ten chapters of varying lengths which give it an open structure very different from the usual forms of treatise-writing; it is part doctrinal exposition, part autobiography and spiritual testament, as well as part precept through counsel and example. It begins with a brief prologue in which Caterina explains the reasons that have led her to write: divine inspiration, and the desire to be useful by assisting in the work of divine Providence. Then follows the illustration of the seven weapons necessary to win the battle that the soul has to fight in order to enter heaven. These are diligence, self-distrust, full trust in God's help, the memory of Christ's passion, thoughts of death and the reward in heaven, and continual remembrance of the Holy Scriptures. Each 'weapon' has an explanatory chapter which is brought to a rapid conclusion by an exhortation. The particular stress in the treatment of the last 'weapon', which itself forms half of the entire treatise, renders it the aim of the work: the true 'most faithful mother' is the Holy Scriptures from which to take advice in the internal travails and troubled events of the monastic community experienced by Caterina. The visions recorded here of the Virgin (Vegri, *Le sette armi*, VII 10), of the crucified Christ (VII 15–20), of the Virgin with the Christ child (VII 28, 116–17) also appear in the exhortation to keep in mind God's word, necessary in the religious life. In this and the last three chapters, the narrative is told in the third person, in such a way as to reduce the autobiographical evidence of Caterina's spiritual experiences, to whose tempted soul God allowed numerous graces also in matters of faith.

The treatise has a strong didactic purpose and contains characteristic insertions of verse or rhymed prose which echo the vitality of the ascetic Franciscan model credited to the Observants. Other works attributed or attributable to Caterina remained unpublished by the convent of Corpus Christi in Bologna; they show how her example acted as a spur in the monastic environment of the city so as to promote the literary activity of an entire convent.[5]

Caterina Vegri's work is regarded as an important turning point in Italian religious life and culture. The religious aspirations of the *devotio moderna*, independently of a direct link with its Dutch namesake, appear in the female world as a tendency towards the 'mixed life', uniting prayer and contemplation with work and charitable acts. It also increased the spread in Italy of communities of tertiaries.[6] Communal life in small groups, often governed by a widow – as is recorded even at the beginning of the sixteenth century in the cases of the Ursulines, Dimesse or other similar communities – also responded to the social needs of women's partial liberation from family and paternal guardianship.[7] From the point of view of spirituality, Caterina's ascetic treatise is the first feminine expression of a typical 'devout' movement of fifteenth-century vernacular literature.[8]

Other reasons exist, however, as to why discussion of sixteenth-century Italian female religious writing should begin with this figure, who is a prototype of Renaissance culture and learning. Educated at one of the most prestigious schools of the Renaissance, that of Guarino Veronese at Ferrara, Caterina contributed to the foundation and diffusion of Poor Clare monasteries, which became true and proper appendages to the Renaissance courts of central-northern Italy, offering hospitality to princesses and companions of the leading families of princes and aristocrats. It was precisely the cultured circle of the Poor Clare monasteries that allowed the rapid manuscript publication of Caterina's work and also led to the birth of the new literary genre of biography. The Venetian noblewoman Illuminata Bembo, a companion of Caterina who had also been in the monastery at Ferrara with her, addressed a letter to the sisters of the various Poor Clare monasteries to announce the death of their abbess, renowned for her sanctity. This letter, expanded to give space to Caterina's life and memory, then became a longer composition which assumed in itself the characteristics of a didactic treatise and of biography. Illuminata's principal aim was to preserve and transmit the saint's 'sayings', the teaching that Caterina had herself frequently communicated in poetic form; but at the same time Illuminata composed a biographical portrait of the saint and highly educated Poor Clare which gave her a place among the illustrious women of the Renaissance.[9] Like other erudite women of the period, Caterina had been able to write 'beyond her sex',[10] but had moreover lived in the period in which women's writing in the vernacular could have access to printing. Her embalmed body, still on show to the public, is an exceptional testimony: seated in a simple armchair ever since the last quarter of the fifteenth century, and placed in a cell where the most precious objects she owned and the manuscripts she illuminated are still assembled, her hand rests on a fifteenth-century printed edition of her *Sette armi spirituali*.

Caterina Vegri also becomes an 'illustrious woman' through Illuminata Bembo's writing. Included in one of the collections of 'famous women' that circulated in the fifteenth-century Renaissance courts, she took on the role of a model of behaviour for Observant nuns.[11] Illuminata's writing, however, remained unpublished, and was to circulate in print only from the beginning of the first decades of the sixteenth century in the version compiled by a friar.[12] Known within Poor Clare circles, Caterina's life was used as an example for the writing of the biography of Eustochia Calefati da Messina, a cultured and saintly abbess of the monastery of Montevergine, whose portrait has been handed down to us by Sister Iacopa Pollicini.[13] In this case, too, the manuscript circulation of the female text in the vernacular compares with a Latin biography prepared, perhaps for printing, in 1543 by the well-known humanist Francesco Maurolico, and published a century later by the Jesuit Ottavio Caetani.[14] We should recall, however, Illuminata Bembo's and Iacopa Pollicino's cultural and literary merit, unrecognised until now, for having begun a biographical genre which was entirely different from both hagiography and the model of the collections of 'famous women'. Within the confines of didactic purpose and memoir, these texts written for female religious communities reproduce the character of the monastic *sacra conversazione* in their structure and style.

Like Caterina Vegri, Eustochia Calafati was the author of writings on the Passion which have come down to us in manuscript form.[15] Between the end of the fifteenth century and beginning of the sixteenth, another Poor Clare came close to Caterina in her production of devout treatises that reached publication: Sister Camilla Battista, born into the unfortunate family of the Varano of Camerino, murdered by Cesare Borgia.[16] The *Dolori mentali di Gesù* ('The mental sufferings of Jesus'), one of Camilla's many writings, appeared anonymously in the last decade of the fifteenth century. Although the first editions of this small work are now quite rare, the text was widely published. Republished in 1593 together with Lorenzo Scupoli's *Battaglia spirituale* ('Spiritual battle'), it was to have a considerable publishing success in the seventeenth century. The *Dolori mentali di Gesù* is a compendium in eight chapters of revelations on the Passion which express the mental sufferings of the Redeemer. The work is in the form of a dialogue between Christ and a devout nun. Behind this is concealed the author, who wrote not for literary reasons but by order of her abbess and through obedience to Christ himself who told her: 'Go and write those sorrowful thoughts of the passion that you know about.' The autobiography, here veiled for reasons of religious reticence, is fully revealed in the *Vita spirituale* written on Camilla Battista's own initiative around 1490. The later treatise *Della purità del cuore* ('Purity of heart') has, however, a subtly rationalising progress. Various poems in Latin and in the vernacular have also been attributed to Battista, on somewhat questionable grounds.[17]

The cultural tradition of the courts of the Po Valley or of the small city-states of the nearby Marche, which extended to women and nuns of high birth, is no less lively and profound in republican and aristocratic Genoa. Between the Quattrocento and Cinquecento the city was at the centre of a religious movement and the organisation of works of charity which also involved women, and made use above all of *Caterina Fieschi Adorno's work and spiritual leadership attracting lay and ecclesiastical followers. Her teaching consisted of a spirituality centred on 'pure love', and her small treatise on purgatory was to take on special significance in the context of criticism against indulgences and the denial of purgatory itself favoured by Protestant reform.[18]

L'Opus Catherinianum was published in 1551, forty years after Fieschi Adorno's death, perhaps the sign of an abiding memory, but also of problems in entering the world of sixteenth-century publishing in a restricted ambience such as that of Genoa. More than a work, it is a collection of writings in which, as often happens in the case of women, it is not easy to ascertain what was written by Fieschi Adorno herself or inspired by her and in part reconstructed on the basis of acounts of her followers and of her confessor. The *Vita e dottrina* ('Life and teaching'), compiled almost certainly by her confessor Cattaneo Marabotto, summarises the events of her life, relating them to her teachings. The first part of the *Dialogo tra anima, corpo, amor proprio, spirito, umanità e Dio* ('Dialogue between the Soul, the Body, Self-love, Spirit, Humanity and God') is, however, almost certainly by her, while the other two parts of the Dialogue are written by followers. The *Trattato del Purgatorio* ('Treatise on Purgatory') was also compiled by followers, inspired by the saint's teachings and the fruits of her mystical experiences.

Two other writers form part of the circle of Caterina Fieschi Adorno's followers, although each is quite different. Mariola Fieschi was the daughter of Innocenzo Fieschi di Savignone and wife of Francesco Fieschi, violently murdered during the wars between factions in Genoa at the end of the fifteenth century. A friend and companion of Caterina, she entered the reformed Dominican cloister of Corpus Christi, where she took vows in 1477 and chose the name of Sister Tommasa. Twenty years later she was also to have the task of introducing Observant reforms into the old city monastery dedicated to Saint James and Saint Philip. Having learned to read and write at home, and in constant contact by letter with religious, sisters of her own order and with her son who had himself become a Dominican, Sister Tommasa widened her knowledge of devout literature and spiritual theology which she then meditated upon and elaborated in an original way. Caterina da Genova's *Life* portrays Sister Tommasa as a nun dedicated to theological and rational meditation and not disposed to abandon herself to mystical experiences. 'She was called Sister Tommasa . . . and felt such love of the spirit that to assuage it she wrote, composed, painted and carried out other devout exercises, has written compositions about the Apocalypse and something about Dionysus the Areopagite, and written other beautiful devout and useful treatises.'[19] Her works were not, however, published, and it is now the critic's task to distinguish between original writings and transcriptions and summaries of works then current.

Equally part of Caterina da Genova's circle, although of a generation later than Caterina Fieschi Adorno, was Tommasina Vernazza, who later became Sister Battista. She was the daughter of the notary Ettore Vernazza, a founder of the Company of Divine Love. During her long life she lived through the most complex and diversified religious experiences of the sixteenth century. Having taken her vows in 1511 in the Congregation of St John Lateran, where spiritual writers and those closer to the spirituality of the *devotio moderna* were most active, Sister Battista experienced the originality and creativity of the first lay movement of Divine Love, took part in the work of editing the *Opus Catherinianum*, and was later involved with post-Tridentine monastic reform.[20]

Sister Battista's spiritual works, centred on divine love, consist of sixteen treatises which almost always begin with a verse from the Bible. They were sent to her confessor, the canon of the basilica at Rome, St John Lateran, Gasparo Scotti of Piacenza, who supervised their publication. She expressed her own judgement on the disposition of the texts for publication, but would not live to see the final outcome. The works in fact saw the light of day between 1588 (the year after her death) and 1610 in four volumes. She also wrote a significant number of letters to nuns in other monasteries to encourage the application of post-Tridentine monastic reform. These were published in an appendix to her works.[21]

Leaving aside the circles of Caterina da Genova's influence for a moment, we see developing between the last decades of the Quattrocento and early Cinquecento in the northern and central regions of Italy the phenomenon of *sante vive*, 'living saints', or charismatics, in demand by the courts for their prophecies and revelations. Although they were listened to for their teaching and looked upon as authorities, they were rarely writers of literary texts, if we exclude letters or manuscript revelations. Their letters, however, were sometimes published after their deaths. The Bolognese Elena Duglioli wrote a letter on the daily practice of the devout life to the Marchesa Anna di Monferrato, which was published in 1521 as a small treatise under the title of *Brieve et singular modo del spiritual vivere*, ('A brief and special way of leading a spiritual life'), while some other writings of well-known mystics remained in manuscript form.[22]

The Florentine Domenica da Paradiso is among the early sixteenth-century women who were famed for their sanctity and distinguished by the commentaries transcribed by their confessors.[23] From Lucia Broccadelli of Narni, who received the stigmata and had ties with Ercole d'Este's court, we have a work of visions and revelations, recently discovered and studied, and which is one of the first and most significant examples of autobiography.[24]

The religious crisis of the sixteenth century, the argument over the spiritual value of monastic vows and the violent suppression of convents in Protestant countries created a deep division in Europe. In the Catholic world, and particularly in Italy, seat of the papacy, a double need was evident: to reform the old institutions and to increase apostolic and missionary activity. Women were not marginalised from these spheres, and were able to adapt their various experiences and religious foundations to the needs of society and Church.

The foundation of the Company of St Ursula by *Angela Merici (born between 1470 and 1475, died 1540) was the most direct expression of the new spiritual tendencies of the early sixteenth century. This was a confraternity formed of young women from middle to lower-middle ranks of society who, while wishing to dedicate themselves to God, were unable to enter monasteries because they did not have dowries. They were protected and governed by noble widows, and were under the Rule dictated by the foundress; this required virginity, but not vows. This rejection of monastic vows was prompted by a return to the ideals of the early Church, where monasteries and the cloister had not existed, while the reason for maintaining virgins who continued to live at home with material and spiritual help from other women was the modern expression of the earlier tension concerning the participation of lay people on the road to perfection.

Set up in 1535, with local episcopal approval in 1536, and papal approval in 1544, the Company spread into the diocese of Brescia. There it encountered much opposition, leading between 1545 and 1565 to the adoption of a more direct form of institutionalisation, such as the wearing of girdles over habits (indicating dedication to God), and a closer dependence on a priest and local bishop. In the post-Tridentine period, when open female monasteries, like those of the tertiaries, were forced to adopt *clausura*, the Brescian confraternity was able to keep its original structure. In fact, as was understood immediately by the bishop of Milan, Carlo Borromeo, the Ursulines living as they did in different areas of the city were able to respond to the Counter-Reformation need to teach children Christian doctrine.[25] He encouraged the institution in his diocese and thus promoted its spread. This apostolic aim would later be accompanied by teaching women reading and writing and other skills, which distinguished it from the aims of other religious institutions, particularly in the seventeenth century.

The Ursulines provided religious education for the young girls enrolled in the confraternity, and two works, drafted by Angela Merici's secretary, the priest Gabriele Cozzano, are extremely important from a conceptual and cultural point of view. Merici's *Ricordi* were written for the use of those members of the order charged with the religious education of the young girls enrolled in the Compagnia, while the *Testamento*, also known as the *Legati*, provided advice for the older women, usually widows, who acted as patrons, supplying the material needs of the young girls. These are not ascetic or mystical writings, nor are they biographical or autobiographical records, but are truly innovative instruction on the level of teaching and education. Finally, it is Angela Merici's understanding of the need for teaching standards in order to impart to young women a useful education with regard to behaviour and morality that must be recognised. Angela is inspired by the example of maternal love. Possibly not yet expressed theoretically, but rather as suggestions and exhortations, Merici's treatises can be defined as being pedagogical.

Apostolic life and charitable activities are also the ideals that inspired the foundation of the Compagnia delle Angeliche, sponsored by the Contessa di Guastalla, Ludovica Torelli (1499–1569), and set up with the priests of San Paolo. The link that united the Barnabites (so-called after the church in which they met) and the Angeliche harks back to the medieval paradigm of separate but linked male and female monasteries, which had a strong female influence in its administration and discipline of the community. A pre-eminent role within the confraternity was assigned to Angelica Paola Antonia Negri (1508–55), who was given the name 'Divina Madre Maestra', and who was somehow spiritual director of both branches of the young congregation.[26] Spiritual letters printed for the first time in 1564 and again, edited by her admirers, in 1576, have been attributed to her. They are addressed to important people on the occasion of liturgical feast days or saints' days and contain theology of an orthodox doctrinal nature. Nevertheless, a deep division within the congregation evolved between Negri's followers, and those who no longer accepted dependence on a woman, in accordance with the dispositions of the Roman Curia. As a result Giampietro Besozzi, one of the superiors of the order, attributed the letters in Negri's name to himself. The true paternity (or perhaps we should say, maternity) of these letters is still under discussion today.

In the course of the sixteenth century, despite the crisis of the Reformation, reactions by the papal Inquisition and the Congregation of the Index (of forbidden books) against suspect mystical teachings, and the beginning of the systematic repression of religious houses of suspect or 'simulated' sanctity, a subterranean vein of mysticism was nurtured, particularly by the Dominicans influenced by their fiery reformer burned at the stake in Florence, Girolamo Savonarola, and by the Capuchins.[27] *Maria Maddalena de' Pazzi, the most prolific writer of mystical texts at the end of the sixteenth century, was educated in a Florence that was still much imbued with the spirit of Savonarola. A Carmelite, even if she did not belong to St Teresa d'Avila's more ascetic 'Discalced' order, she was soon regarded as an exemplary nun and put forward as the model of post-Tridentine observance. The process of beatification began shortly after her death, and she was sanctified during the seventeenth century. As a result, her writings and her *Life* were reprinted several times in the course of that century.

Maria Maddalena de' Pazzi's writings have a spontaneity and character of oral speech which derive from being a transcription of her ecstasies made by the sisters who heard her actual words. These contemplations possess a marked theological character that is not merely spiritual. *Ammaestramenti* (teachings) for novices concerning the regular life accompany the 'words of ecstasy', as well as various letters, never sent, addressed to the pope urging him to reform the Church.[28]

We should add a very special kind of writing to this swift survey of seventeenth-century women's religious writing – that of spiritual poetry. If collections of the Petrarchan type such as those by *Vittoria Colonna have above all a literary value, nuns' verse compositions reveal a more religious inspiration linked to devotional practices associating singing with manual labour.

As has already been noted in chapter 1, correspondence is a literary genre in which there is a strong feminine presence: if spiritual letters appeared in print under the names of Osanna da Mantova and Paola Antonia Negri, collections of letters in manuscript, conserved in archives, bear witness to the important function of spiritual instruction carried on by women addressing princes or religious, who listened to their divinely inspired exhortations or advice.[29]

The relative success of women's religious writings in the fifteenth and sixteenth centuries, evidenced by the publication of many of them, should not blind us to the problems connected to the special status of women's writing: there is, above all, the problem of the audiences, and another of attribution. None of the published writings appeared in print during the writers' lifetimes, but were edited by priests a few or several years after their deaths. The destination of nuns' writings is primarily the circles of the other sisters and within the order. Sometimes the sisters took part directly in writing the texts, such as is shown in the case of Maria Maddalena de' Pazzi's revelations, but more often it was the confessor who took down and transcribed the mystic's experiences. This clearly poses the problem of attribution, sometimes challenged, particularly in the case of editions of spiritual letters published during the sixteenth century.

Generally speaking, however, it is possible to establish that in the two centuries concerned, female religious writing by women enjoyed success and recognition by the Church in accordance with its favourable attitude towards mystical and prophetic sanctity. The change in models of sanctity and the mistrust towards charismatic phenomena found in the Church's hierarchy at the end of the sixteenth and in the early seventeenth century, together with a tighter supervision of spiritual works by the Congregation of the Index, restricted space given to the written expression of female mysticism.[30] In the seventeenth century we find instead a kind of strictly autobiographical writing controlled directly by confessors and destined mostly to remain in manuscript.

NOTES

1. See G. Zarri, 'From prophecy to discipline (1450–1650)', in L. Scaraffia and G. Zarri (eds.), *Women and Faith. Catholic Religious Life in Italy from Late Antiquity to the Present*

(Cambridge, MA, 1999). I owe much in the elaboration of this essay to my friend Elisabetta Graziosi and to collaboration with Susan Haskins, to whom I am extremely grateful.

2. See Florence W. J. Koorn, 'Women Without Vows. The Case of the Beguines and the Sisters of Common Life in the Northern Netherlands', in E. Schulte van Kessel (ed.), *Women and Men in Spiritual Culture XIV–XVII Centuries* (The Hague, 1986), pp. 135–47.

3. See A. Samaritani, 'Ailisia da Baldo e le correnti riformatrici femminili di Ferrara nella prima metà del secolo XV', in *Atti e memorie della Deputazione di Storia Patria di Ferrara*, s.3, 13 (1973), pp. 91–156.

4. See introduction to Caterina Vegri, *Le sette armi spirituali*, ed. C. Foletti; C. Leonardi, 'Caterina Vegri e l'obbedienza del diavolo', in O. Besomi et al. (eds.), *Forme e vicende per Giovanni Pozzi* (Padua, 1988), pp. 119–22.

5. G. Zarri, 'Ecrits inédits de Cathérine de Bologne et de ses soeurs', in G. Brunel-Lobrichon et al. (eds.), *Sainte Claire d'Assise et sa posterité* (Paris, 1995), pp. 119–230.

6. Maiju Lehmijoki-Gardner, *Worldly Saints. Social Interaction of Dominican Penitent Women in Italy, 1200–1500* (Helsinki, 1999).

7. See G. Zarri, 'Il terzo stato', in S. Seidel Menchi et al. (eds.), *Tempi e spazi di vita femminile tra medioevo ed età moderna* (Bologna, 1999), pp. 311–34.

8. See G. Zarri, 'La vita religiosa femminile tra devozione e chiostro', in *Le sante vive. Cultura e religiosità femminile della prima età moderna* (Turin, 1990), pp. 9–50; C. Gill, 'Women and the Production of Religious Literature in the Vernacular 1300–1500', in E. Ann Matter and John Coakley (eds.), *Creative Women in Medieval and Early Modern Italy* (Philadelphia, PA, 1994), pp. 64–104.

9. On Bembo and her work, see Zarri, 'Ecrits inédits de Cathérine de Bologne et de ses soeurs'. A critical edition by S. Mostaccio, *Specchio di illuminatione*, is in preparation.

10. P. H. Labalme (ed.), *Beyond Their Sex. Learned Women of the European Past* (New York–London, 1980).

11. Giovanni Sabadino degli Arienti, *Gynevera de le clare donne*, eds. Ricci and A. Bacchi della Lega (Bologna, 1887).

12. *Vita de la beata Caterina de l'ordine de la diva Clara del Corpo de Christo* (Giovanni Antonio de Benedetti, Bologna, 1502), attributed to the Franciscan Fra Dionisio Paleotti.

13. E. Pispisa, 'Calafato Eustochia', *DBI*, 16 (1973), pp. 402–3; S. Spanò, 'Eustochia Calafato', *GLdS*, 1 (1998), pp. 639–40.

14. M. Catalano (ed.), *La leggenda della Beata Eustochia da Messina* (Messina–Florence, 1950).

15. F. Terrizzi S. J., *Il Libro della passione scritto dalla beata Eustochia Calafato Clarissa messinese (1434–1485)*, (Messina, 1979).

16. See S. Spanò, 'Battista Varano', *GLdS*, 1 (1998), pp. 259–60.

17. Beata Camilla Battista da Varano, *Le opere spirituali*, ed. G. Boccanera (Iesi, 1958).

18. See P. Fontana, *Celebrando Caterina. Santa Caterina Fieschi Adorno e il suo culto nella Genova Barocca* (Turin, 1999).

19. For Tommasina Fieschi, see Umile Bonzi da Genova, 'Fieschi Tommasina, domenicaine italienne', in *DS*, 5 (1964), coll. 332–6, and S. Mostaccio, 'Delle "visitationi spirituali" di una monaca. Le lettere di Tommasina Fieschi O. P.', in G. Zarri (ed.), *Per lettera. La scrittura epistolare femminile tra archivio e tipografia secoli XV–XVII* (Rome, 1999), pp. 287–311, from which this quotation is taken.

20. For Ettore Vernazza, see D. Solfaroli Camillocci, 'La monaca esemplare. Lettere spirituali di madre Battistina Vernazza (1497–1587)' in G. Zarri (ed.), *Per lettera*, pp. 235–61.

21. See G. Zarri, 'L'altra Cecilia. Elena Duglioli dall'Olio (1472–1520)', in *Le sante vive*, pp. 165–96.

22. This rare text was reprinted by G. Melloni, *Atti o memorie degli uomini illustri in santità nati o morti in Bologna*, classe II, vol. III (Bologna, 1780), pp. 436–40. On Duglioli, see entry by M. Romanello in *DBI*, 41 (1992), pp. 799–802.

23. See G. Antignani, *Domenica da Paradiso. Aspetti storici e momenti profetici* (Poggibonsi, 1995), also A. Valerio, *Domenica da Paradiso. Profezia e politica in una mistica del Rinascimento* (Spoleto, 1992).

24. On Brocadelli, see G. Zarri, 'Pietà e profezia alle corti padane: le pie consigliere dei principi', in *Le sante vive*, pp. 51–85.

25. On the role of female educators among the Ursulines in Milan, see A. Turchini, *Sotto l'occhio del padre. Società confessionale e istruzione primaria nello Stato di Milano* (Bologna, 1996).

26. On the Barnabites and the Angeliche, see E. Bonora, *I conflitti della Controriforma* (Florence, 1998).

27. See G. Zarri (ed.), *Finzione e santità tra medioevo e età moderna* (Turin, 1990), and, in the context of inquisitorial action on Italian religious life from the sixteenth to eighteenth century, see A. Prosperi, *Tribunali della coscienza* (Turin, 1996).

28. On her letter, see A. Scattigno, 'Lettere dal convento', in Zarri (ed.), *Per lettera*, pp. 313–57.

29. See Elisabetta Graziosi, 'Scrivere in convento: devozione, encomio, persuasione nelle rime delle monache fra Cinque e Seicento', in G. Zarri (ed.), *Donna disciplina creanza cristiana* (Rome, 1996), pp. 303–31.

30. Apart from the letters used and cited in *Le sante vive* and *Per lettera*, see A. Prosperi, 'Spiritual letters', in Scaraffia and Zarri (eds.), *Women and Faith* (see note 1).

The Enlightenment and Restoration

LUISA RICALDONE
Translated by Peter Brand

7
_____

Eighteenth-century literature

The surge of interest in women and writing generated by the spread of Women's Studies has sparked a great deal of research on women in the eighteenth century, and in the 1990s in particular there has been a remarkable increase in the number of studies on women's culture in the eighteenth century. For example, a register listing Tuscan women writers has been compiled, as has a complete catalogue of all the writings of *Isabella Teotochi Albrizzi as well as works about her. Editions of rare and unpublished texts, as well as several anthologies, have appeared; numerous articles have been published in both academic and popular journals, and there have been monographs and essays on significant figures and on important topics and events of the period.[1] This already considerable output is set to increase further, for research in the literary field has barely begun; studies in the 1980s tended to concentrate on social, ideological and educational aspects of female emancipation in the Enlightenment, to the exclusion of more specifically literary matters.

The omission of this important element in the history of eighteenth-century culture can be explained by the absence, among the large number of female writers, of any really outstanding figures to compare with a *Caterina da Siena, *Gaspara Stampa or *Vittoria Colonna. Even if very few of the aspiring women writers can be considered of the highest quality, the fact that these women existed in such large numbers is in itself highly significant.

But how are we to trace the progress of women's entry into the field of literature at a time when they had to contend with the traditional prejudice condemning them to 'needle and spindle', even though they were appreciated and praised if they shone in their studies? It is difficult to do justice to the great variety of attitudes and achievements, the contradictions, the advances and retreats in a battle which was to prove of decisive significance for the modern age – more important even than the Crusades or the Wars of the Roses, according to Virginia Woolf. We can discover a good deal by attempting to answer several general questions. How, for example, did these women gain access to the language of culture and master the necessary tools? What is the connection between the literary genres favoured by women and the criteria adopted by critics and the public? How can one reconcile the public and private spheres, if at all? What part does ambition for fame and immortality play in women's literary activities? Was literature a predominantly inward-looking experience for them, or was it a means of communication with a wider world? The phenomenon of women applying themselves to their studies worried Catholics and reactionaries alike, who saw it as a threat to the family and the female virtues of obedience and submission. But it also alarmed reformers and revolutionaries, who quickly channelled it into socially useful directions: the improvement of morals, the education of children and marital responsibility.

We should note first of all that, within the immensely rich field of educational and moral treatises on women's education, literature was included in the range of disciplines allowed to them. This holds true for the whole century, from the *Discorsi Accademici di varj autori viventi intorno agli studi delle donne; la maggior parte recitati all'Accademia de' Recovrati di Padova* ('Academic Lectures of Various Living Authors concerning the Education of Women; Mostly Delivered in the Academy of the Recovrati in Padua') in 1723 and published in 1729, down to the contributions appearing during the Republic of 1796–9.[2] Along with music, dance and a few other arts regarded as decorative entertainment, and together with mathematics, which was seen as a subject relevant to domestic economy, the study and the practice of literature made up the complement of *artes foemininae,* provided that it was kept at an amateur level and excluded works deemed harmful to morals. These might include foreign novels, for example, which were considered dangerous, potentially exciting to the imagination, and plays, which presented on the stage situations often at odds with the roles considered appropriate for women. Those who favoured female education did not envisage the social emancipation of women but, rather, the enhancement of their contribution to the family.

There is one important observation to be made in this overall picture, which is that the emergence of the general concept of equality marks a turning point in the history of women's education. This concept is most widespread in Italy in the three years of the Republic, immediately after the French Revolution, but it is already to be found in democratically minded circles at the beginning of the century. We might consider, for example, the case of Aretafila Savini de' Rossi, the only woman to have taken part in the debate of the Accademia dei Recovrati in Padua. There she spoke out in defence of education not only for noble and upper-class ladies, but also for those of the lower classes, following principles of equality with regard to both sex and social class. The right to education was, in fact, included in the code of human rights, but limits were nevertheless laid down within which it could be exercised. The Proceedings of this Academy also contain the Oration delivered by the youthful Milanese scholar, Maria Gaetana Agnesi (1718–99) who, in 1727, recited a contribution in favour of women's education written specially for the occasion by her teacher, and which she translated extempore from Italian into Latin.

Italy differed from other European countries in that very few Italian women at this time earned their living by writing or engaging in cultural activities. There were, nonetheless, a few exceptions to the rule of a female culture kept, for the most part, at arm's length from those sectors offering money and power, and these included *Elisabetta Caminer Turra, director of a journal owned by her father, and *Luisa Bergalli Gozzi, who ventured into the hazardous world of theatre management and took on translations in order to improve her family's disastrous finances. There were also the women improvisers, who merit separate treatment. Improvisation was a profession in its own right ('wonderful and useless' according to Metastasio), for which performers in public places were paid, while those in private houses were rewarded with appropriate gifts. Some of these improvisers, such as Teresa Bandettini Landucci or Fortunata Sulgher Fantastici, were much sought after by the nobility at the end of the century, on account of their bravura, the range of their repertoire, their considerable erudition (especially necessary for classical subjects, for example) and the skill of their versification, which was not limited to brief stanzas of seven-syllable or eight-syllable lines, but extended to the dithyramb and other classical metres. Some of these improvisations were transcribed and published.[3]

Financial independence was not, however, a problem for the aristocracy or the upper-middle classes, that is for those classes of society with the highest degree of literacy, whether because they did not actually need the money or because their ethical conventions did not admit the idea. Those who reaped financial reward from the liberal arts were middle-class males. The dozens of educated women who may have wished to, could not gain access to the sector of paid professional activity, since education, theatre management, politics, diplomacy, journalism, law and medicine all remained male monopolies.

In her essay entitled *Breve difesa dei diritti delle donne* ('Brief Defence of the Rights of Women') Rosa Califronia attributes the willingness of the male to take the limelight, and the female to withdraw to the wings, to the 'particularly Italian' style of education, which, she said, encourages men to be 'loquacious, impetuous, irrational, if anything too forthcoming on the social stage and in polite conversation' while women are obliged to be 'reserved' and to rest on their 'modesty'.[4] Reserve, modesty and self-restraint were the qualities that underpinned a woman's image, to the point that some women declined to publish their work altogether. Elisabetta Credi-Fortini is one of these, and another is Beatrice Cocchi, who wrote under a pseudonym, even pretending to be the translator rather than the author of her own *Lettera ad una sposa* ('Letter to a Bride'). Another was Livia Accarigi, who published her first compositions anonymously. Caterina Augusta Piccolomini, writing to her friend Leonardo Marsili, explained her reluctance to agree to his plan to publish the *Avvertimenti* ('Advice') she had written for her son: 'Here I live in my little study, unknown and quiet, between the four walls of my tiny study, and despite my wish to the contrary you seek to disturb my tranquillity. Your desire to make me famous will perhaps cost me the little fame which my modesty may have earned.'[5]

Prevailing eighteenth-century opinion judged it inappropriate for a married woman to publish her writings. Nonetheless it tolerated, and in some cases even praised, an unmarried woman, or a nun, in other words women without family ties, for doing just that. Because publishing – as the word suggests – put women-writers into the category of public women, it was all the more necessary to reserve for them the epithets 'chaste and learned'. While for those in a religious order society's veto was less stringent, other factors related to their faith or their order made them reluctant to release their writings, usually published posthumously. Such was the case of *Maria Cecilia Baij, whose manuscripts were jealously guarded by the Benedictine nuns of the Most Holy Sacrament in the monastery of San Pietro in Montefiascone, and have even today been published only in part. The same was true of *Saint Veronica Giuliani, canonised in 1870, who compiled a monumental diary of 22,000 pages of manuscript which was not published in its entirety until 1991.

One author, *Giuseppina di Lorena-Carignano, declared she would not 'write with any particular care' or 'correct' her manuscripts because she did not intend them 'to be seen'.[6] Most of her writing was in French, not just because she was of French origin but because French as well as Italian was spoken and written at the Savoy court in Piedmont. The reader is struck by the contrast in her writing between culture and style. While she is familiar with the works of such as Aristotle, the Stoics, Hume and Young, to mention only those she quotes most frequently, her style of writing is imprecise, muddled, clumsy, even incorrect at times. This conflict, surprising in a woman so fond of reading, writing and ideas, is in part due to her enforced move from Paris to the Savoy court in Turin, a change which was likely to have had a considerable impact on the psycho-logical and linguistic development of a sensitive fifteen-year-old girl. It was also connected with her deliberate choice of a solitary and withdrawn style of life, away from the clamour of society. In Giuseppina's case life and letters are closely connected, in the sense that her decision to leave her lan-guage in a tentative, precarious state, even though she was perfectly capable of improving it, together with her refusal to polish her style, nor-mally so important for women writers, leaves us in no doubt about her wish to avoid being compared with others. Throughout her life she main-tained an attitude of proud aloofness from the court, except for a few trusted friends such as Tommaso Valperga di Caluso. One might venture to suggest that the perception she had of herself seemed to be that of an amateur rather than an accomplished writer. 'I like writing as much as reading', she confessed: 'I amuse myself jotting down the various ideas on mostly serious subjects that run through my head.'[7] Giuseppina's son Carlo Emanuele Ferdinando was to be the father of Carlo Alberto, the future King of Italy, and it is important to remember that her key position at the court in Turin is likely to have restrained her against publishing anything controversial concerning the behaviour of the aristocracy and the court circle.

Giuseppina wrote a number of novels, a choice of genre which while lacking a tradition in Italy would have been familiar to her through her French education. Titles include *Les aventures du Marquis de Belmont, écrites par lui-même*; *L'influence des circonstances sur les caractères. Conte moral,* and *La coquette punie par l'amour ou les dangers de la coquetterie.* In some, the princess advances a concept of female identity based on so-called 'manly' qualities: moral strength, pride, constancy under adversity, a refined intelligence, erudition. The idea of fortitude as opposed to delicacy and weakness, and a longing for liberty and independence (further recurrent motifs in her work) complete a picture of qualities closely connected with reason. In one novel and in several of her short compositions the princess stresses the superiority of friendship, which provides a sense of equality, over love, which she sees as an overpowering, destructive and all-consuming force. In other more philosophical novels she examines the craving for power and for wealth, or that most typical of eighteenth-century obsessions: the pursuit of happiness, which for her is to be found within oneself, in an untroubled conscience.

Other aspects of her extensive output are to be seen, for example, in her Utopian novel *Les aventures d'Amélie*, where, significantly, she entrusts a woman, Amélie, with the task of establishing a new society, governed by a set of laws aimed at the abolition of private property, of oppression and violence, and the implementation of modern concepts of equality at all levels of society. Other interests emerge in her *Réflexions sur le suicide*, an exceptionally modern and courageous document, which she probably wrote after reading Hume's treatise *Of Suicide*. These diverse works give this remarkable writer a key position in the cultural and intellectual life of the latter half of the eighteenth century, receptive to the most advanced and radical ideas of her time.

Three contemporaries of Giuseppina di Lorena-Carignano, all born in the Veneto between 1746 and 1751, warrant a brief mention: *Elisabetta Mosconi Contarini, *Silvia Curtoni Verza and *Paolina Secco Suardo Grismondi. The territory under the control of the Serene Republic of Venice experienced a veritable ferment of female culture at this time. It was in Padua that a woman (the Sienese Aretafila Savini De' Rossi) was first given the right of reply in an academic debate on women's education conducted by men; and it was in Venice (and later Vicenza) that Elisabetta Caminer Turra worked as a journalist and translator, that *Giustina Renier Michiel wrote her essays on customs, and Luisa Bergalli Gozzi wrote and staged her plays (a comedy, several melodramas and a tragedy).[8] Also in Venice, Isabella Teotochi Albrizzi presided over one of the most famous salons of the eighteenth century, while the salons of Mosconi Contarini and Curtoni Verza, virtually literary academies according to their distinguished members, were situated in Verona, and the salon of Secco Suardo Grismondi was in Bergamo. The provinces were no less active. Francesca Roberti Franco, for example, friend and correspondent of Clementino Vannetti, was from Bassano. The poet Angela Veronese, a woman of humble origins from the Trevigiano in north-east Italy, whose father was a gardener, taught herself to read and write. A real shepherdess, she quickly established a reputation with cultured Venetians in the early years of the nineteenth century (she was born in 1778, a year before Luisa Bergalli died); at the suggestion of Melchiorre Cesarotti they invited her to their salons, flattered her considerably, and then, once they had satisfied their curiosity, sent her back home.

Elisabetta Mosconi Contarini has left us only a few poems, but her substantial correspondence constitutes perhaps the largest and most important collection of letters of the century. These are addressed to various intellectuals who were also her friends, male and female: Saverio Bettinelli, Ippolito Pindemonte, Giovanni Cristofano Amaduzzi, Clementino Vannetti, Silvia Curtoni Verza, Paolina Suardo Grismondi, as well as her daughter Lauretta, whom she nicknamed 'la Preferita' because she was the offspring of Elisabetta's extra-marital relationship with Aurelio De' Giorgi Bertola, to whom the largest section of the collection is addressed.[9] Recent studies of these letters have emphasised their cultural and literary importance as well as their private and personal nature. Those to her lover, a poet and German scholar from Rimini who travelled a good deal in Italy and the north of Europe, are particularly instructive about the daily life of a noblewoman of the period, whose time was divided between her friends, the theatre, her reading and her children (four in Elisabetta's case). They are of interest both for their insight into the literary tastes of an educated woman in the 1780s (centring especially on Fielding, Sterne, Rousseau and Gessner) and also for the literary quality of the letters themselves. Elisabetta showed considerable stylistic ability in portraying the erotic and emotional aspects of her relationship, and later her friendship, with one of the men most sought after by the noblewomen of the late eighteenth century. In tone and structure they reveal her familiarity with Ovid's *Heroides* and with European models in vogue at that time – the 'lacrimose' drama especially, and also the extensive sentimental literature inspired by Sterne's *Letters from Yorick to Eliza and from Eliza to Yorick* for example. This last was, not surprisingly, a present from Bertola. From the correspondence as a whole a real-life story emerges, but one in which life borrows its narrative method and forms of expression, as well as the perception and experience of love as intense passion and abandon, from literature itself.

We have only a few fragments of the correspondence of Paolina Secco Suardo Grismondi, who was a friend of Elisabetta and, for a while, her rival in love. She emerges as a woman who for her time was a great traveller, well able to form contacts and even emotional relationships with people such as Ippolito Pindemonte and Aurelio Bertola.[10] This is the

bright, sunny aspect of Paolina's personality, while the darker, more nocturnal side is closely tied in with her activities as a woman of letters, torn
between the strongly felt desire to make herself known, and the obstacles,
both social and psychological, which make it difficult for her to appropriate the necessary linguistic tools to express herself through literature,
even though she lacked neither economic nor family support. Her verse in
particular indicates the unease which flowed from her feelings of inadequacy, and clearly point to a complex, problematic relationship with
poetic writing. These tensions are inherent in women of culture, manifest-
ing themselves as the 'vapours', hysterical fevers, depression, 'spleen' and
an entire range of symptoms now recognised as the tribute paid by women
for their emancipation. Paolina Secco Suardo refers to her own poems,
with their notes of pain and suffering, as 'versi da inferma' ('a sick woman's
verse'), and in a letter to Bertola dated 1 May 1785 writes as follows:
'Unfortunately a light but persistent fever has kept me in bed for the past
two months and has even denied me what is my greatest pleasure, writing
to my friends . . . Your letter cheered me, and your charming rhymes, so
dear to me, gave me infinite pleasure and almost stirred me into song.'[11]

With the *Ritratti* and *Terze rime* of Silvia Curtoni Verza we are into the
nineteenth century. The *Ritratti* were published in 1807; this was the
same year not only as Foscolo's *Sepolcri* but, most importantly for this
survey of writing by women, it was also the same year as Isabella Teotochi
Albrizzi's *Ritratti*, while the *Terze rime* appeared in 1822, the year after the
death of Napoleon. That two collections of literary portraits composed
by women should be published in the same year, and in the same region,
cannot be put down to chance, especially as other women in Silvia's and
Isabella's circle tried their hand at this genre. It is of marginal significance that these other writers (Maria Petrettini and Alberta Vendramin,
for example) have not appeared in print. More importantly, the portrait
is indicative of a flourishing literary culture clearly linked with the salon
and the nobility and clearly favoured by Venetian women of culture (see
chapter 10). In its brevity, and its nature of a character sketch, the portrait
is a minor literary genre, linked to private sentiment, belonging thus to a
conceptual and linguistic code considered feminine, dealing with
matters of the heart, of individual feelings and affections. The profiles of
Silvia and Isabella alike turn on a parallel drawn between phsyical
appearance and character, moving from physiognomy to intellectual
inclination. Silvia Curtoni Verza, unlike Isabella Teotochi Albrizzi, tends
to ignore the negative sides of a personality and extol its virtues, thus

obeying the rules of the 'eulogy'. The eulogy is important in this case in its elucidation of the womanly ideal. Silvia's portraits include four female subjects, unlike Isabella who limits herself to depictions of men. In the years between the Hapsburg and Napoleonic regimes, eulogy, rather than this kind of portrait, was used to portray an ideal. So, for example, the campaign against extravagance and on behalf of the poor, two of the leading concerns of speakers in the Assembly between 1796 and 1799, and which later form part of the programme of social welfare of the Napoleonic government to which the upper classes are sympathetic – these concerns are typical of the moral stance of the noble women Silvia depicts. They are related to enlightened Catholic culture and education of the time, which was much concerned with questions of public welfare, a subject widely debated in those sections of Catholic opinion favouring social reform and the involvement of the affluent classes in works of charity. Also included was a denunciation of war, particularly the Napoleonic campaigns which brought much suffering, disease and destruction: 'Marte omicida! in tua feroce possa / dell'orbe madri ai dolorosi gridi / l'alma tua fiera non è mai commossa' ('Homicidal Mars! with your savage power your cruel spirit is never moved by the anguished cries of mothers bereft of their offspring').[12] Silvia also recorded her opposition to Napoleon's despotic conduct in the suppression of monasteries. Her sensitivity to spiritual values (as a young woman she was for a brief time, and of her own volition, a nun) explains her modesty with regard to her poetic achievements. Her conception of the poet as an instrument of the transcendental is clear in the poetic creed she expounds in the quotation prefacing the *Terze rime*, taken from Dante's *Purgatorio* (XXIV, 54): 'a quel modo, / ch'e ditta dentro, vo significando' ('in that manner which he dictates within, I go on to set forth').

This opens up the difficult question of the connection between women's writing and religious-mystical experience generally, which is particularly relevant in the case of Veronica Giuliani and, to a lesser extent, Silvia Curtoni, a sincere believer but without mystical tendencies who disclaims any personal merit for the success of her work and insists on the absence of individuality in intellectual life.

The leitmotiv of *Faustina Maratti Zappi is a secular sense of humility in attributing to others the credit for her poetic vocation and talent. She and *Petronilla Paolini Massimi are the only two women members of the Arcadian Academy included in modern anthologies of eighteenth-century writing. Most of Faustina's poetry is dedicated to Giovanni

Battista Felice Zappi, one of the fourteen founders of the Academy, a distinguished lawyer and poet who enjoyed wide fame in Rome at the turn of the century. The formal admission of women to the Academy dates back to 1708, after which year they play an increasingly active and prominent role in its affairs. Faustina credits her husband (identified here as elsewhere in her writing with the sun) with giving her the necessary courage to undertake the labours and trials of a literary career. Certainly her insistence on her dependence on her husband goes some way towards explaining the favour she found with critics in the first half of the twentieth century. We might wonder if Faustina would have enjoyed the same fame if she had not been married to such an important, if less talented, man, or whether she would have published her poetry alone, when in fact it was published jointly with that of her husband. What we can be sure of is that out of the range of genres available to her, Faustina chose the love-lyric, a conventional enough choice for a woman writer at that time, adapting the traditional image of the unattainable and evasive loved one to the figure of the affectionate and helpful, if sometimes unfaithful, husband.

Petronilla Paolini Massimi adopts an opposite stance. She owes her fame largely to verse which Leopardi is likely to have read, for it bears striking similarity, as in the following: 'Quando dall'urne oscure / placida notte amica / licenzia i sonni e l'ombre molli usate, / ... Per me pace non viene; / e nel comun riposo /sento farsi piú grave il mio tormento' ('When friendly, peaceful night permits sleep and its wonted gentle shade from the dark tombs ... no peace comes to me; and as others rest I feel my suffering grow all the more').[13] Belonging to a circle within Arcadia usually associated with the name of Alessandro Guidi, Petronilla bestows on poetry the sacred task of revealing hidden truths. In one unjustly neglected sonnet, 'Scende il Ver dalle stelle, e adombra e sface' ('Truth descends from the stars, darkens and vanishes'), she takes objection to the banal pastoral motifs of Arcadia and focuses on matters at the very heart of existence: 'l'Autor della natura, e non l'imago' ('the Creator of nature, not its image')[14] should be the subject of the poet's quest. She subscribes to the anti-Baroque, anti-hedonist conception of poetry which developed in the early years of the eighteenth century and received its theoretical exposition in Gianvicenzo Gravina's *Ragion poetica*. She rejects the metres and conventions of Arcadia such as the madrigal and the melodious short-line stanza, seeking a more dramatic type of poetry with a strong moral stance, and to this end she employed the Petrarchan *canzone*, the ode, and, for brief compositions, the sonnet.

The distinctly Stoic posture which Petronilla adopts, issuing a challenge to fate, the stars and mankind, is symptomatic of her challenge to conventions which decreed a weak and submissive female sex. 'Crudeli, io ben saprò nel duolo istesso / ad onta vostra immortalarmi il sesso; / . . . Ancor che donna imbelle / del cimento crudel spero la palma, / che se debole ho il sesso è forte l'alma' ('Cruel men, in my suffering I shall immortalise my sex in spite of you . . . Unwarlike woman though I am I hope to triumph in the bitter trial, for however weak my sex my spirit is strong').[15] Rarely does one find in eighteenth-century women's writing an assertion of personal ability and dignity in such bold terms, or such an unequivocal challenge to the dominance of the male sex. The theme she touches lightly on in the lines quoted above forms the subject of her sonnet 'Sdegna Clorinda a i femminili uffici' ('Clorinda scorns women's tasks'). This poem with its exceptional (for its time) insight into sexual roles, and its strong aggressive charge, is probably one of Petronilla's most successful compositions. Women, she insists, are able to undertake the most difficult intellectual activities: 'Mente capace d'ogni nobil cura / ha il nostro sesso.' ('Our sex is capable of the noblest pursuits of the human mind'). The obstacles faced by women are not posed by a hostile destiny or any natural inferiority: 'So ben che i fati a noi guerra non fanno, / né i suoi doni contende a noi natura' ('Certain it is that the fates do not make war on us, or that nature denies us her gifts'): the only force imposing an inferior and subject status on women is the tyranny of men: 'Sol del nostro valor l'uomo e tiranno' ('Man alone is the tyrant denying our valour').[16]

NOTES

1. See A. Giordano, *Letterate toscane del Settecento. Un regesto* (Florence, 1994). Also A. Forlani and M. Savini (eds.), *Scrittrici d'Italia. Dalle eroine e dalle sante dei primi secoli fino alle donne dei nostri giorni* (Rome, 1991), and M. Cerruti (ed.) *Il 'Genio muliebre'. Percorsi di donne intellettuali fra Settecento e Novecento* (Alessandria, 1993). See also M. A. Macciocchi, *Cara Eleonora. Passione e morte della Fonseca Pimentel nella rivoluzione napoletana* (Milan, 1993), and L. Ricaldone, *La scrittura nascosta. Donne di lettere e loro immagini tra Arcadia e Restaurazione* (Paris–Fiesole, 1996).
2. For literary production by women during the Republic see L. Ricaldone, 'Il dibattito sulla donna nella letteratura patriottica del Triennio (1796–1799)' in *Italienische Studien 7* (1984), pp. 23–46 and A. Buttafuoco, 'La causa delle donne. Cittadinanza e genere nel triennio "giacobino" in Italia', in *Modi di essere* (Bologna, 1991), pp. 79–106. See also L. Guerci, *La discussione sulla donna nell'Italia del Settecento. Aspetti e problemi* (Turin, 1987) and *La sposa obbediente. Donna e matrimonio nella discussione dell'Italia del Settecento* (Turin, 1988).
3. See A. Di Ricco, *L'inutile e meraviglioso mestiere. Poeti improvvisatori di fine Settecento* (Milan, 1990).
4. R. Califronia, *Breve difesa dei diritti delle donne* (Assisi, 1794), p. 109.

5. *Avvertimenti di Augusta Caterina Piccolomini Petra duchessa del Vastogirardi ad Ugone suo figlio ed una lettera sopra se stessa* (Florence, 1784).

6. Giuseppina di Lorena-Carignano, *Portrait 1er de l'auteur de ce recueil fait en 1771*, in L. Ricaldone, *Scelta di inediti di Giuseppina di Lorena-Carignano* (Turin, 1980), p. 10.

7. *Ibid.*

8. See Bergalli's masterpiece, *Le avventure del poeta* (1730) now edited by L. Ricaldone, Turin 1997, the melodramas *Agide* (1725) and *Elenia* (1730), and the tragedy *Teba* (1728).

9. Elisabetta Mosconi Contarini, *Al mio caro e incomparabile amico* (1996). Some letters had already appeared in A. Piromalli, in *Aurelio Bertola nella letteratura del Settecento* (Florence, 1959).

10. For these letters see R. Troiano, 'Paolina Grismondi. Note sulla scrittura femminile del Settecento', in T. Iermano and T. Scappaticci (eds.), *Studi in onore di Antonio Piromalli* (Naples, 1994), pp. 292–326, and F. Tadini, *Lesbia Cidonia. Società, moda e cultura nella vita della contessa Paolina Secco Suardo Grismondi* (Bergamo, 1746–1801; Bergamo, 1995).

11. In R. Troiano, 'Paolina Grismondi', p. 317.

12. 'Pianto d'una madre sul figlio morto in guerra', verses 28–30 in *Terze rime di Silvia Curtoni Verza Guastaverza*.

13. See *Poeti del Settecento*, ed. by R. Solmi (Turin, 1985).

14. See the 1716–22 edition.

15. Paolini Massimi, 'Alcuni inediti', ed. R. Cardini, verses 87–8 and 130–2.

16. See the edition by G. Gronda, 1978. The sonnet is translated into English in B. Allen et al. (eds.), *The Defiant Muse: Italian Feminist Poems from the Middle Ages to the Present* (New York, 1986).

RICCIARDA RICORDA
Translated by Sharon Wood

8
—————

Travel writing, 1750 – 1860

Social and intellectual life in the eighteenth century was marked by the growing presence of women, who found themselves at the centre of philosophical and scientific debate. Nonetheless, the increasing popularity of travel as a valuable learning experience did little to shatter the age-old cliché foreshadowed in the story of Ulysses and Penelope: travel is a man's business, while the woman's place is at home.

This situation was not unique to Italy. With a few exceptions, in the English-speaking world particularly, the female version of the Grand Tour set off some time after its male counterpart. Only in the second half of the nineteenth century, if not indeed at the beginning of the twentieth, did travel become more common for women and begin to take on the characteristics of an educational experience.[1]

Italy did not boast a great tradition of women travellers. The only name frequently cited along with those of her celebrated European sisters is that of *Cristina Trivulzio di Belgiojoso, well into the nineteenth century. Yet the field, on closer viewing, is unexpectedly rich. Even if Italian women travellers were comparatively few in number, it is less travel books themselves than critical interest in them which is lacking. If travel literature in general has struggled until very recently to attract the attention of Italian critics, who have only recently begun to study it, work by women seems still to be left out in the cold.[2]

As far back as the eighteenth century, nonetheless, the question of women's travel became part of a wider debate about women. Naturally, women were still subject to a raft of rules and regulations which certainly did not encourage them to stir. As late as 1840, Paolina Leopardi spoke with regret of her family's total opposition to her desire to travel.[3] Bearing this in mind, it is significant that the late eighteenth-century

Venetian 'journal dedicated to the fair sex', Gioseffa Cornoldi Caminer's
La donna galante ed erudita ('The Genteel and Learned Woman'), makes no
mention of travel as a possible means of education or pleasure for women.
The only substantial reference to travel is in one section of the eloquently
titled *Gl'inconvenienti dei viaggi* ('The hardships of travel').[4] This short
piece refers not to an Italian woman, however, but to a young
Englishman. Convinced as he was that 'a gentleman's spirit can be formed
through travel alone', this young man left for a tour of war-torn Europe,
encountering wherever he went a series of alarming misunderstandings
and misadventures. In this piece, the prospect of travel for women
appears to be exorcised by means of a critique of its more commonly
accepted male form. If even the gentleman's Grand Tour is beset with
such a degree of difficulty, the female reader is left to imagine what would
await her, should she decide to try it for herself.

The difficulty of overcoming the suspicions lingering in women's
minds with regard to travel is underlined by biographies dating from the
early nineteenth century. Ginevra Canonici Fachini, for example, in her
*Prospetto biografico delle donne italiane rinomate in letteratura dal secolo decimo-
quarto fino a' giorni nostri* ('Biographical profile of those Italian women
renowned in literature from the fourteenth century up to the present day'
(Venice, 1824)) is full of praise for Anna Menzolini Morandi: despite her
Chair of Anatomy at the University of Bologna and her renowned skills,
in demand throughout Europe, in creating body parts from wax, she
refused to abandon her homeland in order to visit London, St Petersburg
or even Milan. At another point, with regard to Orintia Sacrat Romagnoli,
Canonici Fachini has no hesitation in concluding that 'she travelled
profitably, and now prospers thanks to that quiet life which is preferable
to any other, more brilliant state'.

While these testimonies demonstrate how unlikely it was that any
form of emancipation was achievable through travel – indeed, the need
for greater freedom and more access to public life was met, rather, by the
salon and by written correspondence – dissenting points of view can also
be detected. In 1793 the writer Ippolito Pindemonte was to berate his contemporaries for their travel mania, reserving his harshest words for
women travellers ('Is there really any need to see how States are governed
throughout Europe, in order better to govern the home?').[5] The novelist
Pietro Chiari, on the other hand, never tired of having his heroines trek
mile after mile, returning repeatedly to the topos of the journey not
simply as a useful narrative device but also in the conviction that it

behoved him to encourage women to venture beyond the narrow domestic and family hearth. Chiari underlined the unique value of travel as educational experience ('Why is it . . . that almost all women are condemned to live lives more sedentary and static even than those of plants, sprouting and growing in the corner of some tiny village where nature happened to deposit them?')[6]

In reality the eighteenth and nineteenth centuries saw no lack of women who refused to remain rooted in 'the corner of some tiny village' even if their reasons for departing cannot always be traced back to the prospect of some form of emancipation. Indeed, we can identify different categories of women travellers. Professional actresses, for example, wandered all over Europe with theatre companies. Other professionals included painters such as *Rosalba Carriera, who visited both France and Austria. A second cohort consists of travellers whose movements are dictated by chance: wives and daughters who travel with their immediate family, as was the case with *Amalia Nizzoli Solla, whose parents journeyed to Egypt when she was still a young girl; or single women such as Cristina di Belgiojoso, exiled for political reasons. Finally, there is a small nucleus of literary women who undertake a cultural tour, sometimes even a Grand Tour, as in the case of *Paolina Secco Suardo Grismondi, who in 1778 went to France to meet with some of the main players on the European intellectual scene. Other cultural tours were limited in scope, as with *Isabella Teotochi Albrizzi, who visited Tuscany where she observed and described monuments and works of art. They headed for the usual destinations of the day – Italian cities with their art treasures, European capitals – but later ventured further towards the Orient.

The cultural tour was a matter for the noble ladies of the salons, and in general only women of the aristocracy went far afield. Nonetheless the middle classes, or at least the upper middle classes, were represented, by high-ranking women such as Rosalba Carriera and Amalia Nizzoli.

There are marked differences in the way these women travellers chose to remember their experiences. Actresses, like their male counterparts, left no record of themselves behind. The same was true of more prestigious travellers: the Marchioness Paola Castiglioni Litta travelled the length and breadth of Italy, France and England before opening her famous salon in Milan, yet never put her experiences down on paper. Others preferred private communication: letters to friends which if not destroyed are yet to be discovered, or diaries, never intended for publication and published after the author's death by someone else.

There are two examples of this kind, significant also in that they occurred at opposite ends of the eighteenth century. These are the *Diario degli anni* MDCCXX *e* MDCCXXI *scritto di propria mano in Parigi da Rosalba Carriera dipintrice famosa* ('Diary of the years MDCCXX and MDCCXXI written in Paris and in her own hand by Rosalba Carriera, famous painter'), published posthumously by Giovanni Vianelli,[7] and the *Diario di viaggio e visita di Firenze* ('Diary of my travels and visit to Florence', 1798) by Isabella Teotochi Albrizzi, which remained unpublished until 1992.[8]

Rosalba Carriera gives only the briefest of notes on her stay in France, largely limiting herself to recording the names of people she met in court and cultural circles. A few terse lines refer to the subject of paintings she has undertaken: 'Tuesday 11th. Portrait of Law's daughter begun', or elsewhere, 'Thursday 1st August. Received order from King to do miniature portrait of himself for Duchess of Vantadour. Today began also another portrait of King himself'; '11th February. Started portrait of Mr Vateau for Mr Crozat.' The 'Vateau' named in the last quotation was the famous painter Antoine Watteau, whose acquaintance was particularly important to Carriera during her stay in Paris.

The pages of the diary do not, then, show us how much Rosalba was painting, nor do they permit fruitful comparisons between the visual realisation of her painterly consciousness and her written comments. Nevertheless, the reader can sense the significance of this working visit for the painter, enabling her to make important contacts but also confirming her reputation as an artist, here acknowledged on the European stage. Although they are rare, personal comments, terse and unexpected, can also be traced. On 14 October, for example, between the laconic reporting of the indisposition of one 'signor Giovanni' and a note of her having begun the 'portrait of an English lady', we have a brief revelation of her state of mind, with no further explanation: 'A sad day for me.'

Rosalba Carriera's writing approximates more closely to the travel diary with the descriptions, again somewhat sparse, of places visited ('Went with sisters to Augustines in Saint-Merri, covered in beautiful tapestries. To San Gervage which has un portage très haut et très magnifique', or events attended ('Went with my mother and sisters to the Comédie Française, given a box by Monsieur de la Carte').[9] The writing style remains fragmentary, as in a traveller's notebook rather than a diary as such, with a few key words and points jotted down. There are some curious turns of phrase in French, and the resulting hybrid linguistic mélange confirms Rosalba's place within an international cultural elite whose *lingua franca* was French.

The diary of Teotochi Albrizzi presents a more articulated narrative than that of Rosalba Carriera. Her tour of Tuscany, in which she was accompanied by her father and her husband, began in March 1798 and finished in October of the same year. Describing the places she stayed in, and the events of the trip, she intersperses travel narrative with jottings of artistic interest. The first pages are taken up with lively descriptions of her journey from the Veneto to Bologna, and on towards Florence. She describes all its difficulties – including snowstorms and accidents to the carriage, which lead Isabella to make deprecating comments on people's desire to travel – but also its pleasures, such as meeting other travellers and intellectuals in the places she visits, as well as the joy of finding herself in cities as splendid as Florence. Monuments and works of art are observed with a keen eye for detail and a highly personal commentary. There are also entries about the landscape as well as narrative passages, such as where the writer speaks of the 'revolt' which blew up with the advent of the Roman Republic, forcing her to interrupt her journey to Rome before getting as far even as Perugia. She returned to Florence where she was to meet, amongst others, the poet and dramatist Vittorio Alfieri, now settled there on his return from Paris, together with his lover Luisa Stolberg, Countess of Albany. In her last diary entry Isabella recounts sitting in Luisa Stolberg's drawing room and hearing the Count reading aloud two sections of *Misogallo* which she greatly admired: 'Various literary events took place in Paris while he was in residence – prose and verse – all of it wonderful.' Teotochi had long admired the Piedmontese writer, whom she had met personally in 1796. Also, in April and May, when her journeys took her to Florence for the first time, she was part of the Countess of Albany's circle and took part in the discussions on Alfieri's tragedies. This would seem to be about the time when she met up with the Spanish Jesuit Stefano Arteaga, her friend and a frequenter of her salon in Venice. First in conversation, later in writing, Isabella sought to rebut Arteaga's objections to Alfieri's masterpiece, *Mirra*. The diary thus illuminates an important moment in Teotochi's literary career: on the verge of trying her hand at 'public' writing with the development of the *Portraits*, her involvement in theatrical and critical debates reveals the soundness of her literary judgement.

The sober elegance of the pages describing her 'tour' suggests they were destined to be read aloud, an appropriate development for this sophisticated salon hostess. Yet even in her case, travel is more than a means of broadening her knowledge. For Teotochi, too, it is a moment of self-affirmation and proof of her own potential.

Another woman of wide culture, with an important salon in her native city of Bergamo, was Paolina Secco Suardo, whose Arcadian name was Lesbia Cidonia. Like Isabella, Paolina, who was friend and correspondent of Ippolito Pindemonte, Aurelio Bertola and Saverio Bettinelli among others, probably saw travel as a unique road to cultural and personal enrichment. She came from an ancient aristocratic family, and her father encouraged her to study languages – French in particular – but also to travel. She began writing poetry at an early age. A lover of the theatre, she had also tried her hand at acting, staging in her salon, as was the fashion of the day, several French tragedies including Le Mierre's *Ipermestra*. An early stay in Verona opened up a stimulating environment, putting her in touch with prominent writers and intellectuals. We see her desire for a journey to France as putting the finishing touches to an exhaustive literary and intellectual education.

Paolina left for France in the spring of 1778 at the head of a group which included her husband, friends, and one chevalier Mocenigo, formerly ambassador to the French court from the Republic of Venice.[10] After a short stay in Turin they headed towards the Alps, passing through Montbard, where Paolina met Buffon, and on to Paris where a particularly sucessful stay was marked by contact with such thinkers and writers as Voltaire, Diderot, Le Mierre and Madame Du Boccage. Information about these very significant encounters is entrusted to the largely unpublished letters, but there is also mention of them in poems, a form rarely adopted by women travellers. One sonnet, 'Al passaggio delle Alpi' ('On Passing through the Alps') preserves for us Paolina's impressions of a disconcerting Alpine landscape, in a tone which mingles classical references with a more modern sensibility: 'Un muto orror qui regna, e sol pel cieco / Sen delle valli s'aprono il viaggio / Gonfi torrenti che mugghiar fan l'eco' ('Mute horror here reigns, and through the blind valleys / Nought but swollen torrents carve their way / With an echoing roar'). Another poem records her arrival in Paris, the 'città regal che fosti ognor de' miei / Desir, benché da lungi, amato obbietto' ('Royal city, even from afar / beloved object of my desires').[11] Other verses are dedicated to the men of stature she meets, including the dramatist Carlo Goldoni. While no reference has yet been found among Goldoni's writings to Paolina, it seems that Voltaire, who met her in the last days of his life, composed some lines in her honour.

The posthumous *Poesie* bear traces of other journeys made by Paolina. A long poem in free verse, entitled 'Viaggio di Genova e di Toscana' ('Journey around Genoa and Tuscany'), portrays the journey Paolina made in the autumn of 1788 through Liguria and various cities in Tuscany and Emilia. It is a work of classical flavour, shot through with mythical references. While much of it is conventional in style, there are interesting moments: the lines dedicated to the risk of shipwreck which was, after all, a commonplace of eighteenth-century travel writing, or, especially, glimpses of Paolina's sense of well-being, as her trip becomes a parenthesis between a long malaise prior to her departure across the Apennines, and the fresh ills which assail her on her return. This view of travel as a moment of physical regeneration, probably correctly understood as an instance of self-fulfilment, is typical of a feminine response which, unsurprisingly, is to be found repeatedly in the work of nineteenth-century European women travellers.

Some hint of a specifically female perspective filters through accounts of journeys written by women in more usual forms, typical of travel literature of the time. While eighteenth-century women travellers linger largely among the silent forms of private writing, whether personal letters or a diary, travel books written by women in the nineteenth century go beyond these forms and approach more orthodox models, such as some kind of report. Marianna Candidi Dionigi, for example, was a highly cultured woman from Rome, a landscape painter with a passion for archaeology, and hostess of a salon frequented in the early years of the nineteenth century by the most noted Italian and European intellectuals, from Monti, Leopardi and Canova to Courier and the young Shelley. In 1809 she published *Viaggi in alcune città del Lazio che diconsi fondate dal Re Saturno* ('Travels through cities in the Lazio region, said to have been founded by the god Saturn', Rome, 1809). In the form of letters to a friend, she describes the journey made through the countryside of Lazio at the age of fifty, visiting archaeological sites. Marianna takes as her model illustrated books of journeys through the classical world, prefacing each letter with one or more etchings by her own hand depicting features of the landscapes she describes. She deals with five cities in the province of Frosinone, to the south of Rome: Ferentino, Anagni, Alatri, Arpino and Atina, all founded, according to legend, by the god Saturn, and joined by a ring of ancient walls. The descriptions are technically accurate and precisely detailed, and illustrated by elevations and plans. Marianna is also attentive to the transcription of epigraphs and inscriptions, and her interest in the frequently overlooked small detail or

oddity makes her book of value to expert as well as lay readers. The etchings, too, reveal an accurate eye for detail, whether depicting buildings,
ruins or the surrounding countryside.

Significantly, Marianna provides her own justification for her writing.
It is intended to answer the request of an anonymous 'dear friend', while
she professes her own modesty, declaring her point of view to be that of a
painter and not of a scholar (her 'comfortable mediocrity') and identifying herself as an amateur, writing for mere pleasure. Moreover, she insists
that every word she writes can be measured against the truth, rejecting
forms of scholarly erudition which proceed by hypothesis alone. These
precautions were most likely prompted by a certain unease in adopting a
wide-sweeping genre rarely taken on by women, and indeed Candidi is
fully able to discuss sources and interpretations of scholars, showing
herself to be fully aware of her own abilities as a woman of learning.

Other feminine traces can be found in her insistence on the value of concrete and direct observation, as opposed to the 'abstract ideas' of those who
are 'devoted only to the study of literature and live permanently shut away
amongst dusty books and papers'. More significant still is the way the
writer's voice occasionally pushes itself to the forefront, interrupting the
dry rhythm of the letter-essay with the description of her own feelings. The
route from Rome to Ferentino opens up before Marianna's eyes a silent and
lonely panorama marked by the remains of antiquity, provoking reflections on the 'empire of time' and on human mortality. The theme of ruins,
so widespread in her era, is of value in this case precisely because it permits
the recovery of a personal dimension: 'with these sweet anxieties I arrived
in Ferentino at dusk and to you, my worthy friend, I have had the courage
to describe more myself than the places I have seen'. If the descriptions of
nature tend to be somewhat conventional in tone, they nonetheless allow
the author's voice to emerge, as she finds in the enjoyment of natural and
artistic splendour compensation for the considerable strains of the journey.

It is rather harder to trace the emergence of the author's personality in
the account of a different 'specialist' journey, this time with a naturalist
bent. Indeed, the *Itinerario della Sicilia riguardante tutt'i rami di storia natu-
rale, e parecchi di antichità ch'essa contiene* ('Itinerary through Sicily having
regard to all branches of natural history and many aspects of antiquity
contained therein'), published in Messina, 1839 by the English scientist
Jeanette Power, presents itself as a serious study guide, with a wealth of
information on the natural and cultural resources of the island, descriptions of stretches of the land, catalogues of insects, shells and fish. While

the structure of the work appears to leave little space for the personal impressions of the traveller, it nonetheless offers a suggestive and evocative image of the researcher, leaving at dawn to roam Sicily, describing and collecting everything she saw, to return in the evening with rich spoils, rarely disappointed.

Women's travel writing now began to explore some of the varied forms of the genre. If the last two writers discussed are located in the higher sphere of the specialist journey, the choices of other nineteenth-century travellers are at the other end of the spectrum. Ottavia Borghese-Masino di Mombello's contribution to the *Strenna femminile italiana per l'anno 1837* ('The Italian Women's Almanac' for 1837), for example, consists of a piece entitled *Il lago di Schède ossia l'oca meravigliosa* ('The Lake of Schède or the Marvellous Goose') which is taken, apparently, from a manuscript called *Mie emozioni nel viaggio da Torino nella Valle d'Aosta e Savoia* ('My sentiments during the trip from Turin through the Val d'Aosta and Savoy'). The very title hints at the figure of a traveller on a sentimental journey, travelling through a romantic landscape described in emphatic tones. The lake and its surroundings become the background to a medieval tale of love and death passed down through local legends and stories. The last lord of this area, Odoardo, who had shut himself away from the world after being refused the hand of the woman he loved, was given a magic egg by an old woman. From this egg hatched a snow-white, intelligent goose which soon became precious to him and his only source of comfort. Nonetheless he found himself compelled to sacrifice the goose in order to provide a banquet suitable to welcome the beautiful lady of the castle, who had withdrawn into the valley to await the return of her husband, and who was, we understand, the young woman whom he once loved. He discovered, however, that the woman was disturbed by his closeness, and had come for the sole purpose of obtaining this very goose, much desired by her daughter. The devastating emotional conflict brought about a series of disasters ending in the woman's death, whilst Odoardo disappeared, cursing the place which had witnessed his cruel suffering.

The traveller's mind is filled with this romantic tale as she observes the lake, formed by the falls of Schède and, according to legend, made by this same Odoardo, who was said to have redirected part of the waterfall towards a sheltered, verdant basin for the amusement of his goose. The novelistic, fairy-tale element is woven into the descriptions of the landscape, giving it particular emotional resonance. And it is worth underlining that while not even here does Ottavia's account of her travels become a mere narrative topos, nonetheless it is 'domesticated' for a female readership, and made pleasurable through its proximity to other forms of writing.

The same is true in the case of the remarkable Giulia Colbert, a benefactress constantly engaged in charitable work. Giulia was French, a former lady-in-waiting at the court of Napoleon before settling in Turin upon her marriage to Carlo Tancredi Falletti, Marquis of Barolo. She travelled through part of Italy around 1815, writing short notes on the places she visited, such as the Lombard countryside, described as rather monotonous, and cities such as Mantova, with its wealth of monuments which were not to her mind adequately preserved. Some years later she went to Switzerland where she produced her *Esquisses* ('Sketches'), in which the landscape, though appreciated in all its beauty, becomes mere background for brief sketches, in which the protagonists are the inhabitants of the places visited. While there are some interesting reflections on the experience of travelling, Giulia's writings, written in French and published posthumously, in translation, are marked by the strength of her religious feeling. More than anything else, the landscape acts as a trigger for meditation and moral reflection, and in natural beauty she sees an image of a beneficent God: 'Quale inimitabile sensazione percorrere un bel paese, lasciare errare i propri sguardi sulle montagne e in fondo alla valle! Chi non sente allora la presenza dell'Amico migliore e più potente, di Colui che solo può dare la felicità' ('What an incomparable sensation to roam a beautiful land, to let your gaze wander over mountain and valley! Who then does not feel the presence of our best and most powerful Friend, who alone grants us happiness.')[12]

Women's travel writing finally finds its own expressive form towards the middle of the nineteenth century, largely thanks to two travellers: Amalia Nizzoli and, above all, Cristina Trivulzio di Belgiojoso, who produced work of a range and depth which can only be touched on here. Their writing depicts places much further afield, as well as crucial experiences in their lives.

Amalia's account, in her *Memorie sull'Egitto e specialmente sui costumi delle donne orientali e gli harem scritte durante il suo soggiorno in quel paese (1819–1828)*, ('Memoirs of Egypt and particularly the Customs of Eastern Women and the Harems, Written during her Sojourn in that Country (1819–1828)') appeared in 1841 and covered a fifteen-year period of her life as a young girl, years profoundly marked by lengthy stays in the east.[13] An initial phase of wonder at a world so different from her own, as well as acute regret for her own far-off land, was followed by the fundamental experiences of marriage and motherhood. The writer adopts a double role. She is the narrator, or rather the essayist who would inform the reader about the country where she now lives, giving detailed descriptions of different regions from the desert to the Nile, its inhabitants, their dress and living conditions, and an idea of the history and politics of the country. But she is also the protagonist of the tale, recounting both positive experiences and more dangerous ones, such as the frequent risk of shipwreck. She describes both her joys and her sorrows, the most profound being the dramatic death of her second daughter during a sea trip to Smyrna, in Turkey. She still demonstrates the wariness we have seen elsewhere, stating that she decided to write on the insistence of 'impartial and educated men'. Her perspective is a limited one, she declares. She does not set out to write a work of scholarship, nor does she wish to tell the story of Egypt; she wishes only to set down some noteworthy events which she has herself witnessed. Nonetheless, the author is well aware that her account, inasmuch as it is the portrayal of things and events seen with her own eyes, will inevitably serve to demystify a rich male tradition constructed around the fabled East. While her descriptions – less central to the text that the title would suggest – of the harems and baths are less corruscating than those of Belgiojoso, they do nonetheless capture a stifling sense of atmosphere, a female condition dominated by passivity and inertia, a state of apathy both physical and moral. That the backward condition of Eastern women is merely an extreme form of the condition of women everywhere is suggested by the uncanny similarity of her accounts of the forced marriage of the odalisque Rossane, and Amalia's own experience, given away in marriage at only fourteen years of age to a man she had never met.

For Amalia too, then, travel becomes an experience of growth and self-discovery. This is even more true for a traveller of exceptional talent such as Cristina di Belgiojoso, heroine of the Risorgimento, who fought for the freedom and independence of her country, from which she was forced to flee at various points in order to escape imprisonment. In 1830 she was an exile in France, on the run from the Austrian police. With the fall of the Roman Republic in 1849 she chose to head east, where she was to remain until 1855. The fruits of these experiences, as well as a series of tales of a 'Turkish-Asiatic' nature (1856–58) are two travel works. Originally published in French newspapers, these were *Souvenirs dans l'exil* ('Memoirs in exile', 1850) and *La vie intime et la vie nomade en Orient* ('Private and nomadic life in the Orient', 1855).

The first of these works is drawn from letters sent to her friend Caroline Jaubert during the first months of exile. Cristina intertwines descriptions of her journey towards Greece and Constantinople with memories of her involvement in recent political events. This dual perspective leads the traveller's gaze to be detailed and questioning, but also somewhat detached. Cristina nonetheless realises that her journey will provide 'sources of interest' enough to act as a substitute for the 'principal food' of her mental faculties: politics. And so she observes above all the inhabitants of the various towns she passes through, the conditions in which they live, their mode of dress. Particular attention is given to women, as is shown by the important episode of her encounter, off Malta, with the Sultaness of Morocco, who provides her with her first glimpse into the lives of Eastern women. Descriptions of landscape, on the other hand, are few and sketchy, and appear to reflect the traveller's state of mind. Her negative depiction of the appearance of Malta, for example, was certainly influenced by the hostile reception offered there to Italian refugees. The narration, fluent and concise even as it swings between a strongly ironic vein and other more reflective tones, concludes with the announcement by Cristina, now settled on the banks of the Bosphorous, of her next journey, to Asia Minor. Here she expects to be moved 'not by the work of man, but by the beauty of nature'.

In the event her journey towards Syria and Jerusalem, in which she was accompanied by her daughter, lasted almost a whole year. And while it doubtless confronted her with unusual and fascinating natural wonders, it offered her above all the chance to familiarise herself with the 'the physiognomy of the people' whom she met. Her perspective as a woman was a privileged one, in that it gave her access to a domestic dimension forbidden to the male visitor. *La vie intime et la vie nomade en Orient* overturns the myths created by the European imagination around the East: there is no room here for exoticism. The dominant features of the human landscape are backwardness, dirt and mud. The traveller attempts to evaluate objectively what she sees, attempting to place both positive and negative in a context so different to the European one. Nowhere is this more evident than in her description of the harems. Described almost with the precision of the sociologist, they lose any aura of a privileged space dedicated to masculine sexuality, taking shape under Cristina's pen as 'places of darkness and confusion, full of smoke and infection', which the traveller can hardly bring herself to enter. Cristina subtly analyses the roles played out in the harem, and the complex relationships operating between the men/owners and the women, forced to accept a condition of utter submission. Cristina refuses to attribute these roles and relationship to the 'nature' of the people, who indeed seem to her more patient and agreeable than Europeans. While on the one hand she relates these roles to the social, religious and political structures of these countries, on the other she implicitly interprets them as paradigmatic of mechanisms which oppress women the whole world over.

In this sense, Belgiojoso's book can be seen as a sort of coming of age of these first expressions of women's travel writing. Balancing a compelling, faithful portrayal of people and places with the recording of the writer's own thoughts and feelings, it relates a process of discovery both of the self and of a wider female condition. Cristina's work overturns the entrenched *topoi* of travel writing: it reveals traces of a specifically female experience in a style which is concise and well constructed, highly eloquent and evocative.

NOTES

1. See L. Borghi et al. (eds.), *Viaggio e scrittura* (Florence, 1988); A. De Clementi and M. Stella (eds.), *Viaggi di donne* (Naples, 1995) and M. Perrot, 'Stepping Out' in G. Fraisse and M. Perrot (eds.), *Emerging Feminism from Revolution to World War* (Cambridge, MA, 1993), pp. 449–81.

2. See Luca Cerlici, 'Alla scoperta del Bel Paese: I titoli delle testimonianze dei viaggiatori in Italia (1750–1900)', *Annali d'Italianistica* 14 (1996), p. 303.

3. G. Ferretti, '[Auto]ritratto con lettere', in *Lettere inedite di Paolina Leopardi*, ed. Giampiero Ferretti (Milan, 1979). See also Michela De Giorgio, *Le italiane dall'Unità ad oggi* (Rome–Bari, 1992), p. 97

4. No. 7, 1788, vol. III, pp. 158–63.

5. *I viaggi* (Venice, 1793).

6. *La Corsara Francese della guerra presente*, in *Trattenimenti dello spirito umano*, vol. XII (Brescia, 1781), p. 4.

7. Venice, 1793. See also Bernardina Sani (ed.), *Rosalba Carriera. Lettere, diari, frammenti*, 2 vols. (Florence, 1985), vol. II, pp. 761–79.

8. Cinzia Giorgetti, 'Il "petit tour" di Isabella Teotochi Albrizzi', *Studi Italiani* 8 (1992), pp. 117–73.

9. Quotations are from Sani, *Rosalba Carriera*, pp. 765 and 766 respectively.

10. See F. Tadini, *Lesbia Cidonia* (Bergamo, 1995), pp. 69–82.

11. 'Giunta in Parigi', in *Poesie della contessa Paolina Secco Suardo* (Bergamo, 1820), p. 58 and p. 59.

12. *Con gli occhi del cuore*, ed. A. Montonati (Milan, 1995), p. 127.

13. Milan, 1841. For a comparison of the work of Amalia and Cristina see M. Scriboni, 'Il viaggio al femminile nell'Ottocento. La principessa di Belgiojoso, Amalia Nizzoli e Carla Serena', *Annali d'italianistica* 14 (1996), pp. 304–25.

9

Journalism, 1750–1850

Some of the writers discussed in this chapter stand out among women writers, on two counts. They were the first women ever to work as journalists in Italy. Also, unlike most other women writers, they were professional writers. They approached writing as a career, with its implications of autonomy and financial independence in a society that saw women as essentially domestic and dependent beings. On both counts, then, they were entering uncharted waters, with no traditions, no role models to imitate.

It is very noticeable that, when these early journalists appeal to a female genealogy, as so many women writers do, they make use of the traditional genre of biographies of 'illustrious women', modified through the elimination of women who were famous in a negative sense, and with the addition of contemporary figures. The eighteen-year-old *Elisabetta Caminer Turra, writing in her father's journal in 1769, produced a spirited roll call of great women, down to the contemporary scientists Maria Gaetana Agnesi and Laura Bassi.[1] And some twenty years later her sister-in-law Gioseffa Cornoldi Caminer peppered her 'women's magazine' with appeals to a tradition of strong, capable, unconventional women, which reaches down to her own times with the great empresses Maria Theresa and 'Catterina, la gloria del nord' (Catherine, the glory of the North),[2] and with the 'donne illustri che nell'età nostra coltivano la lettere, e che non sono poche' ('the far from rare illustrious women who cultivate literature in our own age'), even daring to suggest that she might be one of them (*La donna galante ed erudita*, 'Amena letteratura', 1, 1786). But she, like Elisabetta, stopped short of appealing to the sisterhood of women journalists.

And yet by the time an Italian woman first started working on a periodical (Caminer Turra in 1768), England had been producing well-known women scribblers from the start of the century, with Mary de la Rivière Manley and her *Female Tatler*, Lady Mary Wortley Montagu and her *Nonsense of Commonsense*, Eliza Haywood and her *Female Spectator*, not to mention Jane Hughes, Catherine Cockburn and others who contributed to the *Gentleman's Magazine* in the 1730s, and the anonymous women who contributed to the *Athenian Mercury* as early as the 1690s. And in France the *Journal des Dames* had been edited by women since 1761. This delay, together with the fact that in Italy women journalists remained extremely thin on the ground well into the nineteenth century, is to be explained in terms of structural factors, such as the condition of women, the perception of women, the class system, rather than with any presumed general delay of Italian journalism, which took off from the early seventeenth century as elsewhere in Europe. Women journalists who approached their writing as a career tended to come from classes below the aristocracy and upper middle class, which were still hegemonic in Italy. And they came on the scene at a time when the increase in education was widening the potential readership, down to the urban artisan and professional classes, and even women, posing new challenges to journalism.

Two main types of periodical dominated Italian journalism in the mid-eighteenth century. These were the *gazzette*, which provided news on festivals, the theatre, events at court, and foreign affairs, and the *giornali*, which gave information, although traditionally not critical analyses, on literary, historical and scientific matters through reviews and *estratti* (summaries) of new books. By about 1760 the myth of 'impartiality' was breaking down, and these journals were hosting lively critical debates. Typical of this new, more lively, more militant type of journalism, often directly or indirectly inspired by the model of *The Spectator*, were Baretti's *Frusta letteraria* which took off in Venice in 1763, and, starting in 1764, its great rival, the Milanese *Il caffè*, linked to internationally renowned figures like Pietro Verri and Cesare Beccaria. Political debate, however, did not really feature until the revolutionary period.

Elisabetta Caminer Turra produced a series of such critical *giornali* from the 1760s. Gioseffa Cornoldi Caminer in the 1780s, and *Carolina Lattanzi in the first two decades of the nineteenth century, were responsible for 'women's magazines'. *Eleonora Fonseca Pimentel and *Cristina Trivulzio di Belgiojoso were political journalists writing within revolutionary contexts, Jacobin republicanism and 1848 nationalism respectively. In varying degrees and modes, all concerned themselves with gender issues, with the exception of Fonseca Pimentel. All were reviled with scurrilous accusations, quite independently of whether or not they led unconventional private lives. But were they after all not transgressing merely by leading public lives?

Literary journalism: Elisabetta Caminer Turra

It may be significant that the first Italian women journalists flourished in Venice, with its tradition of freedom from ecclesiastical censorship, its well-established practice of importing, translating, reprinting and selling foreign works, and its family-based publishing networks. Within such a family network flourished Elisabetta Caminer, daughter of a polymath who was also a journalist and a publisher, Domenico Caminer, and Gioseffa Cornoldi Caminer, who was her sister-in-law.

Elisabetta (Bettina as she was generally called) began her journalistic activity in 1768, aged seventeen, as a member of the editorial team of her father's *Europa letteraria*, which transformed itself seamlessly into *Giornale enciclopedico* in May 1773. From 1777, aged twenty-six, she took over the editorship of the *Giornale enciclopedico*, which became *Nuovo Giornale Enciclopedico* in 1782, and finally *Nuovo Giornale Enciclopedico d'Italia* in 1790.

The titles of these periodicals (and even *Europa letteraria* announced itself as a 'giornale' in the frontispiece) proclaimed their nature and function. They had in fact a crucial role in transmitting Enlightenment culture to Italy. All of them were monthly. Their basic format consisted of an *estratto* followed by several book reviews, intermingled with pieces (sometimes in the form of letters) on literary or scientific matters, ending with a rubric entitled 'Novelle letterarie' ('Literary news') listing new books. Sometimes they also carried advertisements for the sale of various products. Many of the pieces published were reproduced from foreign periodicals, as was the custom.

It is often said that Elisabetta, lacking as she was in formal education and largely self-taught, was not really the mind behind the journals, but played a subaltern role to Alberto Fortis, and then to Giovanni Scola, with whom she had long-standing affairs.[3] She was clearly acutely aware of her unorthodox position, as a writer lacking full educational credentials, and a woman writer at that. In response to this problem she adopted one of the strategies traditionally employed by women to present and defend their writing: she makes repeated references to the 'tenuità' ('feebleness') of her 'ingegno' ('intellect'), to her 'deboli forze' and 'scarsezza del suo talento' ('weak powers' and 'paucity of her talent'),[4] accompanied by unashamedly tongue-in-cheek allusions to herself as a 'giovane che non mostra poi d'avere cattiva inclinazione' ('a young woman who does not appear to be of such a bad disposition') (*Europa letteraria*, March 1772), and who therefore deserves encouragement rather than reproach and humiliation.

Her input in the journals is in fact substantial throughout, both as a writer and editor and hands-on manager of the production of the journals, dealing with printing workers, sale of books, customers' bills.[5] And neither should we forget that she was the one who transformed her father's *Giornale enciclopedico* into a vigorous tool in the battle for ideas. When she took over as editor in February 1777, she overtly redefined the nature of the journal through a specific appeal to the culture of the French Enlightenment: while Domenico Caminer, in his announcement of the change of title from *Europa letteraria* to *Giornale enciclopedico* in May 1773, had explained that 'enciclopedico' meant 'universale', that is to say wide-ranging, his daughter stated that the title of the journal was significant because '*Enciclopedia* significa *concatenazione di cognizioni*' ('Encyclopaedia means the inter-relatedness of knowledge', *Giornale enciclopedico*, February 1777).

The topics she wrote on were wide-ranging: literature, with much attention paid to contemporary European literature, scientific matters, pharmaceutics, medicine, botany, agriculture, history, politics, entomology, religion, geography, economics, education, even philosophy (for example she reviewed Soave's Italian translation of John Locke, in *Giornale enciclopedico*, May 1777). There is much emphasis on Voltaire, and on typical Enlightenment concerns, such as issues of legislation and opposition to torture (she wrote in praise of Beccaria in *Giornale enciclopedico*, March 1782), not neglecting current affairs (in October 1789 she expressed guarded approval of the recent revolutionary events in Paris). But her great passion was the theatre. She vigorously publicised her own translations of contemporary European plays (*Europa letteraria*, January 1772, March 1772, *Giornale enciclopedico*, September 1774, January 1775, August 1775), reviewed Goldoni's play which was performed at Drury Lane and praised this 'poeta della natura' ('poet of nature') whose theatre is inspired by 'ordine, verosimiglianza, decenza' ('harmony, verisimilitude, decency') (*Giornale enciclopedico*, March 1777). She also wrote glowing reviews in July–August 1789 of Goldoni's *Mémoirs*, and, beginning in January 1790, of the Zatta edition of his plays which appeared in several volumes.

Much space was also taken up with women's issues. Elisabetta paid special attention to the publication of books by women, on women and for women.[6] She wrote on the condition of women who had been forced to become nuns against their will, on the need for women's education, and generally did not miss a chance to comment on women who had achieved beyond the normal limits of their sex.[7] And she was by no means averse to fashion and adornments, which she analysed with considerable sophistication in their economic dimension. Regarding fashion, in fact, her position was strikingly similar to that of her sister-in-law Gioseffa, whose journal she publicised repeatedly, even going to the extent of listing the contents of the first four issues 'per invogliar le Signore, che debbono essere le principali posseditrici di codesto giornale' ('in order to encourage the Ladies, who are bound to be the principal readers of this journal').[8]

Magazines for the ladies: Gioseffa Cornoldi Caminer and Carolina Lattanzi

When Gioseffa Cornoldi Caminer's *La donna galante ed erudita* appeared in Venice in 1786, on sale at the famous Albrizzi bookshop, it was the first time in Italy that a woman addressed an overtly female readership. Once again, Italy was lagging behind Europe. France had the *Journal des Dames* from 1759 to 1778, and England produced the *Female Tatler* as early as 1709, followed by the much-imitated *Female Spectator* in 1744–6, not to speak of the *Epistles for the Ladies* (1749–50), and the *Lady's Museum* (1760–1).

In Italy the wave of discovery of women as readers, reaching a high point with Francesco Algarotti's *Newtonianismo per le dame* ('Newtonianism for the ladies', 1737), had spread to periodicals in the form of women's magazines: *La Toelette*, *Biblioteca galante* and *Giornale delle Dame*, all three published in Florence in 1770–1, 1775, and 1781 respectively, and the Milanese *Giornale delle nuove mode di Francia e d'Inghilterra* in 1786,[9] and arguably before that with Albrizzi's *Pallade Veneta* (1687–8), each issue of which had the format of a letter addressed to a lady. And Gaspare Gozzi's parodies in his *Gazzetta veneta* from 1760 showed that a female reading public was there to stay.[10] But women had been passive recipients. None of these publications had been written, even less directed, by women.

These magazines for the ladies have generally attracted a negative, or at best patronising judgement, and women in particular have often felt uneasy about them. The quantitative preponderance of fashion plates and articles dedicated to fashion, cosmetics, beauty and such like, have triggered both the criticism of women resenting the 'obligation to be beautiful' and the typecasting of women readers as worthy recipients of 'frivolous material', and scathing comments on the part of men, broken only by grudging and somewhat dismissive recognition of their treatment of 'serious' topics.[11]

Far from being frivolous and superficial these journals are lively, reader-friendly, practical, realistic and also intellectually stimulating, as well as dotted with intriguing advice on matters of health and beauty, and, yes, full of rather splendid fashion plates.

La donna galante ed erudita probably modelled itself on the *Female Spectator*, which had been published in Venice as *La Spettatrice* in 1752.[12] It came out somewhat erratically between 1786 and 1788. Thirty-six issues were published altogether. Each number consisted of thirty-two pages, and regularly included two fashion plates, both preceded by an explanatory piece. Taken together, these pieces amount to an anthropology and history of fashion, relating fashion in clothes to cultural trends and the shifting roles of women and men therein. Cornoldi Caminer analyses and justifies 'lusso' ('luxury goods') in economic terms: luxury goods are both the product of unequal societies and the only means of keeping the poor afloat in them: only if the wealthy will use their surplus profits to purchase consumer goods will it be possible for superfluous wealth to circulate to some degree and therefore be of benefit to the poor.

Besides fashion and luxury goods, other constant topics are beauty and how to achieve it, marriage, family life, the related phenomenon of *cicisbeismo* (whereby married women had a recognised male escort, or *cicisbeo*) and children's education. But one also finds reflections on and a mini-history of journalism, as well as anecdotes, news on literature and the theatre, and, as ever, a number of pieces taken from foreign journals, the *Spectator* in particular.

When Cornoldi Caminer writes on beauty, she also links it to health and hygiene. Among the obstacles to health and therefore beauty she lists excessive use of coffee, over-salty food, lack of exercise, and only washing one's face 'every eight, or twelve days'.[13] She gives advice on how not to be too fat, but also on how to be not too thin, as well as more mundane and somewhat intriguing recipes on the elimination of wrinkles, and on the use of strawberries and chervil water to undo the ominous tanning effects of sunlight, as well as humorous observations on the absurdity of using cosmetics in ways which amount to wearing a mask.[14]

As regards marriage, the journal is pervaded by the dry acknowledgement of its ambivalent status and function, in that young girls will often see it as the only 'gateway to freedom', only to end up in a new form of slavery, especially in the pithy half-page 'matrimonial map', and the spirited history of love and marriage cum analysis of *cicisbeismo* .[15]

Cornoldi Caminer writes very much as a woman, one who is well aware of the material and ideological constraints on women. This is a magazine for the ladies, but she not infrequently addresses men, and their prejudices and stereotypes. She does so in fact in what one could regard as her manifesto, which opens the very first issue of the journal. The tone is allusive and teasing, as it often is, and she endlessly plays with current expectations regarding women writers and in so doing both adopts them and demolishes them at the same time.

Her style is always lively and unpompous, a delight to read, even when she abandons the teasing tone and for once openly basks in female pride, in the 'Breve osservazione sul bel sesso' ('Brief observations on the gentle sex'), where she surveys the history of women, singles out those who have achieved beyond the confines of their assigned roles, and openly challenges the ways in which women of the upper classes have let themselves be suffocated by luxury and inactivity, because, she says: 'Si conclude . . . che una vita ritirata e domestica è la sola che convenga ad una donna in generale; ma io dico di no' ('They claim . . . that women in general are only suited to a withdrawn and domestic life; but I don't think so').[16]

The *Donna galante ed erudita* ceased publication only a few months before the events of the French Revolution in 1789. A decade later its editor re-emerged, as 'la cittadina ('citizen') Gioseffa Cornoldi Caminer', translator of French pro-revolutionary works. A provisional Jacobin government had just been established in Venice.

Carolina Lattanzi was to follow the opposite trajectory. First springing to fame as 'citizen Lattanzi', author of a spirited memoir on 'Schiavitù delle donne' ('Slavery of women') which she delivered in public in Mantua in 1797, 'Anno I. della Libertà d'Italia' ('Year I of the Liberty of Italy'), she then reappeared in 1804, in the far more sedate climate of Napoleonic Milan, as the editor of the *Corriere delle dame*, which she would see through the vicissitudes of the Austrian Restoration until her death in 1818.

The *Corriere delle dame* came out regularly on a weekly basis, and appears to have been very successful. According to a prefect's report, it had 700 subscribers in 1811, which compares well with the 3,000 subscribers to the top contemporary periodical *Corriere milanese* .[17] It was in fact the only paper to survive the transition from the Napoleonic to the returned Austrian regime in 1814.[18] It was undoubtedly a skilfully and vigorously managed journal, both in terms of production and what we would now call marketing.

The *Corriere delle dame* always carries clearly visible information on how and where to subscribe, and the cost thereof, and the format of the announcement keeps changing, clearly with a view to holding the readers' attention. Each number carries an 'enimma' ('riddle'), and refers to the next issue for its solution. As well as, of course, regularly including fashion plates, it also promotes mail-order sales of clothes, patterns and fashion accessories, and often carries advertisements for the most diverse commodities, from candles to French language lessons. Its intended readers clearly were wealthy and reasonably cultured ladies of the upper middle classes, but also their husbands, who might be landowners or members of the emerging entrepreneurial class. In fact it covers a whole variety of topics: from politics (a section entitled 'Termometro politico', usually compiled by Carolina's husband, is a regular feature), to theatrical reviews, to the latest medical discoveries (such as the forceps, smallpox vaccine, remedies for various ailments). There was practical advice (for example on purifying the air in houses, on bringing up and educating children, on breastfeeding), but also information on new inventions such as steamboats, and articles urging Italians to adopt the 'pomi di terra o patate', including an intriguing recipe for a soup based on potato starch.[19]

As was the case with *La donna galante ed erudita*, the *Corriere delle dame* legitimises its preoccupation with fashion and luxury goods in economic terms, seeing them as both products and generators of wealth.[20] From January 1805, it breaks new ground by taking an interest in male fashion as well. But there is also much irony towards fashion and its constraints, and covert challenges to the notion that well-to-do women have an 'oblig-ation' to be idle and bored. In fact, Lattanzi argues against the constraints on women's activities, because 'le donne possono, se lo vogliono, innal-zarsi ad opere maschili' ('women are able, as long as they are willing, to raise themselves to manly activities').[21] It could be said that feminism, or at least female pride, is the one constant thread that runs throughout Carolina's evolution, with frequent challenges to the commonplaces regarding women, and spirited roll calls of women who are managing now or ever have managed to break the constraints imposed by an oppres-sive patriarchal culture. It is in this connection that she mentions, on 10 February 1805, her own oration on the slavery of women published in

Mantua seven short years before, but in fact already in a different age. She even publishes a discussion in dialogue form of her change of views.[22] Carolina the Republican Jacobin had re-emerged as a Napoleonic monarchist, and would later, with the Austrian Restoration, recycle herself as a loyal subject of His Royal and Imperial Majesty. Whether this was the result of political realism or mere opportunism it is difficult to say. Maybe it was a matter of survival.

Political journalism: Eleonora Fonseca Pimentel, Cristina Trivulzio di Belgiojoso and others

Eleonora Fonseca Pimentel is the only woman journalist who has left a detailed record of her work in the Jacobin period. But there may have been others. Two women who worked for Jacobin journals were one Teresa M., who was on the editorial board of the *Quotidiano bolognese* (1797–8), and Vittoria Morano, mentioned in the Turin *La vera repubblicana* (1798) as the person to contact with regard to subscriptions, distribution and submission of articles. While Teresa M., as she signed herself, wrote pieces in which she ironises on current events in Bologna using the style typical of astrological premises to almanacs, and then actually went on to write for *Opuscoletti lunari* (1798) after the closure of the *Quotidiano bolognese*, we do not know whether Vittoria Morano was the author of any of the articles which appeared in the four issues of *La vera repubblicana*, whose intended readership was women, with the aim of educating them to 'virtù repubblicane' ('republican virtues').[23]

Eleonora Fonseca Pimentel was the journalist and opinion-maker of the Repubblica Partenopea, the short-lived Neapolitan Jacobin republic of 1799. In January 1799 she was actively involved in the foundation of the Republic, and soon after was put in charge of *Il monitore napoletano*, which was to be the chief political journal of the regime. From its inception, on 2 February 1799, ten days after the proclamation of the Republic, she was its director and virtually sole writer.

Il monitore appeared generally twice a week, on Tuesdays and Saturdays. It consisted of a leading article, news, miscellany and advertisements. Its source for foreign news was the Parisian *Moniteur*, which was also the obvious model for its title. Its political line was one of broad support for the Jacobin revolutionary government, but Fonseca Pimentel was not identified with any particular Jacobin faction, and was clearly given ample freedom of expression.

In the leading article of the very first number, which begins with the triumphant 'Siam liberi in fine' ('we are free at last'), Fonseca Pimentel takes on board the question of popular hostility, indeed armed resistance, to the Jacobin revolution, which she interprets in terms of popular ignorance, and hence gullibility and vulnerability to reactionary propaganda.[24] Popular hostility was in fact, paradoxically, the chief problem encountered by Jacobins everywhere. Their ideology was based on the conviction of the need to free 'the people' (generally a nebulous, ill-defined but no less powerful concept for that) from tyrannical oppression, while in the eyes of the people they were identified with their class of birth, the landowning nobility. In Naples popular hostility against the Jacobins and their French allies, who were seen as nothing less than an army of occupation, was especially acute. The Jacobin republic was in fact finally defeated by a peasant army, the infamous Esercito della Santa Fede (Army of the Holy Faith) led by Cardinal Ruffo, enthusiastically supported by bands of the urban poor.

The question of popular opposition to the Republic, and what is to be done about it, is in fact the main concern in virtually every number of *Il monitore*. Fonseca Pimentel frequently criticises the government in terms of the speed and effectiveness of their actions: she urges them to abolish the feudal system quickly so the people will see that the revolution really is on their side; she urges them to use repression sparingly and selectively, and focus on skilful propaganda instead. Her parameters remain consistently those of the Enlightenment: there is no Romantic myth of the people as the repositories of wisdom in her thinking. The people are wrong in their hostility to the Jacobin revolution, and they are wrong because they are ignorant. So they need to be educated. But this process of education, in order to suceeed, must happen through a careful and detailed process of mediation through the typical forms of popular culture. She knows very well that a culture of the people does exist, with mental structures totally opposite to those of high culture. Therefore the Jacobins will have to adopt the language, mental structures and typical ways of transmission of popular culture.

So, while the majority of Jacobins were against the dialects, which they saw as socially and regionally divisive, Fonseca Pimentel repeatedly advocates the composition of 'gazzette' in Neapolitan dialect.[25] Her awareness of the widespread illiteracy of the masses and of the particular forms of oral communication leads her to advocate the use of these forms, and therefore their control, by the revolutionary elite. And so she puts forward detailed proposals for the public reading of such *gazzette* both in the towns and in the countryside.[26] She envisages a wide and detailed network of oral communication, controlled by the Jacobins both in terms of its content and form of transmission.

The linchpin of this network of oral communication with the masses should be the clergy, because the people think in religious terms and because of the traditional role of the clergy as the chief mediators between high culture and popular culture. Therefore the Jacobins must make sure that the clergy are on their side (and a significant minority were). They must underline that there is not opposition but continuity between the Gospel and the principles of the Republic, in that both are about fraternity, equality and therefore true democracy. And above all they must adopt the myth-making approach which characterises the religious mentality. In the same way, she wants to channel towards a pro-revolutionary line all the traditional forms of popular street culture. Folk songs, storytelling, puppet theatre, all can be used, she says, to put forward democratic topics.[27]

It is impossible to tell whether, given more time, her ideas could have borne fruit. But time was fast running out for the Jacobins of Naples. Popular armed resistance never ceased during the few months of the life of the Republic, in fact it increased to full-blown warfare. 'La guerra è cotidiana' ('war is endemic'), she writes on 8 June, and she ends the issue with the latest news of the fighting, promising to give more detail later.[28] But that was to be the last issue of *Il monitore*. On 14 June Cardinal Ruffo's army entered Naples, the Republic fell, the Bourbon monarchy was re-established. Eleonora, along with many other Jacobins, was arrested, and imprisoned for a while on a ship anchored in the Bay of Naples. The prisoners were supposed to be given safe passage into exile, and the agreement was guaranteed by Admiral Nelson. But Nelson reneged on the agreement. On 12 August Eleonora was put on trial. On 17 August she and eleven others were condemned to death. Four of them were reprieved. The other eight, Eleonora among them, were hanged in the central market square on 20 August 1799. Her body, before being given burial, was left hanging from the gallows for a whole day, to become the object of much banter on the part of the people of Naples.

What Eleonora was to the Jacobin revolution Cristina Trivulzio di Belgiojoso was to 1848. Even so, her journalistic activities spread well beyond this period. In fact a large number of her writings, including her travel writings, and her essay on the condition of women, first appeared in periodical publications.[29] She was linked to several journals in different capacities, sometimes as editor and financial backer (*Gazzetta italiana*, published in Paris 1844–45, *Ausonio*, published in Paris 1846, *Il crociato*, published in Milan 18 April to 27 July 1848), sometimes as co-founder (as with the Neapolitan *Il nazionale*, March 1848, for which she did not in fact write), and *Italie* (1860), through which she attempted to interpret Italian events to the French reading public. It is also likely that she was a frequent contributor to *La perseveranza* (published from 1859), although it is difficult to know which were her pieces since all articles were anonymous.

Both the *Gazzetta italiana* and the *Ausonio* had as their main concern the question of what kind of patriotism should prevail in the struggles for independence leading up to the events of 1848. The *Ausonio* had a broader approach to topics (it frequently hosted articles on cultural and literary matters as well as politics). Both journals often took on board very concrete issues, linked to agriculture, land tenure systems, the living conditions and lack of education of the peasantry. There was real concern here with the terrible lives of the peasants, and also of course attention to the very real problem of attracting the support of the peasantry to the patriotic cause.

Concreteness, attention to facts, conducting arguments on the basis of factual evidence and concern with the question of popular support, remained constant features of Cristina's political journalism. They all come to the fore in *Il crociato*, which accompanies, analyses and attempts to influence the revolutionary events of 1848 in Milan. The presence of Cristina in *Il crociato*, which came out twice weekly, is massive. From 4 May, when her first signed piece appeared, she consistently signed either the editorial or a shorter article.

While in *Gazzetta italiana* she had advocated a peaceful transition to some form of autonomy, through an agreement with Austria, a position which had unleashed the opprobrium of much patriotic opinion, by 1848 she had firmly embraced the cause of revolution. Her untiring work during the short-lived provisional government in Milan is well attested. She favoured the solution which ultimately prevailed, that is to say, independence from Austria and unification under the Savoy monarchy. To this extent she was opposed to the republican project of Mazzini and his followers, and the *Crociato* stood for the opposite view to Mazzini's republican *Italia del popolo*. She argued that a republican set-up was unrealistic in that in order to succeed it required a level of maturity, education, prosperity and equality that simply did not prevail in the here and now. But precisely because she wanted the revolutionary project to succeed, she was also very critical of the provisional government. She was impatient with their general ineptitude, their lack of initiative, their failure to consult and therefore failure to win over popular support, and also their failure to acknowledge the existence of an alternative, republican, opinion.[30] Although on the one hand she was quite capable of producing a skilful rewriting of history when she deemed this a necessary tool for the creation of consensus around the monarchical project (in the Editorial of 9 May 1848 she presents the house of Savoy as historic defenders of liberty and fighters against foreign invaders), on the other she refused to toe the party line when this involved relinquishing respect for 'i principii e le persone' ('principles and persons'). It is for this reason that she spoke out against the arrest of several republicans on the accusation of being Austrian agents: she reckoned that some may have been, but the majority were just republicans, and, what is more, they were arrested for this very reason.[31] She consistently argued against the views of the republicans, on the grounds that they lacked and always had lacked realism, but she viewed them as mistaken fellow patriots not as enemies, and she wanted to respond to the fraternal challenge of the *Italia del popolo*.[32]

Throughout the short life of the provisional government she both looked ahead to wide-ranging projects of social, cultural and institutional regeneration, and focused on the immediate, urgent and desperate problem of the peasants' lack of support, indeed often outright hostility, to the patriotic revolution. On 15 July, twelve days before the end of the journal, and shortly before the final crushing of the patriotic movement by the Austrian army, she reported that the rural areas, still under the control of Austrian agents, posed a 'sanguinosa minaccia' ('a mortal threat') for the provisional patriotic government in Milan. In the countryside, she says, 'per tutto si ode il canto cupo e funesto di *Viva Radetzky, viva i tedeschi, viva l'imperatore, morte ai signori*' ('everywhere one hears the ominous, dismal song *Long live Radetzky, long live the Germans, long live the Emperor, death to the gentry*'). The destitute masses hated the revolution, made by their oppressors the gentry. There is an uncanny similarity with the plight of the Jacobins surrounded by the hostility of peasants and urban poor. And an uncanny similarity also between the last issue of Eleonora Fonseca Pimentel's *Monitore napoletano* with its ominous statement about war being endemic, and the last issue of *Il crociato* (27 July 1848), in which Cristina reports despondently that defeat is imminent (the Austrians have crossed the Mincio, Valeggio is in Austrian hands).

But unlike Eleonora, Cristina was able to escape and go on to another twenty-three years of battling and writing.

By the mid-nineteenth century, almost a hundred years after the first Italian woman began working for a periodical, women's journalism in Italy had become firmly established, thanks to a small bunch of determined and exceptionally talented women. While the women journalists in this period are too few to allow us to draw firm generalisations, some observations are possible. Firstly, we find them working as 'hard' political journalists only in heroic revolutionary situations (Fonseca Pimentel with the Jacobins in 1799 and Trivulzio di Belgiojoso in the revolutionary wave that swept through Europe around 1848). Secondly, these political journalists were aristocrats, who did not need to earn a living by their writing, while the others, Caminer Turra, Cornoldi Caminer and Lattanzi, opted for the safer venues of literary or 'frivolous' journalism. Their critique, social and even political, is no less sharp for being forced into more oblique ways.

NOTES

1. *Europa letteraria*, November 1769. The research towards this chapter undertaken at the Biblioteca Nazionale Braidense in Milan and the Biblioteca Marciana in Venice was made possible by a British Academy grant.
2. *La donna galante ed erudita*, 16, 1787.
3. See G. Ricuperati, 'Giornali e società nell'Italia dell' "Ancien Régime" (1668–1789)', in V. Castronovo, G. Ricuperati, C. Capra (eds.), *La stampa italiana dal Cinquecento all'Ottocento* (Bari, 1980), pp. 300–6.
4. *Europa letteraria*, January 1772, *Giornale enciclopedico*, February 1777.
5. See S. Stocchiero, 'La redazione di un giornale settecentesco', *Nuovo Archivio Veneto*, N.S., 40, 1920.
6. *Europa letteraria*, September 1771, *Giornale enciclopedico*, January 1778, *Nuovo giornale enciclopedico d'Italia*, October 1790, *Giornale enciclopedico*, June 1779, *Nuovo giornale enciclopedico d'Italia*, June 1794, *Nuovo giornale enciclopedico*, November 1787.
7. *Europa letteraria*, April 1773, *Giornale enciclopedico*, February 1780, September 1779.
8. *Nuovo giornale enciclopedico*, July 1786, June 1787.
9. See U. Bellocchi, *Storia del giornalismo italiano* (Bologna, 1974–80), vol. v, pp. 61, 63, 141, 158, 166.
10. See Ricuperati, 'Giornali e società', pp. 195–8.
11. See for example M. Berengo, *Giornali veneziani del settecento*, (Milan, 1962), p. xlii, and R. M. Colombo, *Lo Spectator e i giornali veneziani del Settecento* (Bari, 1966), pp. 194–200, on *La donna galante ed erudita*, and M. Berengo, *Intellettuali e librai nella Milano della restaurazione* (Turin, 1980), on *Corriere delle Dame*.
12. See Colombo, *Lo Spectator*, p. 109.
13. *La donna galante ed erudita*, 1, 1786.
14. *Ibid.*, 3, 1786; 4, 1786; 18, 1787; 10, 1788; 1, 1787.

15. *Ibid.*, 2, 1788; 17, 1787; 1, 1786.

16. *Ibid.*, 16, 1787.

17. See C. Capra, 'Il giornalismo nell'età rivoluzionaria e napoleonica', in Castronovo et al. (eds.), *La stampa italiana*, p. 495.

18. See S. De Stefanis Ciccone, I. Bonomi, A. Masini, *La stampa periodica milanese della prima metà dell'Ottocento. Testi e concordanze* (Pisa, 1983), vol. I, p. xv.

19. *Corriere delle dame*, 14 October 1804; 7 October 1804; 18 November 1804; July–August 1810; May–June 1806; 5 December 1812; 19 October 1816.

20. *Ibid.*, 5 August 1809.

21. *Ibid.*, 27 October 1804.

22. *Ibid.*, 5 May 1805.

23. I owe the information on both Morano and Teresa M. to Elisa Strumia, who also gave me precious help with Carolina Lattanzi's biography. On Morano see E. Strumia, 'Un giornale per le donne nel Piemonte del 1799: "La vera repubblicana"', *Studi storici*, 30.4 (1989), pp. 917–46.

24. B. Croce (ed.), *Il monitore repubblicano del 1799* (Bari, 1943), pp. 11–12.

25. *Ibid.*, pp. 22–3; p. 109; pp. 148–9.

26. *Ibid.*, pp. 62–3.

27. *Ibid.*, p. 46.

28. *Ibid.*, p. 169; p. 172.

29. 'Delle presenti condizioni delle donne e del loro avvenire' was first published in the first issue of *Nuova antologia* in November 1866. On Belgiojoso's travel writings, see Ricciarda Ricorda in this volume, chapter 8.

30. *Il crociato*, 11 May 1848; 18 May 1848; 20 May 1848.

31. *Ibid.*, 3 June 1848.

32. *Ibid.*, 4 July 1848; 10 June 1848; 13 June 1848.

ADRIANA CHEMELLO
Translated by Peter Brand

10

Literary critics and scholars, 1700–1850

Learned women in eighteenth-century Venice

In a note entitled 'Author to reader', prefacing Goldoni's *Donna di Garbo* ('The Clever Woman'), we find a stout defence of the character of the play's protagonist, criticised by pedantic reviewers for being 'unnatural, and being made to appear *too learned* in too many fields'. Goldoni's comedy was being staged by the San Samuele Theatre company at the height of the Carnival in 1743, and it seemed as though the victory of the female mind over 'the whole arrogant male sex' was almost in sight; the seal was set, on the stage at least, on the heated academic debates of past decades, when the defenders of 'wise and learned women' were opposed by those who maintained that 'learned and virtuous women did not exist'.[1] If in fact the argument in the sixteenth century had been about the excellence and dignity of women, in the eighteenth the question, in academic circles at least, was whether women should be admitted to the study of the Arts and Sciences.

An echo of the controversy that arose in the Accademia dei Recovrati of Padua is to be found in the Dedicatory Letter which Luisa Bergalli sent to Cardinal Pietro Ottoboni, offering him the fruits of her intellectual labours:

> I trust you will accept this offering which, at the kind prompting of others and of my own instinct, I venture to send you . . . knowing that with your erudition and profound wisdom you are free of that almost *universal preconception that we women have no ability* to make our mark in the arts; busy as you are with your high office you can feel confident of finding in my work the style, concepts and thoughts capable of engaging your attention, perhaps on a par with the anthologies of those male authors who add lustre to Italian Poetry.[2] (emphasis mine)

In the most recent histories of literature, Luisa Bergalli appears only in footnotes as the wife of Gasparo Gozzi or at best as the author of *Agide re di Sparta* ('Agis, King of Sparta'), one of the first librettos from a female pen ever to be performed on the stage,[3] or of the later translations of Terence which she published in Venice between 1727 and 1731. In spite of her merits and her literary ability, acknowledged by her first biographers in the eighteenth century, she has enjoyed neither proper recognition nor an adequate critical response in later years. What above all has cast a long shadow over her reputation as a writer of humble and obscure origins, yet one of great erudition and undoubted intelligence, were the hostile comments of her brother-in-law, Carlo Gozzi, in his *Memorie inutili* ('Useless memoirs'). Characterising her as 'a woman of fervid and soaring imagination and thus capable of extremes of poetic rapture', and failing to acknowledge her need to support her large family, Carlo Gozzi savages a woman whose only faults were her lack of any illustrious protector and her passion for literature, deemed excessive in a woman.[4] The part played by her brother-in-law's spiteful comments in transmitting a totally negative image of Luisa to posterity is evident in the criticism of nineteenth-century writers, who reproduce Carlo Gozzi's evident distaste and exaggerate it out of all recognition. Tommaseo presents her to his readers as 'Gozzi's second torment, after his mother' (the aristocrat Angela Tiepolo), commenting ironically on Luisa's straitened circumstances.[5] Other writers refer to her humble origins ('daughter of a Piedmontese cobbler') demoting her to the category of old maid, or even 'femme fatale'. Molmenti calls her a 'tobacco-stained versifier', deliberately ignoring her very substantial output as writer and translator which earned her a considerable reputation in Venice, to the point where her name became synonymous with female culture in the city.[6] It was only in the first decades of the twentieth century that Maria Mioni and Carlotta Tassistro went some way towards redressing the balance with their biographies of 'la sventurata Irminda' ('unhappy Irminda') – as one novelist called her.[7]

Apart from the libretto *Agide re di Sparta*, the amusing comedy *Avventura del poeta* ('The Poet's Adventure')[8] and her numerous translations, Luisa Bergalli's name is associated with a number of editorial projects aimed at reviving the work of famous women of the past. A volume which has not received proper attention hitherto is the collection of *Componimenti poetici delle più illustri rimatrici d'ogni secolo* ('Poetic compositions of the most famous women poets of all ages') which appeared in two volumes in Venice in 1726. It is an anthology comprising poems and miscellaneous compositions by about 250 female poets from the thirteenth to the eighteenth centuries. The first volume contains 112 poets; the second, dedicated to the seventeenth and eighteenth centuries, comprises another 135. This is the first anthology of female poetry designed and edited by a woman. Luisa Bergalli seems conscious of the novelty of her undertaking, citing in her Preface the only two precedents and natural archetypes for her own work: the anthology edited by Domenichi for Busdrago of Lucca in 1559, containing fifty-three women poets, and the more recent one edited by G. B. Recanati, the Arcadian Teleste Ciparissiano.[9] Bergalli links her collection with those of her two famous predecessors, thus combining ancient and modern and including in her own two slim volumes a wide range of poets. Her aim is to trace a 'geography' and a 'genealogy', to provide a sort of map of the terrain and to acknowledge the existence of so many poets, some of them 'quite unknown to the Republic of Letters' so that they, too, will not be forgotten. A prefatory note 'To the reader' explains the criteria the editor has adopted: first, to give due credit to the women writers of the past; second, to gain some recognition for herself.[10]

The importance she attaches to earlier women writers as legitimising her own activities is apparent at various points. In response to those who insisted that women always and everywhere should be prohibited from studying, she declines to waste time on such futile arguments. She prefers, rather, to provide the tangible proof of women's intellectual ability (which men have kept concealed) in the shape of the actual compositions written by those women who have in the past cultivated their passion for the chaste muses of poetry. The 'merits' of these women, which *Moderata Fonte had proclaimed a century previously, are now documented by Luisa Bergalli with the abundant evidence scattered through the history of literature of the vitality, tenacity and fertility of the female mind.

In her references to the 'worthy women' of the past, however, Luisa Bergalli feels obliged to record the problems she has encountered in her task. These arise from two sources, one extrinsic, one intrinsic. The extrinsic problem was that of locating the relevant historical and poetic material. Her close intellectual ties with the outstanding Venetian scholars of her day (the remarkable Apostolo Zeno was her teacher) ensured their approval of her scholarship and gave her access to their libraries. Thus Alvise Mocenigo made the manuscripts of the Marciana Library available to her; Antonio Sforza, who taught her Italian and Latin, allowed her to consult the vast Soranzo library; and Apostolo Zeno opened his own library to her with its rich collection of manuscripts, and above all provided a wealth of advice and suggestions, as we can see from the letters he sent her.[11] The other, intrinsic, difficulty she faced, arose from the inveterate modesty and self-restraint of women, which Recanati confirms. Luisa Bergalli's *Componimenti poetici* was a unique event in Italian literary history, and nothing like it recurred until 1930 when Jolanda De Blasi published her *Antologia delle scrittrici italiane* ('Anthology of Italian Women Writers').

A much more delicate operation was the recovery and publication of the *Rime* of *Gaspara Stampa, almost two hundred years after the first and only posthumous edition (Venice, Pietrasanta, 1554. See chapter 3). Bergalli's edition of Stampa's *Rime*, following the same sequence as in the first edition, was published in Venice by F. Piacentini in 1738. Her name does not appear on the frontispiece, but her signature is given under the dedication in blank verse 'To His Excellency Count Antonio Rambaldo di Collalto', following the contemporary convention of indicating the editorship of a volume. This edition is not just a simple reprint: there is additional biographical and bibliographical material; and in the 1760 edition, *Vittoria Colonna's *Rime* are also printed, and her 'Life' by Giambattista Rota.

In republishing Gaspara's 'sad verses' and 'sombre notes' – referred to in her introductory sonnet – Luisa Bergalli fulfilled two aims: just as Gaspara's love poems had brought *her* glory, now this collection of poems dedicated to Rambaldo would similarly cast lustre and honour on Luisa Bergalli. In aiming to 'renew the acclaim' for Gaspara's *Rime,* Bergalli is conscious of doing herself a good service, because the now 'silent pages' that once brought immortality to Gaspara Stampa would by extension cast some of their glow on herself. But before bidding a final farewell to these poems Luisa sought to raise her message above the level of personal experience and introspection to a broader, more universal female perspective, appealing to other women like herself:

> Se non siete di lei più sagge, e belle,
> Se più degno amator voi non alletta;
> Donne, serbate il cor libero e sciolto.

(Rime, p. 252)

(If you are not wiser, and fairer than her, / If no worthier lover tempts you, / Then, ladies, keep your heart free and unconstrained.)

By symbolically including women in the world of letters, Bergalli sets off a wave of other editorial projects in eighteenth-century Venice. One example was the *Almanacco sacro e profano . . . in difesa delle donne* ('A sacred and secular Almanac . . . in defence of women'), printed in Venice in 1750, clearly an off-shoot of the *Componimenti poetici*. The *Almanacco delle donne* adopted the traditional calendar structure but, beginning with the frontispiece, showed distinctive features motivated by its intended female readership. It cost a modest ten *soldi* and introduced two innovations to the almanac tradition, aimed at exhibiting the 'true glory' of the female sex: every one of its 365 days is dedicated to a female saint and is illustrated with a female figure renowned for her virtue, wisdom and intelligence.

Alongside the best-known female poets and philosophers of ancient Greece (Diotima, Aspasaia, Hypatia, Corinna, Demophila, Agalli) appear the exemplary women of Roman civilisation from Camilla to Cornelia, from Lucrezia to Giulia, from Livia to Placida. But there are also queens and princesses, the founders of religious orders (Caterina de Bar, Orsola Benincasa, *Caterina di Siena, Luisa de Mantlac, Francesca Borrei) and lowly nuns included for their 'learning' and 'sanctity'. Together with the most famous female poets and scholars of the sixteenth century we find *Laura Cereta, *Isotta Nogarola, Paola Antonia Negri and Olimpia Morata, and the Venetians *Moderata Fonte and *Lucrezia Marinella. The numbers increase as we approach Luisa's day with Margherita Costa, Barbara Torelli Benedetti, *Isabella Andreini, Giulia Gonzaga, Beatrice Papafava Cittadella, *Faustina Maratti Zappi and Bergalli herself. Also present are French female poets and scholars from Louise Labé to Madame de La Fayette, who is included for 'the numerous books she published', and the painters from Sofonisba Anguissola to the Venetian *Rosalba Carriera, Bergalli's own teacher.

While the collection of *Componimenti poetici* focused interest on women who dedicated themselves to poetry, the *Almanacco* takes the form of a 'gallery' of famous women, whose biographies are exhibited like medallions for the readers, male and female, to admire. Bergalli departed from tradition in orienting her selection less towards women distinguished for the customary theological and cardinal virtues, and more towards female writers and women of learning and culture; and turned the *Almanacco*, like the *Componimenti poetici*, into a tribute to those women throughout history who managed to make their voice heard.

The salons

The distinguishing feature of the eighteenth century lies in a transition from the private to the public, with boundaries beginning to shift between the two. There is in fact a broadening of social consciousness, with new cultural institutions becoming established, and new spaces emerging which open up the private dimensions of society to the public: the café, the theatre, the library. For women this means an increase in access to social life. The salon greatly expands the confined space of the domestic scene, extending it into the public sphere.[12]

Distancing itself from the bustle and intrigue of the court, the eighteenth-century salon established itself in the city, in private houses, where a noble title, whether hereditary or acquired by marriage, together with substantial wealth, guaranteed women considerable freedom of action. The model of polite conversation for the elite moved from France, from Catherine de Vivonne, Marchioness of Rambouillet's *'chambre bleue d'Arthenice'*, with its learned debates on the happy or hapless vicissitudes of love and on the possibility of women finding a space and a place in a world dominated by men, to Venice, and the palaces and evocative alleys along the Grand Canal.

In the cosmopolitan city of the lagoon, women were the driving force behind the most famous salons. These gatherings acted like a magic lantern, shedding a glow of reflected fame in which the *salonnière* became a much sought-after hostess able to provide opportunities for conversation with the most learned and enlightened men of the age. The salons acquired the aura of an enchanted place beyond the laws of space and time, capable of abolishing, if only temporarily, differences of wealth, status and sex. For women, they represented a much prized if ephemeral emancipation.[13]

The salons of *Isabella Teotochi Albrizzi and her contemporaries, *Giustina Renier Michiel and Marina Querini Benzon, followed the tradition initiated by Caterina Dolfin Tron and Cecilia Zen Tron, and were famous for their unrivalled 'Venetian hospitality'. Isabella Teotochi's long career as a *salonnière* began in 1782 at the Ponte de' Barattieri and continued, even more grandly and proudly, after her marriage to Count Albrizzi in 1796, in Calle Cicogna, where she gathered around her such famous figures as Melchiorre Cesarotti, Ippolito Pindemonte and Ugo Foscolo: to this last she was a 'dolce amica', a 'sweet friend'. There is frequent mention of her great talent for bringing together many different nationalities: on one evening 'at least twenty different languages, Oriental and European, and six Italian dialects' are said to have been spoken.[14] This salon was also famous for its forward thinking, thanks to the presence of some of the most innovative minds in the city. The conversations in Isabella's salon produced the most culturally coherent group, the only one capable of constituting a 'school' in the literary culture of its time.[15]

Isabella Teotochi made good use of the advice lavished on her by Pindemonte and was clearly a careful reader of contemporary as well as classical authors. A good example is her well-known letter on Alfieri's tragedy, *Mirra*, where she reveals not only the finesse of her scholarship but also her sensitivity to contemporary changes in taste. Where this was most evident, however, was in her sparkling conversation, always attuned to contemporary issues, alert to new publications and new writers, and to the presence of famous foreigners passing through the city.

Although Byron called her 'the Venetian Madame de Staël', nineteenth-century critics focused principally on just one of Isabella's works, her *Ritratti* ('Portraits'), several editions of which appeared during the first decades of the century. They were first published in 1807 (only a month before the *Ritratti* of her friend, the Veronese aristocrat *Silvia Curtoni Verza) and enjoyed at least four editions in the space of twenty years – an indication of how popular and successful a genre Teotochi chose. It had developed in a purely oral form in the salons of the late eighteenth century. Out of the literary 'games' based on improvised jokes, aphorisms and witty remarks which had been perfected in the salons of Paris before being transplanted to Italian soil, emerged the convention of describing *caractères*, or sketching the essential characteristics of a person, especially someone present in the salon at the time.

Isabella chose real people for her *Ritratti*, people with recognisable strengths and weaknesses. Beginning with the facial features of her subjects, she went on to uncover their moral stature. Her adoption of the neoclassical principle of 'pictorial' representation is evident not only in her prose and choice of metaphor, but also in the inclusion of copper engravings accompanying the text.

This, then, was the moral aim which guided Teotochi's pen, especially in her *Vita di Vittoria Colonna* ('Life of Vittoria Colonna'). Based primarily on the eighteenth-century biography by Giambattista Rota, it is something more than the tribute to the ideal of the 'faithful wife' which became entrenched in the hagiography of the seventeenth and eighteenth centuries. The pleasure of rereading the life of a famous woman of the past is enhanced by a humanising process, which has very positive implications for contemporary women. Adopting as epigraph the lines from Canto XXXVII of the *Orlando furioso* which Rota had cited,[16] Teotochi begins by deploring a 'universal idea' that 'half of humanity has for centuries taken no part in the

study of science and literature'. The *topos* of the woman destined by biolog-
ical decree to remain illiterate, which is at the root of all Luisa Bergalli's
scholarly work, is Teotochi's starting point, marking a thematic as well as a
chronological continuity. What she wants above all to draw attention to is
Vittoria Colonna's literary merit, which is to be seen not only in the *Rime*
but also in the numerous tributes to her from distinguished writers of her
time, of which Rota prints some of the finest and most interesting extracts
in his book. 'Certainly her very beautiful poetry clearly reveals the richness
and finesse of her intellect and of her imagination, and the delicate and
highly refined temper of her feelings, and it may serve as an example of
how to imitate an original model without servility.'[17]

But the most interesting passages are those where she reconsiders
Colonna's relationship with Michelangelo, censored by sixteenth- and
seventeenth-century biographers. On the basis of the evidence of Ascanio
Condivi, Michelangelo's pupil and first biographer, Teotochi now reconsiders their friendship. In his life of Colonna, Rota passed over this matter
in silence, but Teotochi follows Condivi: 'We are indebted to his pupil and
friend Condivi for telling us that he adored the Marchioness of Pescara and
fell in love with that divine spirit, and that she returned his love and
addressed numerous letters to him, revealing a pure and tender passion.'[18]
We can read this as an indication of Teotochi's desire to justify her own
deep friendships, and the intellectual and emotional relationships in
which she was involved in her own day in Venice. As justification for her
activities she attempts to establish a genealogy of women writers within
the literary tradition. Speaking of Colonna, she says:

> Admirable woman! May your shining example serve as a stimulus to
> those gifted but timid souls who do not have the courage to launch
> themselves on the noble paths of glory. For if the fine arts and poetry,
> and especially the lyric, derive their inspiration and vitality from
> warmth of imagination and spontaneity and delicacy of feeling, why
> should the cultivation of those arts and the gathering of laurels from
> them be denied to the sex which, thanks to exquisite refinement of
> perception and inner harmony of the emotions, is most fitted to depict
> them?[19]

Some years after writing the *Life of Vittoria Colonna* Teotochi resumed
the composition of her much admired word-portraits of the 'characters'
of her friends, and she turned to a fellow Venetian, Giustina Renier
Michiel, like her a devotee of letters and of learned conversation in her
salon, which had become a centre of Venetian culture. The opportunity

arose when the publishing house Vallardi issued their *Strenna* ('New Year's Offering') for 1833, a few months after the death of Giustina Renier, who had been widely acknowledged as the 'peerless great lady of Venice'.[20]

Starting with a brief sketch of the physical appearance of her friend, Teotochi goes on to paint a moral portrait of a woman whose family circumstances required her to assume a public role in the formal ceremonies of the Republic alongside her paternal grandfather, the Doge Polo Renier (1779–89), and who succeeded in maintaining her gentility and affability: 'Her eyes sparkled with a vivacious and at the same time serene radiance, and her rosy lips were constantly parted in a smile that showed the habitual cheerfulness of her disposition. Her slender body seemed all harmony, tending to lean forward attentively, reflecting the kindness which always came naturally to her.'[21]

Giustina Renier Michiel was born into a family that gave the now declining Republic its last Doges (her grandfather Polo Renier, and her maternal uncle Ludovico Manin). She is depicted as being naturally inclined to spontaneous behaviour and simple habits, and Teotochi searches deep into her subject, showing the exceptional moral strength behind her unostentatious benevolence, her courage, her kind-heartedness and generosity.

While she is not primarily concerned with the literary activities of her friend and contemporary, Isabella Teotochi cannot pass over in silence that 'love of country' which inspired Giustina Renier in the gloomy days preceding the fall of Venice. Indeed, Renier dedicated to the 'splendour of the defunct Republic' her work *L'Origine delle feste veneziane* ('The origin of the festivities of Venice', 1829). Here Teotochi recognises the depth of patriotic feeling to which a woman of that time could give voice. But she is not interested in recounting the biography of her subject; what she really wants is to evoke her spirit, to give the most vivid and vibrant picture possible of her simple, strong and noble soul, to provide in other words a perfect equivalent of the engravings and other images of her friend. It was not until several years later that one of Giustina Renier's earliest biographers, Luigi Carrer, produced a fully rounded biography of the woman and her writings, likening her to the great mythical heroine, Antigone.

The original stimulus for the composition of Giustina Renier's book appears to have been an enquiry which the French government addressed to the municipality of Venice, headed *Questions statistiques concernant la ville de Venise*. Jacopo Morelli, Director of the Marciana Library, and the scholar

Count Jacopo Filiasi, first approached her. She readily offered to help, and immediately stamped her own personality on the project in the decision to abandon the normal chronological account of Venetian history in favour of an approach which would allow the magnificence of the city to be illustrated by a description of the games and popular festivities of the Venetians. She laments the reticence or silence of the official sources, never forgetting that she is a woman – witness her close interest in the 'customs' of women, her eagerness to reconstruct the history of Venetian women and to fill as far as possible the numerous gaps and culpable omissions in the official sources in this respect.[22] The Venetian Antigone thus took on the thankless task of scattering the ashes of the now defunct Republic, consigning them to posterity in a monument of erudition.

The 'Alpine Sibyl'

In the combined eulogy and biography *Elogio storico* ('Historical eulogy') written by Count Coriolano di Bagnolo introducing the volume of *Poesie postume* ('Posthumous poems', 1843) by the Piedmontese *Diodata Saluzzo Roero, the Count expatiates on the merits and virtues of the noble and learned poet, citing in support the most famous Italian writers of the time. Diodata was indeed a model figure, admired and loved by her contemporaries, and her literary career acquired great symbolic significance, even influencing Madame de Staël's portrait of the protagonist of her novel, *Corinne*.[23]

Diodata was barely twenty years old when she was catapulted to fame with the publication of her first poetry collection, *Versi* (Turin, 1796), and at first she was trumpeted as the literary prodigy of the century. Her teacher and admirer, Abbot Valperga di Caluso, compared her with the 'famous Tasso whose *Rinaldo* was published *before he was nineteen*'.[24] This was indeed a conspicuous poetic debut which was widely praised and which led to her election in 1801, the first woman ever, to the Accademia delle Scienze of Turin. She had already been one of the first women to be enrolled in the Arcadia of Rome in 1795, with the name of Glaucilla Eurotea, and in the Accademia Reale of Fossano on the nomination of the Abbot of Caluso in 1797. Giuseppe Parini, too, a man not readily given to fits of enthusiasm, found in her poetry evidence of 'natural ability, education, application, sensitivity, ingenuity, delicacy, nobility of spirit, originality of ideas and imagery'.[25]

In 1799 Diodata married Count Massimiliano Roero di Revello, but she became a widow three years later and returned to her family home on the small and geographically isolated Saluzzo estate, where she compensated for her emotional loss by dedicating herself to a quiet life of study. She established a network of correspondents including the most distinguished intellectuals of her time, such as Ludovico di Breme and Alessandro Manzoni. Thanks to her friendship with Di Breme, in fact, she found herself embroiled against her wishes in the disputes between Romantics and Classicists following the publication of her poem 'Le Rovine. Visitando l'autrice l'antico castello di Saluzzo' ('The Ruins: On the Occasion of the Author's Visit to the Ancient Castle of Saluzzo') which Di Breme cited as an example of the perfect Romantic lyric.[26]

A striking feature of the first collection of her *Versi*, an elegant little volume produced with great care, is the young poet's ability to move so easily from one lyric form to another. In addition to the predominant sonnets on Arcadian, pastoral and mythological subjects, there are other traditional forms (eleven *canzoni*, three sequences of *stanze*, a *capitolo*, eleven blank-verse compositions, three *cantate*, six *poemetti* and a *sestina*) written for relatives and friends on the occasion of weddings, birthdays and other similar events. These occasional poems, while following current conventions, represent a genre in which Diodata was particularly prolific and reveal the wide range of her contacts with other women, highlighted in the concluding epigraph:

> Non canto no per gloriosa farmi;
> Ma vo passando mar, passando l'ore
> E in vece degli altrui, canto I miei carmi.

(Versi, fol.1)

('No, I do not sing to win glory; / But while I'm travelling over seas, I pass away the time / Instead of chanting others' poems I sing my own.')

The poems of *Faustina Maratti Zappi, a much-loved and admired friend of Diodata Saluzzo, illustrate two particular themes in Piedmontese poetry and prose in this period: love of glory and the presence of female poets, which Croce mentions in his brief critical essay on her, referring to a 'guild' of women writers.[27]

Two sonnets addressed to Faustina Maratti and *Veronica Gambara show the extent to which Diodata felt herself to be part of a female tradition. In the latter sonnet she celebrates the glorious life of Gambara, whom she pictures with the 'green fronds' of poetry wreathing her brow and marching alongside Bembo and Vittoria Colonna towards the temple of Glory. In the sonnet to Faustina Maratti, Diodata feels she has been explicitly entrusted with her heritage, evoking her with the Arcadian name of Aglauro.

But it is above all in the poem entitled 'Il tempio della gloria' ('The temple of glory') that Saluzzo sets out to reconstruct her own literary genealogy, following in the footsteps of the Muse of History, and declaring herself the daughter of such famous mothers as the Marchioness of Pescara, Veronica Gambara and Faustina Maratti Zappi. In her choice of 'mothers' she follows the traditional literary canon, but she is particularly conscious of the scholarly legacy of the eighteenth century, when the fortunes of Gambara and Colonna were revived by reprinting sixteenth-century editions which made these Renaissance poets accessible to contemporary readers. To these two we should add the name of Gaspara Stampa who had been re-edited, as we have seen, by Luisa Bergalli and to whom Saluzzo dedicates one of her most successful *novelle*.

The enthusiasm for Diodata Saluzzo's *Versi* was not destined to continue after the success of the first two Turin editions and the Pisa reprint of 1802. The fourth edition (4 vols., Turin 1816–17) which included her two tragedies *Erminia* and *Tullia* and her *novella* in prose, *Gaspara Stampa,* met with a very cool reception compared with the triumph of twenty years before. Without abandoning other types of poetry, Saluzzo confined herself mainly to occasional verse. After a brief experiment with tragedy, she shows her metrical versatility in a long poem in twenty *canti* inspired by the female Greek philosopher, Hypatia – an ambitious effort at a genre rarely attempted previously by women.

This historical and philosophical novel in verse, as she tells us in her Preface, is set in Alexandria, Egypt, in the fifth century AD. It was entitled *Ipazia, ovvero delle filosofie* ('Hypatia or the schools of philosophy'), after the famous Hypatia, daughter of Theano, who was the central figure around whom the leaders of the various philosophical schools in Alexandria congregated in her day. The plot of the novel is based on the love of the Christian Hypatia for Isidoro, which ends, after a series of disputes and conspiracies, when Hypatia rejects marriage and meets her death in the chaos of the subsequent civil war. *Ipazia* was written in Piedmont during the period of French domination and the Napoleonic campaigns, and readily lent itself to an ideological and patriotic reading, as the author herself suggests in her explanation of the moral aim of the book.

Diodata Saluzzo takes some liberties with history, and she conflates at least three different historical persons in the figure of Isidoro. Her sources are the studies published by Ludovico Antonio Muratori, Agatopisto

Cromaziano and Le Nain de Tillemond. Saluzzo may also have used two recent neo-Greek novels: Alessandro Verri's *Avventure di Saffo poetessa di Mitilene* ('The adventures of Sappho, poet of Mytilene', 1780), and the later *Platone in Italia* ('Plato in Italy') by Vincenzo Cuoco, published in 1804–6.

Diodata Saluzzo's last literary project, her *Novelle*, is a collection of eight stories which was published thanks to the support of Alessandro Manzoni. Four take their titles from female figures for whom the author undertook detailed scholarly research. One story is dedicated to Isabella Losa, another to Guglielmina Viclaressa and a third to Gaspara Stampa. In her narrative, ruins recur obsessively, creating pseudo-medieval scenarios where courts of love break into the dominant motif of death, and the characters become little more than accessories. She sets her figures in a literary context reminiscent of Manzoni's tragedies, which she read enthusiastically. But the Manzoni of *I promessi sposi* is far away from the romanticised sensibilities of Hypatia and the heroines of Saluzzo's *Novelle*.

In the eighteenth century and beginning of the nineteenth, there is a revival of letters in general, with women's accomplishments appearing in hitherto unrepresented areas such as literary scholarship, social history, biography and philosophy. There is a new consciousness of cultural history and tradition with the editions of work by women poets of the Renaissance, while the emergence of the salon provided a means for social and cultural exchange, enabling women to find at last that longed-for access to a public domain.

NOTES

1. C. Goldoni, *Tutte le opere,* ed. G. Ortolani (Milan, 1943), vol. I, p. 1017.

2. Bergalli, *Componenti poetici delle più illustri Rimatrici d'ogni secolo,* Part I, fol. 2v.

3. A. Bellina and B. Brizzi, 'Il melodramma', in G. Arnaldi and M. Pastore Stocchi (eds.), *Storia della cultura veneta dalla Controriforma alla fine della Repubblica* (Vicenza, 1985), vol. I, p. 393.

4. Carlo Gozzi, *Memorie inutili,* ed. G. Prezzolini (Bari, 1910), pp. 43, 109.

5. 'Della vita e degli scritti di Gasparo Gozzi. Ragionamento', in G. Gozzi, *Scritti con giunta di inediti e rari,* ed. N. Tommaseo (Florence, 1849), p. v.

6. P. Molmenti, *La storia di Venezia nella vita privata* (Bergamo, 1908), vol. III, p. 457.

7. Respectively, M. Mioni, *Una lettera veneziana dal secolo XVIII* (Venice, 1908); and C. Tassistro, *Luisa Bergalli Gozzi, la vita e l'opera sua nel tempo* (Rome, 1920). Alfredo Panzini called his historical novel about Bergalli, *La sventurata Irminda. Romanzo* (Verona, 1932).

8. See L. Ricaldone's recent edition (Rome, 1997).

9. Bergalli also refers to anthologies edited by Baruffalsi (Ferrara, 1713), and Bulifon (Naples, 1693, 1695). The latter, containing verse by fifty women, was itself a version of Domenichi's 1559 collection.

10. Bergalli, *Componimenti poetici*, fol. 4r.

11. Bergalli, *Lettere* (Venice, 1752), vol. II, especially the letter dated 20 July 1726, pp. 436–8.

12. See Dominique Godineau, 'La donna', in M. Vovelle (ed.), *L'uomo dell'Illuminismo* (Rome–Bari, 1992); M. I. Palazzolo, *I salotti di cultura nell'Italia dell'Ottocento. Scene e modelli* (Milan, 1985); G. Rossi, *Salotti letterari in Toscana* (Florence, 1992).

13. Godineau, 'La donna', pp. 472–3.

14. E. Masi, 'Il salotto d'Isabella Albrizzi', in *Parrucche e sanculotti nel secolo XVII* (Milan, 1886), p. 218.

15. G Pizzamiglio, 'Ugo Foscolo nel salotto di Isabella Teotochi Albrizzi', *Quaderni Veneti* 2 (1985), p. 55.

16. 'If those accomplished ladies . . . had devoted themselves to those studies which confer immortality upon mortal virtues / and had been able by themselves to achieve undying reputation without having to beg it from authors, their fame would soar to heights perhaps beyond the reach of any of the male sex', stanzas 1–2, prose translation by G. Waldman (Oxford, 1983), p. 441.

17. 'Vita di Vittoria Colonna', in Albrizzi, *Ritratti,* 4th edn (Pisa, 1826), p. 180.

18. *Ibid.*, p. 190.

19. *Ibid.*, pp. 192–3.

20. Albrizzi, 'Ritratto di Giustina Renier Michiel', in Teotochi, *Strenna*, pp. 185–93.

21. From reprint in *Cosmorama Pittorico*, 6. 16 (1840), p. 122.

22. See her letter to D. Sante Valentina about her research published for *The Treves–Todros wedding* (Venice, 1844).

23. Ludovico di Breme, *Lettere*, ed. P. Camporesi (Turin, 1969), p. 333.

24. Quoted by P. Paravia, 'Saluzzo, Diodata', in *Biografia degli Italiani illustri*, vol. VII (Venice, 1840), pp. 264–70.

25. *Poesie postume,* ed. Corialano di Bagnolo (Turin, 1796), p. 407.

26. Di Breme, *Lettere*, pp. 567–70.

27. B. Croce, 'La Sibilla alpina. Diodata Saluzzo Roero', in *Varietà di storia letteraria e civile* (Bari, 1935), pp. 233–42.

Part III

The Risorgimento and modern Italy, 1850–2000

11
_____

Journalists and essayists, 1850–1915

Maria: 'Would you like to write for the papers like many young women
do?'
Luisina: 'No, I'll be honest with you. I think the name of a modest
young woman should be known only to her parents and to a small
circle of friends.'
Maria: 'But at times there are great minds . . .'
Luisina: 'And I respect those. But the problem is, dear Maria, that
almost all the young women coming out of school these days
believe they are great minds, and they don't rest until they get their
names printed in some two-penny newspaper. That's what my
mother says.'
Maria: 'I certainly won't be tempted like that! After elementary school,
I'm going to be a florist!'[1]

This imaginary dialogue between the wealthy Luisina, daughter of
the aristocratic Beltrami family, and Maria, the anonymous blacksmith's
daughter, appears in a textbook for elementary schools published in the
Italy of the 1880s by *Ida Baccini. The dialogue points on the one hand to a
real phenomenon, the considerable increase in the number of women
writers in liberal Italy, and, at the same time, to the desire to contain this
phenomenon on the part of one who succeeded, yet still thought ill of the
ambitions of others. The dialogue omits to mention that the many
women with a school degree who sent their productions to women's magazines actually found encouragement in these publications.

In fact, there was no real reason for alarm. Although the number of
women writers grew in the first decades after Unification – in line with
the expansion of schooling, the emergence of an information and publishing industry which specifically addressed a female audience and the

rise of feminism – only a small number of women were actually able to find a solid position in the world of journalism, or more generally as writers of non-fiction. Even in the case of men, it would be an anachronism to speak of journalists as such. As Michela De Giorgio has observed, the professional category 'journalist' remained rather ill defined until the period after World War One: still in 1916 the *Annuario della Stampa* (Yearbook of the Press) included quite heterogeneous writers, especially among women.[2]

Even if 'real' journalists were rather few and the category still fairly undefined, a novelty of this period was that some women began to make a living out of writing for periodicals, and in contrast to the previous period, a number of them came from the middle classes or the petit bourgeoisie. Understandably, most women writers tended to cluster around periodicals for a female audience (either feminine or feminist or both) and new and/or expanding fields associated with women, such as children's education and psychology. The women who succeeded in the male world of daily newspapers were very few and tended to write fiction, or on specifically 'female' topics. The same is true in the case of periodicals of 'high' culture. While a more visible category, women writers in liberal Italy had to operate within the boundaries of what was thought acceptable and appropriate for a woman to do and write – although some of them also found ways of overstepping these boundaries, or contesting them from within.

Education became one such appropriate topic – a topic moreover which allowed women to define a public role for themselves – during the Risorgimento. Writings on the subject of education represented an important component of women's essayistic production, beginning in the 1840s and 1850s and continuing through the post-Unification years when new schools and institutions were created by a liberal state engaged – although not without ambiguities – in a conflict with the Church for control of the educational system. From the late 1840s, liberal women of patriotic sentiment advocated new principles for women's education and linked this renewal to an ideal which partook of what is commonly called 'republican motherhood'. The moderate liberal and Catholic *Caterina Franceschi Ferrucci attracted the praise of Vincenzo Gioberti and Carlo Cattaneo for proposing a programme centred around serious readings for women, readings which would prepare them to become 'true Italians in their language, fantasy and thought',[3] and detailing with precision the kind of studies that women of different ages should undertake. She was concerned primarily with creating more responsible mothers of 'citizens', and she assured the reader that she did not want to throw women into the political world, nor to make them into *literati*. The same sentiment was expressed by another educationist, Giulia Molino Colombini (1812–79), ideologically close to Franceschi Ferrucci, in a work which had several reprints: 'I do not intend to transform Italian women into women of letters: but I care that they are not vain, ignorant, superficial and lost in useless amusements . . . we mothers of free citizens will not be able to accomplish our task in a dignified manner unless we are educated . . . to the point of gaining respect for the solid worth of our souls.'[4]

While Franceschi Ferrucci did not conceive of education as a means of widening occupational perspectives to women, focusing instead on what they should learn to become soundly patriotic mothers, Molino Colombini had a more practical orientation, providing guidelines on how to prepare some women to be good governesses and teachers. In her reflections on education, the poet *Erminia Fuà Fusinato was willing to go further. She advocated women's education by insisting on how an expanded and improved education for women, far from transforming them into unbearable pedants and impairing their chances of marrying, could in fact offer a concrete alternative to the numerous women of the middle classes who could not marry, or to those who needed to support their families in difficult times. This sensitivity may well have been a reflection of her own situation. Her writings on women's education appeared mostly after her untimely death, when she was recruited posthumously for the cause of nation-building, and exalted as an example of devotion to the fatherland and to its educational system.[5]

While contributing works which defined the educational model of Italian moderatism, all these women also engaged in fiction and poetry, writing book reviews, travel accounts and occasionally literary essays. Not surprisingly, the latter were devoted to the female figures who featured prominently in the Italian literature of the Middle Ages: Molino Colombini contributed a piece on the women of Dante's poem for an important celebratory volume that the establishment of the new Italy dedicated to their greatest poet,[6] and Fuà Fusinato lectured on Petrarch's Laura before the Ateneo Veneto.[7] Only Franceschi Ferrucci wrote a fully fledged literary history concerning the period from Dante to the sixteenth century, one of those works of which it is difficult to find mention these days in histories of literary criticism, but which enjoyed a certain reputation at the time.[8]

An analogous range of interests and impulses was to be found among other women writers of more radical ideological commitment who operated after Unification. Of these we should recall the founder of the first Italian feminist journal, *Gualberta Alaide Beccari. Although the *Dizionario biografico degli italiani* has forgotten her, she did not fail to find a place in the numerous collections of lives of illustrious Italian women which appeared at the turn of the nineteenth century. In *Stelle femminili* ('Female Stars'), a biographical dictionary published on the eve of the First World War, a passage from Beccari's unpublished autobiography explains the origins of her vocation thus:

> From a very early age, I was eager to be a journalist in order to fight not only for women's rights, but also for those of my fatherland and for all that could improve her political and moral conditions . . . I was filled with enthusiasm by the idea of creating a new woman, made anew by education and a proper upbringing as a citizen for her country, which so needed her to gain moral vigour now that it has become a nation.[9]

These words summarise well the kind of moral and political impetus which stood behind the journalistic work performed by a small but significant number of women in post-Unification Italy. Often immobilised for months in bed through illness, Beccari was able, thanks to a network of friends and supporters, to ensure the publication of *La donna* for almost twenty-three years (1868–91). In its best moments, the journal could count on about 1,200 subscribers, primarily teachers. Besides ensuring the publication of this periodical, Beccari regularly contributed editorials as well as the rubric 'Corrispondenza in famiglia' ('Family Correspondence'), in which she exchanged views with her collaborators and friends. The author of some works of fiction, she also collaborated on other periodicals, and her articles allowed her to make at least for some time a 'fairly good profit'.[10] Another publishing enterprise that she undertook a few years after starting *La donna* was *La mamma* (1876–92). This children's periodical shows the continuing importance that motherhood had even for women who did not completely subordinate women's worth to their maternal function. As a matter of fact, the link between the democratic patriotism of Giuseppe Mazzini (1805–72) and emancipationism distinguished Beccari and many of her collaborators, and culminated in the much extolled figure of the 'patriot mother' or 'citizen mother.'[11]

The most important Italian emancipationist of the nineteenth century, *Anna Maria Mozzoni, a frequent contributor to *La donna*, participated in this political culture although, in contrast to the more orthodox followers

of Mazzini, she stressed rights over duties and rejected the sentimentality
pervading the Mazzinian 'cult of the maternal'. She translated John Stuart
Mill's *On the Subjection of Women* (1870) into Italian. In the late 1870s she also
moved into the socialist camp, though without ever entering the Italian
Socialist Party, established in 1892, because of her conviction that women's
specific struggle needed its own separate organisation and would be
damaged by a complete absorption into the labour ranks. Mozzoni had no
specifically literary or journalistic ambitions – indeed, she had a certain
distrust for 'literary women',[12] but wrote vigorous and at times devastatingly sarcastic prose, published in *La donna* and in several periodicals of the
democratic and socialist left. Thus she summarised the no-win situation
of women:

> If you devote your piously-inclined soul to spiritual exercises, you
> immediately become a hypocrite or a bigot in the eyes of the vulgar
> multitude; if you want to train your innate intelligence through study,
> you are a pedant; if you spend long hours in front of the mirror to
> make yourself beautiful you immediately turn into a vain woman; if
> you need and like to take walks, you'll get the reputation of being an
> idle spirit.[13]

In all her writings, which often originated as public lectures, Mozzoni
forcefully and repeatedly criticised the legal restrictions imposed on
women by the new civil code of the Italian state in 1865, and intervened
repeatedly in favour of suffrage and to oppose the paternalistic nature of
the 'protective' legislation for women workers which would be eventually
introduced in 1902. But her writings went beyond the advocacy of
women's issues, and she spoke and wrote on topics as diverse as physics
(the speciality of her father, a gentleman *savant*), Bonapartism in Italy, the
question of the annexation of Rome to Italy, the Paris Commune.

Mozzoni was also active on the scene of social enquiries. In the framework of the most important investigation of the liberal period, the
Inchiesta Iacini (late 1870s to early 1880s), she was recruited by a deputy of
the democratic left, the physician Agostino Bertani, to collect information on the social and hygienic conditions of the peasantry of Lombardy.
Unfortunately, the material she and Bertani himself collected appears to
have been lost in the bureaucratic labyrinth of the Ministry of
Agriculture.

The same destiny befell the information collected by another woman to
whom Bertani resorted during the Inchiesta, *Jessie White Mario, English
by birth and education but Italian by adoption as well as marriage (to the

democratic federalist Alberto Mario). A protagonist of the Risorgimento, and a close friend of both Mazzini and Garibaldi, White Mario was a prolific writer and journalist whose work was entirely devoted to what she called her 'second fatherland', Italy, made so 'by instinct, by loving intelligence, by the fortunate encounter in youth with some eminent Italians who inspired me with firm faith in Italy's renewal, as well as by law through marriage'.[14] Although a protagonist herself of Italian events, she always felt the need to excuse herself for writing – she who was not born in Italy – about things Italian (she authored the biographies of the main democratic exponents of the Risorgimento). In the preface to her biography of Bertani, she tells the reader that she does not write out of arrogance (*presunzione*), but under pressure from Italian publishers and friends and in order to let her own country know the 'marvellous story of the Italian Risorgimento'. Historians have observed that her biographies were more akin to memoirs than accomplished works of history. She tended to rely excessively on what she saw herself, and her partisan spirit made her silent on the divisions within the Italian democratic camp.[15] Her political agenda clearly dominated her selection of topics and her work of reconstruction.

Thus White Mario's American biographer is right to consider her a better journalist than a historian.[16] A participant in the campaigns of 1859 and 1860, which led to the proclamation of the Kingdom of Italy, White Mario reported on the war operations for the London *Daily News*, where in 1856 she published a Mazzinian history of the Italian revolutions. After Unification she collaborated on Italian political newspapers of the democratic left such as *La lega della democrazia* and became a correspondent for the American weekly *The Nation*. White Mario sent more than 140 articles to this paper between 1866 and 1906, vividly portraying the many vicissitudes of the new nation from Garibaldi's attempts at annexing Rome in the 1860s, to the colonial undertakings of the 1880s and 1890s, to the extensive social unrest and repression of the 1890s, to the political change of the post 1900 years. She also alternated descriptions of Italy's major social and political problems (southern poverty, high illiteracy rates, child labour, social unrest, organised crime), with presentations of significant specimens of Italian 'high culture' and events documenting the progress of the country. Her continuing political engagement and her activity as reporter were behind her 1877 collection of essays on poverty and the poor in the vast southern metropolis, *La miseria in Napoli* ('Destitution in Naples', 1877), which must be placed close to Pasquale

Villari's *Lettere meridionali* ('Letters from the South', 1878), as indicative of the new awareness of the 'social question' which gripped members of the educated elites of Italy after 1871. A chapter on prostitution shows White Mario's matter-of-fact approach to an issue frequently clouded by moralising prose and posturing. In contrast, she observes how prostitution among the 'lowest classes' is an occupation like any other, and, she adds with a characteristic Victorian attitude, that one could not really expect anything different given the 'promiscuity' in which the Neapolitan poor lived.

Beccari, Mozzoni and White Mario centred their lives and their writings around a 'cause', and used newspapers and magazines to propagate their message. They were first of all militants who at times were able to make a living out of their journalistic activity; indeed, White Mario actually relied on this for most of her life. But there were others who made a career out of writing for newspapers and magazines, and in the process developed a fully fledged identity as writers and journalists. *Matilde Serao was the most successful of these. As a young woman, before becoming a highly regarded novelist (see chapter 12) and probably the best-known woman writer of liberal Italy, Serao ardently aspired to a position in the journalistic world. Her ambition was soon fulfilled. She began her career by collaborating on Neapolitan dailies such as *Il Piccolo* and *Giornale di Napoli*, moving then rapidly to other newspapers such as *Capitan Fracassa* and *Roma capitale* and to the literary Sunday supplement *Fanfulla della domenica*. Together with her husband Edoardo Scarfoglio, she founded and directed first the daily *Il corriere di Roma* and later *Il Mattino*. Finally in 1904, after her separation from Scarfoglio, she founded her own daily (the first woman in Italy to do so), *Il giorno*, which was supposed to rival *Il mattino*. Thanks to Serao's ability and reputation and to new forms of promotion, *Il giorno* acquired a considerable readership (about 20,000 subscribers) and appeared until 1927, the year of Serao's death.[17]

As a journalist, Serao shied away from 'high politics' and penned primarily social and literary columns. During her collaboration on *Il corriere di Roma*, she began a popular column entitled 'Api, mosconi e vespe' ('Bees, blowflies and wasps,' later shortened to 'Blowflies') which she brought to all other newspapers for which she worked. In this gossip column, reports on the main events of 'high society' (with detailed lists of all their participants) alternated with advice on good manners for the middle and lower-middle classes, brief correspondence with the readers, and even political and social commentaries. A sizzling style and wit often characterise these short exercises, which became a distinct feature of Serao's contribution to all the newspapers she collaborated on or founded. In this column she appears to identify completely with the life-style of the wealthy and aristocratic elites, although, as Sharon Wood has noted, as a writer she also felt above the world she described, endowed with a kind of moral and cognitive superiority: 'Those elegant ladies don't realize that I know them inside out, that I hold them in my mind, that I will put them in my books: they have no idea of my strength and power' (Wood, p. 44). While her journalism benefited from her literary imagination and skills, it provided the writer material for her numerous novels, some of which she published first in instalments in newspapers and journals. This is very visible, for example, in *Il paese di cuccagna* (*The Land of Cockayne*, 1891), where extensive descriptions of popular life in Naples accompany a narrative centred around the devastating effects that the passion for the lottery has on all classes of society.

Although Serao's influential pen did not write directly on 'high poli-tics', she did use it to oppose women's suffrage, with a variety of trite arguments (from the hopeless ignorance of women to the dirty nature of politics – a man's business *par excellence*) which greatly annoyed her polit-ical adversaries who would have much preferred to have such a writer on their side.[18] A woman who lived an unconventional life and a living testi-mony to the ideas of feminists, as many did not fail to notice, Serao was not only a vocal anti-feminist but also a conservative monarchist who claimed that in matters of politics women do not think, but 'feel', and that they naturally feel love for the monarchy. At the same time, Serao was not insensitive to the plight of the poor, and of poor women espe-cially. In response to Prime Minister Agostino Depretis's comment about the need to 'disembowel' ('sventrare') Naples during the cholera epi-demic of 1884, she wrote what many consider her best work, a series of brief essays depicting the conditions of life among the popular classes in Naples. First published on the pages of *Capitan Fracassa* in September 1884, these short pieces were soon after collected in a book entitled *Il ventre di Napoli* (*The Belly of Naples*), a title clearly modeled after Zola's *Le Ventre de Paris* (1873). The ways the Neapolitan poor had of making ends meet, popular diet, religiosity and superstition, the widespread and very intense passion for gambling, the rituals of the lottery, usury: in a vivid style that had nothing of the aridity and heaviness of certain social inves-tigations, Serao unveiled a suffering humanity (and, in its midst, the suf-fering and exploitation of women in particular) neglected by scores of previous writers who had represented Naples within the conventions of the picturesque.

Yet, as critics have observed, while sensitive to the suffering of the poorer classes, Serao never went beyond a rather generic denunciation which fell short of identifying the complex web of responsibilities which stood behind the problems of the city.[19] Her political conservatism and her loyalty to the South, and to Naples in particular, kept her from condemning a phenomenon such as *camorra*. Even when she took up again the topic of the city's conditions twenty years after the first edition of *Il ventre di Napoli*, her analysis of the causes continued to be generic and her view of Naples's predicaments became in fact increasingly replete with the mawkish brand of Christian sentimentalism she developed in her late years.[20] This was particularly noticeable in her collection of essays on the war entitled *Parla una donna. Diario femminile di guerra Maggio 1915–Marzo 1916* ('A woman speaks. Female war journal May 1915–March 1916'), which reflected Serao's increasingly fatalistic view of the world, probably accentuated by old age and the war itself. In the book she also addressed women with a moralising and emphatically patriotic tone which contrasted with her earlier pacifist stance, although not with the enthusiasm she manifested for the Libyan war.

Serao was unique in the position she was able to carve for herself in the competitive male world of daily newspapers. Without achieving the same level of power and success, other women, however, were able to acquire respectable positions and build writing careers in the new and expanding world of women's and children's magazines. Among the women in charge of this kind of periodical, we should mention Ida Baccini, the director from 1884 to 1911 of the most popular journal for girls of the time, *Cordelia*. This weekly, founded in 1881 by the progressive polygraph Angelo De Gubernatis, achieved the considerable figure of about 10,000 subscribers in 1913.[21] As director of this journal, Baccini did not modify substantially the format devised by De Gubernatis, but made it less smug and more in line with the changing taste of its audience. Educational articles on historical and contemporary issues alternated with short stories, poems and novels in instalment written by well-known and less well-known writers. The readers too – both schoolchildren and teachers – contributed their prose to the magazine.

Baccini was a prolific author of articles for literary journals, and children's books – her *Memorie di un pulcino* ('Memoirs of a chick', 1875) enjoyed dozens of reprints – as well as successful textbooks for elementary schools, also reprinted several times. Baccini wrote a prose exuding the values that the patriotic middle classes intended to instil into the hearts of the Italian people, adapted when necessary to the female gender. Love of order, cleanliness, industriousness, a desire for learning – within limits, to be sure, in the case of women and the lower classes – and patriotism were the virtues exalted in the large number of textbooks and stories published by this author. The readers were reminded again and again of the benefits of economising, the healthiness of country life and the bliss of honest poverty.

A great admirer of Edmondo De Amicis, who undoubtedly inspired her production of textbooks, and of Matilde Serao, Baccini was particularly proud of her language, which her contemporaries praised for its simplicity and purity. Converting to feminism in her later years, she wrote an autobiography centred around the description of her 'conquest' of a position in the publishing industry where she also voiced her complaints about the poor treatment that publishers reserved to authors – a cause of the rather modest lifestyle she claimed she was confined to in her older age, in spite of the large quantity of books sold by her publishers.[22]

Another woman intellectual who carved an important niche for herself in the expanding publishing industry of liberal Italy was *Paola Lombroso, one of the two daughters of Cesare Lombroso, the well-known inventor of criminal anthropology. Paola Lombroso is noteworthy not only because of her essays, but also because as a member of a distinctive *milieu*, the positivistic circle of her famous father in Turin, she represents another important component of the complex intellectual scene of the turn of the century.

Before she was twenty years old, Paola Lombroso started to publish articles and short novels in literary journals such as the *Fanfulla della domenica* of Florence and the *Gazzetta letteraria* of Turin. Between 1895 and 1909 she also sent several scientific contributions to the *Archivio di psichiatria*, the psychiatry periodical founded by her father in 1880, and to the journals of the socialist left, from *Critica sociale* to *Socialismo* to the daily *Avanti!*. She also regularly contributed to newspapers in Milan, Trieste and Turin. While addressing many social and political issues of the day (primarily the conditions of the lower classes and the ways of improving these conditions), Paola Lombroso also used journalism to diffuse her ideas on the female condition, and on psychology, particularly that of children, to which she devoted most of her energies until about 1910.

Although Paola Lombroso's early interest in writing and journalism was a cause of anxiety in the family, her studies in child psychology received the approval of her father. This was a proper field of involvement for a woman, both in terms of subject matter and in terms of degree of difficulty – it did not challenge Cesare Lombroso's conviction of the intellectual inferiority of women. The *Saggi di psicologia del bambino* ('Essays on child psychology', 1894) presented detailed descriptions of children's character, environment and life history. This work looked at children in the light of an evolutionary theory which made them into the equivalent of 'primitive men' whose development echoes the main steps of the evolution of humankind. At the same time, it exhibited the sensitivity of its author towards the emotional world of young people, a sensitivity which would allow her to write successful children's fiction.

Like other members of her milieu, Paola Lombroso conceived the role of intellectual as one directed to a social and humanitarian purpose. Her desire to make scientific knowledge available to a wide public, combined with the conviction that her own task as a woman was simply that of diligently collecting facts, translated into works which one could easily overlook, or classify as 'popular psychology'. Among these works there were *Il problema della felicità* ('The problem of happiness', 1907), in which she attempted to discover what makes an individual happy by examining the life stories of one hundred men and women of the upper middle classes, and *I segni rivelatori della personalità* ('Revealing signs of personality', 1902) in which she used physiognomy and graphology to provide a 'rapid and approximately exact diagnosis of personality'. *I caratteri della femminilità* ('The characteristics of femininity', 1909), while re-asserting the primacy of motherhood for woman's full self-realisation, implicitly challenged some commonly held ideas about women's inferiority to which her own father had contributed. Appearing in a popular series aimed at spreading the findings of the modern sciences,[23] these works were imbued with the axioms and naive assumptions of positivistic science as well as with the common prejudices of the middle classes. At the same time, they were earnest attempts to find sound answers, based on empirical observations, to commonly asked questions and problems. As Delfina Dolza has observed, they were also shaped by a sensitivity to the social context of women's subordination which made the author subvert some of the very convictions of her intellectual milieu.[24]

As an intellectual with left-wing leanings, Paola Lombroso was particularly concerned about the life and beliefs of the lower classes. In the volume she co-authored with her husband in 1906, entitled *Nella penombra della civiltà: da un'inchiesta sul pensiero del popolo* ('In the shadow of civilisation:

from an enquiry on the ideas of the popular classes'), she called attention not only to what she considered the profound ignorance of the lower classes, but also to their political apathy which, she warned, could end up with negative consequences for those responsible for such a state of things. Lack of participation in collective life translated into an atrophied sentiment of patriotism, and the authors lamented the Italian people's failure even to feel the most 'noble and legitimate sentiment of national solidarity' (p. 170). Almost fifty years after Unification, Italian intellectuals were still facing the issue of making Italians. This kind of awareness partly explains Paola Lombroso's engagement in the acculturation of children of the poorer classes, and more generally in developing children's fiction. She originated the idea behind one of the most successful Italian children's weeklies of this century, the *Corriere dei piccoli*, and collaborated on it for about three years (1908–11). She published several collections of short stories and novels for children and adolescents and directed some of the series in which they appeared. Compared with Baccini's production, the children's fiction published by Paola Lombroso was less immediately didactic and moralistic. It reflected a fairly sophisticated understanding the world of children and young people, sensitive to its autonomous values and 'laws'. It was also shaped by a more critical morality, one which did not simply try to make people adapt to the world as it was, but also tried, at times, to make them imagine the world as it could be. In this world, girls, too, were no longer discouraged from writing stories.

Far from constituting a homogeneous whole, the women writers whose work we have considered in this chapter represent a range of actual 'writing careers' or trajectories for women who came to be intellectuals in late Risorgimento and liberal Italy. Most of these women did not rely on writing to make a living, although some did and were proud of it (Baccini, Serao, at times Beccari). Most moved between genres, between fiction and non-fiction. In a century which theorised women's separate sphere, they inevitably privileged certain subjects and discourses. They tended to write for other women and for children, thus performing the educational role that was expected of them. Yet at the same time they asked questions and introduced perspectives which their male counterparts might not have thought of. Although quite diverse in terms of social, intellectual and political backgrounds, for most of these women the choice to be a writer was closely linked to some forms of political engagement, to a mission, a cause, be it making the nation or women's emancipation or more often, as we have seen, both. A woman who wrote without having to justify this act before the world by resorting to some higher moral reason was still the exception in the Italy of the second half of the nineteenth century.

NOTES

1. Ida Baccini, *Quarte letture per le classi elementari maschili* (Florence, 1885), p. 4.
2. Michela De Giorgio, *Le italiane dall'Unità ad oggi* (Rome–Bari, 1992), p. 490.
3. Caterina Franceschi Ferrucci, *Degli studi delle donne*, quoted in Ilaria Porciani (ed.), *Le donne a scuola. L'educazione femminile nell'Italia dell'Ottocento* (Florence, 1987), p. 17.
4. Giulia Molino Colombini, *Sull'educazione della donna*, 3rd revised edn (Turin, 1869), p. vi.
5. See Erminia Fuà Fusinato, *Scritti educativi*, ed. Gaetano Ghivizzani.
6. Giulia Molino Colombini, 'Le donne nel poema di Dante', in *Dante e il suo secolo* (Florence, 1865), pp. 182–201.
7. Erminia Fuà Fusinato, 'La Laura del Petrarca', in *Scritti letterari*, ed. Ghivizzani, pp. 97–114.
8. Caterina Franceschi Ferrucci, *I primi quattro secoli della letteratura italiana dal secolo XIII al XVI. Lezioni.*
9. Carlo Villani, *Stelle femminili. Dizionario bio-bibliografico*, 2nd edn (Naples–Rome–Milan, 1915).
10. De Giorgio, *Le italiane*, p. 391.
11. See Judith J. Howard, 'Patriot Mothers in the Post-Risorgimento: Women After the Italian Revolution', in Carol R. Berkin and Clara Lovett (eds.), *Women, War, and Revolution* (New York, 1980), pp. 237–58.
12. Franca Pieroni Bortolotti, *Alle origini del movimento femminile in Italia, 1848–1892* (Turin, 1963), p. 63.
13. Anna Maria Mozzoni, *La donna e i suoi rapporti sociali*, now in Anna Maria Mozzoni, *La liberazione della donna*, ed. Franca Pieroni Bortolotti (Milan, 1975), from which I quote (p. 42).
14. Jessie White Mario, *Garibaldi e i suoi tempi*, preface.
15. See the introduction by Giovanni Spadolini to the reprint of the 1905 edition of *Garibaldi e i suoi tempi* (Naples, 1982), and the introduction by Guido Gerosa to the reprint (Pordenone, 1986), of the first edition of the same work (1882).
16. Elisabeth Adams Daniels, *Jessie White Mario. Risorgimento Revolutionary* (Athens, OH, 1972), chapter 8.
17. Wanda De Nunzio Schilardi, *Matilde Serao giornalista (con antologia di scritti rari)* (Lecce, 1986).
18. See the 'lettere aperte' written to Serao by Anna Maria Mozzoni and Jessie White Mario in *La lega della democrazia* 1, nos. 132 and 134 (15 and 17 May 1880).
19. See for example Quinto Marini, 'Postfazione', in Matilde Serao, *Il ventre di Napoli*, ed. Quinto Marini (Pisa, 1995).
20. Matilde Serao, *Il ventre di Napoli (Venti anni fa. Adesso. L'anima di Napoli)*.
21. De Giorgio, *Le italiane*, p. 388.
22. Ida Baccini, *La mia vita. Ricordi autobiografici.*
23. See the 'Piccola biblioteca di scienze moderne' of the Turin publisher, Bocca.
24. Delfina Dolza, *Essere figlie di Lombroso. Due donne intellettuali tra '800 e '900* (Milan, 1990), pp. 195 ff.

12

The novel, 1870–1920

In 1892 Italo Svevo, author of *La coscienza di Zeno* (*Confessions of Zeno*, 1923), published his first novel, *Una vita* (*A life*). The protagonist, Alfonso Nitti, commits suicide after the boss's daughter, an aspiring writer, convinces him to write a novel with her; irked by his sexual passivity, she then seduces him. Svevo's portrayal of Annetta Maller, both satirical and deadly serious, reflects two of the most widely-spread clichés of the time about women writers – they were sexual predators and they were 'virile': 'she was not a woman when she spoke of literature, she was a man involved in the struggle for life, a morally muscular being'.[1]

A few years later, the projected theme of Annetta's hypothetical novel – the biography of a woman married to a man unworthy of her – is taken up by a major male writer, Luigi Pirandello (1867–1936) in a novel entitled *Suo marito* ('Her husband', 1911). The protagonist, Silvia Roncella, is neither virile nor a sexual predator, but her rise to fame emasculates her husband nonetheless. Moreover, while she herself writes prolifically, her lover Maurizio Gueli, one of the most prominent authors of the time, has severe writer's block. When Silvia discovers his infidelity, she attacks him with a knife: he loses his right arm, together with any capacity to write at all.

These references to literary representations of women writers by men emphasise the importance of seeing women's writing of this period in the broader context of discourses of gender and culture circulating at the time.[2] The impact of women writers on the collective imagination in this period is a reflection not only of the popularity and timeliness of their work, but also of what they had come to symbolise in a highly conservative, agrarian society suddenly faced with the combined challenges of nationhood and modernisation. The late emergence of a national, popular literary market in the heart of perhaps the most elitist of all the European traditions, was marked by an explosion of women writers unprecedented in Italian history.[3] Every stable institution in sight – from the family to the class system to art and culture – appeared suddenly to be under attack. The rise of women writers in concomitance with these changes conditioned public response to them and cast them into the limelight, often against their will.

Just as women were emerging as a force to be reckoned with, the shifting parameters of gender suggesting that much of what constituted 'femininity' was in fact socially determined, 'science' began an all-out campaign to ground all difference firmly in biology. Its goal was to demonstrate the genetic inferiority of 'real' women and the 'deviant' character of so-called masculine women. Charles Darwin's *The Descent of Man* (1871), by concluding that woman's evolutionary development was stunted, legitimised the ideas of such later propagandists as Mobius (*On the Physiological Debility of Women*, 1898) and Otto Weininger (*Sex and Character*, 1903). In 1893 the famous Italian criminologist Cesare Lombroso, in collaboration with his son-in-law Guglielmo Ferrero, published *La donna delinquente, la prostituta e la donna normale* ('The criminal woman, the prostitute and the normal woman'), which claimed that all women had a natural propensity towards delinquency and prostitution; only maternity could save them from it.[4] Weininger was later to include intellectual women among the 'prostitutes'. Italian intellectuals were enamoured of Weininger, and much male reaction to female writing of the time is characterised by references to the virility or femininity of the writer in question.[5] The anxiety generated by the potential for a blurring of gender boundaries undoubtedly accounts for this obsession with establishing 'difference'. Interestingly, the same writers could be considered masculine or feminine, depending on the critic's point of view: the important thing was that each writer be situated on one side or the other of the great divide. In this game, female writers could rarely win – most often, they were either men in skirts, or 'mere women'. Women writers, too, were self-conscious about their 'transgressions', often going to great lengths to reassure themselves – and everyone else – that they were not forfeiting their femininity by writing. *Neera entitled a collection of essays *Le idee di una donna* ('The ideas of a woman', 1904), and in one of her novels painted a portrait of a 'masculine woman' to whom, significantly, she ascribes a passion for rigorous theoretical works, rather than literature. Corinna, described as the freest and happiest woman in the world, was 'almost six feet tall, (with) a square, angular heavy-boned body that seemed

to have been sculpted with a hatchet . . . She had read a great many theological, philosophical and surgical works . . . She loved Spencer, Darwin,
Nordau, Schopenhauer.'[6]

The perceived threat to male writers posed by the emergence of the
woman writer was readily acknowledged by Luigi Capuana, whose essay
'Letteratura femminile', a review of the previous year's production by
women, was published in the 1 January 1907 issue of *Nuova antologia*.
Capuana rejects the notion that the influx of female novelists was really
the cause for concern that some of their male counterparts – and competi-
tors – seemed to believe. Although women writers may be multiplying
exponentially, quantity has nothing to do with quality or originality:
women who write are doomed only to repeat what men have created
before them.[7]

This was a popular but inaccurate assumption. Italian literature's
elitist history, together with its bias in favour of poetry, conflicted sharply
with the immediate need for a popular, accessible literature. Most Italian
literati were far too steeped in the classical tradition to be able to write for
ordinary Italians. Women, on the other hand, were largely self-taught,
with little or no training in the classics or literary traditions.[8] They were
the ideal labour force for a burgeoning publishing industry anxious to
exploit the growing demand for readable books by a largely female
public. The philosopher and historian Benedetto Croce pointed out
astutely, though not without some disdain, that the immediacy and
naivety of the frequently confessional female register was ideally suited to
the creation of a new, popular literary language.[9]

The premises for the participation of middle-class women in the intellectual life of the nation had been created by the Risorgimento, when
women patriots became an accepted part of the social landscape, and
women's magazines dedicated to them began to appear.[10] After Unification, however, the state promoted the family as the pivotal structure of
the new society and public discourse relegated women forcefully back to
the private sphere. Leading intellectuals set aside bitter political differences to concur that women could best serve the interests of their country
from behind the scenes, by educating their children in the virtues of patriotism and by providing the material and emotional comforts of a home
for their husbands. The angel-of-the hearth, thus suitably empowered
and safely out of the public eye, became a staple of the official rhetoric on
the role of women.[11] At the same time, northern Italy was moving rapidly
towards a modern capitalist economy and by the end of the nineteenth

century one and a half million women were working in factories, the majority of them in the textile industry. It was here, around the struggle for better working conditions, that the feminist movement's first successful attempts to mobilise women took place.[12]

At first the feminist cause found support mainly in the progressive women's journals, but by the turn of the century popular magazines and newspapers were full of articles and even regular columns on the changing role of women, while *Nuova antologia* solicited contributions on the subject from well-known intellectuals. The prestigious *La voce* published two special issues on the various implications of the 'woman question'.[13]

The climate of revolt created by the feminist movement put a great deal of pressure on women writers, novelists in particular. Though the novel was considered by some an important tool which could be exploited for the education of women to 'appropriate' sentiments and values, its rather chequered history and the racy reputation of the highly popular, contemporary French novel tended to overshadow this belief. Moreover the tendency of the press to turn women writers into public figures and spokespersons for women in general was potentially damaging to them, both personally and professionally. Since many of them earned a large part of their income from mainstream women's journalism (see chapter 11), they had to tread lightly through a minefield of sensitive issues. Not surprisingly, they were often insecure and self-conscious, and their stated political positions, for the most part, were anything but radical, and often contradicted their imaginative writings. Neera and *Matilde Serao were both well-known anti-feminists. Even the *Marchesa Colombi, who was involved with a feminist alternative education project for women, was ambiguous in her endorsement of feminist claims. While women writers had greater access to the channels of public discourse than ever before, much of what they really thought and felt has to be read between the lines.

The bulk of the narrative literature written by women in this period belongs to the vast grey zone between late-Romanticism and *verismo*, Italy's version of naturalism. Many works were of a hybrid nature, a mixture of popular elements and serious intentions. The emergence of *verismo*, with its emphasis on the critique of social conditions, provided the first legitimate opportunity to conduct a more overtly critical analysis of women's lives. Paradoxically, inasmuch as it theorised the 'impersonality' of the narrator, whose only task was to record his/her observations from the standpoint of an uninvolved onlooker, *verismo* also allowed women writers to carry out their project with less inhibition and less fear of being identified with their heroines than might otherwise have been the case.

Perhaps the best example of *verismo*'s influence as a liberating force is to be found in the work of Anna Radius Zuccari or Neera, as she was known to the public, one of the most prolific and popular female writers of the time, and a protégée of both Luigi Capuana[14] and Benedetto Croce (who also edited and introduced a selection of her works well after her death).[15] Her early novels are characterised by such ominous titles as *Addio!* ('Farewell!', 1877) and *Il castigo* ('The punishment', 1881), and are all centred on the adultery/punishment motif, in which the intensity of the physical passions – rarely consummated – is matched only by the profound sense of guilt and mortification which they generate in the otherwise morally irreproachable heroines. In spite of her efforts to submit them to appropriate suffering of various sorts as retribution for their transgressions, real or fantasised, Neera was harshly rebuked by the critics for having dared to depict such intense desire, and in a preface to the second edition of *Addio!* defends herself with great vehemence.[16] It is clear that in these novels she is somehow trying to escape the virgin/whore dichotomy. The anguished dilemmas of her heroines, repeatedly caught between the irreconcilable extremes of sacred marital duty and adulterous sexual passion, may also seem to reflect her own sense of having to choose between authenticity as a writer and her reputation as a woman.

Confirmation of this hypothesis is provided by the motif's sudden disappearance as soon as she enters the naturalist phase of her career. For Neera, in fact, *verismo*'s view of the artist as an impersonal observer meant freedom from the confusion – and hence conflict – of roles that had determined the adultery/punishment motif of the early novels. The works belonging to the naturalist period – *Teresa* (1886), *Lydia* (1887), *L'indomani* ('The day after', 1890) – emphasise the social and environmental factors contributing to the misfortunes of their heroines: they are the victims not of their passions, but of what they have been taught, and what they have absorbed from their environments. Most of Neera's other heroines live in anonymous drawing rooms, their pasts consisting of the minimum number of facts necessary to justify their present situations, their vulnerability a given, a 'universal' deriving from their womanliness. In *Teresa*, *Lydia* and *L'indomani*, however, the roots of the extreme vulnerability of the heroines are for the first time critically explored and traced back to upbringing, rather than taken for granted.

Neera never really resolves her own conflicts about writing. Alongside potentially feminist novels, she produces essays and articles aimed at discouraging aspiring women writers (*Le idee di una donna*, pp. 94–107) and denigrating the accomplishments of Georges Sand and George Eliot, while celebrating the unknown mothers of Dante and Leopardi (*Le idee* pp. 63–7). At the same time, paradoxically, *Teresa* bears a striking resemblance to Eliot's *The Mill on the Floss*, and one of its minor characters, the town madwoman, Calliope (the muse of epic poetry), is clearly a tribute to Georges Sand. Calliope's many love affairs and her refusal to accept the strictures of gender roles are suggested as the source of her 'madness' but, significantly, no mention at all is made of a writing career.

The madwoman reappears in *Il tramonto di un ideale* ('The sunset of an ideal', 1883), a novel by Marchesa Colombi, pseudonym for Maria Antonietta Torriani-Torelli. In this deliberate attempt to parody and subvert the sacred cow of Italian novels, Alessandro Manzoni's *I promessi sposi* (*The Betrothed*), the figure of the madwoman is represented by La Matta, a young illiterate servant-girl secretly in love with her master. She unwittingly thwarts his engagement to the virtuous daughter of a town official by failing to deliver a letter to her hidden in a copy of Manzoni's novel.

Torriani first attracted public attention with *In risaia* ('In the ricefields', 1878). The story of a young peasant girl's inability to find a husband because of a disfiguring disease contracted in the rice fields of the Po Valley, it was written in the years when the debate on *verismo* was at its peak, and appeared at the same time as Emma Ferretti Viola's (1844–1929) *Una fra tante* ('One amongst many'), a novel about a prostitute. Torriani was particularly concerned with the influence of the novel on the minds and sensibilities of young women. She berated the novels of her time, hostorical, late-Romantic and naturalist, for their lack of any relationship to 'reality' and in works such as *Prima morire* ('To die first', 1881) warned of their power to elicit false expectations of life, in the manner of Flaubert's *Madame Bovary*.

Torriani produced a strikingly original little masterpiece of sardonic wit, the engaging and startlingly modern *Un matrimonio in provincia* ('A provincial marriage', 1885), republished in 1973 by Italo Calvino for Einaudi, with a preface by Natalia Ginzburg. The novel is narrated by Denza, a housewife and mother of three children. The tone is matter-of-fact, devoid of sentimentalism or any affect other than the self-deprecating irony borne of hindsight. Denza's first heart-throb is described bluntly as 'a sort of elephant';[17] the young girl is clearly deceived by nothing other than her own pressing emotional needs and volatile romantic imagination. After the death of her adolescent dreams, and years of boredom and humiliation, she eagerly marries an older, well-to-do notary, distinguished by a large wart on his forehead. Wart and all, life with the middle-aged notary is preferable to the isolation and degradation of spinsterhood, epitomised for Denza by the fate of her unmarried aunt, presented in the novel's very first paragraph as 'a little old maid, thin as a rail, who slept in the kitchen where she had installed a screen to hide the bed, and who spent her life in the dark behind that screen' (*Un matrimonio*, p. 3). Torriani's unique brand of *verismo* punctures not only the occasional Romantic stereotype, but also the orthodox naturalist motifs that more conventional writers like Neera exploit to the fullest. Where others see tragedy and injustice, Torriani sees only the absurd, implacable logic of life, as it continually fails to live up to our inflated expectations.

Both Neera and the Marchesa Colombi, though certainly well-versed themselves in the current events of the time, tend to depict women whose lives are totally contained within the private sphere. Less popular and more controversial writers, such as the socialist Bruno Sperani (Beatrice Speraz, 1839–1923), engaged openly with such thorny questions as women's careers and class conflict,[18] but the only mainstream writer whose works reflect her awareness of the public sphere is the conservative *Matilde Serao. As much a regional writer as an Italian one, Serao confronts everything from the social problems of quasi third-world Naples in *Il ventre di Napoli* (*The Belly of Naples*, 1884) to the scandalous situation of an elderly nun forced into the streets of Rome by a government decision to close sparsely populated monasteries (*Suor Giovanna della Croce*, 'Sister Joan of the Cross', 1901). *La conquista di Roma* (*The Conquest of Rome*, 1885) describes the corrupt parliamentary world of the new Italy, while *Vita e avventure di Riccardo Joanna* (*The Life and Adventures of Riccardo Joanna*, 1887) exposes the world of journalism which Serao knew so well. Her own, highly unorthodox life was never treated directly in her work, though we do get glimpses of her in such stories as *Scuola normale femminile* ('Grammar school for girls') and *Telegrafi dello stato* ('State Telegraph Offices'), as the irreverent, high-spirited, somewhat masculine young Caterina Borelli, who openly criticises senseless institutional regulations and reads literary journals under her desk. Serao also makes a brief, cameo appearance in the novel *Fantasia* ('Imagination', 1883) as a journalist covering a local agricultural fair and described by the protagonist as a woman who lives for more than just love.[19]

In the second part of her career, with the demise of *verismo*, Serao progressively abandoned the realistic, investigative vein for the guaranteed success of the late Romantic *feuilleton*. However, like other women writers of her time, she did attempt, briefly and under the influence of *verismo*, to escape the strictures of the conventional portrayal of women. The early adultery novel, *Fantasia*, parodies both Emma and Charles Bovary, as well as Mena Malavoglia, glorified by Giovanni Verga in *I Malavoglia (The House By the Medlar Tree*, 1881) as a model of feminine passivity and self-abnegation. Serao pits the wicked adulteress Lucia against the saintly wife Caterina, believing in neither: imaginative, volatile and verbose, Lucia is as wooden as the exasperatingly concrete, passive and laconic Caterina.

The confirmation of *Fantasia*'s status as an early exercise in literary options, designed to mimic the stereotypes deriving from the tradition, comes from the novella that follows immediately on its heels, *La virtù di Checchina* ('The virtue of Checchina', 1884),[20] an ironic rendering of the *Madame Bovary* motif which dispenses with both manipulative, high-strung adulteresses and naive, self-effacing wives. Checchina's virtue is tested when her husband, a miserly physician who smells of formaldehyde, in a fit of *arrivisme* brings temptation into his own home by inviting the debonair Marchese d'Aragona to dinner. Unlike the flighty Isolina, her friend and confidante, Checchina has always been a faithful wife. But the news of the Marchese's imminent visit to her home creates new stirrings of rebellion, and the bulk of the novella is an account of Checchina's struggle with temptation after the Marchese invites her to his luxurious apartment. After much deliberation, she finally submits to the mundane demands of domesticity and to inhibitions provoked by guilt and shame. This low-key tale of the all-too-human Checchina's adulterous non-adventure is generally considered one of Serao's more fully realised works.

In the third and final phase of her challenge to the literary stereotypes of her time, Serao abandons the adulterous woman altogether, in order to represent the difficult but uneventful lives of young unmarried women, *fanciulle*. *Il romanzo della fanciulla* ('The young girl's novel', 1886) is not in fact a novel at all, but a collection of stories in which Serao draws on early personal experiences. In the very important preface to the *Romanzo* she distinguishes her own portraits of young women from those in *Chérie* (1883) by Edmond de Goncourt, whom she criticises for basing his novel not on first-hand observation but on confessions and confidences, 'as if young girls ever confided in anyone, mothers or friends, fiancés or experimental novelists'.[21] Significantly, this high point in her representation of women coincides with the adoption of a choral narrative framework and the recourse to her own memory as an ostensible source of inspiration. Both devices are expedients clearly designed to circumvent standard plot and character development and to emphasise the great variety and complexity of female types.

The dissatisfaction with previous literary representations of women is also the source of inspiration for the most notorious novel written by an Italian woman of the period, *Sibilla Aleramo's autobiographical *Una donna* (*A woman*, 1906). However, while earlier writers were objecting to male representations of women, Aleramo, of a subsequent generation, is equally critical of women writers, and indeed speaks of her novel as a reaction to their mediocre parodies of more fashionable books by men.[22] It is true that *Una donna*, a fictionalised account of the events behind Aleramo's decision to abandon her child in order to escape an abusive husband, was far more overtly polemical than most earlier novels by women, and provoked a great deal of discussion, not of its literary merit, but of its conclusion.[23] Curiously, Luigi Capuana's 1907 review of the previous year's writing by women, 'Letteratura femminile', makes no mention of it at all, in spite of the fact that it was the most controversial novel of the year.

The Italian literary tradition offered women in an unhappy marriage two possibilities: adultery or resignation. In order to find an appropriate model for her tale of 'liberation', Aleramo was thus forced to look elsewhere. Henryk Ibsen's notorious play, *A Doll's House*, also the story of a woman's decision to abandon her family, had been translated for the Italian stage by Luigi Capuana and met with such audience hostility at Nora Helmer's final exit that Capuana subsequently asked Ibsen, in vain, to rewrite the play's ending.[24] Wishing both to distinguish herself from Ibsen and to pay homage to him, Aleramo incorporates the character of Nora into her own novel, as the Norwegian designer, a friend of the protagonist's who has left a dull marriage in her own country and is seeking a new life in Italy. The designer offers moral support and encouragement, but her own happiness is cut short when she suddenly falls ill and dies. Aleramo's 'revolutionary' text is not revolutionary enough to allow for any form of female desire to be endorsed if it is not framed by some form of self-sacrifice. In fact, the protagonist ultimately takes as her model a widowed and childless social activist who devotes herself to the poor and thus performs a nurturing function without actually being a mother or a wife.

For all her apparent revolutionary fervour and her rejection of other women's writings, Aleramo shared with her colleagues of those years a tendency to see the condition and the identity of women in static opposition to the condition of men. At least one of Aleramo's contemporaries, *Grazia Deledda, and another writer belonging to the subsequent generation, *Maria Messina, begin to perceive gender roles as complex, dynamic and interactive, rather than fixed and anchored to biology. Both are writers of the 'periphery', Deledda from Sardinia, Messina from Sicily.

Deledda's novels are mostly set in an almost mythical Sardinia. A rugged natural landscape provides the lyrical backdrop for extreme, elemental passions raging within the rigid confines of archaic and unforgiving societal norms. Her most famous works are undoubtedly *Elias Portolu* (1903) and *Canne al vento* (*Reeds in the Wind*, 1913). Though clearly a reflection of the heightened tensions spawned and nurtured by an insular, entrenched environment, her narrative is also marked by the transformations taking place in the world at large. Two novels, *Marianna Sirca* (1915) and *La madre* (*The Mother*, 1920) both cast transgressive male figures – the bandit, and the priest in love – against two strong female figures, spinsters isolated by a socio-economic independence which makes it impossible for them to find suitable husbands in their immediate milieu. Both of these novels would seem to be stories of love which transgresses the boundaries of class and the law, whether ecclesiastic or secular. Yet, on closer examination, they actually reveal themselves to be stories of truncated or stunted masculinity. Both male characters shrink from love for the women they have compromised. The priest is less afraid of God than he is of his mother, the woman who has sacrificed her life for him. The bandit, whose relationship to his mother is also put into relief, is unable to carry out his promise to Marianna because he is caught up in the dynamics of male bonding and rivalry which in Deledda's view characterise banditry. At every level *Marianna Sirca* is a denunciation of ineffectual and precarious masculinity, the men more preoccupied with the trappings of wealth, 'honour' and independence, than with the real tasks at hand, to say nothing of the welfare of the women they are meant to be protecting. Meanwhile, the women are busy doing the work of 'real' men; Simone's sisters, for example[25] dress as men in order to look out for spies when he is about to return home to see his ailing mother.

If Deledda's novel exposes the false myths of gender espoused by a highly traditional nineteenth-century society, Maria Messina depicts the confusion of roles in an apparently more modern early twentieth-century context, where women seem to enjoy greater economic and sexual freedom. Her most famous and best novel, *La casa nel vicolo* ('The house in the alley', 1921), however, examines the invisible psychological underpinnings of the present confusion – traditional gender arrangements gone awry. It takes place in a timeless Sicily, and depicts a triangular relationship exasperated by the pathological, hot-house atmosphere of confined quarters, a metaphor for the stranglehold grip of the family on the individual in Sicilian society. What emerges is a highly nuanced study of the dynamics of male dominance and female masochism, with victims and oppressors paradoxically changing places in a shifting choreography of life-as-death. Another novel, *Alla deriva* ('Adrift', 1920) presents a situation where the unconscious rejection of traditional masculine and feminine roles by both husband and wife leads, in the absence of alternative models, to the tragic failure of a marriage. Most of the space in the novel is dedicated to the analysis of the male protagonist, in many ways a prototype of the inept early twentieth-century anti-hero paralysed by his ambivalence towards patriarchal expectations. Many short stories, on the other hand, examine the 'new woman', who reveals herself, also, to be inept, incapable of enacting her desires, of turning her new aspirations into a new and different life. Messina has been compared to both Verga and Pirandello, and indeed her work is marked by both fatalism and a sense of the impossibility of real change, in spite of appearances to the contrary. What is new in her work is the awareness of the subtle interactions between masculine and feminine subjectivities, and of the connections between psychic and social structures in the rapidly evolving social and economic landscape of post-World War I Italy.

What emerges from the half century between the completion of Unification (1871) and the onset of Fascism (1922) is a conscious attempt to renegotiate and extend the parameters of female identity, both personal and literary. These are also the years in which European male writers began the often aloof and hermetic modernist experimentations which could make the 'realist' voice of most women writers appear formally antiquated and irrelevant. In fact, writers such as Neera and Serao, once *verismo* was no longer in vogue, returned to the popular novel, while Grazia Deledda continued to write in the naturalist vein in spite of the movement's decline, earning herself the Nobel Prize for literature in 1926, if not the esteem of most literary critics. Certainly Italian women did not have the rich narrative tradition shared by English women writers, nor did they enjoy the respect and relative autonomy of English middle-class women. While Virginia Woolf yearned for 'a room of her own', Italian women in many cases still yearned for the more basic freedoms of movement and of choice, necessary premises for such a desire. Italo Calvino, one of Italy's most illustrious twentieth-century writers, said that the only thing the so-called neo-realists really shared which might justify grouping them into a movement was the need to tell the stories of suffering and injustice stifled by the Fascist regime for twenty years.[26] Perhaps something similar can be said of the women writing in these years. If male writers in this period were experimenting with form and language, women were only just beginning to give voice to their own experience. Tales of symbolic castles and impersonal, invisible bureaucracies might convey the sense of male disorientation and powerlessness in an increasingly impersonal world, but only realistically depicted interiors could represent the anguish of physical enclosure that was still so much a part of women's lives. Recourse to the much maligned confessional register was one of the ways in which they achieved their aims. And yet, paradoxically, precisely because they sensed how alien male representations of the feminine often were to their own reality as women, they could sometimes share a very modern and precocious awareness that literary language and structures are not mimetic and transparent. While Verga and Capuana were still worrying about 'impersonality', their contemporaries Matilde Serao and Marchesa Colombi were using metafiction, parody, pastiche and expressionism to record their own distancing 'voice-overs' for the naturalist scenarios they had inherited.

NOTES

1. Italo Svevo, *Una vita* (Milan, 1964). p. 110.

2. See Bruno Wanrooij, *Storia del pudore. La questione sessuale in Italia 1860–1940* (Venice, 1990).

3. See Antonia Arslan, 'Ideologia e autorappresentazione: Donne intellettuali fra Ottocento e Novecento', in Annamaria Buttafuoco and Marina Zancan (eds.), *Svelamento. Sibilla Aleramo: una biografia intellettuale* (Milan, 1988), pp. 164–77, and Lucienne Kroha, *The Woman Writer in Late-nineteenth Century Italy. Gender and the Formation of Literary Identity* (Lewiston, Queenston and Lampeter, 1992).

4. See Nancy A. Harrowitz, *Antisemitism, Misogyny and the Logic of Cultural Difference: Cesare Lombroso and Matilde Serao* (Lincoln, NE and London, 1994).

5. See Lucienne Kroha, 'Scrittori, scrittrici e industria culturale: *Suo marito* di Luigi Pirandello', *Otto/Novecento* 5 (1995), pp. 167–82.

6. Neera, *Senio* (Milan: Galli, 1892), pp. 48, 50–2.

7. Luigi Capuana, 'Letteratura femminile', in *Luigi Capuana*, ed. G. Finocchiaro Chimirri (Catania, 1988), p. 19.

8. Patrizia Zambon, 'Leggere per scrivere: la formazione autodidattica delle scrittrici tra Otto e Novecento: Neera, Ada Negri, Grazia Deledda, Sibilla Aleramo', *Letteratura e stampa nel secondo Ottocento* (Alessandria, 1993), pp. 125–54.

9. Benedetto Croce, *Storia d'Italia dal 1871 al 1915* (Bari, 1927), 10th edn (Bari, 1953), p. 89. On Croce and the 'woman question' in general see Franco Contorbia, 'Croce e lo spazio del femminile', in Emmanuelle Genevois (ed.), *Les femmes-écrivains en Italie (1870–1920): ordres et libertés* (Paris, 1994), pp. 15–31.

10. See Judith Jeffrey Howard, 'Patriot Mothers in the Post-Risorgimento: Women after the Italian Revolution', in C. R. Berkin and C. M. Lovett (eds.), *Women, War and Revolution* (New York, 1980), pp. 237–58.

11. See Gigliola De Donato, 'Donna e società nella cultura moderata del primo Ottocento', in Gigliola De Donato et al. (eds.), *La parabola della donna nella letteratura italiana dell'Ottocento* (Bari, 1983), pp. 11–86. On the duties of women, pp. 53–63.

12. See F. Pieroni Bortolotti, *Alle origini del movimento femminile in Italia, 1848–1892* (Turin, 1986).

13. See Anna Nozzoli, '*La Voce* e le donne', in Emmanuelle Genevois (ed.), *Les femmes-écrivains en Italie*, pp. 207–22.

14. See Antonia Arslan, 'Luigi Capuana e Neera: corrispondenza inedita 1881–1885', *Miscellanea di studi in onore di Vittore Branca* (Florence, 1983), vol. V, pp. 161–85.

15. Benedetto Croce (ed.), *Neera* (Milan, 1942). See also Antonia Arslan and Anna Folli, *Il concetto che ne informa. Benedetto Croce e Neera. Corrispondenza, 1903–1917* (Naples, 1989).

16. Neera, preface to *Addio!* (Milan, 1904), pp. vii ff.

17. Marchesa Colombi, *Un matrimonio in provincia* (Turin, 1973), p. 41.

18. See Marinella Camerino, '"Donne nell'ingranaggio": la narrativa di Bruno Sperani', in Emmanuelle Genevois (ed.), *Les femmes-écrivains en Italie*, pp. 75–89.

19. Matilde Serao, *Fantasia*; P. Pancrazi (ed.), *Serao* (Milan, 1946), p. 119.

20. Serao, *La virtù di Checchina*, serialised first in *Nuova Antologia* from 25 November to 16 December 1883, now in P. Pancrazi (ed.), *Serao*, vol. I, pp. 863–908. Also in Matilde Serao, *Il romanzo della fanciulla,* ed. Francesco Bruni (Naples, 1985), pp. 209–56.

21. Matilde Serao, Preface to *Il romanzo della fanciulla*, p. 3.

22. Sibilla Aleramo, *Una donna* (Milan, 1985), pp. 122, 135, 150.

23. For a sampling of reviews of the time see Sibilla Aleramo, *La donna e il femminismo*, ed. B. Conti (Rome, 1978), pp. 189–204.

24. Luigi Capuana, preface to *Casa di bambola* (Milan, 1894) as quoted in Laura Caretti, 'Capuana, Ibsen e la Duse', in M. Picone and E. Rossetti (eds.), *L'illusione della realtà: Studi su Luigi Capuana* (Rome, 1990), pp. 199–200.

25. Grazia Deledda, *Marianna Sirca, Opere scelte* (Milan, 1964), vol. II, p. 410.

26. Italo Calvino, Preface to *Il sentiero dei nidi di ragno* (Turin, 1964).

13

The popular novel, 1850–1920

In choosing to concentrate on *Carolina Invernizio (1851–1916), *Annie Vivanti (1868–1942) and *Liala (Amaliana Cambiasi Negretti Odescalchi, 1897–1995) as representatives of popular women novelists, I admit to basing myself partly on personal preferences and interests. Italian critics who tend to subdivide further the notion of 'popular' often do not put these three novelists into the same category. Carolina Invernizio may be seen as an exponent of the *romanzo d'appendice*[1] (more violent, dramatic and adventurous), Liala of the *romanzo rosa*[2] (more sentimental and directed towards a happy ending), whilst Annie Vivanti is considered a notch higher (belonging to an Italian literary canon which neglects Invernizio and Liala), although she too is seen as the creator of *romanzi popolari*. My choice is perhaps parallel to that of Eco's 'Tre donne intorno al cor . . .'[3] – Invernizio, Serao and Liala, with Serao being replaced by Vivanti who, to my mind, has more features in common with the other two.[4] But in either case we are looking at novels written by women, for women, about women ('Tre donne sulle donne per le donne', as Eco says at the opening of his essay).

The *feuilleton*, as the popular novel by instalments was called in France, was born around 1830,[5] shortly after its English model, whose most famous practitioner was Charles Dickens. In turn it preceded and provided inspiration for the Italian *romanzo d'appendice* (so called because it appeared as an 'appendix' or 'supplement' to daily newspapers) with its suspense, frequent twists, black and white characters and social content, as well as the elements which it inherited from various pre-existing traditions, like the Gothic novel of Walpole, Radcliffe and Monk Lewis, and the historical novel of Scott, Dumas, Grossi and Cantù. Eugène Sue, one of the most celebrated *feuilleton* writers, with his *Mystères de Paris* ('Mysteries of Paris', 1842–3), was to inspire countless other city 'mysteries', including Mastriani's I misteri di Napoli ('The mysteries of Naples', 1869) and Invernizio's trilogy Torino misteriosa ('Mysterious Turin', 1903–4).

The development of the novel, first in England and in France, and afterwards in Italy, coinciding with the establishment of the bourgeoisie, implied a readership which was primarily feminine, although to start with, for reasons of education and social convention, the writers were predominantly male. As the nineteenth century progressed, women were more commonly to be found as the authors, and the reading public expanded to include the working classes. In the 1906 enquiry into reading habits carried out by the Milanese bookseller Ermanno Bruciati, it was found that the more educated women read Fogazzaro, Serao, Marchesa Colombi, Neera, while the lower classes read above all Carolina Invernizio.[6]

'This unpretentious hen of popular literature', as Gramsci quite affectionately was to call Invernizio,[7] wrote over 100 novels, the majority of which came out in instalments in the Gazzetta di Torino and in L'opinione nazionale of Florence. Although Invernizio was Piedmontese, she spent her early life in Florence, where her father, a government employee, was transferred and where her husband, Marcello Quinterno, an officer of the bersaglieri, was first posted. True to the genre in which she was writing, the image of the city looms large in her novels, first Florence and then Turin. Firmly middle class herself, she situated her stories in settings full of contrasts, on the one hand in dark and dangerous alleys, the haunts of louche social dregs, including the characteristic 'barabba' (villain), and, on the other, within the glittering salons and theatres of the well-fed and elegantly dressed upper classes. In between were the respectable workplaces of humble artisans, often the ateliers of seamstresses. Invernizio was in fact concerned about the condition of women workers and in 1890 gave a lecture on Le operaie italiane (Italian women workers) to the Naples Società operaia, in which she denounced their subjection and exploitation and recognised their need for escapism: 'The woman of the people has a great yearning for the fantastic, the wonderful, the improbable.'[8]

Invernizio's portrayal of a wide social spectrum has the distinctive feature that no behaviour is confined to one class – both acts of selfless generosity and of vicious destruction can be committed equally by the aristocracy, the bourgeoisie or the workers. Some social conventions are, however, inescapable, such as the one which enforces the power of the upper-class male over the working-class girl: the victims of seduction and betrayal are generally the poor. This sometimes results in the victim becoming the aggressor and committing a crime which is followed by retribution. An example is in *Storia d'una sartina* ('Story of a little seamstress', 1892) where the seamstress, after being abandoned by her aristocratic seducer, secretly gives birth to a child whom she strangles and casts into the Arno; she eventually catches up with her seducer who, before being killed by her, writes a note absolving her and announcing his own suicide (remorse and punishment for past crime); the protagonist then drowns herself in the Arno (meting out her own retribution).

Massimo Romano, in his *Mitologia romantica e letteratura popolare*,[9] lists opposing pairs of structural functions which operate in Invernizio's novels. The first function creates the drama, the second resolves it: exchange of individual roles leads to agnition, or recognition, disguise to unmasking, abduction to discovery, betrayal to punishment or forgiveness, crime to punishment, courtship to conquest etc. The reader recognises these patterns, enjoys being one step ahead of the story and finds reassurance in the expected outcome. But there are a few examples of an alternative or dubious outcome, injecting an element of surprise. While *Storia d'una sartina* illustrates betrayal leading to punishment, in *Il bacio d'una morta* ('Kiss of a dead woman', 1886), the wife forgives the husband's transgressions with an exotic dancer.

Marina Federzoni's essay on Carolina Invernizio[10] contains a section on the presentation of character which makes a similar point about the reader's expectations: the initial description of a character who is making her/his appearance, Federzoni says, is like the dictionary entry for a word we do not know. Even proper names give us hints as to the personality. In *Il bacio d'una morta* for instance, the wronged wife is Clara, symbol of light, whilst the evil temptress is Nara, close to *nera*, black. There is a pattern to the initial descriptions: the rich and powerful are often presented from their own point of view, whereas the poor are spied on as they engage in their menial activities. The information also suggests whether a person is going to be a protagonist or a minor character, with a positive or negative role. One of the attributes which normally goes with positive characters is golden hair, whilst black hair is a mark of evil. Note the first vision of Clara when she is saved from the grave in *Il bacio d'una morta*: 'Now her forehead was revealed in all its purity, her dishevelled golden hair fell attractively on the pillow, casting a halo round the pale, suffering but beautiful, adorably beautiful face.'[11] But, as in the case of structural functions mentioned above, there can always be surprises, unexpected reversals.

One such exceptional case appears in *Storia d'una sartina*, where Amalia, the innocent bride of the faithless seducer is 'very pale, with black hair, beautiful eyes, tall, slim, supple'.[12] This can be compared to the Piedmontese original of *Storia*, that is *Ij delit d'na bela fia* ('The crimes of a beautiful young woman'), which first appeared in *'L Birichin* in weekly instalments between September 1889 and February 1890. Here the bride, Luisa, is 'as fair as an angel, blonde, with black eyes, tall, slim, adorable',[13] her golden hair representing her innocence. Apart from the different golden/black hair convention of the two novels, *Ij delit* (which was probably addressed not to a readership of dialect speakers who knew no Italian, but to a primarily middle-class public for whom the enjoyment of dialect literature was in addition to their normal diet of Italian), strikes one as having greater originality. The *Storia* was more explicit, more melodramatic, being aimed at a more popular readership which expected the conventions of the genre to be strictly followed. While I was working on a comparison between these two novels[14] I was struck by the different effects of the Italian and the Piedmontese, the way in which the language of the *Storia* seemed quite spontaneous until compared with that of *Ij delit*. The juxtaposition made the Italian appear inconsistent, with elements of surprising formality, whereas the Piedmontese had a greater evenness of style, more appropriate to the content. It was this bilingual interest that led me initially to my second author, Annie Vivanti.

Annie Vivanti had a German mother and an Italian father (a 'garibaldino' in exile in England). She spoke English and German before learning Italian. After travelling extensively in Europe she moved to Italy to study singing and acting but, following her marriage to the Irishman John Chartres, she settled with him for a while in America before returning permanently to Italy in 1902. This mixed linguistic background led to her writing novels in both English and Italian and, interestingly, as with Invernizio, some novels had versions in both languages; one was written first in English (*The Devourers*, 1910) and then in Italian (*I divoratori*, 1911) and another vice versa (*Circe*, 1912, English version with the title *Marie Tarnowska*, 1915). Apart from Carducci's constant support of her, other men of letters, too, felt there was a lot to admire in the writings of Vivanti. Benedetto Croce observed that her stories were not taken too seriously by the author, nor should they be by the reader – they ought to be a source of pleasure for both – 'a game of the imagination'.[15] Croce compares Vivanti to Bizet's Carmen, with her sudden violent but fleeting passions. This is picked up by Giuliana Morandini, who, in her volume *La voce che è in lei*,[16] anthologises a passage from Vivanti's first novel *Marion* (1891), presenting the world of the theatre and the contrasting lives of Marion and Anna, the one driven to vice, the other an innocent victim. As Morandini says in her introduction, extending Croce's musical image, the novel opens with a teasing, attractive rhythm, and ends on a note of tragic isolation, a presage of the life of Vivanti herself, who, after her light-hearted early days, was to be persecuted by the racial laws and to lose her family in a bombing raid during the Second World War.

The beginning that promises well but turns to disaster is the subject of a novel written in English, set in both America and Europe, *The Hunt for Happiness* (1896). It has the epigraph *cui bono?* (in whose interest?) and contains a preface which gives an idea of the philosophy which was also to mould many of Vivanti's later books:

> I might have made the story prettier, and finished them all off happily; landed the young ones in a haven of matrimony, the pathetic ones in the grave, and sent the bad ones out, reformed to begin new lives . . . I might have written a story with a moral to it, that would have been improving. But, again, what is the good of improving?[17]

After some years of silence in which Vivanti devoted herself to the upbringing of her daughter, Vivien, who was to become a gifted musician, she produced the novel *The Devourers*, already mentioned, with its Italian version. It was dedicated 'To my wonder-child Vivien to read when she has wonder-children of her own.' It was inspired by her considerations on motherhood, transformed into a stylised and dramatic tale of three generations in which gifted and precocious daughters (publishing a first book of poetry at fifteen, or giving a first concert at nine), 'devour' their mothers, whose whole lives are taken over by their demanding offspring (and, it should be added, they devour anyone else who is involved in their upbringing). The theme of motherhood has rightly been picked out as one of the most characteristic in Vivanti (among others by Anna Nozzoli, who considers this novel 'a monument to motherhood').[18] There is, however, ambiguity in the attitude which emerges: it is true that the mothers are willing victims but not without regrets that their own lives are being eclipsed.

In *Circe*, it is motherhood that leads to the ultimate crime. This novel, based on a real-life scandal of the time, is recounted to the narrator (who is in fact Vivanti herself) as a dream of the protagonist who is confined to a prison in Puglia after having arranged for one of her lovers to murder another. Maria can no longer distinguish reality from dream and is convinced that all her past is part of a dream. In her tormented mind she sees her lover Kamnorovsky as an obstacle to the recovery from scarlet fever of her young son Tioka, and it is to save Tioka that she plots the murder.[19] Opposed to the D'Annunzian destructive sorceress (who in *Circe*, however, is an example of corrupted innocence) is the woman whose virtue is violated by an unscrupulous male. This is a figure who appears in a novel that takes up again the theme of motherhood: *Vae victis!* ('Woe to the vanquished!', 1917), inspired by Vivanti's play *L'invasore* ('The invader', 1915), and later reprinted with the Italian title *Guai ai vinti* ('Woe to the vanquished!', 1926). The action is set in the war and revolves round the rape by German soldiers of Chérie and her sister-in-law Luisa (whose small daughter Mireille is struck dumb by the trauma of witnessing the rape). They escape as refugees from Belgium to England. When the pregnancy of the two women becomes a certainty they react in different ways. Luisa rebels and asks for an abortion; she asserts her autonomy as a woman, and, with the understanding of the doctor and the priest 'free, redeemed, renewed, she walked with winged step back into life, and found that happiness and youth still blossomed for her'.[20] Instead Chérie opts for maternity. She loses forever her husband back from the war but the birth of her child has the effect of a miracle on Mireille, who regains the power of speech. So the value of motherhood is vindicated in this novel too, but the more original element is the respect for Luisa's autonomy, which brings her dignity and independence.[21]

One of the features which seem to me to prevent Vivanti from being considered a 'popular' novelist *par excellence* is that, in spite of the characters and plots which belong to the genre, the endings are often open, leaving the reader with an element of uncertainty, which is contrary to the tradition of this type of fiction. Andrea Molesini Spada, in his chapter on Vivanti's *Naja Tripudians* (1920) in *Dame, droga e galline*, discusses the open ending in this novel, wondering whether it was 'through inexperience, or through an instinct for inconclusiveness'[22] that Vivanti seemed both to suggest and to refrain from an unconventional ending, the corruption of Leslie's virtue, which would have gone against the ethos of the whole story. This seems not to take sufficient account of Vivanti's own statements in the novel. In the introduction she claims that she did not imagine the story, it was reality that conceived it and created it, and to anyone who asked her about the ending she would reply that life ends not only with death, for the story of Leslie ends where it does and 'the rest is silence'.[23] I would see the end as an element which distances Vivanti from conventions, perhaps what Fabio Finotti is referring to in the same volume, *Dame, droga e galline,* when he suggests that Vivanti is pointing towards a new form of novel, one in which situation is becoming more important than plot. He points out, as had Molesini Spada, that *Naja Tripudians* ends just where one would expect a *romanzo d'appendice* to begin.[24]

In fact *Naja Tripudians* has an unusual structure: the first half of the novel is very positive, almost idyllic, with the life, in a village near Leeds, of two small girls with their elderly father who specialises in tropical medicine. There is a flashback to his youth in the tropics which brings in a character, Jean Vital, who never reappears (again contrary to the conventions of the genre). When the girls start reading novels, like *Jane Eyre,* they are surprised at how much can happen in fiction, and comment that their own life is so empty that no one would dream of writing about it. There is another pointer to the opposite when an acquaintance comments on the snake of the title (*Naja Tripudians* being the name of the Indian cobra) as reflecting the moral evil of the time. The second half of the book in fact moves from innocence to corruption. In the London house of Lady Miranda Randolph Gray, the two trusting sisters are witnesses to a vice-ridden society, which tries to suck them under. Vivanti succeeds in building up tension between the sisters and the household which adds zest to the narrative, with figures like the bisexual Dafne Howard and the morphine-addicted cat. The elder sister, Myosotis, escapes and asks a policeman to help her save Leslie, who has been doped. She is however unable to retrace her steps and we are left with the question, which has troubled critics, as to whether Leslie would ever be found again.

As we have seen, Annie Vivanti enjoyed the esteem of established men of letters. On the other hand, Carolina Invernizio and Liala had huge sales but little respect from critics. Invernizio stated 'I take a merry revenge on critics. For my faithful readers and friends are their wives and sisters.'[25] Liala, although she had the goodwill of D'Annunzio (who is reputed to have invented her pen-name with the element 'ala' reflecting her interest in aviation), commented 'Critics bite me',[26] adding that everyone nevertheless read her books, from manual workers to women with degrees. In her autobiographical essays *Diario vagabondo* ('Wandering diary', 1977), she states: 'I do not need critics to talk about me: my readership speaks well of me, and it is to my readership that I am accountable.'[27] Her first novel, *Signorsì* ('Yes, sir', 1931)[28] is reputed to have sold one and a half million copies, and by popular demand she was forced to write a sequel to *Dormire non sognare* ('To sleep but not to dream', 1944) in spite of the awkward detail that she had made her heroine die at the end of that novel.[29] Liala's career spanned over half a century. She began writing after the death of her great love, a pilot she hoped to marry after obtaining a divorce abroad from her husband, by whom she already had one child, Serenella. After the pilot's death she returned to her husband and they later had another daughter, Primavera. This is worth recounting because it is tempting to see her own personal experiences, so different from the strict moral code which ruled Invernizio's married life, as influencing the message conveyed by her fiction: life is not made up of black and white, good and evil; each person acts according to temperament and circumstances and must be understood rather than judged.

In the decades in which Liala was writing, from the 1930s to the 1980s, her novels reflected many historical events and the changes that were taking place in Italian society. In *Brigata di ali* ('Brigade of wings', 1947), there is, as background to the romance between Sisinnia and the pilot Roberto Sarti, the Spanish Civil War in which Sarti takes part, naturally on the Fascist side. In *Sotto le stelle* ('Beneath the stars', pre-1943) Italy is about to declare war: 'The French are being battered, the English are fleeing. Strange war, to be sure. There's only one nation really fighting – the Germans,'[30] says one of the characters, Sini, to which the protagonist, Villagrazia, replies: 'There will soon be two fighting' (p. 112). In *Vecchio smoking* ('Old dinner jacket', 1952), the Italian protagonist has been forced by family circumstances to marry a Spanish heiress who insists on returning to Spain and even makes him lose his Italian nationality. When Italy joins the war he is distraught at not being able to fight. He confides to his small son, 'I won't even get a scratch, as I cannot carry out my duty.'[31] When Italy is defeated he grieves for the beautiful buildings and streets which have been destroyed – streets down which 'people of all races and colours' are now walking (p. 164). It is however noteworthy that references to political events are generally vague and superficial, and even when Liala's novels are set in lands other than Italy, the emphasis is never on the alien or the exotic but rather on human relationships, which she presents as universal.

The world of the 1970s makes its appearance in *Good-bye sirena* (1975). Vico's mother has run off with the ski-instructor, leaving him to be brought up by his father, the owner of a steel works. Vico's series of lovers include a schoolgirl, a married woman and finally the English Margaret who is instead smitten with a gentleman called Everest, at which point Vico says 'Good-bye sirena', and turns to the priesthood. Inserted in the novel are references to the Communists and the Christian Democrats, to strikes in factories and schools, to girls on the pill, sex without contraception, Mao's little red book, tights, bras and miniskirts – a far cry from the elegant society and the impeccable dress codes of Liala's 1930s.

The class structure of Liala's novels is modified with the passing of time as can be seen from this last example, but certain patterns are retained. The men, for instance, continue to be categorised according to social condition, whereas the women are not so confined, because they are more socially mobile, and all that is required is good breeding.[32] We have an example of this in *Una carezza e le strade del mondo* ('A caress and the roads of the world', 1957), where the little fairground attendant finds herself in the position of being able to choose between marriage to a rich elderly business man or to a young writer.

One of the most common criticisms levelled at Liala is that her women are subjugated and inferior. It is true that their ultimate aim is marriage and family (which, it should be noted, is likewise the aim of the men), but her women can also be rebellious and independent, and take their fate into their own hands. In *Signorsì* it is the wife Renata who is shown as more adult and more independent, indulging in none of her husband Furio's childish jealousies or unreasonable demands. When she feels she is being treated as a sexual object, she bursts out:

> What am I? A pretty little thing to be taken when desire torments you, to be insulted when desire is silent. That's my life, Furio, kisses and blows. When you don't fling me on the bed, you crush me on the ground with hands that torture me . . . I am not an animal, I am a woman! I have a soul, I have my pride, I have a heart.[33]

In *Bisbigli del piccolo mondo* ('Whispers of the small world', 1951), two young Italo-American girls with their mother take up residence in Italy in a villa they have inherited. The family is penniless and it is up to the young women to restore their fortunes – naturally, as befits the *rosa* genre, through romance rather than work. But the romance is unconventional in that the initiative and the power of choice are in the hands of the two sisters. At first Chantal has her eye on a rich cheese manufacturer. «Marry me, my giant cheese»,[34] she wills him. (In many of Liala's novels there is this original, shorthand way of expressing thoughts, by putting them in guillemets instead of using the inverted commas or dashes which contain dialogue.) After many near misses in marriage Chantal settles for the one person to whom she feels she belongs, the mechanic, Bruno (who conveniently finds their late great-aunt's pearls, worth a fortune). Apart from the extravaganzas, the novel is well rooted in the village gossip (as the title implies) of the Lombard lakes, the part of the world from which Liala came.

It is intriguing that in this novel, as in so many others, Liala's characters are very hygiene-conscious, always going off to wash their hands, to have baths, commenting that even in poverty one must have cleanliness. This emphasis may emerge in unexpected moments, as in *Signorsì*, when the adulterous relationship between Renata and Furio's best friend, Mino, is about to be consummated: 'His temples were beating as if they were about to burst, his eyes could no longer see, his nostrils were flaring, full of the scent of this beautiful woman, clean, healthy, young, exquisitely perfumed' (p. 317). Liala was proud of her educative role: 'With my novels I've taught good manners, respect for others. I've taught people how to behave at table. And Liala got there before deodorants. There are tons of soap in my books, and many of my readers have learnt that it is important to wash.'[35] This fits into the widely accepted view that women's popular fiction served as conduct literature for its readership.

For both Carolina Invernizio and Annie Vivanti, plot is of primary importance. Their novels exhibit a complex structure with frequent skilful use of flashbacks, surprising the reader with extraordinary opening situations which are then justified with the presentation of the events leading up to them. Liala, on the other hand, favours consecutive narrative. For her, plot is not so relevant, it is the relationships that count, and very often the protagonists' lives are uneventful, apart from their encounters, their separations and their emotions. Because of the way relationships are highlighted, Liala is concerned that the rationale behind them should be understood and she enables her readers to appreciate why attractions are felt, by presenting double focalisation – not only are the men seen through women's eyes, but the women are seen through male eyes and equal importance is given to the psychology of the two sexes.

Liala is mostly true to form in giving her readers the endings they expect, following the conventions of the popular novel, but in *Signorsì*, which has a freshness of touch perhaps coming from its autobiographical nature, it is Renata who, unable to tolerate the strain of two relationships, decides to end her own life by flying so dangerously that she crashes. The reader senses she is at the end of her tether, but does not predict her suicide. Another, even more autobiographical novel written earlier (1926), but not published until the end of Liala's life, is *Ombre di fiori sul mio cammino* ('Shadows of flowers in my path', 1981), a title recalling Proust's *A l'ombre des jeunes filles en fleurs*. This too has a spontaneity about it which is reflected in its style and structure. After the protagonist Liana has married, unenthusiastically, and has had a daughter, she meets the pilot who will be the passion of her life. The novel, which had been in the third person until the meeting, suddenly switches to the first ('It is Liana Egret's heart. It is my heart'),[36] so that the ensuing relationship is focalised through Vita (Liana's new name) as she observes Amore.

The features which stand out in these three novelists are, as we have seen, very varied. If I had to pick out the most striking, I would say it was creative fantasy, sometimes unbridled, sometimes extravagant, but always gripping. All three surprise one with the multiplicity of the story lines which allow them to write innumerable novels which do not repeat themselves in spite of recurring patterns. As each writer had her faithful readers, there had to be a sense of recognition in the novels, which was provided by the type of dramatic situations, culminating in a largely expected outcome – closed in Invernizio and Liala, more open in Vivanti. There was enough sense of adventure (in the case of Liala sometimes only emotional adventure), to take readers out of their normal world but equally there was the 'consolatory' element which reassured them that a certain ethos was being respected or, in the case of Vivanti, that the author shared with them an ambivalent approach to situations and outcome. Above all, the centrality of the women characters, whether as protagonists themselves, or in the lives of the male protagonists, whether they took command of their own destiny or whether they achieved their goals through patience and good judgement, allowed the mainly female readers to project themselves into lives which appeared more successful than their own. Thus the 'popular novel' can be considered popular in two senses: because of its success, and because of its intended readership – it was *for* the people, but in its origins and ideologies it was not *of* the people.

Good general discussions of recent popular novels by women are offered by Antonia Arslan and Maria Pia Pozzato and by Eugenia Roccella. The latter highlights the importance of Liala for the very definition of the genre: according to her, she embodies the 'classical rosa', which differs from the 'popular rosa' represented by Luciana Peverelli (1902–1984), and from the 'new rosa' represented by Brunella Gasperini (1919–1979). Since the Seventies further aspects seem to have emerged (Roccella defines them as 'post-rosa'), with bestselling authors such as Maria Venturi

(1936–), editor of *Novella 2000* and then of *Annabella* (which she changed into *Anna*); Sveva Casati Modignani, a pseudonym used by a journalist husband-and-wife team, Bice Cairati (1938–) and Nullo Cantaroni (1928–); Susanna Tamaro (1957–), whose *Va' dove ti porta il cuore* is not easily classified within the borders of our genre. Now the genre as such seems to have been taken over by American series (*Harmony, Harlequin*) which have reduced even more the space allowed to narrative structure, construction of plot, quality of writing, in favour of a serial, industrial product, leaving little scope for the individuality of different authors.

NOTES

1. See for instance Angela Bianchini, *Il romanzo d'appendice* (Turin, 1969); Giuseppe Zaccaria, ed., *Il romanzo d'appendice* (Turin, 1977); Antonia Arslan, ed., *Dame, droga e galline. Romanzo popolare e romanzo di consumo tra Ottocento e Novecento,* second edition revised by Pier Luigi Renai (Milan, 1986), originally (Padua, 1977).

2. See Maria Pia Pozzato, *Il romanzo rosa,* Espresso Strumenti 16 (Milan, 1982); Antonia Arslan and Maria Pia Pozzato, *Il rosa,* in Alberto Asor Rosa, ed., *Letteratura italiana. Storia e geografia,* vol. III, *L'età contemporanea* (Turin, 1989), pp. 1026–43 (Arslan's section, *Il rosa italiano,* published also in Antonia Arslan, *Dame, galline e regine. La scrittura femminile italiana fra '800 e '900* (Milan, 1998), pp. 29–42; Eugenia Roccella, *La letteratura rosa* (Rome, 1998).

3. Umberto Eco et al., *Carolina Invernizio, Matilde Serao, Liala,* Il Castoro 145 (Florence, 1979). Eco's 'Tre donne intorno al cor . . .' is the introductory chapter, pp. 5–27. Eco's title is taken from the first line of a *canzone* by Dante.

4. This is closer to the line taken by Roccella's *La letteratura rosa,* which sees Invernizio and Vivanti as two predecessors of Liala.

5. See the introduction to Bianchini, *Il romanzo.*

6. See Michela De Giorgio, *Le italiane dall'Unità ad oggi* (Rome–Bari, 1992), p. 42.

7. Antonio Gramsci, *Quaderni del carcere,* I (Turin, 1975), p. 344: 'questa onesta gallina della letteratura'. On Invernizio see Andrea Cantelmo, *Carolina Invernizio e il romanzo d'appendice. L'ininterrotto successo della celebre scrittrice popolare* (Florence, 1992); Guido Davico Bonino and Giovanna Ioli, eds., *Carolina Invernizio. Il romanzo d'appendice,* Proceedings of the Conference 'Homage to Carolina Invernizio', Cuneo, 25–6 February 1983 (Turin, 1983). In this volume the article by Luciano Tamburini, p. 19, corrects the date of birth of Invernizio (usually given as 1858 or 1860), on the basis of her birth certificate, to 18 March 1851.

8. Carolina Invernizio, *Nero per Signora,* contains this speech as an appendix. The quotation comes from p. 271.

9. Massimo Romano, *Mitologia romantica e letteratura popolare. Struttura e sociologia nel romanzo d'appendice* (Ravenna, 1977), pp. 118–22.

10. In Eco et al., *Carolina Invernizio,* pp. 34–40.

11. Carolina Invernizio, *Romanzi del peccato, della perdizione e del delitto,* p. 44. For studies on *Il bacio d'una morta* see the essays by Piero Sola, Patrizia Zambon and Serenella Baggio in Arslan, ed., *Dame, droga e galline.*

12. *Storia d'una sartina,* p. 93.

13. *Ij delit d'na bela fia* (Turin, 1976), p. 73.

14. Anna Laura Lepschy, 'Carolina Invernizio's *Ij delit d'na bela fia* and *Storia d'una sartina*', *Italian Studies* 34 (1979), 93–104; also in Italian, in Anna Laura Lepschy, *Narrativa e teatro fra due secoli. Verga, Invernizio, Svevo, Pirandello* (Florence, 1984), pp. 55–75.

15. Benedetto Croce, *La letteratura della nuova Italia,* vol. VI (Bari, 1950), p. 301.

16. Giuliana Morandini, *La voce che è in lei. Antologia della narrativa femminile italiana tra '800 e '900* (Milan, 1980), pp. 308–19.

17. *The Hunt for Happpiness*, p. v.

18. Anna Nozzoli, *Tabù e coscienza. La condizione femminile nella letteratura italiana del Novecento* (Florence, 1978), p. 12.

19. See Gianni Venturi, 'Serpente e dismisura: la narrativa di Annie Vivanti da *Circe* a *Naja Tripudians*', in Emmanuelle Genevois, ed., *Les femmes écrivains en Italie (1870–1920): ordres et libertés* (Paris, 1994), pp. 292–309.

20. *Vae victis!* (Milan, 1917), pp. 241–2. See Nozzoli, *Tabù e coscienza*, pp. 11–17.

21. See Roccella, *La letteratura rosa*, pp. 26–7.

22. Andrea Molesini Spada, 'Idillio e tragedia: verifica di uno schema', in Arslan, ed., *Dame, droga e galline*, p. 242.

23. *Hamlet*, Act 5, scene 2.

24. Fabio Finotti, '*Naja Tripudians*: strutture e committenza del romanzo di consumo Novecentesco', in Arslan, ed., *Dame, droga e galline*, pp. 257–67.

25. Riccardo Reim's introduction to *Nero per signora*, p. xxxviii.

26. *Tuttolibri,* 6 November 1976, quoted in Eco et al., *Carolina Invernizio*, p. 97.

27. *Diario vagabondo* (Milan, 1977), p. 305.

28. There are problems with the dating of Liala's novels since Sonzogno's archives were destroyed during the war. I am accepting the dating proposed in Eco et al., *Carolina Invernizio*, pp. 119–21.

29. For these details see Isabella Bossi Fedrigotti, *Corriere della Sera,* 29 March 1997, p. 33.

30. *Sotto le stelle* (Milan, 1975), p. 112.

31. *Vecchio smoking*, p. 147.

32. See Maria Pia Pozzato, 'Liala', in Eco et al., *Carolina Invernizio*, p. 100.

33. *Signorsì* (Milan, 1978), pp. 252–3.

34. *Bisbigli del piccolo mondo* (Milan, 1992), p. 67.

35. Pozzato, 'Liala', in Eco et al., *Carolina Invernizio*, p. 97.

36. *Ombre di fiori sul mio cammino* (Milan, 1997), p. 275.

37. Arslan and Pozzato, *Il rosa*; Roccella, *La letteratura rosa*.

14

Futurism and Fascism, 1914–1945

The success of women writers after the Risorgimento generated a backlash in the early twentieth century among male critics and writers, some of whom maintained defensively that 'il pericolo roseo' (the 'pink threat') was in reality not a threat at all, for women could only be inferior writers, or imitators. This gendered ideology of the political and cultural leaders of the new Italy was adopted and adapted by Fascist ideologues, who through the darkest years of the regime tried to argue – even as social and cultural modernisation inevitably altered gender roles and women writers became more than ever public figures of great resonance and appeal – that women were essentially made to be wives and mothers, and that their only natural and politically desirable place was in the home, over whose economy it was their patriotic duty to preside in an orderly and parsimonious fashion.[1]

Benedetto Croce, one of the most consistent commentators on literature written by women, as well as the most influential critic of the first half of the twentieth century, occasionally paid women writers patronising, back-handed compliments, but on the whole had a biased vision of their work. In an essay on the politically and socially *engagée* poet and prose writer *Ada Negri, he asserted that 'lack or imperfection' in artistic work is most particularly a 'feminine flaw' ('difetto femminile'). It is precisely woman's maternal instinct, her 'stupendous and all-consuming' ability to mother a child that prevents her from successfully giving birth to a fully realised literary work. Croce's essay appeared originally in 1906, and was reprinted several times without any changes over the following decades in the monumental *Letteratura della nuova Italia*. Otherwise profoundly anti-Fascist, Croce nonetheless had a view of women intellectuals closely resembling that of the Fascist philosopher Giovanni Gentile and other even more reactionary

Fascist thinkers. In his 1938 treatise on the family, the Fascist sociologist Ferdinando Loffredo, for example, expressed thoughts about women intellectuals that substantially coincide with Croce's.[2] Spokesmen of the regime's cultural politics perpetuated the notion of the superiority of the male creative genius, attributing to women the subsidiary if exalted function of anonymous and obscure mother, sister and bride.[3] In Croce's view, women are unable to render their experiences and feelings universal; their writing tends to remain circumscribed, excessively personal and 'impure', especially when dealing with erotic passion. Croce's *La letteratura della nuova Italia* was republished several times in expanded editions up until the 1950s, and contributed perhaps more than any other single critical text to disseminate in the literary establishment this notion of women's writing, excluding women from the literary canon or relegating them to a marginal position.

At the beginning of the century, Croce typified a new wave of misogyny that resonated particularly in the circle of 'cutting edge' writers and thinkers who gravitated around the journal *La Voce* (1908–16) and who became some of the most influential voices of the following few decades. Giuseppe Prezzolini, Giovanni Papini, Giovanni Amendola, Ardengo Soffici and Giuseppe De Robertis were among them. In 1911, the critic Emilio Cecchi – later the founder of the journal *La Ronda* (1919–25) and among the principal exponents of *prosa d'arte*, the lyrical prose-fragment which to this day is enshrined in the canon of modern Italian as among the most authentic literary achievements of the interwar years – published an essay in *La Voce* entitled 'La donna che si spoglia' ('Women who take their clothes off') that eloquently summarises what both *Vociani* and *Rondisti* thought of women writers. Cecchi compared women's confessional and autobiographical writing to an obscene strip-tease, because women in his view have no interiority and no spiritual depth worth expressing in art. His spiteful reviews of *Sibilla Aleramo's works in the twenties and thirties implicitly reiterated this position. *Solaria* (1926–36), the leading modernist literary magazine that included Montale, Vittorini and Gadda among its collaborators, cultivated a similarly condescending attitude towards women's writing. Women's novels and life-writing (autobiographical fiction, memoirs, diaries and personal reminiscences) were generally associated either with populism and an inferior type of mass culture, or else faulted as impure and formally unrefined. Gadda, for example, in his 1931 review of *Paola Masino's novel *Monte Ignoso* ('Mount Ignoso') attacked the author's 'undisciplined' style, her wave-like mixing of the real with the symbolic and the fantastic, and her way of conveying the flow of sensory perceptions with no sense of a 'deeper understanding', a more authentic dimension. What Gadda perceived as formal 'flaws' are ironically the very elements that make this experimental novel by Masino one of the most interesting modernist texts of the period.

A restricted view of what constituted an authentically modern or modernist literature contributed to the marginalisation of women in the interwar period. The storytelling, well-plotted novel came under suspicion, and the notion developed that the 'successful' novel was inevitably ideologically tainted, an ally of Fascist populism, or a mere consumer product, usually for women. The post-World-War-II literary canon sealed this marginalisation by enshrining the 'pure art' of the prose fragment and the *prosa d'arte* favoured mostly by men authors, as well as the poetry of the inward-looking hermeticist masters, as the only authentic literature produced in the interwar period, to the detriment of other genres and literary modes.[4] *Gianna Manzini, who was close to the *Solaria* circle, and published the lyrical, anti-narrative novel *Tempo innamorato* ('Enamoured time') in 1928 and the prose poems of *Rive Remote* ('Distant shores') in 1940, is the only woman whose name sometimes appears in literary histories of the period, although she is better known for her post-war work. Yet women between the wars explored the creative possibilities of life-writing as well as different kinds of new realism and experimental narrative styles; the literary landscape was therefore much less unified and male-dominated than it would appear from literary histories, where women's names are hardly mentioned.

Despite antagonism and neglect, women in Italy in the interwar period nevertheless continued to write in ever-larger numbers, and in some cases received recognition from abroad. When *Grazia Deledda was awarded the Nobel Prize for Literature in 1926, the reaction in the Italian literary establishment was one of stunned surprise.[5] Deledda nonetheless continued to be labelled a 'regionalist' writer and a belated off-shoot of male-dominated *verismo* and *decadentismo*. Like most categories used to account for literary works by women, the description is symptomatic of literary criticism's failure to account for the multiplicity and diversity of the modernist mutations of realism in the twentieth century.[6]

Women writers themselves often felt that there was something illegitimate about their writing, as if it constituted the invasion of a masculine terrain and a betrayal of femininity for which they had constantly to apologise. *Matilde Serao and Sibilla Aleramo both expressed feelings of this kind. Serao separated from her husband (the writer Edoardo Scarfoglio) in 1904, but ran her own successful newspaper (*Il Giorno*) until her death in 1927 and wrote several novels. Her last one, *Mors tua* ('Your death') published in 1926, was a deeply felt meditation on the Great War from the contrasting points of view of the soldiers at the front, and the women who stayed behind. Serao regarded herself as an exceptional being, a kind of man in women's clothes, while she repeatedly affirmed that woman's proper place, where she could best perform her natural role and fulfil her mission as wife and mother, was in the home. After the international success in 1906 of *Una donna* ('A Woman'), a bestseller that sold tens of thousands of copies even in the interwar years, Aleramo became a professional writer. She painstakingly constructed her own original kind of life-writing, producing a series of autobiographically-based narrative texts in the interwar years. These included *Il passaggio* ('The passage', 1919), *Amo, dunque sono* ('I love, therefore I am', 1927), *Gioie d'occasione* ('Occasional joys', 1930) and *Il frustino* ('The whip', 1932), as well as poetry, essays and drama. *Una donna* was reprinted in 1931 and 1938; *Amo, dunque sono* in 1933; *Il passaggio* in 1934. Yet she endlessly questioned her femininity and pathetically solicited the elusive approval of the male critical establishment, including Croce and Cecchi. Croce had written her a devastating letter in 1913, questioning the sincerity of *Una donna* and the motives that led her to leave her husband and child and to become a writer. He accused her of being sick and inauthentic, the victim of an uncontrolled sexual passion and moral lassitude.[7] The typology of the woman writer as sexually dissolute, which goes back to the Renaissance, was to have a long history under Fascism, with women writers and intellectuals, including Aleramo, routinely accused by right-wing Fascist critics of being deviant, promiscuous, masculinised and sterile.[8] Some women, for example Amalia Guglielminetti, ironised and capitalised on this kind of reputation, at the cost of being relegated, however unfairly, to the status of 'unserious' writers.

To both Serao and Aleramo, critical approval came with reservations and begrudgingly. Serao was a good narrator, critics would and still do often say, but she was sloppy, got lost in too many details and was eager to please the sentimental masses of women, an exponent of mass, inferior literature as opposed to (male) high culture. Whatever was good about Serao's writing, or other women's whose qualities could not be denied, was ascribed to their exceptional, man-like nature. In 1925, Ada Negri revealed that she 'always thought of a woman writer as a man condemned to live in a woman's body'.[9] Aleramo could hardly be accused of being a mass writer, for her seemingly spontaneous autobiographical texts after *Una donna* were well-wrought and writerly, filled with literary allusions. Some readers – Piero Gobetti for example – were able to discern what Aleramo was doing with language and autobiography in texts such as *Il passaggio*,[10] yet critics through the 1920s dismissed her as a minor D'Annunzian, decadent prose writer who unduly mixed life and erotic passion with literature. While she became an icon of the emancipated creative woman among female readers, the regime found it convenient to hail her as 'exceptional'. Aleramo is usually remembered only for *Una donna*, while the rest of her long writing career is hardly mentioned. Only in the 1980s did feminist critics begin to look at her work with different eyes, partly because her concerns with female experience, autobiography and eroticism anticipated some of the key themes of contemporary feminist thought.[11]

In opening her book *Parla una donna* ('A woman speaks') in 1916, in the midst of the Great War, Serao welcomed the radical change that in her eyes the war was causing among women writers, who were abandoning their ill-placed ambitions, she claimed, and returning to their naturally feminine mission as anonymous soldiers' wives, mothers, nurses and seamstresses. But as it turned out, Serao was wrong, for while Italian women (and women who happened to live in Italy, such as Mina Loy) did indeed display courage and strength in assisting the wounded and the veterans, they did not at all abandon their literary ambitions. On the contrary, established writers from before the war, like Serao herself, continued publishing with renewed energy. Grazia Deledda, *Clarice Tartufari, Ada Negri, *Paola Drigo, *Amalia Guglielminetti, *Annie Vivanti, *Maria Messina and Carola Prosperi were among them. Especially remarkable for their incisive realism and focus on the social problems of women were Tartufari's novel *La rete d'acciaio* ('The steel net', 1919) and Maria Messina's collection of short stories, *Le briciole del destino* ('The crumbs of destiny', 1918). Deledda published *L'incendio nell'uliveto* ('Fire in the olive grove', 1919) and *La madre* ('The mother', 1920), among the strongest novels of her career. Aleramo's *Andando e stando* ('Moving and staying'), a collection of short creative and critical prose texts that included her famous 'Apologia dello spirito femminile' ('Apology for the feminine spirit') – an impassioned call for women to construct their own feminine and feminist aesthetic – appeared in 1921.

The social and cultural turmoil caused by the war jump-started a new generation of young women who came of age during the conflict, many of them maturing their literary vocations precisely in response to the war. The Futurists were among the most ardent supporters of the war as a revolutionary and liberating outburst of energy, and many women found their iconoclasm refreshing. Despite its misogynist rhetoric, Futurism's radical rejection of the past (including the cultural stereotypes of the angel of the hearth and of the *femme fatale*, and the rituals and taboos of bourgeois sexuality) and its critique of marriage, family values and traditional morality, appealed to a group of emancipated young women who saw in Futurism a potentially liberating aesthetic and cultural avant-garde movement. Futurism, which saw in Croce a reactionary figure was also the first movement in Italy that did not discriminate between high and low, between literary culture and mass culture, thus erasing a distinction that had been used to contain and discriminate against women's works.

In the turbulent war and post-war years a substantial contingent of women Futurists emerged around *L'Italia Futurista* (1916–18), *Roma Futurista* (1918–20), and a few other avant-garde journals in Florence and Rome. These women enjoyed substantial critical success at the time and were highly visible within the Futurist ranks, but have been all but forgotten in literary histories, which still tend to identify the Italian Futurist avant-garde almost exclusively with male authors.[12]

The poet and prose writer *Maria Ginanni, married at the time to the Futurist painter, writer and film-maker Arnaldo Ginna, was the principal editor of *L'Italia Futurista*. Around her, a circle of young Futurist women writers and intellectuals gathered, including fiction writers, novelists, prose-poetry writers and free-word poets such as Irma Valeria, Fanny Dini, Eva Kühn Amendola (the wife of Giorgio Amendola, the anti-Fascist leader who died in 1926 in France after severe Fascist beatings), *Rosa Rosà (also a visual artist and illustrator) and *Enif Robert (also an actress). The Futurist actress Fulvia Giuliani – later a star of Bragaglia's 'Teatro degli Indipendenti' in Rome – wrote for *L'Italia Futurista*, as did the avant-garde playwright and poet Mina della Pergola, author of satirical and playful *sintesi teatrali* (synthetic theatre), whose action was concentrated within a few minutes. The Futurists Bruno Corra, Mario Carli and Primo Conti were also part of the journal's circle, where men and women worked together in an unprecedented communal atmosphere.

The often ludicrously exaggerated virilistic misogyny of Futurists like Volt and Marinetti was vigorously rebuked by women Futurists on the pages of *L'Italia Futurista* and *Roma Futurista*. The critique of Marinetti's wartime libertine manual *Come si seducono le donne* ('How to seduce women', 1917), a book that was symptomatic of some of the profoundest male paranoia with regard to women and sexuality generated by the war and the fear of gender inversion, gave women like Enif Robert, Rosa Rosà and Shara Marini the opportunity to articulate their views on women. For them, she was no longer a mere object of exchange, but a strong and independent being with her own identity and potential for greatness on an equal level with men. In a typical move, Marinetti proceeded to incorporate the women's critiques in subsequent editions of his book, and in an unprecedented opening to women in Italian culture, he continued throughout the 1920s and 1930s to encourage and welcome women Futurists – writers as well as artists and performers. His wife, *Benedetta (Benedetta Cappa Marinetti), whom he met in 1919 in the studio of the painter Giacomo Balla and married in 1923, went on to become a major Futurist writer and painter whose work, which she signed simply 'Benedetta,' has only recently begun to resurface and be studied by critics.[13]

A desire to experiment with language and genres along the lines inspired by Futurist iconoclasm and avant-garde modernist themes, and at the same time to give a distinctly feminine/feminist imprint to their texts, can be identified in the works of several women writers of the immediate post-war period. Rosa Rosà's feminist articles in *L'Italia Futurista* were followed by the short synthetic novel *Una donna con tre anime* ('A woman with three souls', 1918), the most interesting of Rosà's prose works. The very notion that a woman could not only have a soul (rather than be, simply, body – whether erotic or maternal), but indeed have multiple and reciprocally contradictory souls, defied the cultural assumptions about femininity still being promoted by Croce and the *Vociani*, among others. Rosà's novel, which experiments parodically with a series of different sylistic registers, tells of a series of strange behavioural and linguistic metamorphoses undergone by a young petit-bourgeois housewife, whose perceptions are radically transformed by the new perspectives disclosed by a Futuristic vision of the city and of the liberatory potential of technology and science. Rosà's interest in science, like that of her entire circle, intersected with a fascination for theosophy, the occult and the esoteric, as well as for metapsychic phenomena and the unconscious, and prefigured similar interests among the French surrealists. In dealing with the oneiric and extrasensorial, however, the Futurists tended to be whimsical and ironic, as can be seen for example in Arnaldo

Ginna's 1919 *Le locomotive con le calze* ('Locomotives wearing stockings'), wittily illustrated by Rosà's black and white drawings. Irma Valeria's article on 'Occultismo e arte nuova', ('Occultism and the new art', *L'Italia Futurista*, 1917) encapsulated the group's interest in a new poetic language capable of penetrating occult mysteries beyond the reach of traditional scientific discourse. Irma Valeria's 1917 book of poetic prose, *Morbidezze in agguato* ('Softness ready to spring') exemplifies the strange mix of parodic irony and theosophic concerns prevalent (although not universal) in the group. The title toyed ironically with the Futurist (and later Fascist) obsession with hardness and virility and abhorrence of 'softness' and effeminacy. The book has an almost dadaist tone, and its irreverent wit is often directed at the author herself.

Unlike the surrealists, the Futurists of *L'Italia Futurista* were not inspired by Freud, and they eschewed any positivistic vision of science, privileging instead a more imaginative, almost delirious approach to the unconscious. The poetic-narrative works by Maria Ginanni, dubbed a 'prodigious brain' by Marinetti and other prominent Futurists, represents the most interesting Futurist experiments in this vein. In *Montagne trasparenti* ('Transparent mountains', 1917) Ginanni created a language of abstract and surreal images to express previously uncoded sensations and unconscious mental associations, projecting them on to the world of external phenomena. In the less compressed but still fragmentary *Il poema dello spazio* ('Poem of space', 1919), on the other hand, Ginanni developed a new kind of analytical poetic language to probe the depths of her unconscious and explore in seeming slow-motion its elaborate links with sensory perceptions, as well as the dynamic interchange between the unconscious and the dilemmas posed to her conscious self by questions of philosophy and religion.

Questions of identity and gender were paramount to women Futurists in this period before the Fascist seizure of power in 1922, when Italy itself was undergoing an identity crisis following the trauma of the war, and revolutionary hopes and expectations were heightened by the violent, exciting rhetoric of socialists and (at the time) left-wing Fascists. Enif Robert's 1919 experimental and semi-autobiographical montage novel, *Un ventre di donna* ('A woman's belly') included a small number of letters from her lovers Marinetti and Eleonora Duse and, for the sake of publicity, was presented as co-written by Marinetti himself. The book foregrounds the question of female creative identity along with that of the political identity of Italy. Robert tells the story of her initiation into

Futurism as a tale of liberation from the oppressiveness of her patriarchal family and the bourgeois gender system, and compares her recovery from a painful hysterectomy for uterine cancer to the forthcoming healing of Italy itself after the war. Her ability to write about the body and the physical sensations caused by the operation, and her use of experimental language and free-word prose, make this one of the most interesting of all Futurist texts.

Robert's seemingly proto-Fascist enthusiasm for the war, together with several women Futurists' endorsement of the Fascist movement, led critics to erase them from post-World-War-II history. In hindsight, knowing the history of Fascism's totalitarian transformation and the horrors brought about by the regime, it is difficult to grasp the feelings of excitement during the interwar period, to say nothing of reasons why women Futurists such as Eva Kühn Amendola and Benedetta embraced Fascism in the 1920s, along with feminist intellectuals such as Teresa Labriola (daughter of the Marxist thinker Antonio Labriola and the first woman lawyer in Italy, as well as the first to hold a university chair) and *Margherita Sarfatti. Sarfatti, a Venetian Jew, a socialist, and a brilliant and influential critic, was Mussolini's closest adviser in matters of literature and art in the 1920s, and the author of the immensely successful *Dux* (1926) – a mythologising biography of Mussolini – as well as an allegorical Fascist propaganda novel, *Il palazzone* ('The great palace', 1929). Sarfatti championed the anti-Futurist *Novecento* movement in the arts (a kind of spectral realism that had its literary equivalent in Bontempelli's magic realism) and edited the influential journal *Gerarchia* '(Hierarchy').

The enthusiasm generated among intellectual women by early Fascism was due in part to its libertarian and even feminist agenda, which coincided in part with Futurism's own programme. Only with the great depression and the demographic campaign to boost the large family did Fascism revert increasingly to reactionary misogynistic and discriminatory policies. Contradictory, 'imperfect' and flexible enough to tolerate a wide spectrum of relatively emancipated social and cultural modes of behaviour and expression, Fascism still maintained a substantial consensus among women, including many Futurists, and, until 1943, contained opposition and resistance mostly within non-violent limits.[14] Teresa Labriola became the apostle of a 'Latin' Fascist feminism, idealistically calling for a new kind of 'virile but not masculine' woman for the New Italy. Even so, Fascist feminists Sarfatti and Labriola grew disenchanted with the regime and were increasingly isolated and ostracised in the 1930s.[15]

Benedetta's first novel, the autobiographical *Le forze umane* ('Human forces', 1924), an instant critical success, combines synthetic lyrical and impressionistic prose fragments in a proto-surrealist, painterly vein with philosophical dialogues about abstraction and sexuality, as well as extended narrative passages written in a compressed, cinematic style. The novel tells in fictionalised form the story of her family's ordeal during the war (Benedetta's father had a mental breakdown and died shortly after the war) and of Benedetta's own experience as a teacher of underprivileged children, while subtly tracing her coming of age and her increasingly self-confident sense of intellectual and sexual identity, which led her finally to become interested in Futurism. The protagonist's emancipated character is set subtly in contrast to that of her mother, a lovingly portrayed but austere woman entirely devoted to her patriotic husband and children and the care of the home. The character of the mother in Benedetta's novel corresponds uncannily to the model of the exemplary wife and mother eventually adopted by Fascist propaganda. Even in her Fascist years, Benedetta herself refused to be just that, and she tried to be both a Futurist woman and a good Fascist at the same time – but she was caught in a glaring contradiction. Benedetta's juggling of family, work and politics in the 1930s gave, as she herself wittily remarked, a new meaning to the term 'Futurist simultaneity'. She had three daughters with Marinetti, assisted him in his endless projects on behalf of Futurist and avant-garde art, and continued to be a very productive writer and artist as well as (eventually) a propagandist for the regime among women, calling for their patriotic cooperation and sacrifice in times of approaching war. None of her creative writings or paintings were works of propaganda, however; she continued to experiment with abstraction and surrealism, producing two astonishingly different and strong experimental novels, *Viaggio di Gararà* ('Gararà's voyage', 1931) and *Astra e il sottomarino* ('Astra and the submarine', 1935) while also working as a set designer for some of Marinetti's plays.

A number of the later women Futurists, like Benedetta herself, never stopped hoping that Fascism would eventually bring to women and to Italy the changes that it had promised in its revolutionary phase. In the 1930s and early 1940s, women like Marisa Mori (painter, stage designer and photographer), Barbara (pseudonym for Olga Biglieri, painter and aviator), Giannina Censi (dancer), Laura Serra and Dina Cucini (poets), and Maria Goretti (prose writer, critic and poet) attempted to integrate Fascism and Futurism through an art inspired by aviation and technology.

This flight-inspired art, practised by Benedetta herself in some of her paintings, expressed a contradictory consciousness, conveying a desire for a liberated feminine space and time quite 'other' than that which Fascism offered to women. Maria Goretti's 1941 book entitled *La donna e il futurismo* ('Women and Futurism'), an experimental montage work combining a critical overview of the history of Futurist women with autobiographical narrative and Goretti's own acrobatic, playful poetry, articulated a new vision (inspired by some of Benedetta's views) of female literary and artistic creativity as an expansion of woman's role as life-giver, mother and *generatrix*. The book was published during World War II, when women were being rallied to resume their roles as guardian angels of the family while the men were away fighting. It epitomises in many ways the kind of ideological and cultural negotiations with Fascism and the creative solutions to which women writers resorted in order to carve out a space for their writing.

Under Fascism more works by women were published than ever before, although post-war literary histories tend to ignore or dismiss this fact. Many major writers of the period, Aleramo included, shared the Futurists' interest in questions of identity and life-writing, and while less inclined towards montage and linguistic pyrotechnics their work nevertheless exhibits a good deal of formal experimentation. Ada Negri's autobiographical novel, *Stella mattutina* ('Morning star', 1912) was an immediate success and went through several subsequent editions over the following two decades. Negri's text was one of the most effective examples of the kind of life-writing in which women excelled in the interwar years. Written in the third person, it tells the story of Dinin, a young girl whose growth is traced through a series of concentrated, lyrically compressed episodes marking her ritual encounters with nature, puberty, love and death, and the discovery of her intellectual and literary vocation, which concludes the novel and signals the girl's entrance into adulthood and maturity. Unlike Benedetta's first novel, where the mother figure is antithetical to the protagonist, here it is the mother who, through her story-telling, inspires Dinin's own narrative vein. It is through the mother's voice that even violent and unbearable aspects of life and experience are subject to the ordering and finally pleasurable control of narrative shape, and contribute in turn to form the young girl's intelligence and sense of self. Negri opened the way for other life-stories in a similar mode. Clarice Tartufari's autobiographical *Il gomitolo d'oro* ('The golden skein') appeared in 1924, and Paola Drigo's *Fine d'anno* ('Year's end') in 1936. Like Negri's

Stella mattutina and Aleramo's *Il frustino*, Deledda's *Cosima* (published post-humously in 1937) tells an autobiographical story in the third person, reconstructing the author's girlhood in Sardinia and her initiation to liter-ary writing. The protagonist is cast as a veritable rebel, and the narrative belies the rural myths that Fascism painstakingly attempted to construct in that period.[16]

Women's experimentation with realism in the interwar years included blends of realism with archetypal symbolism, allegory, surrealism and expressionism. Women wrote novels and, especially, short stories and novellas. Although short fiction is considered often a minor and implicitly inferior mode in Italian literary histories, this is where some women truly excelled in the interwar period. Collections of short stories that deserve to be reread and re-evaluated include *Finestre alte* ('High windows', 1923) and *Sorelle* ('Sisters', 1929) by Ada Negri; the short narratives of *Maria Messina (whose work was compared by Leonardo Sciascia to that of Katherine Mansfield); *Angelici dolori* ('Angelic sorrows', 1937) by *Anna Maria Ortese; *Itinerario di Paolina* ('Paolina's itinerary', 1937) *Il coraggio delle donne* ('The courage of women', 1940) *Sette lune* ('Seven moons', 1941) and *Le monache cantano* ('The nuns sing', 1942) by *Anna Banti, still known mostly for her novel *Artemisia*; *L'anima degli altri* ('The soul of others', 1935) and *Concerto* ('Concerto', 1937) by *Alba De Céspedes; and the novellas 'Marianna' (1930) and 'Pamela o la bella estate' ('Pamela or the fine summer', 1935) by *Fausta Cialente. Many of these short narrative texts appeared originally in news-papers, literary journals and women's magazines, some of which – espe-cially the *Almanacco della donna italiana* – held progressive positions which encouraged women's literary work and countered the regime's policy of cultural autarchy.

Paradoxically, women authors benefited from the Fascist restrictions on the press. Many anti-Fascist and independent periodicals and newspapers survived under Fascism by avoiding explicit political issues and themes, turning instead to literature. More fiction by women than ever before was published in the cultural pages of Italian newspapers and periodicals. The authors were established writers from before the war, such as Deledda, Negri, Vivanti, Tartufari and Prosperi, as well as new ones including Banti, Masino, Manzini, Cialente, De Céspedes and Ortese. Although their styles differed substantially, the women who published short narrative and auto-biographical texts in newspapers tended to address issues that related to the contemporary reality of their readers, such as love, maternity, social class and ethnicity. They developed, moreover, communicative skills that made their literary prose clear, effective and gripping. These works had enormous resonance, especially among women readers, for they exposed violence against women, discrimination and the constraints of the patriarchal culture of which the regime constituted a modern mutation. Some were decidedly oppositional and anti-Fascist in their implications.[17] Yet, despite its anti-feminist policies and its attempts to intimidate women who, like Alba De Céspedes, had a 'rebellious and indomitable character' (De Céspedes was placed under arrest for six days in 1936), Fascism on the whole tolerated and sometimes found it convenient even to extol writers such as Ada Negri and Sibilla Aleramo. The censors did not prevent the publication of De Céspedes's short stories in the press until 1943, three days before Mussolini was ousted. De Céspedes's novel *Nessuno torna indietro* ('None turn back'), a text that implicitly took an adversarial position *vis-à-vis* the regime's image of women's roles and sexuality, was published in 1938 and became a bestseller.

Although after 1933 nothing could be published without prior authorisation, Fascist censorship tended (at least until the 1940s, when there was a considerable crackdown) to be rather haphazard as well as literal-minded. As long as texts made no explicit negative references to Mussolini, the Pope, Catholicism or any other clearly 'political' subject, censors glossed over the rest. Paola Masino, for example, was able to publish in 1933 the devastating short story 'Fame' ('Hunger'), on what was a very sensitive issue at the time, as well as other disturbing short stories later collected in *Racconto grosso* ('Grand tale',) in 1941. *Monte Ignoso* inexplicably passed the Fascist censors, even though it portrays a radically dysfunctional family and includes a mother's killing of her own daughter together with episodes of sexual violence. But her masterpiece, the experimental surrealist/expressionist novel *Nascita e morte della massaia* ('Birth and death of the housewife'), written in 1938–39, was censored when already in proofs, and she was asked to remove all negative political references to Italy, and all 'disrespectful' quotations from the Bible, before the book could be published. The novel, a brilliant satire of the bourgeois and Fascist glorification of the housewife as exemplary wife and mother, eventually appeared in 1945. On the other hand, however, the name of Annie Vivanti, whose mother was Jewish, was officially banned from all publications after 1938, although this did not prevent Croce from publishing his thoughts on her in 1940.

Women's achievements in the novel, if placed alongside those of Borgese, Bontempelli, Moravia, Alvaro, Silone, Gadda and Vittorini, give the impression of a far more diverse literary era than that which emerges from traditional literary histories emphasising the modernist lyric and *prosa d'arte*. Grazia Deledda wrote nearly one-third of her archetypal–realist–symbolist short fiction and novels after the First World War (she died in 1936), yet the mistaken perception persists that she was not a 'modern' writer. Nevertheless, her later work suggests analogies with those of great modernists such as Eudora Welty and Faulkner. Paola Masino's writing from this period is routinely mentioned at the margins of Bontempelli's *realismo magico*, as is that of Anna Maria Ortese. Yet Masino's novels *Monte Ignoso, Periferia* ('Periphery', 1933) and *Nascita e morte della massaia* clearly belong to a different and unusual experimental register, a modernist realism infused with surrealist and expressionist elements. Ortese, despite her considerable post-war reputation, is also still poorly understood. Other experimental realists of the interwar period include Paola Drigo and Marise Ferro. Previously the author of four collections of short fiction, in 1936 Drigo published the novel *Maria Zef*, whose stark realism, explicit violence and laconic style make it a striking antecedent to the best post-war neo-realist prose (as well as a feminist and implicitly anti-Fascist text). Marise Ferro's central theme also concerns violence against women. She published three modernist–realist novels, *Disordine* ('Disorder', 1932), *Barbara* (1934) and *Trent'anni* ('Thirty years', 1940), yet her name has all but vanished from literary histories. The history of twentieth-century realism and post-war neo-realism in Italy needs to be reconsidered in the light of the work of women authors whose texts, either because they did not fit prevalent critical categories and literary trends, or (as in the case of Ada Negri), because after World War Two they were perceived as politically tainted by Fascism, were removed from the canon. Individual novels such as *Cortile a Cleopatra* ('Courtyard in Cleopatra', 1936) by Fausta Cialente, *Nessuno torna indietro* by Alba De Céspedes, and Masino's *Nascita e morte della massaia*, have in recent years been the object of renewed critical attention, due in part to the anti-Fascist credentials of the authors. Yet these texts, unique literary achievements in many ways, are in fact also part of a vast and complex literary production by women that still awaits reappraisal and its rightful place in the canon of Italian literature.

NOTES

1. A collection of texts exemplifying the attitude towards women in the Fascist era is in Piero Meldini, *Sposa e madre esemplare. Ideologia e politica della donna e della famiglia durante il Fascismo* (Florence, 1975).

2. See Ferdinando Loffredo, *Politica della famiglia* (Milan, 1938).

3. See for example Acuzio Sacconi's lecture on 'La cultura della donna' ('Women's culture') given in 1929 and republished in Elisabetta Mondello's *La nuova italiana: la donna nella stampa e nella cultura del ventenni* (Rome, 1987).

4. See Lino Pertile's 'Literature and Fascism', in David Forgacs (ed.), *Rethinking Italian Fascism. Capitalism, Populism and Culture* (London, 1986), pp. 162–84; the only female writer mentioned in passing is Liala. See chapter 13 in this volume by Laura Lepschy.

5. See, for example, Tilde Nicolai, 'Cronache letterarie', in *Donna italiana* 6, I (1928), p. 34, quoted in Mondello, *La nuova italiana*, pp. 152–3.

6. Maria Luisa Astaldi, herself a prominent fiction writer and critic, pointed out this inadequacy as early as 1939 in her *Nascita e vicende del romanzo italiano* (Milan), calling for a more gender-specific interpretation of Deledda's work, and making a similar case for Serao. For a recent feminist rereading of Deledda, see Neria De Giovanni, *L'ora di Lilith. Su Grazia Deledda e la letteratura femminile del secondo Novecento* (Rome, 1987).

7. The letter is reproduced in Bruna Conti and Alba Morino (eds.), *Sibilla Aleramo e il suo tempo. Vita raccontata e illustrata*, pp. 83–4.

8. See for example Nicola Pende, 'Femminilità e cultura femminile', in *Gerarchia*, May 1941, cited in Meldini, *Sposa e madre*, p. 27.

9. Quoted in Ugo Ojetti, *Cose viste* (Milan, 1923–39), p. 190.

10. Piero Gobetti, 'Sibilla', in *Il lavoro*, 12 July 1924, reprinted in Conti and Morino, eds., *Sibilla Aleramo e il suo tempo*, pp. 200–1.

11. See the essays in Annarita Buttafuoco and Marina Zancan, *Svelamento. Sibilla Aleramo: una biografia intellettuale*.

12. See especially the anthology *Le Futuriste. Donne e letteratura d'avanguardia in Italia (1909–1944)*, ed. Claudia Salaris (Milan, 1982).

13. On Benedetta, see my 'Fascist Theories of "Woman" and the Construction of Gender', in Robin Pickering-Iazzi (ed.), *Mothers of Invention: Women, Italian Fascism, and Culture* (Minneapolis, MI, 1995), pp. 76–99, and the exhibition catalogue *La Futurista: Benedetta Cappa Marinetti*, The Galleries at Moore (Philadelphia: Moore College of Art and Design, 1998), which includes essays on Benedetta as both artist and writer. See also the introductory essay written by Simona Cigliana for the new edition of Benedetta's three novels entitled *Le forze umane, Viaggio di Gararà, Astra e il sottomarino* (Rome, 1998)

14. Recent scholarship, particularly research by Luisa Passerini, Giovanni De Luna, Robin Pickering-Iazzi, and the more cautious Victoria De Grazia, has started to question the previously widespread notion that women passively accepted the regime or, as argued by Maria Antonietta Macciocchi, were collectively seduced by the Duce's image and the regime's propaganda.

15. On Labriola, 'Fascist feminism', and in general on women's attitudes towards Fascism and vice versa, see Victoria De Grazia, *How Fascism Ruled Women: Italy 1922–1945* (Berkeley, CA, 1992).

16. See Robin Pickering-Iazzi, *Politics of the Visible: Writing Women, Culture and Fascism* (Minneapolis, MI, 1997), pp. 57–88.

17. See Robin Pickering-Iazzi, *Unspeakable Women. Selected Short Stories Written by Italian Women During Fascism* (New York, 1993).

15

The novel, 1945–1965

In 1965 Giorgio Pullini published an informative study of the Italian novel between 1940 and 1960 in which he organises writers and their novels according to themes or issues.[1] Unlike many other literary surveys, gender is not used as a criterion for classification; instead of being grouped in a chapter of their own, the work of women writers is discussed alongside that of their male peers. In all, Pullini discusses the work of 137 male writers and fifteen female writers. That there was a significantly higher proportion of men to women publishing novels in this period is not in question, but the issues identified by Pullini and other literary historians as dominating the period – namely, narrative and war (the novel of socioideological commitment), narrative and the South (language and dialect in the novel) and, after 1960, literature and industry and the avant-garde – ill accomodate the work of women writers. Women's writing between 1945 and 1965 is distinctive: the divergence is present from the beginning of the period under discussion when many Italian male writers turned (or in some cases returned) to the practices of neo-realism, while women writers, with rare exceptions – the best known being Renata Viganò in her popular novel about the Resistance, *L'Agnese va a morire* ('Agnese goes to her death', 1949) – are drawn neither to its aesthetics nor to its subject matter.

Women's writing between 1945 and 1965 was in many cases the outcome of a long apprenticeship served as readers and translators of the best that European literature could offer from the previous decades. As such their work, which can often be uncompromising in the demands it makes of the reader, represents a decisive, if persistently undervalued, step in the deprovincialisation of Italian culture.

Writing by women in this period is both stylistically and thematically distinctive. This is in part because most of the women writers who came to the fore in the post-war period were born before or during the First World War; they include *Anna Banti, *Elsa Morante, *Natalia Ginzburg, *Lalla Romano, *Anna Maria Ortese, *Alba De Céspedes and *Maria Bellonci. *Gianna Manzini and *Fausta Cialente continued or resumed writing after the war but are also closely associated with the pre-war period.[2] In many cases their literary formation came in the high noon of 1930s modernism when, despite the advance of Fascism, cultural life in Italy was very open to European and indeed international writing. Proust and Woolf alongside Gide, Mansfield and Joyce are just a few of the writers whose work came to the attention of Italian readers and writers through the pages of the courageous Florentine literary journal *Solaria*, which between 1926 and 1936 also published contributions from Gianna Manzini and one of the earliest short stories by an eighteen-year-old Natalia Ginzburg.

The writings of Proust and Woolf with their exploration of inchoate states of being and consciousness were particularly important in stimulating a renewed interest in the novel and its capacity to translate into language the complexities of subjectivity. Manzini, Romano, Banti and Ginzburg were all enthusiastic readers of Proust. Banti was later to refer to her literary encounter with the French author as a *coup de foudre*, a bolt of lightning.[3] During the war years most of these writers were working as literary translators trying as best they could to make ends meet, as Maria Bellonci, at that time translating Stendhal's *Cronache italiane*, was later to point out. Such work provided a demanding but exhilarating literary and stylistic apprenticeship. In her autobiographical memoir *Lessico famigliare* (*Family Sayings*, 1963) Natalia Ginzburg, whose translation of the first volume of Proust was published in 1946 (errors of translation expunged by Einaudi from the first edition were deliberately reintroduced by her when the book was later republished) mentions several times the respect, even passion, displayed by her mother for *A la recherche du temps perdu*. Her father on the other hand merely skimmed through the book, declaring it so boring that their daughter Paola could come to no harm through reading it. Lalla Romano, who claimed she was 'converted' from poetry to prose by the experience of translating Flaubert's *Trois contes*, took the title of the first of her major novels, *La penombra che abbiamo attraversato* ('The twilight we have passed through', 1964) from Proust. Anna Banti's translation of *Jacob's room* (1922) appeared in 1950, followed two years later by the essay 'Umanità della Woolf', 'The Humanity of Virginia Woolf', in which she adopts Woolf's stance in *Orlando* and addresses all those women who for lack of time, self-confidence, support or simply paper are themselves unable to write.[4] Gianna Manzini's first encounter with Virginia Woolf's writing came in 1932 when she read *Mrs Dalloway*, by which time she was an established writer with a novel and two collections of short stories to her name. The claim she made at the end of the war in *Forte come un leone* ('Strong as a lion', 1947), that 'all that was added to my interpretation of the world I owe to her' testifies to the strength of her attachment to Woolf, even while it is not strictly true.[5] In the essay on Woolf her attention is directed to the English writer's technique and style. Her own work shared in the aesthetics of literary modernism with the emphasis falling on an introspective subjectivity, such as can be seen in *Lettera all'editore* ('Letter to the publisher', 1945), where the writing itself becomes the vehicle for self-discovery. What Woolf's example gave her was the excitement of discovering another major writer who held views on the practice of writing that she herself had reached independently.

The case of Virginia Woolf was distinct from other literary influences in that her Italian readers were highly conscious of her significance as a role model for the committed woman writer. It must nevertheless be acknowledged that with the notable exception of De Céspedes, women writers of this period did not see themselves as feminists. Indeed, both Banti and Ginzburg distanced themselves from the politics of feminism and what Ginzburg referred to as its limited spiritual outlook. When it came to cultural matters, however, they, like many others of this period, were alert to the inequalities of treatment meted out to women writers by a predominantly male literary establishment, and they wrote with feeling on the difficulties encountered by all women with creative aspirations. Manzini refers to her commitment to writing as 'a taking of the veil, a kind of invisible taking of the veil'.[6] Their sense of commitment embraces not only their own standing within Italy's literary life, but also their vision of the role of culture in the life of the nation. This is why Woolf the essayist and in particular the author of *A Room of One's Own* was of such importance. The Italian writers were unashamedly highbrow, some might say elitist. At a conference held by 'Noi donne' on 'La donna e la cultura' in 1953, Anna Banti claimed that mass culture was 'a practice that is probably more harmful than illiteracy'.[7]

A further reason why women's writing is distinctive is that their experiences as women, even in times, of war, are inevitably different. The war years 1939 to 1945 brought deprivation, displacement (particularly after 1943) and loss to men and women: Ginzburg lived in internal exile after

1941, her husband Leone died in prison in Rome in 1943 and the German Occupation put the lives of her and her children at risk; De Céspedes in 1943 crossed enemy lines in the South and worked as broadcaster for the Resistance; Banti's apartment in Florence was hit in a bombing raid in 1943 which also saw the destruction of the manuscript of *Artemisia*, while Morante returned to occupied Rome fearful for the safety of her manuscript of *Menzogna e sortilegio* (*The House of Lies*). Sometimes their experiences were woven into the fabric of their post-war writings, but often they remained silent. There are very few novels by women that take the war, or the Resistance, as subject. The storytelling or the anecdotes that those years gave rise to, and that Calvino refers to in his preface to *Il sentiero dei nidi di ragno* (*The Path to the Spiders' Nests*), are rarely written by women. Much of the narrative within this period falls within two main areas – the memoir/autobiography and the historical novel, whether fictitious or factual. The end of the war did not see a break in women's writing but a continuing preoccupation with questions first raised in the 1930s although often applied to a different reality; it sometimes led to fundamental misunderstandings on the part of critics, and dismissal of women's writing as intimist, autobiographical and introverted.

Silence, or the refusal to speak on behalf of others, is most marked in the immediate post-war novels of Natalia Ginzburg. Neither *La strada che va in città* ('Road into the city', 1942) nor *E' stato così* (*The Dry Heart*, 1947) ever touch directly on the public domain. Written in a minimalist, laconic style, too terse for sentimentality, her narratives often adopt the point of view of a young woman living a suppressed but obedient life within a patriarchal family. In *E' stato così* a woman sits on a park bench meditating on a marriage that has led her to shoot her husband dead. Her confession and the novel end with her implied suicide. The short story 'La madre' ('The mother') tells the story of a young widow who fails to conform to the traditional ideas of motherhood; she is too thin even to look like a proper mother. The narrative is focalised largely through the combined consciousness of her two sons, and this technique serves to heighten the reader's awareness of the appalling isolation which will drive her to suicide. With the exception of *Valentino*, where the subject is a homosexual man, Ginzburg's narratives tell of family life in which women, far from being at the heart of the family, are themselves the outsiders and misfits. Ginzburg's chilling domestic novels which ended in either resignation or suicide were published at the end of two decades which had seen women as the objects of a deeply oppressive ideological conformism, for whom self-realisation was measured in terms of marriage, children and the home. In 1961 Ginzburg accompanied her second husband to the Italian Institute in London, and here her sense of displacement freed her to draw for the first time in her writing on memory. Chekhov had always exercised a strong literary influence and he was now joined by Ivy Compton-Burnett. From the influence of these two authors came *Le voci della sera* (*Voices in the Evening*, 1961) where through the narrator Elsa and her lover Tommasino we glimpse the lives of two middle-class families in the post-war period. Two years later appeared Ginzburg's best-selling memoir of family life as she experienced it as the youngest of five children, *Lessico famigliare* (*Family Sayings*, 1963).

Lalla Romano's first narrative work, *Le metamorfosi* ('Metamorphoses', 1951) consisted of sixty-one transcriptions – with no psychoanalytic intentions – of dreams in a space outside time, and marks the stop-off point in her evolution from poet to novelist. It was followed by a series of narratives which if ordered according to the narrating subject's age rather than publication date can be read as stages in a fictional autobiography. Published a year after *Lessico famigliare*, *La penombra che abbiamo attraversato* is a journey, undertaken after the death of her mother, back to the small town in the Piedmontese hills and her pre-World War I childhood. Despite the Proustian title which the author claimed she chose for its allusive mysteriousness, her own style is concise, reticent even, and her description of the way in which her mother spoke is an accurate representation of her own writing: 'However, Mother never made things up, on the contrary she stripped them down, she laid them bare, she did not exactly "tell stories": she just hinted'.[8] The quest for childhood which the reader is invited to share is conducted in the knowledge that the past is unreachable, and is always filtered through the present. This multiple point of view ensures that while the search for the past may itself generate melancholy nostalgia, the narrative it produces does not. In common with Bellonci and Banti, Romano trained in the visual arts (and indeed is herself an artist) and her writing has a painterly quality which contributes towards the aura of stillness that her prose generates.

Nonetheless, it is a misapprehension to think that these women writers were not engaged with events that also fall within the purview of the public domain. Post-war literature in Italy was caught up in the ideological debates of the day, and the absence of an overt ideological engagement in much of the narrative by women was at odds with the cultural climate. This is not the same as saying that the writers were apolitical:

Anna Banti was one of the founding members in 1948 of a group of writers of the left who created a 'cultural alliance'; Natalia Ginzburg joined the Italian Communist Party at the end of the war but resigned in 1951. Their writing bears testimony to an interest less in some abstract notion of history than the ways events come to make their mark on an individual's life and consciousness. History is seen refracted through the experiencing self, and takes its place alongside the many other processes that shape a life. In Ginzburg's ambitious novel *Tutti i nostri ieri* (*All Our Yesterdays*, 1952), the public and private become intermeshed in the story of a generation in the history of two families, the one wealthy, the other poor, whose houses at the start of the novel face each other in a small provincial town in Northern Italy. Unusually for this author, the narrative is given a historical dimension by being presented in the third person, while a collective sense is communicated through the absence of direct speech. Where we watch the male characters get steadily drawn into the politics of their country, in the case of the two sisters pregnancy, and then motherhood, become the determining events in their lives. Concettina finds it difficult to sustain an interest in politics when her morning sickness persists throughout the day and ideology is not so compelling when food shortages give rise to her fear that her milk will fail. When in *Lessico famigliare* Natalia Ginzburg recreates her childhood years at home in Turin in the 1930s, family friends such as Turati, Kuliscioff and Pavese, all of them well-known public figures whose presence in her memoir would have intrigued her Italian readership, are here seen in an entirely private capacity through the eyes of a bright and observant, but unworldly young girl. Where public and private come together in a profoundly painful way, with the recording of her husband's death in the cells of Regina Coeli in German-occupied Rome, the information is compressed into one sentence. This autobiography, which the author asks us in the preface to read as a work of fiction, evokes the past through the family sayings and anecdotes that bond its members across time and place.

Lalla Romano's novel *Tetto murato* (1957), named after a small town in Piedmont, covers the period during the Occupation from July 1943 to autumn 1947. In this novel 'Grand History' as Romano called it, adopting a term used by Stendhal, is not present simply as a literary or psychological frame.[9] Told by Giulia, a young woman who is temporarily separated from her husband, the narrative traces the relationships between four people, that is, two married couples who have been thrown together by circumstance. Paolo, formerly in the Resistance but now sick and destitute, finds himself living with his wife in semi-clandestinity in a mountainous Piedmont region contested by partisans and Germans. Exceptional circumstances have created an unusual and delicate psychological equilibrium between the four of them which could never exist or be sustained in normal circumstances.

Alba De Céspedes stands out in such company for the role she gives to ideology both in the cultural formation of her characters and in the direction her narrative takes. The title of a novel she published in 1955, *Prima e dopo* ('Before and after'), is indicative; the hiatus separating the two moments of the title refers to the experiences of the protagonist, Irene, in the Resistance, which become the defining moment in her life and lead to far-reaching changes of lifestyle and choice. She abandons a rich upper-class fiancé and with him a pampered lifestyle, choosing instead an economically precarious life as a left-wing writer with an intellectual for lover. It is noticeable that where other writers turn to Virginia Woolf, De Céspedes is much closer to Simone de Beauvoir. Her most important novel, *Il rimorso* (*Remorse*, 1963), provides a portrait of the post-war era in Italy through letters exchanged among friends and entries from the protagonist Valeria's diaries. The novel has affinities in terms of both scope and ambition with Simone de Beauvoir's *The Mandarins* (1954).

The protagonists of the books referred to so far are educated middle-class women. *Laudomia Bonanni's two collections of short stories, *Il fosso* ('The ditch', 1949) and *Palma e sorelle* ('Palma and her sisters', 1954) take as their subject, on the contrary, women from the dispossessed, poverty-stricken rural communities. Without sentimentality, she writes of the lives of women and girls for whom World War II and the German Occupation brought respite from the sexual abuse of their menfolk, now in hiding or at war, and the continuous exhausting cycle of pregnancy, child-birth, lactation and frequent infant death. Gifts from German soldiers, or money from townsfolk fleeing the bombs and grateful for refuge in any hovel, provided temporary relief from grinding poverty and the constant struggle to provide food. For the protagonists of these tales, politics and ideology are meaningless words that do not form part of their own language. *L'adultera* ('The adulterer', 1964) is a novel that follows the mind of a working woman travelling to Rome to meet her lover, and whose thoughts turn to the bombings of Rome, her sexual life, her abortion. Her pragmatic attitude to life, with its tough unsparing attention to women's sexuality and male incomprehension, prefigures *Dacia Maraini's early realist novels *La vacanza* (*The Holiday*, 1962) and *L'età del malessere* (*The Age of*

Discontent, 1963). Maraini focuses on the new generation of young women who find themselves trapped, unable either to react or to initiate change. During this post-war period, there appears for the first time in Italian narrative an explicitness about women's sexuality and this is perhaps nowhere more evident than in Milena Milani's *Storia di Anna Drei* ('Story of Anna Drei', 1947). The novel caused something of a sensation in its day by replacing the customary sexual triangle of two men competing for the same woman with two young women competing for the same man, and indeed their interest in each other is much stronger than their interest in the ostensible object of attraction.

Cultural formation and experience on the part of women contributed to a different configuration of aesthetic concerns and practices, which in the ideologically charged cultural climate of those post-war years did not gain for women the sustained recognition they merit. If we break away from the systemisation of the literature of the period as adopted by Pullini, we can take our argument a stage further and abandon the grouping of novels according to established genres. Only in this way can we approach women's writing through its most conspicuous property – the recourse to subjectivity as the organising principle of the narrative work. Unlike Anglo-Saxon narrative, a fundamental distinction in Italian fiction has traditionally been drawn between the historical novel (the first indisputable narrative masterpiece in Italy was a historical novel, Manzoni's *I promessi sposi* (*The Betrothed*), and the genre has continued in its wake to enjoy a prestige that has never been attained by other narrative genres), and the novel of contemporary mores or life. Such a division is posited in the first instance on the acceptance of historical or chronological time and seen as a succession of minutes, days, months and years, which for Anna Banti is *cronaca*. What really matters for Banti is to depict time as it is mediated through the subjective experience of time passing, 'hour by hour, particularly those days history is silent on', where memory often becomes the agent of organisation.[10]

The period saw the publication of a number of novels which took as their subject an episode or character from the past, yet do not fit the mould of the historical novel. If one leaves aside for a moment aesthetic considerations, this new approach provided an opportunity to write about powerful women whose lives extended far beyond the range decreed acceptable by a Fascist ideology which persisted, at least as far as its thinking on women was concerned, well into the post-war years. Maria Bellonci is the author most closely associated with the traditional historical novel. Her first novel, *Lucrezia Borgia* (1939), was stimulated by her study of the Gonzaga family and Mantegna's frescoes in the 'Camera degli sposi' in Mantua. *Segreti dei Gonzaga* '(Secrets of the Gonzagas', 1947) a book made up of three discrete sections that have subsequently also been published separately, returns to the scene fifty years on. It is the most closely researched of her writings, although the closure of the archives from the end of 1940 to 1942 led her to a sustained meditation on the nature of the characters making up this extraordinary family, in particular Isabella D'Este. After regaining limited access to the archives in 1942, she describes how she would travel by train between Mantua, Modena and Florence. As she listened to the soldiers' tales of war, in her mind the unhappiness of the past would graft on to the misery of the present. This most historical of writers thus renounces all claims to omniscience, and the most carefully researched events appear to occur openly and spontaneously. In an interview of 6 February 1951, in answer to the question why she always took her characters from the past, she replied 'because the past is a continuous present! Imaginary characters do not exist just as historical characters do not exist: there are just vital characters and non-vital characters.'[11]

Like Maria Bellonci, Anna Banti's (pseudonym for Lucia Lopresti) training was in art history. Her husband, the art historian Roberto Longhi, has commented on Bellonci's unusually visual literary style amounting to an almost tactile plasticity, a comment which could equally be applied to Banti. In her most acclaimed novel *Artemisia* (1947) the writing is intensely visual; unilinear plot is replaced by an episodic structure which draws together recurrent motifs, creating the verbal equivalent of portraiture. The protagonist is the seventeenth-century artist Artemisia Gentileschi, then virtually unknown, whose life Banti researched and wrote up during the war (it is interesting in this respect that Banti refers to Woolf's work on *Orlando* (1928) as being for her a release from the 'piccolo tempo' and short-termism of her day). The novel is a reworking from memory of an earlier manuscript that was destroyed in an air bombardment over Florence in 1944. The episode is recalled in the opening pages of the book when Artemisia's shade, Banti's 'companion of three centuries ago' appears in the Boboli Gardens alongside a distraught Banti urging her to make a fresh start, refusing to be consigned once again to oblivion. This is not a biography where the author tells the life of a non-narrating subject: Artemisia has her own voice that is heard addressing the author in the book's opening words: 'Do not cry.'[12] The work draws its remarkable intensity both from its narration of moments from Artemisia's life, and equally from the dialogue born of the difficult and often delicate relationship between the two women. The relationship is tough, completely devoid of sentimentality, but far from the conventional relationship between biographer and subject. The protagonist of a biography as much as an autobiography is a product of the processes of writing, and cannot be the same, nor should she be confused with, the living person. Banti takes advantage of the distinction by creating in the Artemisia Gentileschi who steps forward to console her a woman whose life is not in all its factual details the same as the historical figure. It is a fictional biography as well as a historical novel, raising interesting questions as to how far dissimulation or fabrication is permissible in respect of another's life. Banti rescues Gentileschi from oblivion for the second time, while in the novel Gentileschi paints from memory a portrait of a close friend and talented artist, Annella de Rosa, murdered by her husband, thus immortalising her on canvas. But as befits a work where the author had no more power than her subject, the posthumous fame conferred on Artemisia Gentileschi belongs equally to Anna Banti: they both speak through their work but they need each other to exist.

The author's admiration for her subject is not reserved for her painting or her person but for her position as 'one of the first women to support with her words and her paintings the right to congenial work and an equality of spirit between the sexes' (from the novel's preface). The work is a vindication of female creativity and equal worth – in her lifetime Gentileschi's canvases brought her autonomy and self-determination. Her fate contrasts with the heroine of the remarkable long story 'Lavinia fuggita', first published in the collection *Le donne muoiono* ('Women die') in 1952. The story tells of a young woman, *maestra* of the choir of orphan girls at the *Pietà* in Venice in Vivaldi's day, for whom her music can never be anything other than sound she carries in her head. Unable to translate it into performance, her extraordinary creativity turns inwards, destroying mind and reason.[13]

I have tried to give some indication of how and why women's narratives of this period are distinct from those of their male colleagues and where they share stylistic and/or thematic affinities. The two authors I shall close with stand alone; each in her own way resists assimilation. Both Anna Maria Ortese and Elsa Morante are unsettling writers. Anna Maria Ortese's work criss-crosses the line that traditionally divides travel writing and 'literature': in Italian culture the border dividing literary writing, 'scrittura', from journalistic writing is closely guarded by the academies and critics. In her fictions, too, she crosses boundaries, alternating mimesis and the fantastic. Between 1948 and 1962, at the start of a literary career marked by long periods of acute poverty, Anna Maria Ortese tried to earn her living through her travel writing. One of her most striking narratives from this period was a Gorkyesque descent into the lower depths (the *bassifondi*) of Naples, *Il mare non bagna Napoli* (*The Bay is Not Naples*, 1953), where she brought to public attention the appalling conditions that reigned in the war-hit city – including a graphic description of her own family's apartment. The book was received by many critics as a neo-realist work, but the author herself claimed that Naples represented her own metaphysical malaise. The city became the screen against which she could project her own metaphysical neurosis – an inability to understand where and what reality is – a state of mind that she described as ('this nothingness of knowledge of the real').[14] After several further collections of stories and travel writings, in 1965 Ortese published *L'iguana* (*The Iguana*), the tale of one Carlo Ludovico Aleardo di Grees of the Dukes of Estremadura and Count of Milan, architect and orphan, who sails the seas in search of land to build villas and yachting clubs for the wealthy of Milan. Poised on a knife-edge between fantasy and reality, the tale has the lightness of fable and the cutting edge of an allegory of human destruction.

Anna Banti, Natalia Ginzburg and Lalla Romano saw women as custodians of the past. Elsa Morante's *Menzogna e sortilegio* (*The House of Lies*, 1948), which ranks as one of the major novels to appear in Europe this century, is also the product of a young woman's memory, but all similarities end here. She has one of her protagonists ask if the past and 'this kingdom of the dead' is not a trick, and imagination and memory instruments or illusion.[15] The narrative voice belongs to Elisa, who has immured herself in a small room with just her cat Alvaro for company, where she lives in a state of partial consciousness, listening to the 'memory's whisper' which transforms a petit-bourgeois family drama into the stuff of legend: 'and as happens to a people without history, I exalt over this legend'. Much of the novel presents the 'romance-like memories' through the point of view of self-deluded members of the family themselves; a family fatally contaminated by the *morbo* (germ) of the *menzogna* (lie) – a disease that has now been transmitted to Elisa. These are not stories passed down through the generations, for her ancestors did not communicate with each other, nor is she gathering the stories for future generations, for there will be none.

Elisa's narrative covers three generations in the history of her Sicilian family and of the island, beginning in the 1890s with her maternal grand-mother, then governess to an aristocratic family in rapid decline, who erroneously believes herself to be the heroine of a romantic novel. Morante's novel presents a historical and social analysis of a phantasma-goric, obsessional and claustrophobic world paralysed by the immobility of its class and caste system, and by the bigotry that passed for religion. Morante was steeped in the great realist tradition of the nineteenth century, the works of Dostoevsky in particular, and the all-inclusiveness of *Menzogna e sortilegio* includes genre as well as subject matter, sweeping together the *feuilleton*, realism, the Gothic, the supernatural and even a censored epistolary novel which we know about only through the narra-tor's own comments. But the genres are not only those traditionally asso-ciated with narrative, for at the heart of the writing are the performing arts – opera, puppet-theatre and above all melodrama. There is a theatri-cal substratum to the novel, but with the failure of the sacred, the tragic is now the stuff of melodrama. In the later novel *L'isola di Arturo* (*Arturo's Island*, 1957) lies, deceptions and myth continue to play their part in sus-taining the family romance, and in particular the relationship between the young protagonist, Arturo, and his homosexual father. Reared like Romulus on goat's milk, Arturo roams the island of Procida a free spirit until adolescence and initiation into adulthood take away the freedom of innocence.

Morante's next novel, *La storia* (*History*, 1974), was the first twentieth-century Italian novel to become a bestseller, with close on an unprece-dented million copies sold in the first year alone. Its presentation of history as a succession of persecutions, wars and acts of violence against defenceless individuals, stirred up an ideological controversy among the parties on the left, dominated at that time by the powerful Communist Party. The simplicity of the title belies its complexity, for *storia* refers in equal measure to fabulation and history; the second always appears capi-talised in the text, and is damned in the subtitle with the epithet: 'A scandal that has lasted ten thousand years'. The novel revisits a painful and contested period in Italy's recent history, for the final years of the war, the Occupation of Rome and the battle between Fascists, Nazis and Communists are the setting for the tragic story of a primary school-teacher, Isa Raimundo, and her two children, the younger of whom, Useppe, is the result of her rape by a German soldier. Useppe is a magical, other-world child touched by special powers of communication with animals and nature, a repository of myth and fable who is destined to an early death. Where sceptical contemporaries read the novel as an historical epic revisiting the classical sites of neo-realism (the proletarian apartment block, the huge anonymous buildings given over to refugees from the bombings), for today's reader what emerges most powerfully from the darkness in the magic-realist evocation of the dead in the narration of a ghetto after the round-up of 16 October 1943, is the celebration of a visionary state of grace that accompanies innocence and makes possible the act of storytelling itself.

NOTES

1. Giorgio Pullini, *Il romanzo italiano del dopoguerra (1940–1960)* (Padua, 1965).
2. Fausta Cialente published just one novel, *Ballata levantina* (1961), during this period. Gianna Manzini's *Lettera all'editore* and *Forte come un leone* were both published in 1945; *La sparviera* in 1956.
3. Anna Banti in a letter to Giuseppe Leonelli of 4 February 1973.
4. Anna Banti, 'Umanità della Woolf', in *Opinioni* (Milan, 1961), pp. 72–3.
5. See Gianna Manzini, 'La lezione della Woolf', in *Forte come un leone*, pp. 76–96,
6. *Ibid.*, p. 78.
7. Conference held by 'Noi donne', proceedings published as *'La donna e la cultura'* (Rome, 1953), p. 92.
8. Lalla Romano, *La penombra che abbiamo attraversato* (Turin, 1964), p. 91.
9. Lalla Romano had previously written two stories about the Resistance, 'I tedeschi a Boves' and 'Una strada qualunque', which were published in a partisan journal in 1945.
10. For an excellent discussion of the 'Romanzo e romanzo storico' see Anna Banti, *Opinioni*, pp. 38–43. The essay was written in 1951.
11. Maria Bellonci, *Opere*, vol. I (Milan, 1994), p. lvi.
12. Anna Banti, *Artemisia* (Milan, 1989), p. 7.
13. Anna Banti, 'Lavinia fuggita', in *Il coraggio delle donne*, pp. 13–42.
14. Anna Maria Ortese, *Il mare non bagna Napoli* (Milan, 1994).
15. Elsa Morante, *Menzogna e sortilegio*, in *Opere*, vol. I, p. 307.

16

The novel, 1965–2000

The reaction to experimentalism and the feminist revolution

Published on the eve of the students' and women's movements of 1968, and in the middle of the Italian avant-garde's debate on structuralism, Marxism and psychoanalysis, *Alice Ceresa's experimental novel *La figlia prodiga* ('The prodigal daughter', 1967) is an ironic, pseudo-philosophical discussion of the (un)representability of the prodigal daughter, a hypothetical character whose existence is implied only by that of her counterpart, the prodigal son.[1] Ceresa's meta-narrative is an attack on the Italian neo-avant-garde's lack of concern with gender and social reality; it is also a critique of the contemporary social and cultural orders which deny daughters autonomy, and an exhortation to put literary form to the service of the representation/creation of a new female subjectivity. *La figlia prodiga* was almost prophetic in denouncing a political and cultural situation which Italian women were setting out to analyse and change. This chapter attempts to trace women's continued efforts to appropriate and adapt the Italian literary institutions to their artistic and social aims during the last three decades of the twentieth century. While in the second half of the 1960s women's issues played second fiddle to the crisis of bourgeois capitalist ideology, the 1970s saw the appearance of a literature which openly denounced the oppressed condition of women, deconstructing the current notions of femininity which kept women imprisoned in their body and the home. In the 1980s, women writers moved on to construct alternative female identities. The search for a voice capable of expressing a difference rooted in the body is an integral part of these narratives. Writing in this decade parallels the shift in Italian feminism from the political phase of emancipation and equality to the more cultural phase of affirming female difference in the imaginary (psychic) and symbolic (linguistic and intellectual) structures of society. With the 1990s, issues relating to sexual difference become bound up with investigating the post-modern disintegration of the systems which traditionally structured our perception of the world. We shall see how writers turn the consequent decentering and fragmentation of the self from an alarming into a liberating and enriching process.

The early work of two now established writers – *Francesca Sanvitale and *Maria Corti – illustrates the Italian cultural and political climate immediately prior to the students', workers' and feminist movements, a set of events which played a crucial role in empowering women to speak and write in the 1970s and beyond. Sanvitale views her first novel *Il cuore borghese* ('The middle-class heart', 1972) as a deconstruction of the psychological novel.[2] Originating, like Ceresa's book, in the intellectual context of 1960s experimentalism, this novel dissects the 1950s crisis of bourgeois institutions – the couple, marriage, family – and the failure of Marxist/left-wing ideology to provide alternatives in either the private sphere or the political arena. Beneath the intellectualism of *Il cuore borghese*, however, women are represented as having a greater potential than men to reach reality: Olimpia, its protagonist, finds continuity between past, present and future in her female family genealogy. She invokes her dead grandmother as her household god and concludes that her decision to live away from her mother, 'only to reach this inner void so similar to despair, was associated with the sense of an irreparable sin against love. But such an interpretation may be incorrect or much too simplistic: perhaps remorse towards one's mother is an incomprehensible feeling, which has always been in the subconscious and is never to go away' (p. 136).[3] *Il cuore borghese* anticipates Sanvitale's second novel *Madre e figlia* ('Mother and daughter', 1980), which explores, lyrically rather than intellectually, the complexities of the mother–daughter relationship and sets the tone for an important strand of women's narratives in the 1980s.

Corti's *Il ballo dei sapienti* ('The dance of the sages', 1966), set in the early 1960s, is an ironically comic but pessimistic account of the mounting discontent of both students and teachers with an education system bogged down by bureaucracy and corruption, and a society in which meaningful relationships are impossible. It is symptomatic of the social and cultural subordination of women that they appear only as the supporting props and objects of desire of the three male characters whose intellectual, personal and sexual frustrations guide the narrative throughout. Women are either oblivious to their condition, or do not know how to escape it, or, like the few existing women professors, are 'convinced, like the dear departed Madame de Staël, that the brain has no sex' (p. 237).

In these two novels, interest in women's plight is subordinate to a wider dissection of bourgeois values and institutions increasingly under attack, reaching crisis-point in 1968, when Italy was swept by demonstrations and strikes. Just as a strong feminist movement emerged, a new group of writers came to the fore in the 1970s, whose works engaged with the concerns of post-1968 cultural and political debates. They focus on the dichotomy between women's new public and traditional private roles, calling for a fundamental change in male–female relationships to parallel the dramatic economic and political transformations of Italy. Even while many of their characters are working women, these writers concentrate on the oppression they suffer within the family in their domestic roles as wives and mothers. Their narratives also exhibit a number of common formal features. The adoption of first-person narration by working-class as well as middle-class characters, as a means of self-reflection and self-knowledge, recalls the feminist practice of consciousness-raising. Their fragmented, a-temporal structures convey the protagonists' fragmented perception of self and reality; conversely, the form of an explicit or implicit diary underlines the monotonous and repetitive quality of women's lives. The consequent predominance of the present tense or present perfect and the employment of a syntax and style resonant of spoken language suggest the topicality and urgency of what is narrated.[4]

An example of this trend is *Dacia Maraini's *Donna in guerra* (*Woman at War*, 1975). Here Vannina embarks upon a journey which, through the encounter with the feminist Suna, brings her to question the notion of femininity she has always unquestioningly conformed to. She reports a conversation with her husband about her 'sexual listlessness':

> 'You're going against your own nature, love.'
> 'What nature?'
> 'Your nature is good, soft, sensitive and you're making it hard and aggressive.'
> 'Am I being aggressive if I don't feel like making love to you?'
> 'Yes, you're aggressive against yourself, you're repressing your own character.'
> 'Perhaps my character was moulded on yours, it wasn't really my own.'
> (*Woman at War*, p. 248)

Donna in guerra offers no facile solutions to women's sexual and cultural oppression. While showing the importance of countering the inability of male politics, whether traditional or revolutionary left-wing, to engage with women's issues, it also demonstrates the need for grassroots renewal. At the end of the novel, Vannina, a primary-school teacher, puts her hope for new gender relations in a younger generation. Maraini here goes beyond the individualistic coming to consciousness of the bourgeois protagonists of, for instance, Carla Cerati's or Giuliana Ferri's novels, or the angry but impotent denunciations made by their lower-class counterparts, such as *Armanda Guiducci's housewife in *Due donne da buttare* ('Two disposable women', 1976). The latter's apocalyptic monologue shows how women's traditional efforts as life-givers and nurturers are made vain by a man-made industrial society which poisons and pollutes: 'all those wooden dried fish decapitated frozen mountains of plastic mountains of cans minced meat maybe rat meat in aspic . . . mountains of peas closed in cans . . . like me closed fleshless sealed suffocated' (pp. 28–9).

This literature is commonly considered stylistically and structurally unsophisticated. Writers certainly aspired to a style suitable for the dissemination of ideas and experiences which affected all women: it was anti-elitist, anti-rhetorical and a counter to the obscure avant-garde productions of the 1960s. However, recent studies have emphasised the experimentalism of women's writing during this decade, and suggested that Italian women's writing from 1968 onwards engages in a complex relationship with the traditional genres of confession, romance, picaresque, the quest novel, the *Bildungsroman*, the historical novel and the detective novel (Lazzaro-Weiss, 1993). Guiducci's writings, for example, cross the boundaries between sociological/anthropological essay, confession, testimony, autobiography and fiction, and create a kind of *récit* in which the writing subject finds perfect correspondence with the narrated subject and the reader. This contamination between genres is characteristic of the output of many writers throughout the period we are considering. Maraini's novel is also deceptive in its alleged realism. Her stylised story of Vannina's emancipation contains a subtext rich in symbolism which draws attention to the spaces of female difference and anticipates the concerns of the narrative of the next decade.

By no means all writing in the 1970s fits into the paradigm illustrated above. *Gina Lagorio's bestselling *La spiaggia del lupo* ('The wolf's beach', 1977) adopts a traditional third-person/past-tense structure to present, elegantly and suggestively, a young woman's twofold struggle against bourgeois hypocrisy and the new goals of female independence and sexual freedom. This is the *Bildungsroman* of a young woman whose innocent, fairy-tale existence on a magical beach along the Ligurian coast is abruptly interrupted by her falling in love with, and becoming pregnant by, a married stranger. In deciding to have the baby, Angela defies both bourgeois respectability and the pressures of the emerging lay mentality in favour of abortion. She also finds the strength to pursue an artistic vocation against the odds. The story follows Angela to Milan during a period of strikes and occupations; here she becomes involved with young people of her own generation and slowly gains the strength to rebuild her life and career together with her child. Lagorio had already dealt with the theme of positive motherhood in her autobiographical *Un ciclone chiamato Titti* ('A cyclone named Titti', 1969), which explores the effects of an unexpected pregnancy on a not-so-young couple. Lagorio's characters are not afraid of going against the grain, at a time when women, in real life and in literature, start to express their ambivalence *vis-à-vis* motherhood and to affirm their right to self-determination and to abortion. *Oriana Fallaci's controversial *Lettera a un bambino mai nato* (*Letter to a Child Never Born*, 1975), a dramatic monologue from a woman to the foetus she carries in her womb, broaches the painful issues of abortion, miscarriage and motherhood from numerous angles – emotional, physical, social, political, scientific, ethical and religious – and from the mother's as well as the child's point of view. *Lidia Ravera's *Bambino mio* ('My dear child', 1979) imitates Fallaci's rhetorical strategy to present a 1968 political activist and writer torn first between the desire for motherhood and its ideological rejection by her peer group, and then between the conflicting demands of motherhood and her writing career. All these novels broach a fundamental issue in women's lives: without dismissing the importance of feminism, they appeal to women to make a truly free choice and to search for deeper inner independence.

Before moving on to the next decade, another group of narratives must be mentioned which, according to Silvana Castelli, propose self-willed physical and linguistic segregation in a hospital, an asylum or a convent.[5] Castelli's own novel *Pitonessa* ('The female python', 1978) exemplifies the type of text she analyses. Its third-person narrative originates in the mind of a woman who is segregated within the walls of her bedroom. The description of her present isolation is mixed with fragments of her past and the past of other women, and with memories of the forays of a gang of six rebellious young girls to which she belonged. In

Bambine ('Young girls', 1990), Ceresa continued her investigation of whether female rebelliousness is at all possible in a society organised in such a way as to quash individual character. Castelli, on the other hand, proposes childhood as a space of female transgression which is subsequently erased through the superimposition of orthodox gender roles. This theme is, of course, not new in the literature of this period. *Marina Jarre's *Negli occhi di una ragazza* ('In the eyes of a young girl', 1971) follows the process of domestication of a young girl who steps into her dead mother's place as carer of her father and brother. The novel ends on an unproblematically optimistic tone, as Maria Cristina succeeds in pursuing her own inclinations and artistic talent. Castelli's text, however, shows that the fight is far from over: her character, once a rebellious little girl, is now trapped in a physical and linguistic enclosure, a neurotic state which she does not want to, or perhaps cannot, leave. She remains 'inside this room where by remaining still she exists without needing anything else . . . and where not even the telephone dares ring in order not to disturb her with the very sound of her name' (p. 33).

Castelli's novel begs the question of how liberating the protagonist's isolation is. The issue at stake here is women's relationship with language and writing.[6] Rather than opting for Castelli's uncommunicative reclusion and experimentation, women writers have chosen to work from within more representational modes of writing, while still being profoundly committed to both the search for new forms and styles and to the critique of women's social and cultural marginalisation.

The investigation of the female self

As feminism in the 1980s turned its attention away from the battle for political equality to the question of sexual difference, writers set out to question women's traditional exclusion from writing, and to develop a language and a literature bearing the imprint of the female body and Self. *Biancamaria Frabotta's *Velocità di fuga* ('Velocities of flight', 1989) exemplifies this search, staging the struggle of a young aspiring writer to free herself from traditional images of womanhood and to find alternative literary forms to communicate female difference.[7] Many narratives of the late 1970s and early 1980s share these thematic and aesthetic concerns. The protagonist-narrator of *Laudòmia Bonanni's *Il bambino di pietra: una nevrosi femminile* ('The stone child: a female neurosis', 1979) uses writing as a therapeutic tool of female self-discovery; indeed, she compares herself to

Zeno, the protagonist of Italo Svevo's *The Confessions of Zeno*. The narrator writes about herself for the benefit of her psychoanalyst, seeking the causes of her neurosis in her family and marriage. The book we read becomes a possible life alibi, replacing a woman's most important life alibi: a child ('I did not make a child for myself. Have I perhaps written a book?', p. 162). *In Grazia Livi's *L'approdo invisibile* ('The invisible landing', 1980) a jaded thirty-eight-year old journalist leaves Milan, a city obsessed by money at the expense of human relationships. Over the course of this physical and metaphorical journey aimed at reconstructing the self, she must peel off many layers of myths and ideologies, including feminism and its fallacious belief that women can become 'whole' through work and emotional independence. This process triggers a chain of questions on what the self is, on whether it has an inner centre, on the relationship between writing and motherhood and the place of both within the self. The narrator is also searching for a voice as a writer, in order to move from ephemeral journalism to literature. She finds inspiration in Jane Austen who, without a female tradition behind her, was nonetheless able to find a voice of her own (pp. 214–15). The endeavour to find one's place in a female genealogy unites the work of women writers, feminist theorists and literary critics in the 1980s. Frabotta's and Livi's narratives stress the importance of the mediation of literary mothers in order for women to gain access to writing, while Frabotta's aspiring writer engages secretly in nocturnal written conversations with Katherine Mansfield, Virginia Woolf, Karen Blixen and Simone de Beauvoir.

Blood genealogies and the female family lineage are the focus of another strand of narratives in the 1980s and the early 1990s. Francesca Sanvitale and *Fabrizia Ramondino were pioneers in delving into mother–daughter relationships where, as feminists had realised since their consciousness-raising days, identity and sense of self were rooted. Their novels revolve around the daughter's need for differentiation from, and her simultaneous desire for, identification with the body of the mother. Sanvitale's *Madre e figlia* ('Mother and daughter', 1980) portrays a daughter's struggle to circumscribe her own self against complete identification with her mother. The isolation into which this mother and daughter are forced as a consequence of illegitimacy creates an extreme situation of psychical and physical con-fusion, so much so that the disease that ravages the old mother's body and her death threaten the daughter's own existence. Ramondino's *Althénopis* (1981) focuses on female subjectivity with reference to a specific social context. The free, genderless childhood of the protagonist is threatened by the prospect first of an oppressive model of Mediterranean womanhood, and later of an apparently free, non-gendered model of personhood based on money and career. The young woman rejects the first, tries the second, but rejects that too. She returns home in a neurotic state of mind. The search for self resumes, but from within the confines of her relationship with her mother: 'Defeated she had come back to the Mother – almost as if to ask her the reason for living . . . They survived, but their fates divided. They had become two, but in an unequal way . . . The Daughter discovered her destiny, but the Mother vanished' (pp. 232–4).

Writing about the mother is a substitute for her lost body and a path to autonomy in these two novels. A rich cluster of texts followed in their wake, which unashamedly explore the whole spectrum of daughters' feelings towards mothers, from the classic love/hate conflict to outright hatred and obsessive attachment.[8] *Elisabetta Rasy's first novel, *La prima estasi* ('The first ecstasy', 1985), reconstructs Saint Teresa of Lisieux's progress towards death as a rejection of womanhood originating in the loss of her mother at a young age. The self-willed wasting of her body is presented as a controlled pursuit of annihilation motivated by her desire to re-unite with her mother and re-enter the lost maternal pre-linguistic space. Teresa favours silence over speech and prayer, and finds gratification in the rhythmic repetition of tones and sounds of the rosary: 'the magnificent re-enactment of childhood games' (p. 97). She is ordered to write down her life before she becomes ill. Her simple language refuses to establish links and to look for a plot in her life. As her disease progresses, her increasingly childish and almost incoherent language conveys 'the ultimate essence of her passion' (p. 129), while Rasy's sophisticated narrative powerfully evokes Teresa's endeavour to silence her body in order to make the chosen dereliction of her life complete.

In stressing the physical nature of the mother–daughter bond, the literature on mothers and daughters represents a significant advance in the creation of a new literary language. While in the feminist literature of the 1970s the corporeal nature of women's experiences was expressed through an anti-rhetorical and unadorned style, in the 1980s, on the other hand, it was associated with complex narrative structures and sophisticated style and vocabulary. Sanvitale, for example, employs a highly lyrical style to convey the physical quality of dreams, symbols and memories which form the texture of her writing, while Ramondino's baroque sentence structure and composite language, incorporating Neapolitan dialect, describe places and people in their materiality with both poetic cadence and dazzling lexical precision.

Sisters and grandmothers also feature in the narratives of the two decades. Some of Ramondino's stories in *Storie di patio* ('Short stories from the patio', 1983) and Ravera's *Sorelle* ('Sisters', 1994) delve into the tensions and rivalries which accompany the parallel or diverging paths of sisters. While relationships between mothers and daughters and between sisters are inherently ambivalent, the ones between grandmothers and grand-daughters are generally portrayed as positive. Margaret Mazzantini's *Il catino di zinco* ('The zinc basin', 1994) employs a style in turn precious and colloquial to talk about a heroic grandmother figure from the grand-daughter's point of view, whereas *Susanna Tamaro's *Va' dove ti porta il cuore* (*Follow Your Heart,* 1994) is indeed narrated by a grandmother. Family histories rich in strong female figures are the subject matter of *Passione di famiglia* ('Family passion', 1994), Cristina Comencini's novel about three generations of women united by a visceral passion for love, cards and food, of *Francesca e Nunziata* ('Francesca and Nunziata', 1995), Maria Orsini Natale's historical novel about a Southern family of pasta-makers, and of *Le viceregine di Napoli* ('The Neapolitan vicereines', 1997), Luciana Viviani's recollection of two influential women in her family.

Dacia Maraini's *oeuvre* exemplifies women's acquisition of a language and literary forms capable of representing a new female speaking subject which reclaims the body from the domination of biology and sees it as a site of social stratification and resistance. One of the few writers to have made the transition from the feminist modes of writing of the 1970s to the more diverse aesthetics of the 1980s and 1990s, Maraini consistently addresses the issue of patriarchy's silencing of women. *Isolina* (1985) deals with the real-life case of a working-class young woman in Verona at the beginning of the nineteenth century. Made pregnant by an upper-class army officer, Isolina dies after her lover and his drunken fellow officers insert a fork inside her in order to induce an abortion. Her body is subse-quently cut into pieces and disposed of in the river. The book is a text in the process of being woven, as the author-turned-investigator records her difficulties in unearthing documents, piecing together information in the official documents, and uncovering the way important evidence was suppressed in order to protect the honour of the army, the prestige of the officer's family and his career (the case was dismissed as suicide). *Voci* (*Voices,* 1994) returns to the problem of violence against women, at a time when the Italian political parties and women's groups were involved in negotiating a satisfactory law on sexual violence. Once again, the mysterious murder of a woman shows up a social and political system which does its best to silence the victims. *La lunga vita di Marianna Ucrìa* (*The Silent Duchess*, 1990), inspired by Maraini's eighteenth-century Sicilian ancestress, moves beyond the mutilations inflicted on women's bodies to speak of its potential for pleasure and liberation. Marianna Ucrìa becomes deaf-mute in childhood after being raped by an elderly uncle. She is later given to him in marriage. She learns to read and write and turns these skills into means of communication and learning. However, the novel is not concerned with women's exclusion from culture in eighteenth-century Sicily, but with Marianna's discovery and re-invention of her body, therefore with the release of 'female desire in a society which would deny it' (Wood, p. 230). Marianna overcomes her mutilation, discovers her sexuality, brings to consciousness the memory of the physical abuse at the root of it, finds the lost connection with her mother, and finally leaves her family to travel freely with a female companion. At the end of the story, she is no longer a victim, but a free agent. This novel is generally considered Maraini's best achievement to date for the depth and breadth of her aesthetic and historical commitment. Nevertheless, the dry and spare style which characterised her earlier work earned Maraini the coveted Strega Prize with *Buio* ('Darkness', 1999). This is a collection of stories inspired by real cases of violence and structured around the police superintendent who investigates them (the same female figure appears in *Voci*), in which the author extends her denunciation of abuse against women to children, adolescents and other vulnerable groups.

While Maraini's *La lunga vita di Marianna Ucrìa* is about the constitution of a subject, another strand of women's writing focuses on the disintegration of the self from a post-modern perspective. *Francesca Duranti, *Ginevra Bompiani, *Sandra Petrignani, and *Paola Capriolo write self-conscious and fragmented novels dealing with precarious identities and unstable inner and outer realities, with characters who continually revisit the past in the attempt to grasp the 'reality' behind the façade and with the relationship between art and life. In Bompiani's parodic and surreal tales in *Mondanità* ('Worldliness', 1980), *L'incanto* ('Enchanted', 1987), and *Vecchio cielo, nuova terra* ('Old sky, new earth', 1988), mysterious characters, strange events and magical transformations speak of the instability of the self and delve into the feminine and masculine unconscious, through a continuous overturning of reality, appearance and imagination, often controlled by an extradiegetic narrator. In *Navigazioni di Circe*

('Navigations of Circe', 1987), Petrignani redraws the figure of Circe as a woman in whom female desire and sexual seduction are played out in a writing and rewriting of her life, causing continuous deferral of pleasure and narrative closure. Her liaison with Ulysses is an exploration of the battle of the sexes, where each party yearns both to appropriate and enslave the other, and to annul him/herself in the illusory union of the sexual act. When Circe realises that Ulysses, and indeed every human being, is separate and different, she is free to leave his island and start her own navigations. While this narrative records the destabilising effects of writing on the self and life ('Writing is a process of fission, it causes all sorts of splits, it breaks up unity . . . Since I started writing I'm not the same; a fracture has gradually appeared between me and my heroic past', p. 103), on the other hand it makes female difference the warrant of Circe's new identity. Starting from Petrignani's claim that Circe represents woman before feminism, recent criticism has interpreted the book as her process of liberation through becoming aware of sexual difference, which is posited as the foundation of a true equality between the sexes (Wood, pp. 261–6). Yet, while the text ends with Circe looking at her reflection and seeing a healthy and beautiful woman free and ready to embark on her voyages ('There, I see only Circe, her hair ruffled by the wind, the suntan which never fades, her healthy teeth, her beautiful arms', p. 133), the reader also sees a woman alone and may wonder whether her freedom will turn into yet another enclosure.

Duranti's characters are tormented by the conflict between the search for a true self and the demands of the social persona. Their inner search for a place in which they can feel at one with reality is consistently frustrated by the pressures to fit into bourgeois conformism. In her *La casa sul lago della luna* (*The House on Moon Lake*, 1984) and in the novels which followed, this theme becomes intertwined with a preoccupation with the relationship between art and life, the power of literature to shape and control life, and the interplay between self and textuality. In *Ultima stesura* ('Final draft', 1991), a woman writer reconstructs the history of her writing and her life by putting together a number of her short stories and recalling the context in which they were produced and given their final form. The resulting meta-narrative is interspersed with intertextual references to Duranti's previous work, thus telling the history of its creator's own life and career through a close-knit game of self-concealments and self-revelations. As well as being a reflection on the difficulty of combining living and writing experienced by all writers and on the artist's troubled search for identity, *Ultima stesura* also highlights the impact of the specifically female experiences of love, marriage, separation and motherhood on creative work, and resumes the theme of women's search for an autonomous identity, a concern of Duranti's earlier work.

Paola Capriolo's *Il doppio regno* ('The double kingdom', 1991) explores the shifting boundaries between reality and illusion, dream and consciousness, art and life. The only guest in a mysterious hotel where she finds herself after escaping a giant sea wave, Capriolo's narrator wavers between the desire to remember her former life through dreams and flashes of memory, and simultaneously the yearning for the anonymity offered by the isolated hotel. The text is an attempt to record these memories and a psychological investigation into the nature and seductions of two kingdoms, the hotel and the world outside it. The nameless, genderless, ageless, desireless hotel waiters whom the protagonist quickly comes to resemble are the counterparts of her previous dismembered self fraught with emotional trauma, sexual strife, loss and death. Each kingdom is at one time perceived as a prison and at another cherished as a place of freedom. In the end, the narrator decides not to leave the hotel, thus choosing timeless, undifferentiated, harmonious life over time, difference, and anguish and art (she recites poetry by Foscolo, Leopardi and others as if it were her own creation) over reality and the contingent.

In these post-modern narratives the self is understood as a stratification of conflicting experiences leading to existential anguish and psychological disorientation. In other narratives the effort to understand these stratifications widens to include the analysis of one's family and cultural roots. In *Casalinghitudine* ('Housewifery', 1987) and *Il gioco dei regni* ('The game of kingdoms', 1993), *Clara Sereni puts the feminine arts of cooking and sewing respectively to the service of recomposing the conflicting cultural components of her identity. In the former, she mixes ingredients and reinvents recipes from her Jewish and Russian heritages to suit the practical and ideological needs of her present life, thus turning 'housewifery' from drudgery (as for the protagonists of *Donna in guerra* and *Due donne da buttare*) into positive difference and creativity, and loosening the psychological hold of her dead father, a rigid Marxist and Communist Party ideologue who also dictated the family diet. In the latter novel, Sereni reconstructs her family history by cutting and pasting together extracts from texts left behind by its members, exceptional men and women who lived through the revolutionary movements in Russia, two world wars,

Fascism, the persecution of the Jews, Communism and the creation of Israel. The result is a collage exploring the private face of a family who pursued high civic and political ideals at the expense of personal feelings and family affections. The book ends with the recuperation of Sereni's Jewish and maternal heritage, and the discovery of 'the emotion of an uninterrupted female genealogy' (p. 446) in which she has found her place. This is not a historical novel, since Sereni's engagement with the past is subordinate to her interest in family and personal history. However, many writers during the 1980s and 1990s have increasingly turned to the past to produce a wide variety of 'historical' narratives. The next section will outline women's appropriation and transformation of this genre.

Reinventing the past

Women writers, both new and established, have given enormous impulse to the resurgence and renewal of the historical novel in Italy.[9] Their narratives share with Sereni's text the ideological and aesthetic post-modern tenet that the present must be understood through a process of continuous critical re-interpretation of the past and recontextualisation of the self. In the tradition established by *Anna Banti with her innovative *Artemisia* (1947), these writers blend history and imagination to draw parallels with the present, bringing to light women's forgotten contribution to official history, giving voice to lesser-known historical figures, delving into their own cultural and geographical roots and reflecting on the historical process itself. As in *Artemisia*, these narratives often establish a link between narrated self and narrating self whose circumstances are illuminated by the vicissitudes of the character, thus bringing past and present together. While the historical novel in the 1990s was accused of merely evading the present, women's narratives demonstrate both how much the past looms over the present and the depth of women's commitment to contemporary reality.

*Maria Bellonci's *Rinascimento privato* ('Private Renaissance', 1985), which reconstructs the life of Isabella d'Este in Renaissance Mantua, and Maria Rosa Cutrufelli's *La briganta* ('The female brigand', 1990), which traces the 'feminist' development of a fictional character modelled on real-life nineteenth-century women brigands, respond to the need to include women's viewpoint in official history. Laura Mancinelli's *Gli occhi dell'imperatore* ('The emperor's eyes', 1993) recreates the private world of Frederick II of Swabia and his love for Bianca Lancia of Gagliano: it is a story of unfulfilled love and desire, of physical and sentimental journeys and adventures, told through the revelations afforded by silences, looks, minimal gestures and sounds. The political intrigues of the age of Frederick II are evoked in *Silvana La Spina's historical detective novel *Quando Marte è in Capricorno* ('When Mars is in Capricorn', 1994), which, together with her *Un inganno dei sensi malizioso* ('A mischievous trick of the senses', 1995) and *L'amante del paradiso* ('The lover of paradise', 1997), conjures up the mixture of cultures within Sicily. Minor or forgotten artists, whose lives are reinvented in Marta Morazzoni's *Ragazza col turbante* (*Girl in a Turban*, 1986) and in *Marisa Volpi's *Il maestro della betulla* ('The birch tree painter', 1986), are pretexts for an exercise in imagination aimed at constructing inner worlds against carefully and elegantly drawn backgrounds. Rasy's *Il finale della battaglia* ('The end of the battle', 1988), set during World War I, is concerned with language, narration and their possibilities in dealing with the uncertainties of history. *L'altra amante* ('The other lover', 1990), a modern adaptation of Balzac's *La fausse maîtresse*, originated in Rasy's desire to give presence to a character which in the original existed only as an absence and a narrative device. The protagonist of *Rosetta Loy's *Le strade di polvere* (*The Dust Roads of Monferrato*, 1987) is not history, although history affects the life of four generations of a fictional Piedmontese peasant family, but time itself; not linear historical time, but a cyclical time which becomes an eternal, magical present, where the past repeats itself for ever.[10] Maria Corti's *Il canto delle sirene* ('The song of the Sirens', 1989), a history of the representation of the Sirens and the effect of their seduction on people's destinies from ancient Greece to the present, places itself on the borders between intellectual history, mythology, iconography, fiction and autobiography.

*Isabella Bossi Fedrigotti addresses the issue of regional identity in conflict with or as a complement to national identity. Her novels are set in the frontier region of Trentino-Alto-Adige, a battleground of wars between Italians, Germans and Austrians, at different times between the Third War of Independence and the Second World War. The protagonists of *Amore mio uccidi Garibaldi* ('Darling, kill Garibaldi', 1980) and *Casa di guerra* ('House of war', 1983) face political and personal choices that contradict their sense of linguistic and geographical belonging and confuse their loyalties to people, families, armies and nations: 'I was German but also *trentino*, and those June days were for me the worst in the whole wartime. My heart was divided. I could see that the situation was beyond repair: *trentini* and Germans had now become enemies, while, I know for sure, the people asked simply to be left alone' (*Casa di guerra*, p. 134). Bossi Fedrigotti consistently uses an internal multiple point of view to give her characters equal voice, to underline their inner anguish when they must sacrifice human relationships to political choices. However, in *Casa di guerra*, the writer subtly makes the impact of the narrated events on a woman's life and sexual desire (the spinster Miss Firmian) the centre of her narrative. Similarly, in *Amore mio uccidi Garibaldi*, the main focus is on the disruption historical events bring to family relationships and women's lives. Fabrizia Ramondino's narratives, from *Althénopis* (1981) to *L'isola riflessa* ('The inward-looking island', 1998), and other works, poetic mixtures of essay and autobiography, depict the transformation of the South into a mass industrial society, leading to cultural and linguistic loss and self-estrangement. Her *In viaggio* ('On the road', 1995) explores nomadism as a privileged condition through which to overcome provincialism, while *L'isola riflessa* stresses the need for rootedness: only through the preservation of cultural identity and contact with our origins will we survive an alienating reality and grasp the challenges of an increasingly global society.

Frontiers and cultural, political and linguistic diversity are explored consistently by *Giuliana Morandini, whose expressionistic style, rich in imagery and symbolism, conjures up multi-layered and complex realities. Her novels are set in liminal places: Friuli during the last war, Trieste, Berlin. Like many of her contemporaries, this writer has progressively moved away from autobiographically based plots and protagonists to produce narratives which go deeply into the historical roots of identity. *Sogno a Herrenberg* ('Dream at Herrenberg', 1991) and *Giocando a dama con la luna* ('Playing draughts with the moon', 1996), respectively about the sixteenth-century German painter Jörg Ratgeb and the eighteenth-century German archaeologist Karl Humann, respond to the need to understand conflict in a particular place by interrogating those who have witnessed its history. All Morandini's novels engage in an open dialogue with history. *I cristalli di Vienna* (*Blood Stains*, 1978), set in Friuli and Vienna, looks at the horrors of World War II through the eyes of a young girl and her memories as a young woman. The protagonist of *Caffè specchi* (*The Café of Mirrors*, 1983) attempts to recompose her fragmented identity while visiting an unnamed border city (Trieste), whose fragmented culture and history have reached a point of crisis. *Angelo a Berlino* ('Angel in Berlin', 1987) is a penetrating representation of the effects of political and ideological division on every aspect of life: art, architecture, housing, culture, psychic life, family, personal and sexual relationships. The latter novels uncannily prefigure the later conflict in ex-Yugoslavia and the fall of the Berlin wall. Morandini is a sharp interpreter and scholar of the history and culture of central Europe. Her work is highly topical within the context of a Europe where regional, ethnic and linguistic diversities are being defended against increasing homogeneity.

Not only sexual difference

The preceding section has highlighted an increasing interest among women writers in other differences together with or beyond sexual difference. Jewishness, for example, has been explored by Sereni, *Giacoma Limentani, Lia Levi, and *Edith Bruck. The narratives of the latter, who survived Auschwitz, are informed by the dilemmas posed by Holocaust writing, in particular the problematic relationship between experience of the concentration camps and its representation in writing. Her *Lettera alla madre* ('Letter to my mother', 1988) addresses these issues, while attempting to bring back to life, by means of the rhetorical trope of apostrophe, her mother who died in Auschwitz. In Bruck's *Lettera* and in Levi's *Una bambina e basta* ('A girl and nothing else', 1994), the traditional conflicts in mother–daughter relationships are compounded by race, religion, history and war. In *Luce D'Eramo's autobiographical *Deviazione* ('Deviation', 1979), racial discrimination sheds light on discrimination against other diversities. Nineteen-year-old Lucia, wishing to find out the truth about Nazism and Fascism, flees her bourgeois Fascist family and embarks upon a surreal journey through German labour and concentration camps. An Italian non-Jewish volunteer, she must fight for her survival together with Jews, Poles and Russians, although her efforts to shed her social identity prove more difficult than she had imagined. After she is seriously injured in an accident which leaves her trapped and helpless in a wheelchair, she must fight for her social rehabilitation, for her right to love, marriage and work, against the prejudices of a society which treats the disabled as non-persons. The book, a harrowing narrative of the process of shattering and recomposing a social and personal identity, records this struggle with extraordinary emotional intensity. D'Eramo's subsequent novels also explore Otherness, under the guise of terrorism, old age, immigration, disability and the young neo-Nazis. Women in prisons, women and terrorism, drugs, immigration and lesbianism are the subject matter of Goliarda Sapienza's *L'Università di Rebibbia* ('The university of Rebibbia', 1982) and *Le* *certezze del dubbio* ('The certainties of doubt', 1987). Old people in homes receive literary treatment in Petrignani's *Vecchi* ('Old people', 1994), a collection of short prose pieces based on real interviews, while several short stories from Sanvitale's collection *La realtà è un dono* ('Reality is a gift', 1987) deal with sexuality and old age. *Silvana Grasso's *Ninna nanna del lupo* ('Lullaby of the wolf', 1995) is a superb linguistic experiment fusing Sicilian dialect with Italian to produce a mixture of high and low registers suitable to convey the dignity of the decaying body of ninety-year-old Mosca, struck by tuberculosis in adolescence. Mental handicap is the subject matter of a collective book, *Mi riguarda* ('It concerns me', 1994), to which Bossi Fedrigotti and Sereni have contributed as a political, more than a literary, project aimed at lifting a social and linguistic taboo. The weak and the defenceless, the victims and the innocents of today's world are the subject matter of Susanna Tamaro's *La testa fra le nuvole* ('Head in the clouds', 1989), a philosophical-picaresque, fable-like *Bildungsroman* reminiscent of Voltaire's *Candide*, emphasising the lack of sense in the adult world, and of *Per voce sola* (*For solo voice*, 1991), her best book to date, which analyses the violence and horror beneath the surface of everyday life through the languages and perspectives of children and old people.

*Anna Maria Ortese, whose work spans six decades, stands apart from all trends and fashions, making her a solitary giant in Italian letters, has also concentrated on the exploited and vulnerable creatures of this world. Already in her acclaimed *Il mare non bagna Napoli* (*The Bay is Not Naples*, 1953), she observed the physical and moral degradation of the Neapolitan sub-proletariat with a hallucinatory hyper-realist eye, portraying a surreal city governed by destructive and irrational forces. In *L'iguana* (*The Iguana*, 1965), *Il cardillo addolorato* (*The Lament of the Linnet*, 1993), and *Alonso e i visionari* ('Alonso and the visionaries', 1996), Ortese has developed her distinctive brand of 'magic realism' and a vision of the world as subjected to evil forces, a consequence no longer of the 'silence of reason' (the title of the concluding piece in *Il mare non bagna Napoli*), but of the exercise of reason by humanity which has killed nature. Her novels regularly feature suffering creatures, half human and half animal, which are in turn innocent vestiges of a past time of harmony between humans and nature, and demonic incarnations of evil brought about by culture. In *Il cardillo*, set in Naples immediately after the 1799 revolution, and in *Alonso*, Ortese identifies the Age of Enlightenment, the exaltation of reason and progress, as the critical moment lying at the origin of today's corruption, materialism and hatred of nature. Ortese's vision of existence translates itself into a literary search for understanding a metaphysical reality which recedes indefinitely behind illusory masks and self-destroying interpretations. She does not offer solutions on how to improve the world, but suggests that the oppressed, corrupted Mediterranean South (Naples, Sicily, the island of Ocaña) is the site from which the regeneration of values should start. As opposed to the industrialist, capitalist, corrupting North, the South still preserves strong associations with nature. In *Alonso*, the North–South opposition is replaced by a generalised nature–culture opposition, where culture, comprising Europe and the United States, is seen as a progression towards a 'disamore universale' ('universal loss of love'), a deepening of the 'dolore del mondo' ('world's suffering'), and an aggravation of humanity's 'disconoscimento dello Spirito del mondo' ('disavowal of the Spirit of the world') (p. 245).

The new generation

A group of young writers has recently burst on the Italian literary scene whose work must be interpreted with reference to a different set of intellectual and cultural parameters. Identity and writing are played out against the codes and languages which make up the society in which their young protagonists live. References to highbrow literature, kitsch, technological and mass-medial subcultures, the local cultures and dialects, youth cultures and their jargons, music, comics, Italian provincial punk, American pulp, trash and splatter, combine in explosive mixtures to produce parodic, iconoclastic narratives, evoking a fragmented and multi-faceted reality through images and tones ranging from the comic to the grotesque, the gothic and the macabre. These are the ingredients of *Silvia Ballestra's self-ironical and self-referential *Gli orsi* ('The bears', 1994), which conveniently provides the cultural co-ordinates of her writing. The protagonist of the title story 'Gli orsi (63–93)' makes herself part of the new 'youth literature' which claims Pier Vittorio Tondelli and, further back, the avant-garde Gruppo 63 as its forefathers. She also distances herself from it by means of the irreverent language and tone she uses to relate the 1993 Reggio Emilia meeting sanctioning the existence of this new narrative (hence the 63–93 of the title). No critic or writer is hallowed enough to be spared Ballestra's cutting mockery, nor does she spare the cultural industry for its role in manufacturing the success that the young writers attending the meeting and the narrator herself seek. Literary success is an obsession for the protagonists of these new narratives, all penniless aspiring writers, searching also for fulfilling sexual relationships. Writing and female identity pose no problematic exclusions for Rossana Campo's narrator in *In principio erano le mutande* ('In the beginnning were the underpants', 1992), an exuberant first-person picaresque account of a young woman's quest for love, sex and success. In *Mai sentita così bene* ('Never felt so good', 1995), Campo appropriates and subverts stereotypical sexist male language to represent female sexuality and desire.[11] *Carmen Covito's *La bruttina stagionata* ('A seasoned ugly little woman', 1992) is a middle-aged woman's search for Eros amidst metropolitan loneliness, conveyed through a mixture of high and low tones, of drama and farcical comedy. It is still early to predict the impact these narratives will have on Italian mainstream literature, but their major strength is their ability to convey the sense of a reality which increasingly eludes linguistic representation.

At the end of this outline of thirty years of women's writing in Italy, it appears that Ceresa's call for a new female subjectivity and for literary forms capable of representing it has been answered. Women writers have steadily gained ground, slowly moving from the margins to the centre, engaging in increasingly more ambitious literary projects, occupying an increasingly prominent position on the literary scene, and obtaining public recognition through the many literary prizes they have reaped in the past fifteen years. Women's writing has been a laboratory for finding new forms to convey a reality specific to women and, more importantly, for transforming reality through the manipulation of the writer's tools. This chapter attests to the seriousness and quality of the results. Women have made an enormous contribution to the regeneration of the novel in Italy by making its form, content and language more pliable and thus able to represent and interpret the concerns of men and women in a fast changing world. The critical ground is also fertile, with more and more attention being devoted by academics, critics and reviewers, both in Italy and abroad, to the appraisal of this literature, thus ensuring its inclusion in the Italian literary canon.

NOTES

1. See Teresa De Lauretis, 'Figlie prodighe', *DonnaWomanFemme: Omelie di donne* 2–3 (1996), pp. 80–90. De Lauretis takes Ceresa's prodigality to refer to a daughter's most extreme transgression, lesbianism. Research in Rome, 1997, for this chapter was made possible by a British Academy grant.
2. During a meeting at the Italian Cultural Institute, London, 20 February 1997.
3. All translations unpublished in English are mine, except Petrignani's *Navigazioni di Circe*, taken from Sharon Wood (1995).

4. Some examples are Giuliana Ferri's *Un quarto di donna* ('A quarter of a woman', 1973), Carla Cerati's *Un matrimonio perfetto* ('A perfect marriage', 1975) and Gabriella Magrini's *Lunga giovinezza* ('Long childhood', 1976). See also Anna Nozzoli, *Tabù e Coscienza* (Florence, 1978), pp. 147–70.

5. See Castelli's 'Miti, forme e modelli della nuova narrativa', in Walter Pedullà, Silvana Castelli and Stefano Giovanardi, *La letteratura emarginata. I narratori giovani degli anni '70* (Rome, 1978), pp. 111–200 (pp. 123–32), in which she examines texts by Maria Paola Cantele, Leila Baiardo, Rosetta Loy and Toni Maraini.

6. Carol Lazzaro-Weiss discusses Castelli's work in 'From margins to mainstream: some perspectives on women and literature in Italy in the 1980s', in Aricò, pp. 197–217 (p. 201).

7. See Manuela Gieri, 'Frabotta', in Bondanella, pp. 229–31.

8. Carla Cerati's *La cattiva figlia* ('The bad daughter', 1990), Elena Ferrante's *L'amore molesto* ('An uneasy love', 1992) and Marisa Bulgheroni's *Gli orti della Regina* ('The Queen's Gardens', 1993), are the most prominent examples. The quest for the mother is a significant, structuring component of Rosetta Loy's *Sogni d'inverno* ('Winter dreams', 1992), Francesca Duranti's *Effetti personali* ('Personal effects', 1988), Fleur Jaeggy's *I beati anni del castigo* (*Sweet Days of Discipline*, 1989), and Mariateresa Di Lascia's *Passaggio in ombra* ('Passage in the shadow', 1995).

9. See Lazzaro-Weiss (1993), pp. 120–57, Della Fazia Amoia, pp. 37–56 and Neria De Giovanni, *Carta di donna. Narratrici italiane del '900* (Turin, 1996), pp. 5–14.

10. See Sharon Wood, 'Rosetta Loy: The paradox of the past', in Zygmunt Barański and Lino Pertile (eds.), *The New Italian Novel* (Edinburgh, 1993), pp. 121–38.

11. See Claudia Bernardi, 'Pulp and Other Fictions: the Critical Debate on the New Italian Narrative of the Nineties', *Bulletin of the Society for Italian Studies* 30 (1997), pp. 4–11.

17

Poetry, 1870–2000

In the closing decades of the twentieth century the number of women who write poetry has greatly increased, as has critical attention to their work. The most dominant characteristic of this generation's work is probably its absence of any canon or tradition. Since the late 1940s, Italian women poets have defined their own point of view and experimented with poetic forms. Their poetry bristles with a new self-confidence; it is mature, fertile, pliable and stylistically varied, with the poets themselves willing and able to defend their point of view.[1] Italian women poets have been given an equal voice, and any difficulties encountered are similar to those faced by their fellow male poets. These women have redefined the thematic nature of poetry, while the most persistent note in their work is an increased anxiety for the personal, social and environmental issues that face humanity, regardless of gender, in the new millennium.

This new position contrasts strongly with that of women writers in Italy in the late nineteenth and early twentieth centuries. During that period, poetry was the most popular literary genre and women chose it as a vehicle for lyrics that were mostly sentimental and devotional in character.[2] The poetry written by these women was mostly decorative, tentative in its approach to the canon, and consequently thematically conservative and stylistically imitative.[3] Poetry written by women in the late 1880s reflected their subordinate social position. Collections produced at that time either marked milestones in family life such as births, weddings and deaths, or they were devotional or pedagogical in intent. Many of the titles used, such as *Canti e ghirlande* ('Songs and garlands') and *Petali e lacrime* ('Petals and tears') reflect the peripheral, lachrymose and sentimental nature of much of the work. Unsure of themselves from a literary and social point of view they fell back on the non-threatening themes of domesticity with its occasional happiness but also its loneliness, isolation and melancholia.

I intend to divide this overview of poetry into three sections. The first deals with those poets, often influenced by symbolism, who wrote in the era before the appearance of the ground-breaking work of *Antonia Pozzi in the 1930s, and whose often restricted position within society accounts for the way in which they wrote and the subject matter they presented. The second examines the change apparent in the poetry of those women who were affected not just by the war but also by the poetry of Ungaretti, Montale and the hermetic movement (see chapter 14). The final grouping looks at the work of those who reacted to the women's movement and who have advanced the cause of women's poetry by achieving equality and recognition. There is little difference thematically or stylistically from that of their male counterparts.

The twenty years that separate the death of the poet *Erminia Fuà Fusinato (1876) from that of *Contessa Lara (1896), the Byronic pseudonym of Evelina Cattermole Mancini, mark a notable change in the lifestyle of late nineteenth-century women poets. Fusinato's poetry was conservative, moralistic and pedagogical, while her position in the political, cultural and social life of Rome conformed to the dictates of prevailing social mores. Fusinato's funeral in Rome was attended by high-ranking political authorities, intellectuals, schoolgirls and a wide cross-section of society, and was a sign of the esteemed position she held in that city. The life of Contessa Lara, on the other hand, was marked by various scandals, and her writing in both prose and poetry touched a vibrant chord among her many enthusiastic female readers. Two murders at the start and end of her career dominated her personal life. Her first lover was killed by her husband, while she herself was murdered by the young lover she was about to discard in 1896. Born into a cultured and aristocratic background, Contessa Lara could have opted for a privileged life but chose writing as a career – indeed, she was one of the first women to use writing as her main source of income.[4] Following her separation from her husband, she returned to Florence, the city of her birth, where she published her first poems, *Canti e ghirlande*, in 1867. She wrote three further collections, but despite her wide readership, she was referred to as a 'Stecchetti in gonnella' ('Stecchetti in a skirt').[5] This denigrating comparison – Stecchetti was a male poet and literary critic – insinuated that her writings simply mimicked the canon proposed by men. More dramatically, Contessa Lara's coffin bore a single wreath of white roses from young girls in that city who empathised with her poetry and prose writings, and who chose to mark her tragic death with this symbolic gesture of solidarity. It symbolised female indignation with Italian law which, at that time, indulged men involved in crimes of passion and criticised women who did not conform to the then accepted norms of female behaviour.[6]

What captivated the imagination of her readers was the courage she used to express her emotions. After patronising her earlier work, Benedetto Croce later admitted that her poetry had a serious lyrical dimension that closely paralleled French symbolist poetry at that time.[7] As Emmanuella Tandello points out, Contessa Lara's second collection of poetry, *Versi*, also anticipates many of the major thematic keys subsequently found in D'Annunzio's *Poema paradisiaco*.[8] The attraction of her poetry owes much to its intimate, overtly autobiographical nature. As a poet and novelist she was convinced that women had a right, like men, to participate actively in writing, and her success can be attributed to her ability to appeal beyond her largely female audience.

*Maria Alinda Bonacci Brunamonti from Perugia was also popular. A well-educated, occasional poet, different in every way from Contessa Lara, Brunamonti chose the motto 'innovare serbando'[9] ('innovation through conservation') for her poetry, because she attempted to combine classical metre and verse forms with the artistic, aesthetic and scientific concerns that were topical at the time. She expanded the language of poetry to include technical vocabulary as indicated by titles such as *Flora*, *Fosforescenza marina* ('Marine phosphorescence') and *Zaffiri d'acqua* ('Water sapphires'). She saw poetry as a commentary on contemporary, public and private concerns while Croce praised her critical evaluation of Raphael's art.[10] In 1901, the critic Guido Pompilj openly expressed his preference for Brunamonti's lyrics as opposed to those of his future wife Vittoria Aganoor.[11]

Contessa Lara and Bonacci Brunamonti were models for a later generation such as *Annie Vivanti, *Ada Negri, *Neera and *Vittoria Aganoor. Vivanti (see chapter 13) was born in London (her mother was German, her father Italian), and her fortune as a poet was linked to her friendship with Giosuè Carducci, who wrote the preface to *Lirica* in 1890 and greatly admired the romantic amalgam of contrast and passion in her poetry. In his introduction Carducci made it clear that although women lacked the talent to write successful poetry, Vivanti, with her gifted ear for the rhythms of speech, was an exception to the rule. The opening poem of

Lirica introduces a sharply ironic tone unusual among women poets at that time. Vivanti makes it clear that her intent is infringement of the canon:

> Sono in contravvenzione, o Mondo astuto.
> Volea truffarti con la merce mia:
> Non è tabacco, sigari o liquori,
> Nulla di spiritoso: è poesia!

> (I am in contravention, oh shrewd World. / I meant to trick you with my wares: / It is neither tobacco, cigars or spirits, / nothing witty: it is poetry!)

By contrast Neera, the pseudonym of Anna Radius Zuccari, was a highly successful novelist (see chapter 12) whose collections of poetry addressed the personal sphere. Thus she used poetry to express her maternal emotion – one collection was written to commemorate her daughter's marriage (*Poesie*, 1898) while a second was dedicated to her grandson: *Il canzoniere della nonna* ('A Grandmother's Book of Poems', 1908). Vittoria Aganoor Pompilj, a Paduan of Armenian origin, hesitated for a long time before publishing *Leggenda eterna* ('Eternal Legend') in 1900 at the age of forty-five. Dedicated to her mother, it reflects her frustration at having sacrificed the possibility of marriage and motherhood in order to care for her. Aganoor's dilemma was that she sought spiritual peace through writing poetry which found its driving force in the unhappiness of her unrealised longing for love and parenthood. Despite this aspiration Aganoor rejected all attempts to find parallels between her lyrics and her life, and remained emotionally reticent in her poetry. Her correspondence with Domenico Gnoli reveals the poetic and realistic side of her nature. In one such letter she said: 'I am too complicated and my life too simple for discussion . . . My life consists of little activity and a lot of dreaming.'[12]

Her life, however, was not as empty as suggested in this letter. Aganoor's extensive literary studies owed much to the cultural life of Padua where she lived in the early part of her life. She was given a solid foundation in classical theory and meter, and she was also aware of contemporary developments in poetry and metrics, often adopting ironic and sarcastic tones, as can be seen in poem titles such as *Ribellione* ('Rebellion') and *A Monsieur Verslibre* ('To Mr Free-verse'). Shortly before her marriage, Aganoor wrote the poem *Trasimeno* (as part of *Poesie complete*) to praise Pompilj's reclamation work in that area of Italy which she had visited with him. The poem is traditional in rhyme and metre, but the images used are deliberate symbols of the change for the better not just in the area around Trasimeno but in her life too:

> Il dolce ricordo si perde
> nel sogno. Ecco siede la scorta
> a poppa, e la barca mi porta
> incontro a un'isola verde . . .
>
> (Sweet memory is lost / in dream. Behold the guide sits / at the stern, and the boat takes me / towards a green island.)

*Luisa Giaconi and *Amalia Guglielminetti, while significantly different in poetic temperament, share the coincidence of being recognised in their own right thanks to their connection with the poets Dino Campana and Guido Gozzano respectively. Guglielminetti's sensual verse was heavily influenced by D'Annunzio's poetry while her fortune and acceptance as a poet and writer were aided by her relationship with Gozzano. Giaconi's only collection, *Tebaide* ('Thebaid'), was published one year after her death and is a moving meditation on female unhappiness. The symbolic dimension to her poetry is found in the repeated presentation of dreams that contrast with reality. The final poem, *Dianora,* presents love as an unstable passion which brings happiness and anguish in its tow:

> La tua giornata d'amore
> passò, la tua ora di sole si spense, Dianora;
> la soglia che un giorno segreta
> al tuo piede errante fu mèta,
> si chiuse, il tuo regno d'amore
> finì . . .
> Chi al suo sogno eterno sorrise con un'altra aurora
> d'amore?
>
> (Your day of love / ended, your hour in the sun died too, Dianora; / the secret threshold once / the target for your wandering foot/ closed, your kingdom of love / ended . . . / Who smiled at her eternal dream with another dawn / of love?)

This poem is a shocking example of 'male' appropriation: Dino Campana read it in 1911 and republished it in 1916 with a note stating it had been written years earlier by a woman from Florence. He presented it without its original title, changed the punctuation and made certain adjustments to the text. The line 'Al tuo piede errante fu mèta' is suggestive of movement and wandering, but Campana substitutes 'spirito' ('spirit') for 'piede' ('foot') thereby making a substantive textual change. Yet another alteration is made when Giaconi's line 'né ancora di dubbi s'adombra' ('nor is she overshadowed yet with doubts') is changed to 'un'àncora di dubbi l'adombra' ('an anchor of doubts hangs over her') in the Campana text. Campana signed the 'adjusted' poem as his own; only later was the truth regarding its origin established.[13]

A decisive break with the past becomes apparent in the work of Ada Negri, Sibilla Aleramo and Antonia Pozzi. Ada Negri received considerable recognition over several decades. Her talent for instructing underprivileged children motivated her to write poems on the theme of social injustice, particularly in her 1895 collection *Tempeste* ('Storms'). The harshness of eviction is highlighted in these lines from *Sgombero forzato* ('Enforced eviction'):

> Miseria. – La pigione non fu pagata -
> a rifascio, nel mezzo della via,
> la scarsa roba squallida è gettata.
> Quello sgombero sembra un'agonia.

> (Destitution. – The rent was not paid – / dumped, in the middle of the street, / the few wretched belongings are being thrown. / That eviction seems a death rattle.)

Acclaimed for both what she did and what she wrote, Ada Negri was initially popular with the Socialists, who called her the 'vergine rossa', ('the red maiden') but later accused her of betraying their political cause. Her subsequent marriage to a wealthy industrialist ended unsuccessfully. The titles of many early poems (*Piccola mano* ('Tiny hand'), *Notturno nuziale* ('A wedding nocturn'), *Stanchezza* ('Weariness')) show how Negri concentrates on emotions felt by women who must come to terms with the mixed emotions that often accompany marriage and motherhood. Her doubts regarding her position as a wife and writer surface in later poems, and this honesty and frankness was new among poets in Italy at that time. In the poem, *Il sole e l'ombra*, ('Sun and shadow'), from a collection, *Il libro di Mara* ('Mara's book') describing the rapture of her brief but tragic love for a man whose life was cut short by premature death, the radiance of shared love is threatened by the shadow that accompanies it:

> Sole di mezzogiorno, nel luglio felice, sulla piazza deserta . . .
> il resto è ombra e polvere d'ombra.

> (Mid-day sun, in happy July, on the deserted square . . . / The rest is shadow and shadow's dust.)

While Negri's early work concentrated on spiritual loneliness and the need for social liberation for the less fortunate in society, her later work took on the broader dimension where joy and sorrow are shared not isolated experiences. Despite the social progress apparent in her work she was later criticised for her political ambivalence. Courted by the Fascist regime, she was awarded the title 'poetessa d'Italia' and, on Mussolini's insistence, was admitted to the Italian Academy in 1940, the first and only woman so honoured in those years. Despite this, hers was the only voice that emerged unscathed from the cultural trends and political upheavals of the first half of this century, and for many years she was the only woman poet represented in manuals and anthologies, just as Grazia Deledda was regarded as the only woman novelist worthy of attention. Interest in Negri's work declined rapidly in the post-war period when her link with Mussolini and the Fascists was severely criticised.

Sibilla Aleramo's poetry also caught the attention of the public. Aleramo, pseudonym of Rina Faccio, belongs to that exceptional generation of feminists who played a crucial role in the emancipation of women in Italy (see chapter 12). Instinctively drawn to poetry, which she saw as a vehicle of self-expression,[14] she remained unaffected by changes introduced by Futurist and Hermetic poets. Her poems document a longing for love and power that life does not deliver. Forced to live with herself and that 'mestissima cosa' ('saddest of all things')[15] which freedom represents, she found loneliness all around.[16] For her, life and poetry were inseparable, with the result that her lyrics display a wealth of the human and emotional.[17] In the collection *Selva d'amore*, the poem 'Nello specchio' ('In the mirror') is a good example of how she concentrates on feeling:

> Più cupi i miei occhi
> ma insieme più roridi
> or nello specchio, e li adoro,
> tali li ha fatti l'amore di te.
>
> (Darker are my eyes / but also glistening / now in the mirror, and I adore them, / for my love for you has made them so.)

By contrast the poem 'Dolce sangue' ('Sweet blood') highlights the sensuality that much of her poetry exuded:

> Dolce dolce sangue
> ne le vene mi langue.
> Oh vigor lontano,
> se vieni di delizia vi gemi!
>
> (Sweet sweet blood / languishes in my veins. / Oh distant strength / if you come you will moan with pleasure there.)

Antonia Pozzi's poetry achieved much notoriety in the late 1930s and early 1940s. She took a degree in aesthetics at the University of Milan but her subsequent work as a part-time teacher offered little challenge to her potential or ability, while the constraints placed on her emotional and intellectual life were at variance with the emancipation of her largely misogynist fellow university students. She saw suicide as the only alternative to the emotional void around her. After her death it was discovered that she had written poetry secretly over the years, and ninety-one of these poems were published in 1939. The public response was enthusiastic, and other editions followed. However, Pozzi's poetry was significantly tampered with after her death: it was first expurgated and heavily edited by her own father, then in recent years by Onorina Dino, a nun in Milan to whom her manuscripts were subsequently entrusted. It is thus not clear to what extent we have an authentic text.

The topics that interest Pozzi are childhood, love, death, religion, the sense of void and the suggestive beauty of nature. There is a new register in the poems, *Parole* ('Words'), with precise images, natural eloquence and purity of sound to the fore:

> Forse la vita è davvero
> quale la scopri nei giorni giovani:
> un soffio eterno che cerca
> di cielo in cielo
> chissà che altezza.
>
> (Perhaps life really is / as you discover in your early days: / an eternal breath that searches / from sky to sky / who knows what heights.)

Pozzi's poetry reflects some influence of the crepuscular and hermetic poets, but she maintains an independent voice. Part of its attraction is the immediate rapport established with the reader: 'Poesia, mi confesso con te / che sei la mia voce profonda' ('Poetry, I open myself to you / who are my innermost voice'). Biancamaria Frabotta, who published *Donne in Poesia* in 1976, the first anthology devoted exclusively to women poets, cites Pozzi as an example of a poet who spoke clearly and unambiguously, and this volume played an important role in raising the profile of Pozzi's reputation.[18] Together with the editorial efforts of Onorina Dino and Alessandra Cenni, it has rekindled interest in Pozzi's poetry.

*Margherita Guidacci ushers in significant changes in post-war women's poetry, and her work reflects the challenges and difficulties faced by women.[19] Her first poems were published in 1946, and by the time she died in 1992 she had a further eighteen collections to her credit. After the war, poetry became for her a liberating and vital force; her early work was an attempt both to free herself of the anguish accumulated during the war years,[20] and also to reclaim the value of poetry:

> Chi grida sull'alto spartiacque è udito da entrambe le valli.
> Perciò la voce dei poeti intendono i viventi ed i morti.

> (The one who cries from the watershed on high is heard in the valleys on either side. / Thus do both the living and the dead hear the poets' voice.)

Deeply moved by the work of Ungaretti, she nevertheless remained outside the poetic forms which hermeticism advocated. This independence of spirit marked her work in prose and poetry, but such personal, stylistic and thematic individuality came at a price. She placed herself outside prevailing trends and consequently found it difficult to have her work published, despite being one of the most productive poets of her time. A prolific translator, she was drawn to poets such as John Donne, Emily Dickinson, Emmanuel Monnier and Jorge Guillén.

In the 1960s Guidacci's voice remained isolated, but in the 1970s and 1980s her work returned to the fore, and reflected an increasingly positive attitude towards life. *Inno alla gioia* ('Hymn to Joy') revolves around the themes of joy and love, and culminates in *Il buio e lo splendore* ('Darkness and Brightness') where Guidacci states her belief that, with the intervention of poetry, darkness eventually gives way to light:

> Dopo la notte stellata, l'attesa
> piena di gioia, ecco,
> come sorge splendente
> il nostro giorno delfico!

> (After the star-studded night, the waiting / full of joy, behold, / how resplendent rises up / our delphic day!)

Her career echoes that of other women poets whose work spans several decades from the 1950s to the 1990s, and who managed to remain largely independent of prevalent trends and styles. This often caused them to be consigned to the margins and created significant difficulties in terms of publication and distribution. Both Daria Menicanti (1914–1995) and Biagia Marniti (b. Puglia, 1921) fall within this category.

Another well-known post-war poet who defies easy classification is *Maria Luisa Spaziani. Emilio Cecchi has praised her pursuit of the individual's experience, the striking immediacy of her language and the vibrant structural rhythm of her poems.[21] The ambivalent allusiveness of enigmatic titles such as *Utilità della memoria* ('Usefulness of memory'), *Geometria del disordine* ('Geometry of disorder') and *La stella del libero arbitrio* ('The star of free will') allows her to adopt a range of symbols, figures and allegories that indicate the influence of Montale. Spaziani has never been drawn to the more fragmented style of poetry, so favoured in the second half of the twentieth century. Hers is a balanced and controlled verse that imposes its own rigour and discipline, while the importance of the written word is paramount in these lines from *Poesie*:

> Ci scambiammo tesori senza prezzo.
> Sprecai genio e speranze, notti e fede
> per lanciare quel ponte luminoso.
>
> Raggiungerti è impossibile a ritroso.
> Ogni passo s'impiglia – o serpe, o fogna -
> nella fitta gramigna del disprezzo.
>
> (We exchanged priceless treasures. / I lavished my talent and hopes, my nights and trust / to cast that radiant bridge. / To reach back to you is impossible. / Each step becomes entangled – either viper or sewer – / in the dense morass of contempt.)

Throughout her life Spaziani has fought for due recognition for women's poetry, founding the Montale Centre in Rome to ensure that poets, regardless of sex, would have a united platform and thereby reach a wider audience.

*Amelia Rosselli was one of the most original and linguistically adventurous Italian poets of this century. Forced to flee the Fascist regime, her family found refuge in Paris where her father was assassinated on Fascist orders when she was seven. Her first languages were French and Italian and she later acquired English when the family moved to England and the United States. Rosselli's life was marked by trauma and unhappiness; in her case, memory was synonymous with violent death and painful personal recollections that finally proved too powerful. She took her own life in 1996.

One of the most unusual features of her work is the impact that her triple linguistic background had on the language she used for poetry.[22] It was directly responsible for a certain amount of slippage between her use of English and Italian and led to the creation of the accidental or Freudian lapsus which so characterises her poetry. This lapsus can consist of Italian phrases where an English word is deliberately or incorrectly used in place of an equivalent in Italian. Rosselli speaks of a 'retrograde amore', 'tantrums segreti' and in the following lines from *Sonno-Sleep* the English is determined by the Italian:

> you seem to hear angels mocking you
> you seem to cry out look the stars!
> and run out rapid against a fence of spine.

The omission of the preposition 'at' makes the expression 'look the stars' a direct translation of the Italian ('guarda le stelle') while both 'rapid' and the 'fence of spine' are suggestive of the Italian equivalents of 'rapida' and either 'siepe di spine' ('fence of thorn') or 'recinto di fil spinato' (' barbed-wire fence'). Equally striking was the way her knowledge of music and musical composition had a strong input on the space, verse, rhyme, rhythm, stress and cadence of her psychologically complex poetry. In *Spazi metrici* ('Metrical spaces', 1962) Rosselli outlined the links between music and poetry while the title of her 1981 poetry collection, *Impromptu*, deliberately recalls a piece of music. What strikes the reader in the final composition of *Variazioni belliche* ('Warlike variations', 1964) is the circular, musical movement, where the repeated key words *mondo, tutto, vedovo, tu, sono* become dominant chords which strike the reader's mind. The effectiveness of this verbal exercise is further emphasised by the repetition of the musical stress and cadence in each line:

> Tutto il mondo è vedovo se è vero che tu cammini ancora
> tutto il mondo è vedovo se è vero! Tutto il mondo
> è vero se è vero che tu cammini ancora, tutto il
> mondo è vedovo se tu non muori! Tutto il mondo
> è mio se è vero che tu non sei vivo ma solo
> una lanterna per i miei occhi obliqui . . .
>
> (All the world is widowed if it is true that you are still on your feet / all
> the world is widowed if it is true! All the world / is true if it is true that
> you are still on your feet, all the / world is widowed if you are not
> dying! All the world / is mine if it is true that you are not alive but just /
> a lantern for my sidelong glances . . .)

When Rosselli came to Italy, her non-Italian cultural and linguistic background led her to stand apart from all schools of poetry, and little attention was paid to her work in the 1960s and early 1970s. Her early work was written when linguistic experimentalism was dominant, and although she had some contact with members of *Gruppo 63* promoting experimentalism, her poetry was not shaped by them despite its creative exploration of the ambiguity of language and languages. However, in 1963 Pier Paolo Pasolini singled out her use of the Freudian lapsus as a distinguishing and uniquely valuable feature of her language;[23] in 1978 Pier Vincenzo Mengaldo praised her linguistic independence and the informal conversational tone of her deeply evocative poetry. For him, she was the only woman poet worthy of mention in his anthology of twentieth-century Italian poetry.[24]

For Rosselli and *Alda Merini, memory brought fear and terror in its wake, and both attempted to escape its clutches. In Merini's case it is the memory of twenty years spent voluntarily and involuntarily in asylums in Italy. In 'Fogli bianchi' ('White pages') she attempts to liberate herself from the past and come to terms with the future:

> La mia poesia mi è cara come la mia stessa
> vita, è la mia parola interiore, la mia vita . . .
> La poesia, semmai, è la liberazione dal male . . .
>
> (My poetry is as dear to me as life itself, / it is my inner voice, my very life . . . / If anything, poetry is deliverance from evil . . .)

When Merini's early poetry appeared in the 1950s, critics enthusiastically valued its spontaneity: 'Sono nata il ventuno a primavera / ma non sapevo che nascere folle . . . / potesse scatenar tempesta' ('I was born on the twenty-first, in springtime / but I was unaware that to be born mad . . . / could unleash a storm'). Merini's later work, published in the early 1980s, provides a frank account of the frightening and humiliating experiences in mental institutions that have left an indelible mark on her and her work, as in 'Vuoto d'amore' ('Void of love'):

> Il manicomio è il monte Sinai
> maledetto, su cui tu ricevi
> le tavole di una legge
> agli uomini sconosciuta.
>
> (The madhouse is the accursed / Mount Sinai on which you receive/ the tables of a law/ unknown to mankind.)

Although the poetry of Guidacci, Marniti, Spaziani, Rosselli, Merini and many others spanned several decades, the World War II and Fascism lent it a coherence, keeping alive a feeling of civic and moral responsibility. A marked change, however, is apparent in the generation that followed. The establishment of women's cultural centres throughout Italy in the late 1970s provided a platform for women to voice their ideas and present their work. Many of them were actively involved in the political, social and cultural sphere, and this gave them a new self-confidence not apparent in their predecessors. *Biancamaria Frabotta did much to further the case of women and poets in Italy. Frustrated by their quasi exclusion from manuals and anthologies, she threw down the gauntlet with *La politica del femminismo* ('The politics of feminism') and *Donne in Poesia* ('Women in poetry') in 1976, two volumes that stimulated considerable debate.

Several women have made their mark in the 1980s and 1990s. In the case of Vivian Lamarque (b. Tesero 1946), fable and reality provided inspiration for her early poetry. Like Umberto Saba she plays with the banal and everyday. Her poems are short, succinct and playfully humorous, especially in this extract from *Il signore d'oro* ('The man of gold'):

> Era una signora che aveva quarant'anni, come
>   mai?
> Va bene era nata quarant'anni fa. Però gli anni
>   non erano durati veramente un anno e i mesi
>   non erano durati veramente un mese.
> Così i quarant'anni erano arrivati in due tre minu-
>   ti, non era giusto, protestò la signora.

> (She was a lady and was forty, how come?/ All right, she was born forty
> years ago. However the years / had not really lasted a year and the
> months / had not really lasted a month./ And so she had become forty
> in two or three / minutes, it was not fair, the lady protested.)

Lamarque's earlier poetry had the therapeutic objective of helping her come to terms with problems rooted in her family. Her most recent work, whose title *Una quieta polvere* ('A quiet dust') is taken from an Emily Dickinson poem, shows a change of direction. No longer centred on the self, these recent poems show a new interest in urgent civil themes in our times.

A complete contrast is found in the work of *Jolanda Insana. Its most striking feature is her dexterous use of language with its multiple plays on words. The title given to *Fendenti fonici* ('Phonic daggers') suggests that words are like blades that wound and scar. Her creation of new words (many forged from Sicilian dialect), together with a rejection of punctuation, is indicative of her dissatisfaction with the language at her disposal. In *Sciarra amara* ('Bitter feud') where people seek out conflict and dissension, she uses language to highlight the absurdity of life:

non finiremo mai di fare
sciarra amara
nessun compare ci metterà
la buona parola
tu stuti le candele
che io allumo

(we will never cease / to carry on our bitter feud / no godfather will
bring kind words to our lips / you quench the candles / that I light)

Whereas contemporary poets have opted, like many of their male colleagues, for a verse form that pays little attention to traditional rhyme or
versification, Patrizia Valduga (b. Castelfranco Veneto 1953) is a notable
exception. She digs deep into the tradition of Italian poetry, using the
sonnet and octave for her poetry. In *La Tentazione* ('Temptation') she
employs *terza rima* and hendecasyllabic verse to give structure and voice to
her sense of suffering and oppression:

In nome di Dio, apri quella porta!
la notte fissa in me il suo occhio nero;
apri per tempo, la mia vita è corta,

è un vomito d'inferno il mio pensiero
e l'anima mi giace pietra al fondo
e invischia di spropositi ogni vero.

(For God's sake, open that door! / night stares inside me with its dark
eye; / open up in time, my life is short, / my thoughts are a vomit from
hell / and my soul is like a sunken stone/ and it entangles everything
true in errors.)

This contrasts dramatically with *Maura Del Serra who is influenced
by the Tuscan poetic environment, particularly the poetry of Mario Luzi
and Margherita Guidacci. Quasi-hermetic in style, her language is dense
and concentrated with a strong, intuitive dimension as in *La mente* ('The
mind') from the symbolically entitled *Meridiana* ('Sundial'):

Io, regina in catene
da me stessa forgiate nella notte
ed in trecce di fiori mutate al mio risveglio,
siedo sul trono d'acqua terra fuoco
ed aria fluttuante fra mondi noti e ignoti . . .

(I, a queen in chains / that I myself forged in the night / and
transformed into braided flowers on my awakening, / I sit on the
throne of water earth fire/ and air, fluctuating between worlds known
and unknown.)

Further diversity is apparent in Patrizia Cavalli's (b. Todi 1947) epi-grammatic style and uniquely personal poetic message. Her self-deprecating reply to the provocative suggestion that her poetry will not change anything – 'le mie poesie/ non cambieranno il mondo' ('my poems / will not change the world') – is typical of her independence.[25] However, the real sign of advancement and independence in Italian women's poetry can be detected in the work of *Franca Grisoni who writes poetry in her native dialect. A self-taught poet, her first collection *La böba* ('The idiot') was published in 1986 and provoked a lively discussion on the role of dialect poetry within mainstream Italian poetry. Grisoni's work, together with that of Franco Loi, Raffaello Baldini and Franco Scataglini, is now a driving force in the revival and popularity of dialect poetry in Italy. She is natural and spontaneous in expression, displays great metrical skill in her use of the Sirmione dialect (which abounds in monosyllables), and is linguistically original and inventive in what she writes. These lines from *La böba* illustrate how she uses dialect to present the metaphor of impris-onment and the chains of love:

> Gho fat en prizuner
> e 'l encadene al let.
> El parla forester,
> vòi che 'l me 'nsegnes
> a me, che prizunera a lü
> me do da tegner.

> (I have taken a prisoner / and am tying him to the bed. / He speaks a foreign tongue, / I want him to teach it / to me, who give myself / as a prisoner into his hands.)

Grisoni was awarded the Viareggio poetry prize in 1997, a tangible and important acknowledgement of the high value currently placed on her work within the canon of modern Italian poetry. With such recognition it is clear that the use of dialect has become accepted, and it is now valued for the unique contribution it makes to poetry. The courage displayed by Grisoni in using dialect as the language of poetic communication is further evidence of a newly acquired confidence and self-assuredness that Italian women poets now possess.

NOTES

1. See Mariella Bettarini, 'Donna e poesia', *Poesia* 12, n. 124 (January 1999), p. 45.
2. M. De Giorgio, *Le italiane dall'Unità ad oggi* (Rome–Bari, 1992), p. 379.
3. See G. Morandini, *La voce che è in lei*, pp. 43–4; and L. Baldacci, *Poeti minori dell'Ottocento* (Milan–Naples, 1958), vol. I.

4. See Antonia Arslan, *Dame, galline e regine. La scrittura femminile italiana fra '800 e '900*, (Milan, 1998), p. 156.

5. 'L'Illustrazione Italiana', 1 semestre (1886), p. 248.

6. M. De Giorgio, *Le italiane*, p. 381.

7. B. Croce, *La letteratura della nuova Italia* (Bari, 1943), vol. II, p. 330.

8. See E. Tandello, 'Tradition and Innovation in the 1880s: Annie Vivanti and Contessa Lara', forthcoming in V. Jones and A. L. Lepschy (eds.), *A Pen in Her Hand. Nineteenth-Century Women Writers in Italy* (Leeds, forthcoming).

9. M. Alinda Bonacci Brunamonti, *Raffaello Sanzio ossia dell'arte perfetta*, (Urbino, 1879), p. 17.

10. B. Croce, *La letteratura*, p. 342.

11. V. Aganoor, *Lettere a Domenico Gnoli*, p. 357.

12. *Ibid.*, p. 75.

13. *Chroniques italiennes* 39/40; E. Genevois (ed.), *Les femmes écrivains en Italie (1870–1920): ordres et libertés* (Paris, 1994), p. 119.

14. F. A. Bassanese, 'Sibilla Aleramo', in *Dictionary of Literary Biography, 114*, p. 4.

15. S. Aleramo, *Diario di una donna*, p. 27.

16. See *ibid.*

17. N. Sapegno quoted in V. Esposito, *L'altro Novecento*, vol. II (Foggia, 1997), p. 35.

18. B. Frabotta (ed.), *Donne in Poesia* (Rome, 1976), p. 14.

19. See M. Zancan, *Il doppio itinerario della scrittura. La donna nella tradizione letteraria italiana* (Turin, 1998), pp. 101–3.

20. L. Pupolin offers a good discussion of her reasons for writing poetry in: 'Margherita Guidacci: poesia come liberazione e gioia', *Idea* 40, 2 (1984), p. 39.

21. E. Cecchi, *Corriere della Sera*, 23 December 1962.

22. See *Poesia* 93 (March 1996), pp. 21–6.

23. *Il Menabò* 6 (1963), p. 66.

24. P. V. Mengaldo (ed.), *Poeti italiani del Novecento* (Milan, 1987), p. 995.

25. See D. Attanasio in *Leggere* 50 (May 1993), p. 68.

18
_____

Theatre and cinema, 1945–2000

Although the twentieth century witnessed a substantial increase in the publication and critical evaluation of women's writing across a range of literary genres, the number of women involved in writing for performance remained disproportionately small at least until mid-century. The delayed achievement of female writers in theatre and cinema is undoubtedly linked to the hybrid nature of these media. Writing for performance is part of an interdisciplinary process usually requiring the collaboration of several artists and professionals as well as access to specific agencies and material resources, and this access has historically been more difficult for women writers than for men. By the end of the 1950s, however, many of the cultural and economic restraints that had impeded the visibility of women as writers within the performing arts had begun to change throughout the Western world, and there has been a significant increase in the production of work by female playwrights and screenwriters since that time.

The emergence of female dramatists occurred slightly later in Italy than in Britain or the United States. Indeed, not until in the early 1970s was there a perceptible shift in the production and publication of theatrical texts authored by Italian women. Renowned for its opera, Italy has a comparatively weak tradition of conventional drama. In mainstream theatre, directors and leading actors have always enjoyed greater power and prestige than writers, and there has been a corresponding absence of institutional support for dramatic writing. For women writing for the stage, this aspect of the national theatrical tradition compounds the already significant obstacles that face women playwrights everywhere. Although a small number of Italian women writers authored plays in the nineteenth century and throughout the first half of the twentieth century, their work was infrequently published or critically discussed.

The comedies of the Neapolitan actress and writer Titina De Filippo present an interesting case of historical erasure and subsequent recovery. The sister of Eduardo, one of Italy's most famous playwrights, and of the less widely known Peppino, Titina De Filippo wrote several successful plays in the 1930s, when she and her brothers directed a theatre company in Naples. Her plays are similar in style and setting to those of Eduardo, drawing on the generic conventions of the comedy of manners, with distinctive Neapolitan elements, including extensive use of dialect. Though Titina continued her theatrical career as actress during the post-war period, her reputation as a writer was soon eclipsed by that of Eduardo, and her comedies were gradually forgotten. In the 1990s, however, these plays were rescued from oblivion and appeared in print for the first time.[1]

The eventual recognition and publication of Titina De Filippo's work is clearly an exception. In fact, by the end of the 1960s, *Natalia Ginzburg was still the only female writer in Italy who had succeeded both in publishing and staging more than a handful of plays. With the development of radio, film, television, and alternative performance spaces, however, additional venues were becoming available for aspiring writers of material intended for performance. Given the particularly conservative tendencies of theatrical institutions in Italy, it is hardly surprising that in the course of the past half century, many of the dramatic texts and comedies authored by Italian women were created for venues other than the traditional stage.

In the early 1950s Franca Valeri began performing her own monologues in cabaret shows, on radio and on television. Throughout the 1950s and 1960s, she contributed scripts to a range of television shows, while continuing her career as an actress. Famous during this period was her repertoire of comic character sketches, and particularly for her one-woman show *Le donne* ('Women'),[2] which she performed on tour. The most celebrated of Valeri's characters were La Signorina Snob, a pretentious member of the Milanese bourgeoisie, and La Signora Cecioni, a resident of the Tiburtina neighbourhood in Rome. Cecioni's exuberant linguistic mannerisms were modelled on the language of the Roman lower-middle class, and are reminiscent of the elaborate speech patterns found in the narratives of Carlo Emilio Gadda. More recent plays for mainstream theatre include *Sorelle, ma solo due* ('Sisters, but only two', 1998), a satirical portrait of two ageing sisters haunted by uneasy memories and fierce resentments. The most distinctive traits of Valeri's writing are a refined sense of irony and a keen ear for the social and regional variations of the spoken language. Valeri was clearly a pioneer. Her one-woman shows anticipated a trend embraced in the 1980s and 1990s by comediennes such as *Franca Rame and Lella Costa, as well as by performers of dramatic monologues such as Valeria Moretti and Lucia Poli.

Among the handful of Italian women playwrights whose work was produced in mainstream theatre by the end of the 1960s, only one, Natalia Ginzburg, had achieved international recognition. Already established as a novelist, Ginzburg wrote her first play *Ti ho sposato per allegria* ('I married you for fun',) in 1963. By her own admission, she knew little about writing for the theatre, but welcomed the opportunity to escape the limitations of a single, focalising consciousness, which she had until then considered a necessary aspect of writing fiction. A light-hearted comedy, the play blends elements of the theatre of the absurd with conventions reminiscent of the traditional comedy of manners, such as the humorous enactment of class differences. Many of the themes that dominate Ginzburg's subsequent work for the stage are already present here, such as the haphazard motivations and hidden dependencies that inform the life of the couple, and the enduring effect of parental ties on children who have reached adulthood.

Ginzburg's subsequent nine plays offer a contrastingly bleak view of human relationships. Similar to the dialogue found in Pinter – to which her work is sometimes compared – the conversations between her characters mix inconsequential details and important information in a chaotic flow of communication. Audiences abroad often proved more receptive than Italians to the formal idiosyncrasies of this early work in which monologues prevail over dialogue, as the characters unburden themselves at great length while virtually ignoring their interlocutors. Ginzburg's second play *L'inserzione* ('The Advertisement'), which met with a mixed response in Italy, enjoyed considerable success in its first British production, with Joan Plowright in the leading role. A structurally anomalous work, the play features an initial monologue that occupies at least twenty minutes of the opening act. A middle-aged woman, separated from her husband, relates the sad story of her life to a younger woman who arrives at her home in response to an advertisement seeking a lodger or au pair. Between the acts, the husband becomes romantically involved with the younger woman. Little else occurs until the play's concluding moments, when an unexpected outburst of murderous violence reveals the level of tension underpinning the apparent banality of the preceding chatter and rambling self-revelation.

If Ginzburg saw herself as a writer who never felt entirely comfortable in the theatre, Franca Rame, by contrast, sees herself primarily as a creature of the theatre and has been slow to claim her work as a writer. As the personal and professional partner of Dario Fo, Rame has been for many years one of the most prominent figures in Italian theatre, performing on stage with Fo since the 1950s, and sharing his commitment to radical left-wing politics. Along with Fo, she left mainstream theatre to participate in a distinctive theatrical practice, creating comedies rooted in traditions of popular farce and inflected with provocative political satire. It was only in the late 1970s that she began to acknowledge her creative contribution by signing the scripts that were generally finalised on the page by Fo. The attribution of sole authorship to Rame is problematical, however, since Fo's name continues to appear as co-author on all of her work. Nonetheless, there is no doubt that several texts they have produced since the 1970s focusing on a critique of gender arrangements in contemporary society are largely of Rame's inspiration.

Tutta casa, letto e chiesa ('She's all house, bed and church'), the first collection of monologues on which Rame's name appears, was published in 1977 at the height of the women's movement in Italy. Written in the voices of a variety of female characters, the monologues implicitly address several aspects of women's oppression in a male-dominated world. One of the most hilarious of these sketches, *Una donna sola* (*A Woman Alone*), presents a housewife ironing her negligée, surrounded by sleek appliances and a host of products provided by her jealous husband in exchange for her servitude to him and to his lecherous brother, his whole body encased in plaster cast, only his hand free. Although the woman still fantasises with passionate tenderness about her young lover, she insists that she has a good, happy life. As she makes this preposterous claim, the audience has ample opportunity to observe her isolation and pitiful self-delusion. Hilariously ironic throughout, *Una donna sola* parodies women's position within traditional marriage as well as their contemporary capitulation to consumerism.

The humorous impact of *Coppia aperta, quasi spalancata* ('Open couple, almost wide open'), a one-act play published by Rame and Fo in 1983, hinges on the contrasting attitudes of a man and his wife towards the climate of greater sexual freedom that had begun to manifest itself in Italy by the 1970s. As the action begins, it seems that both partners in the 'open' marriage alluded to in the title are attempting to cast off the shackles of conjugal fidelity by pursuing extra-marital affairs. The husband is astonished to discover that his wife has similarly exerted her freedom and taken on a lover, by all accounts a formidable rival. The wife, however, appears to have been propelled into her affair by the desire for revenge on her philandering husband. An escalating war of nerves ends with the crazed husband electrocuting himself in the bathroom. Vindicating neither monogamy nor the new permissiveness, *Coppia aperta* offers an implicit condemnation of the old-fashioned double standard, which, in this play, is still sought after by the male protagonist for his own selfish ends.

In a contrastingly serious vein, *Lo stupro* ('Rape'), the most riveting monologue written by Rame to date, offers a first-person account of a woman's sexual violation, and was inspired by Rame's experience of being gang-raped by neo-Fascist thugs in 1973. Her more recent play *Parliamo di donne* ('Let's talk about women'), combines an undercurrent of pathos with the satirical inflection considered more characteristic of her work. The protagonist of the first act, 'L'eroina' ('Heroin/Heroine'), is the self-sacrificing mother of a heroin addict. Having lost two children to heroin, she endeavours to keep her surviving daughter alive by locking her up and providing the necessary heroin injections herself. To finance this regimen she must resort to prostitution, and, in the course of an encounter with drug dealers, is shot to death in the street. The devastation caused by heroin addiction is a recurrent theme in the work of contemporary Italian women writers, and is found most recently in *Francesca Archibugi's film *L'albero delle pere* ('The pear tree', 1998). No other writer has approached it, however, in the tragicomic register of Rame's powerful sketch. The second act of *Parliamo di donne*, 'La donna grassa' ('The fat woman'), explores women's fraught relationship with their ageing bodies. The protagonist is Mattea, an obese, fifty-year-old woman. Much of the action is devoted to Mattea's encounter with her adult daughter, who is deaf to the lessons inherent in the mother's painful experiences. What emerges most forcefully from their conversation is their mutual hostility and lack of support. This aspect of the play expressly subverts the myth of female solidarity and the centrality of the mother–daughter bond valorised by Italian feminism. Rame, who identifies more closely with the materialist perspective of radical left-wing politics than with the specific aspirations of the women's movement, seems resistant to the utopian tendencies within feminism, and especially suspicious of the idea that women are readily supportive of each other.

Though Rame supported many of the juridical battles fought by Italian feminism over the years, such as the fight to legalise divorce and abortion, she remained distant from most of the cultural initiatives associated with the movement, including the feminist theatre groups that began to emerge in the Italian cities by the early 1970s. In Italy, to a greater extent than in other countries, women's theatre functioned as a forum for political protest and cultural change, since the majority of its participants were motivated by a shared commitment to 'double militancy', namely, to left-wing politics and to feminism. Indeed, theatre companies such as the Maddalena in Rome and Le Nemesiache in Naples offered not only a collective reflection on the erasure of women by Western culture but also a critique of pressing social issues and a stimulus for political action.

*Dacia Maraini was the most prominent participant in this theatrical initiative and one of its most prolific writers. In 1973 she co-founded the Maddalena Theatre, which functioned as venue for feminist creativity and debate until 1990. Other women writers associated with the Maddalena were Maricla Boggio, *Edith Bruck, *Adele Cambria, Annabella Cerliani, *Sandra Petrignani and Lucia Poli. Of these, Boggio and Cambria later went on achieve widespread recognition as playwrights in mainstream theatre. In addition to staging plays and offering workshops in playwriting, the Maddalena organised forums on issues of interest to the women's movement, such as abortion, sexual violence and prostitution, eliciting the participation of international feminists such as Luce Irigaray, Hélène Cixous, Kate Millett and Germaine Greer.

Maraini's initial commitment to theatre was closely linked with her social and political activism, and she rejected the experimental practices of avant-garde performance, currently fashionable in Italy due to the influence of the Living Theatre. Though open to formal experimentation, she upheld the primacy of language in theatre in order to raise consciousness and stimulate debate, in contrast to the emphasis on movement, gesture and improvisation in the contemporary avant-garde. Maraini's dramatic writings have a distinctly dialectical quality, and occasionally deploy self-reflective, distancing devices. Her approach to formal experimentation is guided by the need to challenge dominant cultural discourses whose tools of signification are closely linked to patriarchal ideology.

Maraini's earliest plays are sharply polemical in their inspiration. *Manifesto* ('Manifesto'), which resulted from an investigative enquiry into the incarceration of women, focuses on the plight of female prisoners. The dialogue is written in verse, bestowing on the events the sombre tone of a passion play. One of her most widely performed works, *Dialogo di una prostituta con il suo cliente* ('Dialogue between a prostitute and her client'), inspired by the writings of Kate Millett, sets out to debunk prevailing myths of female prostitution, suggesting parallels between women's position in a masculinist society and the practice of selling sex for money. The focus of the play is the challenging encounter between Manila, educated, dignified in her work, and a client, a member of the supposedly enlightened left. Manila gradually exposes the man's ideological hypocrisy and his reluctance to surrender a sense of masculinist entitlement. In the original production, the actress interrupted the play three times to initiate audience discussion, a strategy also adopted when the play was staged in London in 1980 by the feminist theatre group Monstrous Regiment. The more recent *Stravaganza* ('Freakshow') was inspired by an issue of pressing concern to contemporary society, namely the fate of the mentally ill following the closure of state psychiatric hospitals in Italy in the early 1980s. Unlike Maraini's earlier plays with a strong social position, however, *Stravaganza* is not overtly didactic. Rather, the tone is tragicomic, and the characters developed with a mixture of broad humour and psychological insight. Furthermore, in contrast to many of her previous plays, equal sympathy is accorded to male and female characters.

In keeping with the trend towards mythic revisionism echoed in the work of several women writers, Maraini's *I sogni di Clitennestra* ('Dreams of Clytemnestra') recasts the classical figures of Clytemnestra and Electra in contemporary feminist terms. Her characters function simultaneously as the mythic personages originally presented by Aeschylus and as their imagined contemporary counterparts, women of the lower-middle class living in the Tuscan town of Prato. The play brilliantly suggests the perpetuation of an ancient patriarchal system of male privilege in today's world, and adds a historical/materialist dimension to the analysis of sexual politics. Maraini has also written plays featuring historical figures, such as Queen Elizabeth I and Mary Stuart, Sor Juana Iñez de la Cruz, Erzbeth Bathory, Isabella Morra, and *Veronica Franco. These are presented, not as a rewriting of history, but as an opportunity to reflect on issues of power and authority, subordination and silence, that have affected the lives of women throughout the centuries.

In the 1980s Maraini also co-wrote screenplays for three feature films, echoing themes that dominate much of her dramatic writings. The films are *Storia di Piera* ('Piera's story', 1981), *Il futuro è donna* ('The future is a woman', 1984), both of which were directed by Marco Ferreri, and *Paura e amore* (*Three Sisters*, 1988), a contemporary adaptation of Chekhov's *Three*

Sisters directed by Margarethe von Trotta. All three films explore issues linked to feminist debates, such as motherhood and the family, sexuality and desire, and the tensions inherent in women's relationships with each other in a male-dominated society.

Among the several important plays that emerged from the group of playwrights associated with the Maddalena Theatre was Adele Cambria's *Nonostante Gramsci* ('In spite of Gramsci'). Based on the details of Antonio Gramsci's relationship with his Russian wife and sisters-in-law, the play provides both a critique of family ties in a revolutionary and yet staunchly patriarchal environment and a reassessment of the historical figure of Gramsci from a feminist point of view. Cambria's interest in the Schucht sisters – Julia (Gramsci's wife), Genia (or Eugenia) and Tatiana – was inspired by her discovery of the letters written by Julia and Tatiana Schucht to Gramsci during his long incarceration. This correspondence provided Cambria with a fascinating corollary to the political leader's published writings. The play that emerged from her reading of the material offers a sustained meditation on the relationship of the political and the personal, and a consideration of the erasure of women by history.

The action unfolds in the course of Gramsci's imprisonment at the hands of the Fascist government, during which his wife returned to the Soviet Union to raise her sons with the help of her younger sister Genia, before capitulating to a severe depression and ceasing to write to her husband. Meanwhile, the other sister, Tatiana, stayed in Italy to attend to his needs as best she could. Cambria's drama thus explores the issue of wifely 'sacrifice', both Tatiana's and Julia's, in a masculinist revolutionary context. There are five characters in the play: Gramsci, Giulia (Julia), Genia, Tatiana, and a choral figure, 'La ragazza' (The girl), who is assigned a variety of functions, including the voicing of sentiments felt but not expressed by the other characters. All of the statements made by the male protagonist are excerpted from letters and other published texts by the Communist leader. Gramsci's voice is a dominant element in the performance – the disembodied voice of masculine authority, whose emotions are carefully mediated and rationalised according to the demands of his ideological beliefs. In its implicit questioning both of women's commitment to the male-dominated left, and the left's commitment to women's interests, Cambria's work offered a challenge to contemporary feminists subscribing to the concept of 'double militancy'. The play was subsequently published in the volume *Amore come rivoluzione* ('Love as revolution'), along with Cambria's own commentary and excerpts from the

Schucht–Gramsci correspondence.³ This complex text provides one of the most compelling documents to emerge from Italian feminism.

If the gendered voice of female playwrights has become increasingly audible in Italian theatre over the past forty years, the voice of women screenwriters, as writers, is not as easily identified or accounted for. This is linked to the fact that screenwriting, also a collaborative process, enjoys even less autonomy than playwriting. Scriptwriters rarely see their work produced on screen in a fashion that corresponds to their original vision, since a screenplay is likely to undergo numerous modifications carried out by other writers or imposed by the director, the producer or the editor. In Italian cinema, the term 'autore' (author) generally designates the director rather than the screenwriter, and it is used most often to describe film-makers who direct their own scripts.

In the history of the national cinema only one woman, *Suso Cecchi D'Amico, has won widespread recognition exclusively for her work as a screenwriter. Spanning more than fifty years, her career, which began in 1946, involved close collaboration with some of the most accomplished directors of cinema history, including Luchino Visconti, Vittorio De Sica, Luigi Zampa and Michelangelo Antonioni. Cecchi D'Amico's screenplays belong to a variety of genres, from comedy to melodrama, and include both literary adaptations and original work. Yet she never directed her own material, and her name has always appeared in film credits as co-scenarist rather than as solo screenwriter. A consummate professional, she understood the intensely collaborative nature of the screenwriter's function in the national cinema of the post-war era. If she has left a distinctive mark on the great films of that period, this is to be sought, according to Gian Piero Brunetta, in the delineation of the complex female characters that dominate such post-war classics as *L'onorevole Angelina* ('The Honourable Angelina', Zampa, 1947) and *Senso* (*Wanton Contessa*, Visconti, 1954).⁴ These figures are constructed with a mixture of keen psychological insight and a quest for social and historical accuracy. Among the screenwriters that emerged during the post-war era, Cecchi D'Amico was most admired for her impressive literary background and her careful historical research.

The elusive voice of Italian women screenwriters can be traced with greatest assurance in films written and directed by the same artist, since it is in these films that the script is most likely to reach the screen in a version that reflects the creative vision of its author. Elvira Notari, who founded the Dora production company in Naples along with her husband in 1909, was the first woman to enjoy a long and productive career as a film-maker. In spite of her remarkable productivity and commercial success, however, like other women directors from the silent era such as the distinguished Alice Guy Blaché, she has, until recently, been largely forgotten.[5] Though the screenplay was not developed as an independent form during the silent era, Notari provided ideas and stories for dozens of films, and wrote the intertitles in Neapolitan dialect. Shot on location in Naples, her films were loosely modelled on the popular melodramas and *sceneggiate* of Neapolitan theatre.

In the 1960s Italian audiences saw the almost simultaneous emergence of the two most successful female directors and screenwriters in Italy to date, *Lina Wertmüller and *Liliana Cavani. Both of these very different directors worked for RAI in the early 1960s, and made a successful transition to cinema partly as the result of their success in television. Wertmüller first commanded the attention of a broad national audience in 1964 with a popular series adapted from a novel by the children's author Vamba. She subsequently made two musicals, also for television, *Rita la zanzara* ('Rita the mosquito') and *Non stuzzicate la zanzara* ('Don't tease the mosquito') featuring comic actor Giancarlo Giannini. Her earliest feature films *I basilischi* ('The basilisks', 1963) and *Adesso parliamo di uomini* ('Now let's talk about men', 1964) were released around the same time. These revealed her gift as a social satirist, most striking in her parodic commentary of Italian masculinity, or *gallismo*.

Wertmüller's 'discovery' of Giannini while wording at RAI proved to be a decisive turning point in her career. In her feature films of the 1970s, from *Mimì metallurgico ferito nell'onore* ('The seduction of Mimì', 1972) to *La fine del mondo nel nostro solito letto* ('The end of the world in our usual bed', 1978), her dynamic collaboration with the gifted actor helped to establish her distinctive cinematic signature. Though she has always written her own material, occasionally in collaboration with other screenwriters, she attaches less importance to the authority of the screenplay than to the dynamics that may emerge while working with actors during rehearsal or shooting, and she frequently alters her scripts during the production process. Rooted in the anti-realist conventions of grotesque comedy, Wertmüller's narratives rely on broad humorous effects to deliver a hard-hitting critique of Italian society. These films explore in darkly humorous tones the intersection of sexuality and politics in a variety of settings, from a brothel of the Fascist era in *Film d'amore e anarchia* ('Love and anarchy', 1974) to a small, Northern town during the recent secessionist campaigns of the Lega Nord in *Metalmeccanico e parrucchiera* ('The metal-worker and the hairdresser', 1996). Decidedly left-leaning in her ideological tendencies, Wertmüller nonetheless pokes fun at both right and left of the political spectrum. Although she can be devastatingly critical of the masculinist ethos that dominates social interaction in Italy, she also satirises female behaviour. Her approach is devoid of any concern for feminist orthodoxy, and her work often conveys a sense of authorial indulgence towards her flawed male protagonists.

Though very different from Wertmüller's approach in most respects, Cavani's work is similarly independent in its vision. Cavani began her career writing and producing documentaries for RAI, for which she won immediate recognition. Her best-known feature film, *Il portiere di notte* ('The night porter'), opened internationally in 1974. Although a major commercial success, the film provoked considerable critical controversy. Set in Vienna in the 1950s, it focuses on the accidental reunion of a female concentration camp survivor and the former Gestapo officer with whom she was forced into an erotic alliance as a girl of fourteen. The film avoids a clear-cut condemnation of the former officer, and its principal thematic focus is the powerful, ambivalent bond that continues to link the two characters to each other. Through extensive use of flashbacks, Cavani's script foregrounds not only the victim's compulsion to repeat the scene of her earlier, enforced submission, but also the officer's fascinated identification with the young woman's vulnerability and powerlessness. Another of Cavani's feature films, *Al di là del bene e del male* ('Beyond good and evil', 1978), also deals in a provocative way with the dynamics of sadomaschism. The narrative offers a fictionalised account of Friedrich Nietzsche's triangular relationship with Paul Ree and Lou Salome in the 1880s, emphasising the negotiation of power and eroticism among the three central characters. Those critics who expected a conventional historical drama were disappointed in the film, failing to recognise that Cavani's interest lay not in historical details, but in the opportunity to re-explore thematic paradigms that had emerged in her own earlier work.

Cavani's predilection for contextualising private sexual dramas against a backdrop of socio-historical crisis, and her emphasis on the connections among sex, politics, power and knowledge, have often provoked a scandalised reaction. The violent depiction of war in her adaptation of Curzio Malaparte's *La pelle* ('Skin', 1981), which provides no clearly marked heroes to relieve the depressing panorama of human degradation, has also met with criticism. Yet her work has been defended as challenging the model of masculinity promoted by dominant culture through the creation of unconventional, 'unmasculine' yet usually appealing, male characters. Attempting in her own way to transcend conventional constructions of gender, she has nonetheless distanced herself from the rhetoric of official feminism.

Over the past twenty-five years an unprecedented number of women film-makers have succeeded in directing their own screenplays. These include Francesca Archibugi, Cristina Comencini, Giovanna Gagliardo, Lina Mangiacapre, Wilma Labate, Antonietta De Lillo and Roberta Torre. Some of the most interesting films written and directed by Italian women are closely linked to the themes of feminism. Gagliardo's *Maternale* ('Maternal', 1978), for example, was inspired by the director's experience in consciousness-raising groups organised within the women's movement during the 1970s. In subjective, dream-like imagery, the film offers a thought-provoking meditation on the conflicts characteristic of motherhood in a patriarchal system by focusing specifically on the complexities of the mother–daughter relationship. Exploring the daughter's muteness, hysterical symptoms and relationship to food as symptomatic of the tensions between women, *Maternale* is influenced by psychoanalytic theory and French feminism. Gagliardo's published screenplay is, in fact, accompanied by an essay written by Luce Irigaray, 'L'una non sogna senza l'altra' ('One can't dream without the other') which supplies the words unspoken by the daughter in the film, simultaneously theorising the sense of estrangement and exile from the mother felt by daughters in a world where all relationships are ultimately mediated by men.[6]

Archibugi is the only member of the new generation of women film-makers with a body of work that has commanded international attention. To date, she has made five features, all based on screenplays that she authored, either collaboratively or alone. Uninterested in technical virtuosity or formal experimentation, she is primarily a storyteller, and her films unfold as solid, traditionally wrought narratives. Aimed at a broad popular audience, her work is for the most part firmly rooted in the contemporary Italian experience. Four of Archibugi's films made between 1988 and 1998 are set in Rome in the present or recent past, with characters drawn from various strata of the middle classes. In each of these films at least one young character is positioned as both victim and judge of adult behaviour. Archibugi's remaining feature – an adaptation of Federigo Tozzi's novel *Con gli occhi chiusi* ('With eyes closed', 1995) – is, by contrast, a story of lost innocence set in the Tuscan countryside at the turn of the century. Despite the difference in setting, in its emphasis on the difficult coming of age of its two principal characters this film is linked thematically to the film-maker's *oeuvre* as a whole.

The figure of the wounded child has become the most distinctive aspect of Archibugi's cinematic signature. Her recent film *L'albero delle pere* ('The pear tree') presents the story of two children, an adolescent boy and his five-year-old half-sister, who become victims of their mother's struggle with heroin addiction. Wise beyond his years, the teenage protagonist feels obliged to compensate for the deficiencies of irresponsible parents by taking care of his small sister, who may have contracted a deadly disease. The immaturity of adults and the precocious responsibility of children is implicitly linked in this film and in *Verso sera* ('Towards evening', 1990) with the excessive sense of personal freedom promoted by the youth movement of the 1970s. *Il grande cocomero* ('The great water melon', 1993), by contrast, considers the positive legacies of that period in its depiction of a radical practitioner of child psychiatry who came of age in the 1960s. Inspired by a deep ethical commitment to the most vulnerable members of society, Archibugi's films pay homage both to neo-realism and to Italian comedy, while also resonating with François Truffaut's much admired films about childhood.

The concern with liberation from a dominantly masculine system, together with traces of a shared ethical impulse, emerges in most of the textual production of Italian women writing in the performance genres, whether it is expressed in the satire of Rame's sketches and Wertmüller's films, the absurdist irony of Ginzburg's plays, or as a dramatic meditation on women in history, myth or the environment as in the work of Valeria Moretti, Maraini, Cambria, Boggio and Mangiacapre.

NOTES

1. Titina De Filippo, *Il teatro* (Naples, 1993).
2. The text of the show was later published as *Le donne* (Milan, 1961).
3. Adele Cambria, *Amore come rivoluzione* (Milan, 1976).
4. Gian Piero Brunetta, *Storia del cinema italiano*, vol. II (Rome, 1993), p. 286.
5. See Giuliana Bruno, *Streetwalking on a Ruined Map* (Princeton, 1993).
6. Giovanna Gagliardo, *Maternale* (Milan, 1978).

19

Aesthetics and critical theory

In our contemporary and post-modern times, 'culture' has emerged as a key frame of reference. Art's ambivalent status as, on the one hand, representation and affirmation of the hegemonic social and political order, and on the other as potentially disruptive in its undoing of domi-nant forms, has been addressed within numerous disciplinary contexts, and indeed one of the difficulties faced by a discussion of aesthetics is delimiting the field of enquiry. Since the Enlightenment the question of aesthetics has played a significant role in Western philosophy, an interest echoed as far afield as Freudian psychoanalysis and the revolutionary practice of Marxism, where art holds a privileged place. This chapter seeks to place women's thinking about contemporary aesthetics and cul-tural practice, theoretical considerations on women and literature and by necessary extension on women and language, within a historical and philosophical context. While the considerable space devoted to aesthetics may surprise in philosophers such as Plato (who would banish poetry altogether from his ideal Republic) or Hegel (who assigned art a lowly place in the order of things), the attention paid by women theorists and practitioners to the dynamic relationship between women and art – whether to women as artists, to the representations of women in art, or to speculation about a gendered theory of art and literature – marks out the primary significance of the cultural sphere for women's understanding of themselves, the pre-eminence of the cultural and artistic as a mode of cog-nition.

In 1959 the novelist, critic and philosopher *Armanda Guiducci pub-lished an essay reviewing Antonio Gramsci's contribution to the field of aesthetics. Gramsci, she recalls, deplored the gulf in Italy between the intel-lectuals and the working classes, a structural weakness which resulted not only in economic precariousness but the lack of an organic culture which might express the life of an entire nation. Culture in post-Unification Italy was a matter of privilege, of hermetic intellectualism, a struggle for dominance between fragmentary vested interests. Gramsci engaged directly with Benedetto Croce's idealist aesthetics, seeking a new humanity – and a renewed culture both national and 'popular' – in revolutionary activity and revitalised social relationships, refusing to sanction the divorce of art from its socio-political context. Literary criticism for Gramsci, Guiducci points out, is fundamental in the struggle for a new culture: 'each act of criticism is ethics in action, socially important if it has the courage to face the present, if it doesn't claim to arbitrate between poetry and non-poetry but dares to burst the dams of a normative theory of art, if it is willing to engage in criticism of the everyday'. Gramsci, concludes Guiducci, 'chooses ethically'.[1] The link between aesthetics and ethics is thus firmly rooted in practical politics, and it is hard not to see here the roots of a feminist praxis. The dominant post-war tradition in Italy was rooted in anti-Fascism and firmly opposed to any idealistic attempt, whether Crocian or Hegelian, to devalue the 'material' essence of art. Artistic experience was to include social and historical foundations as well as the manipulation and deployment of materials. While Marxist aesthetics embraces a range of positions and vigorous argument, it is the connection between literature and politics which underpins the thinking of Italian women born in the post-war period about their own cultural practice.

The rapid shifts in positions taken with regard to aesthetics by neo-feminism – from the active political struggles of the 1960s and early 1970s to the present day – bear witness to the dramatic transformation which has seen women's politics broaden from a range of specific civil and legal issues to an increasingly theoretical preoccupation with structures of form and language, subjectivity and sexual difference within the ambit of the modern and post-modern. They also point to the growing sophistication of a feminist discourse which is inherently interdisciplinary in its approach. Early Marxist materialist perspectives have given way to the exploration of the place occupied by women in the symbolic order. The huge task of recovering the work of women forgotten by official cultural history moves hand in hand with an ongoing debate as to how to interpret these writings within a wider cultural context. Emphasis has shifted from the study of women as a sociological and political category, or from the empowering perspective of psychoanalysis, to a study of gender in philosophical terms rather than as political militancy. In this context, aesthetics, as a philosophical approach to literature and to the arts, and as critical practice, has returned centre-stage.

Militant 1970s feminist criticism rejected both Crocean idealism and avant-garde experimentalism. If the resulting texts recalled critical opinion about the writing of novelists such as Alberto Moravia and Ignazio Silone – that it was beautiful because it was not beautiful, insofar as it refused the belle-lettristic preoccupation of the hermeticists – the intention of these women was to turn attention away from the text and towards the private reality of women's lives. The 1970s saw an aesthetic that was an anti-aesthetic, a refusal of literary language as mediating between writer and reader. The identification of the reader with the text in terms both of content and of ideological perspective was solicited through the extensive use of first-person narratives. This was the genre of choice for women of the 1970s, a continuation in symbolic form of the practice of consciousness-raising, a technique suspended between narrative and orality. Autobiography became a form of collective knowledge rather than the assertion of individual and separate identity notable precisely for its difference. Conventional interpretive codes and aesthetic judgements were no longer applicable to work which was cultural and anthropological rather than literary. Aesthetics deferred to politics, and to direct intervention in the institutions and rhythms of cultural production. New journals were set up – *Sottosopra* ('Upside down'), which experimented with collective writing in an attempt to short-circuit the simple substitution of the male 'I' with a female competitive equivalent (an experiment also tried by the Milan-based group *A zig zag* ('In a zig zag')), *Effe* ('F') *Differenze* ('Differences') and *Donnawomanfemme* among others. While *Donnawomanfemme* was highly theoretical, *Effe* and *Differenze* privileged the spoken word, frequently transcribing statements by women who sign with just their first name, in an attempt to forge a communication which bypasses the distorting lens of written forms and speaks from the body. Radio Donna began broadcasting in 1976. Women's publishing houses were set up, such as La Tartaruga (The Tortoise) and *edizioni delle donne,* which sought to promote women as 'political subjects'. This is the moment at which women's struggle becomes a matter of culture, and the specific culture of women becomes a site of political struggle. While other publishers sought to integrate texts on women within their booklists, integrating feminism within authorising institutions, women's publishing houses sought to reveal not homogeneity but the plural dissonance of the women's movement, rejecting the fictitious discourse of harmonious univocity. When *Dacia Maraini and Germaine Greer opened the women-only theatre in Rome, La Maddalena, the opening statement defined the new theatre as a space in which women could begin to construct their own reality, discover an autonomous language created by women for women. Its reflection of the separatism of much Italian feminism was articulated in its message to men: not against them, but without them. Culture lies at the heart of feminist analysis: culture understood as epistemology and ethics, ways of knowing and evaluating, culture as the reproduction of the social. Feminists sought to deconstruct those ideological apparatuses, institutions of civil society, which affect the formation of consciousness.

Poetry by women in the 1970s was perhaps more cautious in jettisoning notions of form, an identifiably aesthetic dimension to their work, possibly because of the strength of the poetic tradition in Italy. While some observers and practitioners saw feminist practice as bringing poetry down from timeless space into a specific social context, a moment of recovery of the suppressed female 'I', a poetry of violence and menstrual blood (Laura di Nola's *Poesia femminista,* for example), other practitioners were less willing to label their poetry as 'feminist', unconvinced of the possibility of gendered aesthetic forms (see chapter 17).[2]

Women critics in the 1970s were also grappling with the complexities of women's relationship to language and to culture. In 1977 Nadia Fusini meditated on the risks of associating the terms 'women' and 'literature' too closely. Language is only a system, a set of symbols: the association risks imposing unwelcome essentialism on both terms. The purpose of literature, says Fusini, is not specular, mimetic, nor is language gendered in itself. The dyad woman/literature swiftly opens up into the broader question of woman/language. Fusini notes that in philosophical discourse from Aristotle onwards the word belongs to the male, the body to the female: if woman procreates, man opposes the symbolic – language, art and the systems through which we perceive ourselves – to his fear of death. Writing, as substitution for the body, is seen to be more problematic for women, already so tied to the concept of the corporeal. For Fusini herself, language is not sexed; rather, it marks sexual difference, intervening in the structuring of subjectivity.[3]

Other critics, too, were debating the conjunction of women and literature. In *La lingua della nutrice* ('Language and the nourisher', 1978) *Elisabetta Rasy, novelist, critic and founding member of *edizioni delle donne*, describes the study of women and literature as less philology than archaeology, a question of privileging not general abstract categories but hints, traces, details. A woman who writes engages in an activity which takes place in darkness, silence and secrecy, like Penelope at her loom. Women approach writing through domestic and craft work – weaving, embroidering – not to mention the art of the body. Rasy, too, asks what might thread together women's artistic production. The constant element is not ideology or style, but the anomalous position held by women in relation to their specific social and cultural contexts, the violation of the complex of rites and behaviours by which women are the liminal component of male culture, defining it by their absence. Refusing to privilege writing by women, Rasy describes investigating women in literature as 'investigating the dead times of literary discourse: the times of secret elaboration, this side of any form, school or fashion. It's a question of recuperating the weakest and most private of literary genres.'[4] Rasy's alertness to the fragment and the detail anticipates the approach of Naomi Schor in her *Reading in Detail: Aesthetics and the Feminine* (London, 1987).

Rasy notes that the question of language tends to recur after each historical high-point of political action. The demand for equality is substituted by the recognition of difference in a shift from political militancy to symbolic practice. For Rasy, Cixous's belief in an exclusively feminine language based on the materiality of the body, following its inner rhythms and times, ignores the material conditions in which women write, their precarious insertion into the social. Rasy's theoretical position articulates in miniature the ability of Italian feminism to look simultaneously at the theoretical abstractions of the French tradition and the more pragmatic social and political emphasis of the Anglo-American tradition. Rasy refuses to recognise in writing by women either the eternal feminine identified by Benedetto Croce or the traces of an ancient maternity conjured up by Cixous, recalling Virginia Woolf's demand that women be given the capacity to listen to their own female desire in a way which does not travesty male culture or function as collaborationism. There are clear echoes here too of *Sibilla Aleramo, who also called for women to stop speaking through a foreign tongue and create their own language.

Rasy is in sympathy with Julia Kristeva's notion of the semiotic, denoting the pre-linguistic rhythms and pulses of the body. Women's alienation takes place not in the factory (work was always the panacea of the emancipationists) but in the chain of reproduction. If 'woman' is the alienation within each society, 'feminism' – as the organisation of all that is hidden, secret, silent – is the condition of alienation within each revolutionary movement. Rasy is interested in the 'structural otherness' of femininity, that female 'elsewhere' which evades all consoling narratives of complementarity or more modern narratives of otherness.

The attempt to annex art to a specifically feminist cultural practice was comparatively short-lived. This was not because of the opprobrium of reviewers when faced with an avalanche of diaries, autobiographies and pamphlets which self-consciously disclaimed artistic status, or the hostility of Marxist critics who saw women's writing slipping away from an engagement with the 'real' as defined by orthodox Marxist theory towards a debased and solipsistic version of realism. Rather, it became clear that art which consciously refuses aesthetics has nowhere to go. *Biancamaria Frabotta speculates that the 'sameness' of these works, the risk of homologisation, the loss of individual voice, was the driving force behind the rapid shift in emphasis seen over the 1980s from literature to philosophy, from the investigation of the female imaginary to a study of the symbolic representation of thought.[5]

One of the most striking features of Italian feminist writing from an English-speaking perspective is the intensely theoretical nature of some of the best writing. If recent international feminist scholarship and research draws above all not on literature or psychoanalysis but philosophy,[6] feminist writing in Italy has long exhibited an awareness of philosophical and literary traditions – whether political philosophy, metaphysics or classical culture – and in some recent work has sought to reunite philosophy with literature. A powerful voice of the early phases of neo-feminism was that of *Carla Lonzi, who was vigorous in her attack on the political philosophy of Marxism as inherited from Hegel. In one of the early pieces of the group Rivolta femminile, 'Let's spit on Hegel', Lonzi states the case for rejecting emancipation as alienation for women, as coopting their difference under the sign of the Same. To be equal to men is to disappear as women: 'equality is what is offered as legal rights to colonized people. And what is imposed on them as culture.'[7] Equality is oppression, a mask for the inferiority of women: difference offers multiplicity, variety, and opens the way to a woman as subject, which is a new birth and which will profoundly change culture. Lonzi's radical feminism informs her spirited attack on Hegel, who understands the master–slave dialectic but promotes a patriarchal political culture based on women's inferiority and an oppressive family culture. Lonzi, who left the Italian Communist Party in 1956 following the Soviet invasion of Hungary, was vociferous in her condemnation of Marxism, Catholicism and psychoanalysis, all discourses of considerable authority in Italy. She anticipates the work of later feminist philosophers such as *Adriana Cavarero in her anti-metaphysical stance, her profound conviction that to undo women's oppression the structuring discourses of Western culture have to be traced back to their origins and refuted. Philosophers – says Lonzi tartly – have spoken too much.

Lonzi's advocation of separatism translates itself into cultural as well as political terms. Lonzi trained as an art historian: she published studies of Georges Seurat and Henri Rousseau, and one of her co-founders of Rivolta femminile was the artist Carla Accardi. For Lonzi there are two possible positions for women in relation to culture. One is to seek parity on a cultural level as historically defined by men. This allows exceptional women privileged, if provisional, access to the esteem reserved for men and distributed by men. This is the path of all earlier women writers, and is chosen in fiction by Anna Banti's Artemisia (see chapter 15). The other path is to begin with the 'degree zero' of a creativity which has been repressed. Lonzi refuses the comforting platitude of a creative female space somehow 'outside' male culture, and is aware of the difficulty of defining an essence, an imaginary, distinct from centuries of historical sedimentation. Nonetheless she prefers the harder path as a 'birth' of culture by women.

While Lonzi was convinced that 'philosophers have already spoken too much', it is to philosophy that other thinkers have turned in order to investigate the relationship of the woman to the symbolic order, to deconstruct the net of symbolic relations and structures of discourse which keep women in a subaltern position, and to elaborate the concept of sexual difference. Nor is philosophy some overarching discourse disconnected from the real world: Adriana Cavarero, for example, was a member of the Communist and then the Social Democratic Party with the demise of the PCI, and a regular contributor to the left-wing and communist newspapers L'Unità and Il manifesto. Like Luce Irigaray, to whom she acknowledges her intellectual and conceptual indebtedness, Cavarero seeks to transform socio-symbolic structures, to turn women into philosophical and linguistic as well as political subjects. Adriana Cavarero and the group known as Diotima – a group of women philosophers based in Verona – start from the premise that Western philosophy is not neutral or gender-free knowledge. Philosophy, insofar as it reveals the mechanisms by which Western culture perpetuates the identification of human consciousness with rationality and both of these with male consciousness, is thus the quintessence of male discourse, to be deconstructed from within. For Cavarero, the male claim to universality conceals sexual difference which thus remains unthought, excluding the female from subjectivity. Diotima counter the Hegelian theory of sexual difference by which woman is transformed into the 'eternal feminine', with men and women having a different relation to the unconscious, and the Freudian view which would see sexual difference as a consequence of the castration complex, resulting in male castration anxiety and female penis envy. Cavarero calls for a sexed thought which nonetheless does not claim to assimilate the other sex, which is not reducible to the logic of a single, neutral, universal subject, which refuses the homologisation of the male subject.

Contemporary philosophy, with its notorious crisis of the subject, for all its postulated and posturing decentring of the subject, still holds little possibility of woman as active subject, producing her own self-representations. All philosophies, up to and including post-modernism and its Italian inflection, 'il pensiero debole' or 'weak thought', exclude the female point of view, deny sexual difference. For Cavarero, the flirtation with 'weakness' can only interest the subject who feels himself 'strong' to begin with. Her aim to deconstruct philosophy from within recalls Lonzi's belief that women's culture cannot be made in the void, but only by undoing the discursive and psychic binds which entrap women. The point is made repeatedly by Italian cultural theorists, and put succinctly by the psychoanalyst Silvia Vegetti Finzi:

> The woman who produces culture has the difficult task of deploying the female imaginary within a symbolic network preconstituted for her very exclusion. If she withdraws from this all that is left her is silence or symptom. The effort therefore is to express female alterity on the 'reverse' side of discourse, in silence, in ellipsis, in effects of style, in repetition, in discordance . . . to burst the banks which male culture has built in terms of intellectual disciplines, codes, rhetoric, in order to speak everything, in order to speak herself. This is why, when women produce female culture, they create myths above all, because myth is the site of the possibility of the impossible.[8]

Cavarero's consideration of language is strikingly similar to that of Aleramo's fifty years before: 'I, like every woman, am now writing and thinking in the language of the other, which is simply the language, nor could I do otherwise. This language, since I happen to be a woman, denies me as a subject, it stands on categories which compromise my self-identification. How, then, can I speak myself through that which, structurally, does not speak me? How can I think sexual difference through, and in, a system of thought which is founded on not thinking it?'[9] Cavarero conceives of a missing language whose echoes can be faintly heard through narrative or poetry, but it is to one of the founding fathers of philosophy, Plato, that she turns in order to explore the erasure of the female from Western thought and to trace the residue of that erasure. Hers is a 'strategy of repossession', a 'purposeful and conceptual theft',[10] and it is this strategy of recovery, a project which Cavarero shares with French thinkers such as Irigaray, which informs *In Spite of Plato*.

In Spite of Plato notes the absence of powerful positive female mythic females in Western culture, figures of the stature of Ulysses or Don Juan, who express in crystalline and condensed form the social and structuring discourses which hold them. The compelling fascination of mythic figures lies in their ability both to withstand and to transcend time, to alter their own intellectual and historical contexts, to be constantly reread, like Italo Calvino's definition of a classic book. Cavarero's aim as a philosopher, rather than to invent new mythic figures, is to 'steal' figures from classical culture, reread the context of their first appearance, and simultaneously deconstruct the development of classical philosophy on which all subsequent metaphysical thinking – and it is metaphysical thinking which Cavarero has in her sights – is based. What Cavarero achieves in this and subsequent works is a simultaneously deconstructive and creative rereading which blurs the boundaries between literature and philosophy.

Cavarero's four mythic figures are Penelope, the Thracian maidservant who laughed at the philosopher, Diotima and Demeter. Penelope, weaving at her loom while awaiting Ulysses, here functions as a condensed metaphor for Cavarero's entire project. Cavarero's reworking of the myth has Penelope weaving together what has been rent asunder by originating metaphysics – the body and the soul, illusion or appearance and reality, material and ideal. Metaphysics is the harbinger of death, the definite separation of body and soul, and male thought seeks to inscribe that death in philosophy and to evade it by a male (homosexual) tradition of parturition of knowledge and heritage. If Penelope undoes the patriarchal order in her weaving she simultaneously works on a different loom which signifies a new feminine symbolic order. One aspect of this is the relationship to time – if men's time is of action, marked by events, Penelope's is a 'quiet time of self-belonging' (*In Spite of Plato*, p. 14), while Penelope waiting on the shore for Ulysses marks not a limit but liminality, the threshold between the death-dealing metaphysics of male thought and the life-affirming quietude of a female symbolic order. Penelope 'tangles and holds together what philosophy wants to separate ... She intertwines and holds together the elements of the living world, the only real world, allowing the philosophers to persist in their desire to inhabit the world above' (*In Spite of Plato*, p. 29).

Cavarero's rereading of the fragment about the maidservant from Thrace, while tracing the development of metaphysics from Parmenides through to Plato, similarly sites the roots of women's existence in a corporeal materiality, and the fundamental doctrine of Platonic philosophy in a denial of the empirical, the everyday, the *real*, which is the realm of women *par excellence*. The woman's laughter exposes the mendacity of philosophical discourse. The chapter on Demeter and her daughter Persephone, abducted by Hades, explores in detail the mother–daughter relationship as the foundation of a female symbolic order, and mother–daughter relationships have been much explored by contemporary women's writing in Italy. For Cavarero this myth is more than an agricultural myth about the revolving seasons. It encapsulates the violent wrenching of power away from women, as a matriarchal order is overturned. Matricide rather than patricide is the original crime. Cavarero's reading, which owes much to Irigaray's *Sexes et parentés* (*Sexes and Genealogies*, 1993), invests Demeter with will, power and authority: she is the giver of life, at her own discretion, and can withdraw this gift, and her emphasis on the mother figure follows Hannah Arendt, who attempts to overturn death as the liminal threshold of philosophy and replace it with birth. Maternity, and with it a female genealogy to challenge the relegation of women by history, is restored to its central position.

The rejection of overarching narratives marks much contemporary writing, whether fictional or theoretical, and leads writers to challenge, from within, hegemonic master discourses. In a recent work of 1997 *Tu che mi guardi, tu che mi racconti* (*Relating Narratives: Storytelling and Selfhood*), Adriana Cavarero moves between philosophy and literature: for her, literature reveals significance without defining it, while philosophy insists on capturing the universe in the trap of definition. Poet and historian both 'turn to the unrepeatable single moment, not to the universal or the general' (*Tu che mi guardi*, p. 40). In her discussion of the stories told by Scheherezade, she notes that the weaver of tales bears several children over the years: sex is here followed not by death but by storytelling, allowing time for fecundity and productivity. For Cavarero, post-structuralists merely want the fragmented woman that patriarchy has always required, and she refuses an aesthetic view which sees in fragmentary, multiple narration an exquisitely feminine practice. While contemporary theoretical practice clearly engages with post-modernism's decentering of subjectivity and undoing of the ties between language and reality, Cavarero still insists that the text refers to something outside, pre-existing, and she rejects the tendency of Anglo-American feminist criticism to negate the unified subject, in an appeal both to common sense and to the pleasure of reading itself.

The potential of a female symbolic order based on the mother is central to the work of another philosopher, *Luisa Muraro, a member of the Libreria delle donne (The Women's Bookshop) of Milan and also of Diotima. The 1987 publication *Non credere di avere dei diritti* ('Don't believe you have any rights') collectively authored by the Libreria, and indebted particularly to Luce Irigaray's *Ethique de la différence sexuelle* (*An Ethics of Sexual Difference*, 1984), aligned itself with radical feminism's rejection of emancipation as incapable of dealing with the differences between women, and argued for an elaboration of sexual difference which alone would account for the disparity between women, a diversity to be exploited through the proposed *affidamento* or 'entrustment' which would see women as figures of authority (the symbolic mother) rather than power in the lives of other women.

While Cavarero's writing is patiently allusive, teasing out meanings, Muraro's *L'ordine simbolico della madre* ('Symbolic order of the mother', 1991) is written in a style designed to debunk the forms of philosophical discourse. Part autobiography, the book also includes ripostes to its own arguments, inviting a questioning, dialectical approach rather than attempting to become itself another master discourse. Like Cavarero, Muraro has been considerably influenced by Luce Irigaray, whose work she has indeed translated into Italian[11] and also edited (*Speculum: L'altra donna*, 1975). Muraro posits a female symbolic order based on the mother which has been repressed. In *Guglielma e Maifreda: storia di un'eresia femminista* ('Guglielma and Maifreda: story of a feminist heresy', 1985) and *Lingua materna scienza divina: scritti sulla filosofia mistica di Margherita Porete* ('Maternal language divine knowledge: writings on the mystical philosophy of Margherite Porete', 1995) she turns to the mystics – a largely female tradition – to give some sense of what cannot be said within the language of patriarchy, while the earlier *La signora del gioco: episodi della caccia alle streghe* ('Lady of the game: episodes from witch-hunts', 1976) delivers a feminist interpretation of the witch-hunt as a means of destroying specifically female knowledge handed down through the generations. Once again, the revealing detail, the individual story, attempts to root history in subjective experience.

Muraro takes Cavarero's thesis of matricide into the area of language: it is in relation to the mother that the child enters into the symbolic order, and the Lacanian notion that entry into the symbolic necessitates a turning away from the mother is thus false. Her attempt to establish a female genealogy, a symbolic order based on the mother rather than the father, has been accused of replicating old dichotomies, while her optimistic celebration of the end of male oppression within the symbolic, expressed in the journal *Via Dogana* in 1995, left some puzzled. Yet Muraro's positive affirmation of maternal love as the primary source of empowerment strongly challenges what she sees as the double negative of patriarchy, whose usurpation of maternal power drives a wedge between mother and daughter to the extent that to learn to love one's mother is to move in the opposite direction to the search for knowledge.

Other writers sought stylistic and methodological solutions to the problems of hierarchy and authority in an attempt to make a break with discourses sanctioned by patriarchal institutions. Lea Melandri took issue with Muraro's elaboration of *affidamento* as repeating all-too-familiar patterns in female dress. *L'infamia originale* ('Original sin', 1977) seeks to deconstruct the misrepresentation by psychoanalysis of women's sexuality. Melandri's critical work on Sibilla Aleramo (a reading of Aleramo's diaries (1979) and a co-edited collection of essays on Aleramo (1986)) led to the experimental *Come nasce il sogno d'amore* ('How a dream of love is born', 1988). Part autobiography, part biography, part literary criticism, she weaves her own text into Aleramo's autobiography, subverting notions of both academic discourse and self-writing, and simultaneously rejecting any hierarchical mentoring across the generations. *Lo strabismo della memoria* ('Cross-eyed memory', 1991) is a similarly hybrid text which, in recreating Melandri's own path from the 1960s through the 1980s, mixes biography, autobiography, fiction and memoir.

Historical as well as psychoanalytical and literary discourse came under scrutiny and challenge. In *Storia della donna, una scienza possibile* ('History of woman, a possible science', 1988) Maria Addis Saba seeks to establish a methodological framework through which to reconsider women's minor role in official history. To insert women into official history would be to confirm their lesser status; what is required is a post-structuralist weaving of plural histories to challenge the notion of unitary history itself. Gianna Pomata refused a version of history which would seek to interpret feminism as an outcome of bourgeois 'progress', with its grand narratives of industrialisation and modernisation. Nonetheless Pomata refuses a unified, unitary history of women and the women's movement, mistrusting 'the whig version of history, the history that searches for and sees in the past the very anticipations, the vanguards, of that which it has overcome and today controls'.[12] In her later work Pomata offers a critique of the view that the development of the sciences and medicine is necessarily beneficial to women; women's history exposes the way in which this ambiguous process simultaneously closes off areas of female autonomy. Pomata recalls Michel Foucault in her analysis of science and medicine as a means of social control, and the construction of 'woman' as a sexual category,[13] while her interventions on abortion reflect her search for a dynamic interaction of past and present. Other historians such as Annarita Buttafuoco have joined in the massive task of bringing to light women's history, cataloguing texts on women in the libraries of Milan, or studying the social rights of women in the post-Unification period.[14]

If Adriana Cavarero explores the borders of literature and philosophy, Luisa Passerini, professor of history and novelist, seeks to overturn conventional hierarchies of literary and historical discourse. Passerini produces a hybrid discourse which mixes history and autobiography, thus bringing a marginal practice centre-stage and crossing boundaries between the public and private, the internal and external. In her historical work Passerini privileges the marginal. Her fragmented narratives of oral and collective memory seek to undermine a grand historical design, while her *Autoritratto di un gruppo* ('Group self-portrait', 1988) is an attempt to fuse theory and practice, positing a post-structuralist subject whose identity can be approached only through a plurality of voices and registers.

By the 1980s women's interest with regard to literature had extended to all spheres of cultural production: editing, publishing, journalism, academic. The academic and novelist Maria Corti, for example, based in Pavia, has probably been one of the most influential of contemporary Italian critics, promoting a renovation of Italian criticism, a deprovincialisation and an opening up to deconstruction and semiotics, as well as setting up the influential journal *Strumenti critici*. Corti refuses the notion that art is gendered – the better the artist, the more distant the work from any gendered *parti pris*. Yet she, too, acknowledges the different treatment meted out to the two sexes, and muses on the neglect of great writers such as Djuna Barnes and Gianna Manzini.

Criticism and readings of writing by women has changed dramatically in recent years, influenced mainly by the concerted effort of scholars and writers to rediscover and reread work of all genres and types. Political denunciation and the marginalisation of women from literature in the 1970s gave way in the 1980s to a process of analysis and theoretical reflection on the symbolic, on the question of women and language: the problem of sexual difference took centre stage in the cultural debate on women. The image of Virginia Woolf's 'room' was expanded from a physical space in which to write, to a language from which to write, as in Marina Zancan's *Il doppio itinerario della scrittura: la donna nella tradizione letteraria italiana* ('The double itinerary of writing: women in the Italian literary tradition', Turin, 1998). At the same time, women's voices began to be heard, through the scholarship of such as Giuliana Morandini's *La voce che è in lei* ('The voice within her', 1980) and Claudia Salaris's writings on the women Futurists. Works of scholarship such as Anna Santoro's *Guida al catalogo delle scrittrici italiane* ('Guide to the catalogue of Italian women writers', Naples, 1990) and *Le stanze ritrovate. Antologia di scrittrici venete dal Quattrocento al Novecento* ('Rediscovered rooms: anthology of Venetian women writers from the fifteenth century to the twentieth century', Milan, Venice, 1991), edited by A. Arslan, A. Chemello and G. Pizzamiglio, are invaluable contributions in that they bring to the attention of both scholars and the reading public voices long dismissed by more orthodox literary histories. Within the space of a few years, previous generations of women as writers were no longer notable by their absence, their minor or inconsequential status, but were undeniably and vividly present in all periods, in a hitherto unimaginable range of forms and genres. The work of rediscovery is ongoing, and promises not only to rewrite the history of Italian women's writing, but to reshape our reading of Italian literature itself.

NOTES

1. Armanda Guiducci, 'A proposito di estetica in Gramsci', in A. Caracciolo and R. Scalia (eds.), *La città futura* (Milan, 1959) (pp. 371–89); p. 374 and p. 379.
2. See Biancamaria Frabotta (ed.), *La politica del femminismo*.
3. Nadia Fusini, 'Sulle donne e il loro poetare', *Donnawomanfemme* 5 (1977), pp. 5–21.
4. *Le donne e la letteratura* (Rome, 1976), p. 11.
5. Frabotta, in Daniel Corona (ed.), *Donne e scrittura* (Palermo, 1990), p. 147.
6. See the Introduction to Sandra Kemp and Judith Squires, *Feminisms* (Oxford, 1997).
7. Carla Lonzi, 'Let's Spit on Hegel', in Paula Bono and Sandra Kemp (eds.), *Italian Feminist Thought: a Reader* (Oxford 1991), p. 41.

8. Silvia Veggetti Finzi, *Il romanzo della famiglia: passioni e ragioni del vivere insieme* (Milan, 1993), p. 236.

9. In Bono and Kemp, *Italian Feminist Thought*, p. 194.

10. Rosi Braidotti, 'Introduction to Cavarero', *In Spite of Plato*.

11. *Ce Sexe qui n'en est pas un* (1997) was translated as *Questo sesso che non è un sesso* in 1980, and *Sexes et parentés* (1987) appeared as *Sessi e genealogie* in 1989.

12. In Bono and Kemp, *The Lonely Mirror* (London, 1993), p. 164.

13. See Gianna Pomata, *Contracting a Cure: Patients, Healers, and the Law in Early Modern Bologna*, translated by Pomata, with the assistance of Rosemarie Foy and Anna Ta (Baltimore, 1998).

14. Elvira Badaracco and Annarita Buttafuoco (eds.), *Testi sulle donne nelle biblioteche milanesi: catalogo-repertorio* (Milan, 1991), and Annarita Buttafuocco, *Questioni di cittadinanza: donne e diritti sociali nell'Italia liberale* (Siena, 1997).

Bibliographical guide to women writers and their work

Aganoor Pompilj, Vittoria (Padua 1855–1910 Rome)

Poet and letter writer. Of Armenian origin, studied in Padua with Giacomo Zanella and Enrico Nencioni. Familiar with French poetry, published her first collection at turn of century. Married Guido Pompilj (1901), well-known deputy and man of letters from Umbria, who shot himself after she died.

Major works

Leggenda eterna, Milan, 1900; Turin, 1903
Nuove liriche, Rome, 1908
Poesie complete, ed. L. Grilli, Florence, 1912, 1927
Lettere a Domenico Gnoli, ed. B. Marniti, Caltanissetta–Rome, 1967
Lettere a Giacomo Zanella (1876–1888), ed. A. Chemello, Venice, 1996

Selected criticism

A. Russi in *DBI* (I), pp. 360–2; Costa-Zalessow, pp. 248–53; G. Sanguinetti Katz in Russell, pp. 1–8.

Aleramo, Sibilla (Rina Faccio) (Alessandria 1876–1960 Rome)

Novelist, poet, diarist, letter writer, polemicist, journalist. Her early years recounted in *Una donna*, the novel which brought her notoriety and fame as a feminist writer. After abusive marriage to clerk from father's factory who had raped her, left husband and small son and developed career as writer. Contributed to many national political and feminist publications. Social activist. Famous for many love affairs with prominent writers and artists.

Major works

Una donna, Rome–Turin, 1906; Milan, 1919; Florence, 1921; Milan, 1931, 1938, 1944, 1950 (preface E. Cecchi); 1973 (preface M. A. Macciocchi); ed. R. Ghiaroni, Turin, 1978; Milan, 1982 (preface M. Corti); Milan, 1985; trans. Rosalind Delmar, *A Woman*, London, 1979
Il passaggio, Milan, 1919; Florence, 1921; Milan, 1932, 1985
Momenti, Florence, 1921, 1922
Andando e stando, Florence, 1921, 1922; Milan, 1942

Amo dunque sono, Milan, 1927, 1933, 1940, 1947, 1982
Sì alla terra: Nuove poesie (1928–1934), Milan, 1935
Selva d'amore, Milan, 1947; Rome, 1980 (preface B. Corti)
La donna e il femminismo. Scritti 1897–1910, ed. B. Conti, Rome, 1978
Diario di una donna. Inediti 1945–1960, ed. A. Morino, Milan, 1978
Un amore insolito. Diario 1940–1944, ed. A. Morino, Milan, 1979

Selected criticism

Guerricchio, R., *Storia di Sibilla*, Pisa, 1974
Federzoni, M., I. Pezzini and M. P. Pozzato, *Sibilla Aleramo*, Florence, 1980
Conti, B., and A. Morino, *Sibilla Aleramo e il suo tempo. Vita raccontata e illustrata*, Milan, 1981
Contorbia, F., L. Melandri and A. Morino (eds.), *Sibilla Aleramo. Coscienza e scrittura*,
    Milan, 1986
Buttafuoco, A. and M. Zancan, *Svelamento. Sibilla Aleramo: una biografia intellettuale*,
    Milan, 1988
Bassanese, F., '*Una donna*: Autobiography as Exemplary Text', in A. Testaferri (ed.),
    Donna: Women in Italian Culture, Ottawa, 1989, pp. 131–52
Kroha, L., 'Strategies of Intertextuality in Sibilla Aleramo's *Una donna*', in *The Woman
    Writer in Late-Nineteenth Century Italy. Gender and the Formation of Literary Identity*,
    Lewiston and Lampeter, 1992, pp. 123–42
Luciano, B., 'The Diaries of Sibilla Aleramo: Constructing Female Subjectivity', in M. O.
    Marotti (ed.), *Italian Women Writers from the Renaissance to the Present. Revising the
    Canon*, University Park, PA, 1996, pp. 95–110
L. Strappini in *DBI* (XLIV), pp. 57–65; F. A. Bassanese in Russell, pp. 9–17; Wood, pp.
    74–89

Andreini, Isabella Canali (Venice 1562–1604 Lyons)

Actress, poet, dramatist. From 1576, actress with the Gelosi, the most famous Italian
theatrical troupe of the day. Married fellow actor Francesco Andreini (1578). One of
earliest theatrical divas, acclaimed in Italy and beyond. Toured France in 1603–4. On
return journey, died in childbirth aged forty-two. Her numerous children included
dramatist Giambattista Andreini.

Major works

Mirtilla, Verona, 1588; Ferrara, 1590; Mantua, 1590; Bergamo, 1594; Venice, 1598, 1602;
    Milan, 1605; Venice, 1616; crit. edn M. L. Doglio, Lucca, 1995
Rime, Milan, 1601
Lettere, Venice, 1607, 1610; Turin, 1611; Venice, 1612; Turin, 1616
Lettere . . . aggiuntovi li Ragionamenti piacevoli, Venice, 1617; Turin, 1620; Venice, 1620, 1627,
    1634, 1638, 1647, 1652, 1663
Frammenti di alcune scritture . . . raccolti da Francesco Andreini, Venice, 1617, 1627

Selected criticism

Schio, M., and F. Taviani, *Il segreto della Commedia dell'Arte. La memoria delle compagnie
    italiane del XVI, XVII e XVIII secolo*, Florence, 1982
Tylus, J., 'Natural Woman: Isabella Andreini and the First Italian Actresses', *Italian
    Culture* 13 (1995), pp. 75–85
MacNeil, A., 'The Divine Madness of Isabella Andreini', *Journal of the Royal Musical
    Association* 120 (1995), pp. 195–215.

L. Pannella in *DBI* (XVII), pp. 704–5; Costa-Zalessow, 117–22; S. Longman in Wilson
(1991), vol. I, pp. 38–9; P. Vescovo in *Stanze*, pp. 83–94; F. A. Bassanese in Russell,
pp. 18–25

Archibugi, Francesca (Rome 1960–   )

Took part in political and cultural activities of Italian youth movement of late 1970s,
an experience that marked most of her work. First feature film, *Mignon è partita* (1988),
an instant success. Soon regarded as one of most promising voices in contemporary
Italian cinema. Co-wrote screenplay of first two features with two other writers, but
wrote subsequent films independently. Films include
Il grande cocomero, 1993, *Con gli occhi chiusi*, 1995 and *L'albero delle pere*, 1998.

Baccini, Ida (Florence 1850–1911 Florence)

Journalist and prolific writer of elementary school textbooks and children's fiction.
Began as elementary school teacher and went on to collaborate with journals such as
Rivista europea, *Gazzetta d'Italia*, *Gazzetta letteraria*. From 1884 directed *Cordelia*, a weekly
for girls, and in 1895 founded *Il giornale dei bambini*, a children's magazine.

Major works

Le memorie di un pulcino, Florence, 1875
La fanciulla massaia, Florence, 1880
La mia vita. Ricordi autobiografici, Rome–Milan, 1904
La vita dei bambini. Racconti, Milan, n.d.

Selected criticism

Catanzaro, C., *La donna italiana nelle scienze, nelle lettere, nelle arti. Dizionario biografico delle
    scrittrici e delle artiste viventi*, Florence, 1890
Porciani, I. (ed.), *Le donne a scuola: l'educazione femminile nell'Italia dell'Ottocento: mostra
    documentaria e iconografica*, Florence, 1987

Baij, Maria Cecilia (Viterbo 1694–1766 Montefiascone)

Mystic and letter writer. Studied music and became a singer. Lost her voice and entered
Cistercian convent. Subsequently entered Benedictine convent in Montefiascone, where
was elected abbess. Wrote about her spiritual and mystical experiences, leaving around
a thousand letters.

Major works

Scrittrici mistiche italiane, ed. G. Pozzi and C. Leonardi, Genoa, 1988, pp. 564–80
Scrittrici d'Italia, ed. A. Forlani and M. Savini, Rome, 1991, pp. 103–6

Ballestra, Silvia (San Benedetto del Tronto 1969–   )

Novelist and short story writer. Lives and studies in Bologna. First two short stories
appeared in Pier Vittorio Tondelli's *Giovani blues. Progetto Under 25* (Ancona, 1985).

Major works

Compleanno dell'iguana, Ancona–Bologna, 1991; Milan, 1991
La guerra degli Antò, Bologna, 1992; Milan, 1992
Gli orsi, Milan, 1994
Il disastro degli Antò, Milan, 1997
La signorina N.N. Una storia d'amore, Milan, 1998

Banti, Anna (Lucia Lopresti Longhi) (Florence 1895–1985 Florence)

Novelist, biographer, art historian, literary and film critic. Studied history of art at University of Rome where met and married eminent art historian Roberto Longhi. Last novel, *Un grido lacerante* (1981), is a fictionalised account of their marriage. Co-founder and co-editor of prestigious journal *Paragone*. Best known today for historical novels, in particular her version of the life of Renaissance artist Artemisia Gentileschi.

Major works
Artemisia, Florence, 1947; Milan, 1953, 1974, 1989; trans. S. D. Caracciolo, Lincoln, 1988.
Le donne muoiono, Milan, 1952; Florence, 1998
La camicia bruciata, Milan, 1973
Il grido lacerante, Milan, 1981
Il coraggio delle donne, Milan, 1940

Selected criticism
Biagini, E., *Anna Banti*, Milan, 1978
Nozzoli, pp. 85–111; D. Heller in Aricò, pp. 45–60; B. Ballaro in Russell, pp. 35–43;
    Wood, pp. 119–34

Beccari, Gualberta Alaide (Venice 1850–1906 Turin)

Journalist, playwright, short story writer. Founder of (and contributor to) the most important Italian women's journal of the second half of the nineteenth century, *La donna* (1868–91). Also directed the children's periodical *Mamma* (1876–92).

Major works
Pasquale Paoli. Un dramma in cinque atti, Venice, 1870
Un caso di divorzio, Milan, 1883
Ragazzi del popolo. Racconti con disegno, Bologna, 1884

Selected criticism
Jeffrey Howard, J., 'Patriot Mothers in the Post-Risorgimento: Women After the Italian
    Revolution', in C. R. Berkin and C. R. Lovett (eds.), *Women, War and Revolution*,
    New York, 1980, pp. 237–58
Gazzetta, L., 'Madre e cittadina. Una concezione dell'emancipazione alle origini del
    primo movimento politico delle donne in Italia', *Venetica. Annuario delle Venezie in
    età contemporanea* 11 (1994), pp. 133–61

Bellonci, Maria (Bellonci Villavecchia) (Rome 1902–1986 Rome)

Novelist and journalist. Best known today for scrupulously researched historical novels. Founded, with husband Goffredo, famous literary salon 'Gli amici della domenica' (1944) which led to Strega prize (1947). Was awarded Viareggio prize (*Lucrezia Borgia*) and Strega prize (*Rinascimento privato*) posthumously.

Major works
Lucrezia Borgia: la sua vita e i suoi tempi, Milan, 1939; rev. edn 1941, 1983; trans. B. Wall,
    London, 1953
Segreti dei Gonzaga, Milan, 1947, 1991
Pubblici segreti, Milan, 1965, 1990
Tu vipera gentile, Milan, 1972, 1986, 1995
Marco Polo, Milan, 1982, 1984; trans. T. Waugh, London 1984

Rinascimento privato, Milan, 1985, 1995
Opere, ed. E. Ferrero, Milan, 1994–7

Benedetta (Benedetta Cappa Marinetti) (Rome 1897–1977 Venice)

Best known as Futurist painter and writer of experimental novels. Studied with Giacomo Balla, in whose studio met husband, F. T. Marinetti, leader of Italian Futurism. Took part in several Venice Biennale exhibitions and all principal Futurist exhibitions of 1920s and 1930s. During Ethiopian war, and at outset of World War II, publicly addressed women in support of Fascist cause.

Major works
Le forze umane. Romanzo astratto con sintesi grafiche, Foligno, 1924
Viaggio di Gararà. Romanzo cosmico per il teatro, Milan, 1931
Astra e il sottomarino. Vita trasognata, Naples, 1935

Selected criticism
Re, L., 'Impure Abstraction: Benedetta As Visual Artist and Novelist', in *La Futurista: Benedetta Cappa Marinetti (exhibition catalogue)*, Philadelphia, 1998–9, pp. 31–47
Re, L., 'Fascist Theories of Woman and the Construction of Gender', in R. Pickering-Iazzi (ed.), *Mothers of Invention. Women, Italian Fascism, and Culture*, Minneapolis, MI, 1995, pp. 76–99
Bentivoglio, M. and F. Zoccoli, *Women Artists of Italian Futurism. Almost Lost To History . . .* New York, 1997

F. Artizzu in *DBI* (VIII), pp. 240–2

Bergalli Gozzi, Luisa (Venice 1703–1779 Venice)

Poet, playwright, translator and critic. Received good education. Apostolo Zeno allowed her to use his library and was an attentive reviser of her first plays. Married Gasparo Gozzi (1738), had numerous children and worked as translator because of financial difficulties. Her attempt with husband to run Sant'Angelo theatre, Venice (1746–8), ended in failure. Died of Black Death.

Major works
Componimenti Poetici delle più illustri Rimatrici d'ogni secolo, Venice, 1726
La Teba. Tragedia, Venice, 1728
Le avventure del poeta. Commedia, Venice, 1730; ed. L. Ricaldone, Manziana, Rome, 1997
Le rime di Gaspara Stampa, Venice, 1738
Elettra: tragedia da rappresentarsi nel Teatro di San Samuele, Venice, 1743
L'Almanacco delle donne, Venice, 1750; ed. T. Plebani, Venice, 1991
Le Amazzoni. Tragedia della Signora Du Boccage tradotta in versi martelliani, Venice, 1756

Selected criticism
Tassistro, C. E., *Luisa Bergalli Gozzi, la vita e l'opera sua nel suo tempo*, Rome, 1919
Panzini, A., *La sventurata Irminda!*, Milan, 1932
Soldini, F., 'Contributo agli studi su Gasparo Gozzi. Gli inediti frammenti di memorie di Francesco Gozzi', *GSLI* 449 (1968), pp. 369–402
Steward, P. D., 'Eroine della dissimulazione. Il teatro di Luisa Bergalli', *Quaderni Veneti* 19 (1994), pp. 73–92
Ricaldone, L., *La scrittura nascosta*, Paris–Fiesole, 1996

C. Mutini in *DBI* (IX), pp. 63–8; *Stanze*, pp. 128–37; P. D. Stewart in Russell, pp. 50–7

Bompiani, Ginevra (Milan 1939–   )

Novelist, short story writer, and literary critic. Teaches English literature at University of Siena.

Major works

Bàrtelemi all'ombra, Milan, 1967
Le specie del sonno, Milan, 1975
Lo spazio narrante, Milan, 1978
Mondanità, Milan, 1980
L'incantato, Milan, 1987
Vecchio cielo, nuova terra, Milan, 1988
L'orso maggiore, Milan, 1994

Selected criticism

N. De Giovanni in De Giovanni, pp. 105–13

Bonacci Brunamonti, Maria Alinda (Perugia 1841–1903 Perugia)

Poet, prose writer and critic. Student of Giacomo Zanella, published her first poems aged fifteen. Was also well respected for writings on art.

Major works

Canti, Perugia, 1856
Canti nazionali, Recanati, 1860
Versi, Florence, 1875; 1876
Versi campestri, Perugia, 1876
Nuovi canti, Città di Castello, 1887
Discorsi d'arte, Città di Castello, 1898
Flora, Rome, 1898
Alinda. Ricordi di viaggio, Florence, 1905

Selected criticism

P. Fasano in *DBI* (XI), pp. 453–4

Bonanni Caione, Laudòmia (L'Aquila 1908–   )

Novelist, short story writer, journalist. Taught in primary schools and has been a member and judge of the Juvenile Court. Work praised by Montale, who compared her short stories to James Joyce's *Dubliners*. Awarded Bagutta and Amici della Domenica prizes (1949) and Viareggio prize (1960).

Major works

Men: avventura al Nuovo Fiore, Milan, 1939
Il fosso, Milan, 1949
Palma e sorelle, Rome, 1954
L'imputata, Milan, 1960
L'adultera, Milan, 1964
Il bambino di pietra: una nevrosi femminile, Milan, 1979
Le droghe, Milan, 1982

Selected criticism

Petrignani, S., 'La vita solitaria', in S. Petrignani (ed.), *Le signore della scrittura*, Milan, 1984, pp. 57–64

Bossi Fedrigotti, Isabella (Rovereto 1948–   )

Novelist and journalist. Austrian mother, Italian father. Received Super Campiello prize in 1991.

Major works

Amore mio uccidi Garibaldi, Milan, 1980, 1982
Casa di guerra, Milan, 1983
Diario di una dama di corte, Milan, 1984, 1996
Di buona famiglia, Milan, 1991
'Arlecchino', in Bossi Fedrigotti et al. (eds.), *Mi riguarda*, Rome, 1994, pp. 15–20
Magazzino vita, Milan, 1996

Selected criticism

Beverly, J., 'I luoghi del cuore e le molte verità: An Introduction to the Novels of Isabella Bossi Fedrigotti', *Tuttitalia* 11 (1995), pp. 35–9

Bruck, Edith (Edith Steinschreiber) (Tiszabércel, Hungary 1932–   )

Novelist, poet, journalist. Born into poor Hungarian Jewish family, survived deportation to Auschwitz. Settled in Italy in 1954. Has worked for Italian television and has directed feature films. Among founders of Centro Femminista Maddalena in Rome. *Lettera alla madre* won Rapallo-Carige prize (1989) and was made into a play (1991).

Major works

Chi ti ama così, Milan, 1959; Venice, 1974, 1994
Andremo in città, Milan, 1962; Rome, 1982
Le sacre nozze, Milan, 1969
Transit, Milan, 1978; Venice, 1995
In difesa del padre, Milan, 1980
Lettera alla madre, Milan, 1988
Nuda proprietà, Venice, 1993
Signora Auschwitz: il dono della parola, Venice, 1999

Selected criticism

Giorgio, A., 'Strategies for Remembering: Auschwitz, Mother, and Writing in Edith Bruck', in C. Burdett, C. Gorrara and H. Peitsch (eds.), *European Memories of the Second World War: New Perspectives on Post-War Literature*, Oxford, 1999
Giorgio, A., 'Dall'autobiografia al romanzo. La rappresentazione della Shoah nell'opera di Edith Bruck', in C. Honess and V. Jones (eds.), *Le donne delle minoranze. Le ebree e protestanti d'Italia*, Turin, 1999, pp. 297–307

Cambria, Adele (1931–   )

Playwright. Became important figure in Italian cultural feminism during 1970s. Founding member of Maddalena theatre (Rome), where staged first plays. Most important work *Nonostante Gramsci*, written from point of view of a writer sympathetic to Marxism, but provides implicit critique of patriarchal attitudes inherent in revolutionary politics. Most recent work, *La regina dei cartoni*, based on story of a bourgeois woman who left family to live on streets of Rome in 1970s and died there in 1983.

Major works

Amore come rivoluzione (contains play *Nonostante Gramsci*), Milan, 1976
Marx, la moglie e la fedele governante, Padua, 1980

Selected criticism

de Lauretis, Teresa, 'Gramsci Notwithstanding', in *Technologies of Gender*, Bloomington, IN, 1983

Caminer Turra, Elisabetta (Venice 1751–1796 Orgiano (Vicenza))

Journalist. Daughter of Domenico Caminer, received very little formal education. Started working as teenager in Venice for father's *Europa letteraria*, then *Giornale enciclopedico*, taking over editorship aged twenty-six. Moved to Vicenza after marrying Antonio Turra, with whom set up a printing shop. Her house was an important meeting place for contemporary intellectuals; in her later years she established a theatrical school there. Translated many theatrical works.

Major works

Composizioni teatrali moderne tradotte da Elisabetta Caminer, Venice, 1772,
Giornale enciclopedico, Venice, 1774–82
Nuovo giornale enciclopedico, Vicenza, 1782–9
Nuovo giornale enciclopedico d'Italia, Venice, 1790–6
Drammi trasportati dal francese idioma ad uso del teatro italiano da Elisabetta Caminer Turra, Venice, 1794

Selected criticism

Lattes, L., 'Una letterata veneziana del sec. XVIII (Elisabetta Caminer Turra)', *Nuovo Archivio Veneto* 27 (1914), pp. 1–35
Stocchiero, S., 'La redazione di un giornale settecentesco', *Nuovo Archivio Veneto* 40 (1920), pp. 173–81
Berengo, M., *Giornali veneziani del settecento*, Milano, 1962
Ricuperati, G., 'Giornali e società nell'Italia dell'Ancien Régime (1668–1789)', in V. Castronovo, G. Ricuperati and C. Capra (eds.), *La stampa italiana dal Cinquecento all'Ottocento*, Bari, 1980, pp. 299–307

C. De Michelis in *DBI* (XVII), pp. 236–41

Campiglia, Maddalena (Vicenza 1553–1595 Vicenza)

Poet, dramatist. Born into nobility, but as result of irregular union. Married local nobleman, Dionisio Colzè, in 1576. In 1580, following failure of marriage, moved back into family home. Despite anomalous social situation, seems to have participated actively in literary life of Veneto and beyond, maintaining close contacts with circles of Accademia Olimpica in Venice, and of Isabella Pallavicino Lupi in Parma.

Major works

Discorso sopra l'annonciatione della B. Vergine e la Incarnatione del S. N. Giesù Christo, Vicenza, 1585
Flori, Vicenza, 1588
Calisa, Vicenza, 1589

Selected criticism

Mantese, G., 'Per un profilo storico della poetessa vicentina Maddalena Campiglia: aggiunte e rettifiche', *Archivio veneto* 5, 81 (1967), pp. 89–123
Morsolin, B., 'Maddalena Campiglia, poetessa vicentina del secolo XVI. Episodio biografico', *Atti dell'Accademia Olimpica* 17 (1982), pp. 5–76
De Marco, G., *Maddalena Campiglia. La figura e l'opera*, Vicenza, 1988

Perrone, C-C., 'So che donna ama donna: La *Calisa* di M. Campiglia', in G. Ulysse (ed.),
    Les femmes écrivains en Italie au Moyen Age et à la Renaissance, Aix-en-Provence, 1994,
    pp. 293–314

D. Sartori in *Stanze*, pp. 57–68; C. Mutini in *DBI* (xvii), 541–2

Capriolo, Paola (Milan 1962–   )

Novelist, journalist, and translator (from German). Her novels have been awarded
numerous prizes (including Giuseppe Berto, Rapallo-Carige, Grinzane Cavour).

Major works

La grande Eulalia, Milan, 1988, 1991
Il nocchiero, Milan, 1989, 1991
Il doppio regno, Milan, 1991, 1993
Vissi d'amore, Milan, 1992, 1995
La spettatrice, Milan, 1995; trans. L. Heron, *The Woman Who Watches*, London, 1998
Floria Tosca, London, 1997
Il sogno dell'agnello, Milan, 1999

Selected criticism

'Un altro mondo': interview with Paola Capriola by Gillian Ania. *The Italianist* 18 (1998),
    pp. 304–34
Ania, Gillian, 'At Capriolo's Hotel: Heaven, Hell and Other Worlds in *Il doppio regno*',
    Italian Studies (1999), pp. 132–56
Wilson, Rita, 'The Space(s) of Myth in Paola Capriolo's *Con i miei mille occhi*', *ITS in
    Southern Africa* 12.2 (1999), pp. 37–57

Wood, pp. 266–74

Carriera, Rosalba (Venice 1675–1757 Venice)

Painter. Distinguished in painting of minatures and pastels, both in Italy and abroad.
Travelled to Paris in 1720 and painted most important people at court, including king.
Influenced eighteenth-century portrait painters.

Major work

Diario degli anni MDCCXX *e* MDCCXXI *scritto di propria mano in Parigi da Rosalba Carriera
    dipintrice famosa posseduto, illustrato e pubblicato dal signor D.n Giovanni Vianelli
    canonico della cattedrale di Chioggia*, Venice, 1793; rev. edn in V. Malamani, *Rosalba
    Carriera*, Bergamo, 1910; new edn 'Diari', in B. Sani, *Rosalba Carriera. Lettere, diari,
    frammenti*, vol. II, Florence, 1985

Selected criticism

Malamani, V., *Rosalba Carriera*, Bergamo, 1910
Da Pozzo, G., 'Tra cultura e avventura: dall'Algarotti al Da Ponte', in *Storia della cultura
    veneta. Il Settecento*, Vicenza, 1985, pp. 518–19
Sani, B., *Rosalba Carriera*, Milano, 1988
Zava Boccazzi, F., 'Rosalba Carriera', in C. Limentani Virdis (ed.), *Le tele svelate. Antologia
    di pittrici venete dal Cinquecento al Novecento*, Mirano, 1996

G. Gatto in *DBI* (xx), pp. 745–9

Caterina Benincasa da Siena, St (1347–1380)

Daughter of a dyer, entered Dominican order aged seventeen. Immediately dedicated herself to charitable works, and was soon surrounded by a 'family' of followers. Dictated letters to religious and powerful figures of the time, giving advice even on political matters. In 1374, was given her spiritual advisor, brother Raimondo da Capua, who would also be her first biographer. Having persuaded Gregorio XI to bring papacy back to Rome from Avignon, she devoted herself until her death to cause of unity and reform of the Church.

Major works

Le lettere, ed. N. Tommaseo, Florence, 1860
Epistolario, ed. P. Misciattelli, Siena, 1913–21
Epistolario, ed. E. Dupré Theseider, Rome, 1940
The Dialogue of Divine Providence, New York, 1980
'*I Catherine': Selected Writings of St Catherine of Siena*, ed. K. Foster and M. J. Ronayne, London, 1980
Lettere alle religiose, Milan, 1982
The Letters of Catherine of Siena, Binghamton, NY, 1988

Selected criticism

Dupré Theseider, E., *Il problema critico delle lettere di Santa Caterina*, Rome, 1933
Gardner, E. S., *Saint Catherine of Siena*, London–New York, 1907
Getto, G., *Letteratura religiosa del Trecento*, Florence, 1967

Dupré Theseider in *DBI* (xxii), pp. 361–79; Costa-Zalessow, pp. 34–8; S. Noffke in Russell, pp. 58–66

Cavani, Liliana (Carpi (Modena) 1937–)

Film director, scriptwriter. Worked for Italian television (RAI) on documentaries and feature films. First independent film was *I cannibali* in 1970. Best known film, *Il portiere di notte* (1974), met with considerable financial success, but, like her other films, was subject of critical controversy. She now prefers to direct opera. Other films include *Al di là del bene e del male* (1978), *La pelle* (1981), *Oltre la porta* (1982) and *Francesco* (1989). Published screenplays are listed here.

Major works

Francesco e Galileo: due film, Turin, 1970
Il portiere di notte, Turin, 1974
with E. Medioli, *Oltre la porta*, Turin, 1982
with R. Mazzoni, *Francesco*, Milan, 1989

Selected criticism

Tiso, C., *Cavani*, Florence, 1975
Buscemi, F., *Invito al cinema di Liliana Cavani*, Milan, 1997

Cavarero, Adriana (Bra, Turin 1947–)

Feminist philosopher and founding member of the group of feminist philosophers based in Verona, Diotima.

Major works

Dialettica e politica in Platone, Padova, 1976

L'interpretazione hegeliana di Parmenide, Turin, 1984

with L. Menapace, *Incontri sul tema: cultura della differenza sessuale*, Rome, 1988

Nonostante Platone: figure femminili nella fisosofia antica, Rome, 1990; trans. S. Anderlini
     d'Onofrio and Á. O'Healy (foreword R. Braidotti), *In Spite of Plato*, Cambridge, 1995

Corpo in figure: filosofia e politica della corporeità, Milan, 1995

Tu che mi guardi, tu che mi racconti: filosofia della narrazione, Milan, 1997; trans. and intro.
     Paul A. Kottman, *Relating Narratives: Storytelling and Selfhood*, Cambridge 2000

with F. Restaino, *Le filosofie femministe*, Turin, 1999

Selected criticism

Braidotti, Rosi, *Patterns of Dissonance*, Cambridge, 1991

Re, L., 'Mythic Revisionism: Women Poets and Philosophers in Italy Today', in M. O.
     Marotti (ed.), *Italian Women Writers from the Renaissance to the Present: Revising the
     Canon*, Pennsylvania, 1996

Cecchi D'Amico, Suso (Rome 1914–   )

Screenwriter. Daughter of writer Emilio Cecchi. Worked as a journalist and translator, began writing for screen in 1946. Collaborating with some of the country's best-known directors, she co-wrote script of several classics of Italian cinema in 1940s and 1950s. Has continued writing screenplays and, occasionally, scripts for television, including Franco Zeffirelli's *Gesù di Nazareth* in 1977. Screenplays include *L'onorevole Angelina* (dir. Zampa, 1947), *Ladri di biciclette* (dir. De Sica, 1948), *Bellissima* (Visconti, 1950), *I vinti* (Antonioni, 1953), *Kean* (Gassman, 1956) and *I magliari* (Rosi, 1959).

Ceresa, Alice (Basel, Switzerland 1923–   )

Novelist, journalist and translator (from German). Born of Swiss Italian father and Swiss German mother, has lived in Rome since 1950, working for Silone's journal *Tempo presente* and for the publisher Longanesi. Won Viareggio prize 'Opera prima' in 1967.

Major works

La figlia prodiga, Turin, 1967

Bambine, Turin, 1990

'La morte del padre', *Nuovi Argomenti* 62 (April-May 1979), pp. 69–92

Selected criticism

Cohen-Tanugi, J., 'La famille dans l'oeuvre d'Alice Ceresa', in Centre Aixois de
     Recherches Italiennes (ed.), *Les femmes écrivains en Italie aux xixe et xxe siècles*, Aix-
     en-Provence, 1993, pp. 273–85

De Lauretis, T., 'Figlie prodighe', *DonnaWomanFemme: Omelie di donne* 2–3 (1996), pp. 80–90

Wilkin, A., 'New Women's Writing in Italian-Speaking Switzerland', in J. Charnley, M.
     Pender and A. Wilkin (eds.), *25 Years of Emancipation? Women in Switzerland 1971 to
     1996*, Bern, 1997

Cereta, Laura (Brescia 1469–1499)

Precocious humanist, educated in convent and then by father, a jurist and magistrate, who guided her Latin and Greek studies. At fifteen, married Venetian merchant who died of plague eighteen months later. Did not remarry, or enter convent. When only eighteen years old, a collection of her essay-letters was circulated. Attacked for writing by both men and women, she seemingly fell silent. Some eighty-two letters and a dialogue were left in manuscript at her death.

Major work
Laurae Ceretae epistolae, crit. ed. F. Tomasini, Padua, 1640; *Collected Letters of a Renaissance Feminist*, transcr., trans. and ed. D. Robin, Chicago, 1997

Selected criticism
A. Rabil, Jr., *Laura Cereta: Quattrocento Humanist*, Binghamton, NY, 1981
M. King and A. Rabil (eds.), *Her Immaculate Hand*, Binghampton, NY, 1983, pp. 77–86
D. Robin, 'Humanism and Feminism in Laura Cereta's Public Letters', in L. Panizza (ed.), *Women in Italian Renaissance*, Oxford, 2000, pp. 368–84

M. Palma in *DBI* (XXIII), pp. 729–30; A. Rabil Jr. in Russell, pp. 67–75

Cialente, Fausta (Cagliari 1898–1993 London)
Novelist, translator. After peripatetic childhood moved to Alexandria, Egypt, with husband, composer Enrico Terni. Anti-fascist. During the war gave daily broadcasts on Radio Cairo and wrote for a newspaper for Italian war prisoners. After husband's death, returned to Rome and later moved to England. Her novels gradually became more introspective and autobiographical, culminating in her most famous work, *Le quattro ragazze Wieselberger.*

Major works
Natalia, Rome, 1930
Cortile a Cleopatra, Milan, 1936
Ballata levantina, Milan, 1961
Un inverno freddissimo, Milan, 1966
Le quattro ragazze Wieselberger, Milan, 1976

Selected criticism
Consoli, V., *Il romanzo di Fausta Cialente*, Milan, 1985

P. Malpezzi Price in Aricò, pp. 108–22; B. Merry in Russell, pp. 76–84.

Colonna, Vittoria (Marino (Rome) 1490–1547 Rome)
Daughter of Fabrizio Colonna and Agnese di Montefeltro, married Ferrante d'Avalos, Marquis of Pescara (1509). Widowed in 1525, dedicated herself ever more to studies, poetry and religious meditation. From 1530 drawn to preaching of evangelical reformers Juan de Valdés and Bernardo Ochino. With close friend Cardinal Reginald Pole established a reforming religious circle at Viterbo. In later years withdrew to convent, developing artistic interests and friendship with Michelangelo Buonarroti.

Major works
Carteggio, ed. E. Ferrero and G. Muller, Turin, 1892
Rime, ed. A. Bullock, Bari, 1982
Sonnetti in morte di Francesco Ferrante d'Avalos Marchese di Pescara, ed. T. R. Toscano, Milan, 1997

Selected criticism
Bainton, R. H., 'Vittoria Colonna', in *Women of the Reformation in Germany and Italy*, Minneapolis, 1971, pp. 201–18
Bullock, A., 'Vittoria Colonna and Francesco Maria Molza: Conflict in Communication', *IT* 32 (1977), pp. 41–51

Borsetto, L., 'Narciso ed Eco. Figura e scrittura nella lirica femminile del Cinquecento: esemplificazioni ed appunti', in M. Zancan (ed.), *Nel cerchio della luna: Figure di donna in alcuni testi del XVI secolo*, Venice, 1983, pp. 171–233

Bullock, A., 'Vittoria Colonna: Note e aggiunte alla edizione critica del 1982', *GSLI* 162 (1985), pp. 407–19

G. Patrizi in *DBI* (XXVII), pp. 448–57; Costa-Zalessow, pp. 63–7; F. A. Bassanese in Russell, pp. 85–94

Contessa Lara (Evelina Cattermole Mancini) (Florence 1849–1896 Rome)

Poet. Father was of Scottish descent and surname Cattermole was Italianised form of family name Kattermohl. Adulated as a poet, her personal life was the source of much gossip and scandal.

Major works

Canti e ghirlande, Florence, 1867
Versi, Rome, 1883
E ancora versi, Florence, 1886
Nuovi versi, Milan, 1897

Selected criticism

Borghese, M., *La Contessa Lara, una vita di passione e di poesia nell'Ottocento italiano*, Milan, 1930

A. Briganti in *DBI* (XXII), pp. 514–16; Costa-Zalessow, pp. 234–9; B. Merry in Russell, pp. 95–103

Copio Sullam, Sara (Venice 1588/90–1641)

Poet, letter writer, philosopher, scholar. Lived in Venice's Ghetto, where distinguished Hebrew scholar, Rabbi Leone da Modena, was family friend and her tutor. Married Giacobbe Sullam around 1613. Exchanged literary letters with epic poet, Ansaldo Cebà; disputed on immortality of soul with priest and literary figure, Baldassare Bonifacio. Resisted attempts of both writers to convert her.

Major work

Manifesto di Sarra Copia Sulam Hebrea, nel quale è da lei riprovata e detestata l'opinione negante l'immortalità dell'Anima falsamente attribuitale dal Sig. Baldassare Bonifaccio, Venice, 1621

Selected criticism

Da Fonseca-Wollheim, C., 'Acque di Parnaso, Acque di battesimo: fede e fama nell'opera di Sara Copio Sullam', in C. Honess and V. Jones (eds.), *Le donne delle minoranze*, Turin, 1999, pp. 159–70

Da Fonseca-Wollheim, C., *Faith and Fame in the Life and Works of the Venetian Jewish Poet Sara Copio Sullam*, University of Cambridge PhD, 2000

G. Busetto in *DBI* (XXVIII), 582–4; Costa-Zalessow, pp. 123–7; G. Busetto in *Stanze*, pp. 109–16

Corti, Maria (Milan 1915–)

Novelist, literary critic, philologist, semiotician. Professor of History of the Italian Language at University of Pavia, where created Fondo Manoscritti. Has published

extensively on problems of literary Italian and on dialects. In 1957, was awarded
National Academy of the Lincei prize for criticism and philology. A central figure in
Italian culture, she is an Academician of Crusca, Arcadia and Brera.

Major works

L'ora di tutti, Milan, 1962, 1971, 1991
Il ballo dei sapienti, Milan, 1966
Principi della comunicazione letteraria, Milan, 1976; trans. M. Bogart and A. Mandelbaum,
     Principles of Literary Communication, London and Bloomington, IN, 1978
Il canto delle sirene, Milan, 1989, 1992
Cantare nel buio, Milan, 1991
Dialogo in pubblico: intervista di Cristina Nesi, Milan, 1995

Selected criticism

Urbani, B., 'Maria Corti a l'écoute du chant de sirènes', in Centre Aixois de Recherches
     Italiennes (ed.), *Les Femmes écrivains en Italie aux xixe et xxe siècles*, Aix-en-Provence,
     1993, pp. 259–72

Covito, Carmen (Castellammare di Stabia 1948–)

Novelist and literary critic. Lives and works in Milan. Won Rapallo-Carige 'Opera
prima' and Bancarella prizes in 1993 for first novel.

Major works

La bruttina stagionata, Milan, 1992, 1995
Del perchè i porcospini attraversano la strada, Milan, 1995
Benvenuti in questo ambiente, Milan, 1997

Curtoni Verza, Silvia (Verona 1751–1835 Verona)

Poet. After brief period in a convent, she married, dedicated herself to literature and
created one of most brilliant salons in Verona and surrounding area. During
Napoleonic campaigns, became enthusiastic promoter of charitable works. Founded a
private theatre in Verona, in which she herself performed.

Major works

Ritratti di alcuni illustri amici di Silvia Curtoni Verza in Arcadia Flaminda Caritea, Verona, 1807
Terze Rime di Silvia Curtoni Verza Guastaverza in Arcadia Flaminda Caritea, Verona, 1822
Carteggio inedito d'una gentildonna veronese, ed. G. Biadego, Verona, 1884

Selected criticism

Montanari, B., *Vita di Silvia Curtoni Verza veronese*, Verona, 1851
Biadego, G., 'Donna Silvia Curtoni Verza a Milano e a Napoli', in *Da libri e manoscritti.*
     Spigolature, Verona, 1883, pp. 107–16
Foscolo, U., *Epistolario*, ed. P. Carli, Florence, 1952
Ricaldone, L., *La scrittura nascosta*, Paris–Fiesole, 1996

F. Petrucci in *DBI* (XXXI), pp. 490–4

Cutrufelli, Maria Rosa (Messina 1946–)

Essayist, literary critic and novelist. Founder and director of women's narrative
periodical, *Tuttestorie*. Lives in Rome where works for publishers and collaborates with
Noi Donne. Has written many sociological essays on women.

Major works

Disoccupata con onore: lavoro e condizione della donna, Milan, 1974

L'invenzione della donna: miti e tecniche di uno sfruttamento, Milan, 1974

Donna, perchè piangi? Imperialismo e condizione femminile nell'Africa nera, Milan, 1976; trans.
N. Romano, *Woman, Why Do You Weep?*, London, 1983

Il cliente. Inchiesta sulla domanda di prostituzione, Milan, 1980

ed., *Scritture, scrittrici*, Milan, 1988

Mama Africa. Storia di donne e di utopie, Milan, 1989, 1993

ed. with R. Guacci and M. Rusconi, *Il pozzo segreto. Cinquanta scrittrici italiane*, Florence, 1993

ed., *Nella città proibita*, Milan, 1997

d'Aragona, Tullia (Rome 1510–1556 Rome)

Writer of letters and a dialogue, poet. Cultivated courtesan. Spent periods of life in
Venice; Ferrara, where Girolamo Muzio sang her praises in his *Rime diverse* (1551); Siena
and Florence. Developed close literary friendship with Benedetto Varchi. Married
Silvestro Guicciardini in 1543, and was released from legal obligation of wearing
courtesan's yellow veil. In 1548, returned to Rome where she died.

Major works

Dialogo della infinità d'amore, Venice: G. Giolito, 1547; 1552; crit. edn G. Zonta, in *Trattati
d'amore del Cinquecento*, Rome–Bari, 1912, pp. 185–248; reprint (intro. M. Pozzi),
1980; *Dialogue on the Infinity of Love*, ed. and trans. R. Russell and B. Merry, intro.
R. Russell, Chicago, 1997

Rime della signora Tullia di Aragona, et di diversi a lei, Venice: G. Giolito, 1547; 1549

Il Meschino, altramente detto il Guerrino, Venice, 1560

Selected criticism

Cox, V., *The Renaissance Dialogue*, Cambridge, 1992

Cox, V., 'Women and Chivalric Poetry', in G. Bedani et al. (eds.), *Sguardi sull'Italia*, Leeds,
1997, pp. 134–45

Costa-Zalessow, p. 737; R. Russell in Russell, pp. 26–34

D'Eramo, Luce (Reims (France) 1925–)

Novelist, literary critic and journalist. Born of Italian parents, brought up in Paris.
Family moved to Italy in 1939. In 1944, went to work in a German labour camp as a
volunteer, returned to Italy in a wheelchair in 1946. Lives in Rome.

Major works

La straniera, Milan, 1955

Finchè la testa vive, Milan, 1964

Cruciverba politico: come funziona in Italia la strategia della diversione, Rimini, 1974

Deviazione, Milan, 1979, 1995

Partiranno, Milan, 1986

ed. with G. Sobrino, *Europa in versi: la poesia femminile del '900*, Rome, 1989

Si prega di non disturbare, Milan, 1995

Una strana fortuna, Milan, 1997

Selected criticism

Caputo, I., 'Luce D'Eramo. E se io fossi nata formica?' in I. Caputo and L. Lepri (eds.),
Conversazioni di fine secolo: 12 interviste con 12 scrittrici contemporanee, Milan, 1995, pp.
17–33

De Céspedes, Alba (Rome 1911–1997 Paris)

Novelist, poet, journalist. Cuban father, Italian mother. Second novel, *Nessuno torna indietro*, fell foul of Fascist censorship. Joined the Resistance in 1943 and broadcast for a clandestine wireless station in the South. Best-known for *Quaderno proibito* (1952), diary of a middle-aged woman, and for partly epistolary, partly diaristic novel, *Il rimorso*, about intellectuals in Rome in 1950s.

Major works
Nessuno torna indietro, Milan, 1938
Quaderno proibito, Milan, 1952
Il rimorso, Milan, 1963
La bambolona, Milan, 1969

Selected criticism
Merry, B., *Women in Italian Literature: Four Studies Based on the Work of Grazia Deledda, Alba de Céspedes, Natalia Ginzburg and Dacia Maraini*, Townsville, Australia, 1990
Carroli, P., *Esperienza e narrazione nella scrittura di Alba de Céspedes*, Ravenna, 1993

D. Radcliff Umstead in Wilson (1991); E. Nerenberg in Russell (1994), pp. 104–10.

de' Pazzi, Maria Maddalena (Florence 1566–1607 Florence)

Carmelite author of spiritual writings. Born into one of oldest aristocratic, Florentine families. Was educated in monastery of S. Giovannino in Florence by women knights of Malta. Entered Carmelite monastery in 1583, aged sixteen, and took vows the following year. Had mystical experiences accompanied by ecstasies during which she declared out loud her meditations or visions, collected and transcribed by the sisters. Canonized.

Major works
Vita della Veneranda Madre Suor Maria Maddalena . . . con l'aggiunta della terza, quarta, quinta, sesta parte . . . che contengono le mirabili intelligenze e molti suoi documenti per la perfezione della vita spirituale, ed. V. Puccini, Florence, 1611
Avvertimenti et avvisi dati da santa Maria Maddalena de' Pazzi a diverse Religiose, Rome, 1683; Bassano, 1699
Lettere spirituali, Crema, 1795
Tutte le opere di S. Maria Maddalena de' Pazzi dai manoscritti originali, 7 vols., Florence, 1960–6

Selected criticism
Secondin, B., *Esperienza e dottrina di S. Maria Maddalena de' Pazzi*, Rome, 1974
Pozzi, G., *Maria Maddalena de' Pazzi. Le parole dell'estasi*, Milan, 1984
Scattigno, A., 'Maria Maddalena de' Pazzi. Tra esperienza e modello', in G. Zarri (ed.), *Donna disciplina creanza cristiana tra xv e xvii secolo. Studi e testi a stampa*, Rome, 1996, pp. 85–103

Del Serra, Maura (Pistoia 1948–   )

Poet, prose writer and dramatist. Strongly influenced by modern Tuscan poetry, her poetry is full of metaphors and symbols, and has a strong religious dimension. Teaches Italian literature at Florence University.

Major works
L'Arco, Florence, 1978
La Gloria Oscura, Florence, 1983

Concordanze, Florence, 1985
Meridiana, Florence, 1987
Infinito presente, Florence, 1992
Corale, Rome, 1994
L'età che non dà ombra, Florence, 1997

Deledda, Grazia (Nuoro 1871–1936 Rome)

Novelist, short story writer. Born in Sardinia. Began writing very early. Left for the mainland in 1900, married a civil servant, settled in Rome. Bore two sons and wrote prolifically, winning the Nobel Prize in 1926. Pirandello's novel *Suo marito* (1911) said to be inspired by her life (following her threats to sue, it was withdrawn from circulation).

Major works

Dopo il divorzio, Turin, 1902; republished as *Naufraghi in porto*, Milan, 1920; trans. M. Lansdale, *After the Divorce*, New York, 1905
Elias Portolu, Turin, 1903
Cenere, Rome, 1904; trans. H, Colvill, *Ashes,* New York, 1908
L'edera, Rome, 1908
Canne al vento, Milan, 1913
Marianna Sirca, Milan, 1915
La madre, Milan, 1920
Romanzi e novelle, Milan, 1941, 1945, 1950, 1955, 1969; ed. N. Sapegno, 1971
Cosima (1936); Milan, 1937 (posthumous)

Selected criticism

Balducci, C., *A Self-made Woman*, Boston, 1975
Dolfi, A., *Grazia Deledda*, Milan, 1979
Pellegrino, A. (ed.), *Metafora e biografia nell'opera di Grazia Deledda, Atti del Convegno: Grazia Deledda, Biografia e romanzo, Roma 19–20 giugno, 1987*, Rome, 1990
Collu, U. (ed.), 'Grazia Deledda nella cultura nazionale ed internazionale', in *Grazia Deledda nella cultura contemporanea*, Nuoro, 1992, vol. II

A. Pellegrino in *DBI* (XXXVI), pp. 491–6; Costa-Zalessow, pp. 268–76; M. Migiel in Russell, pp. 111–18; Wood, pp. 58–73

Drigo, Paola (born Bianchetti) (Castelfranco Veneto 1876–1938 Padua)

Novelist, short story writer. From educated family, married engineer, Giulio Drigo, aged twenty and had one son. Lived in Bassano del Grappa, travelling frequently to Rome, Milan and Padua. Started literary career with short stories in journals such as *Nuova antologia* and *L'Illustrazione Italiana*. Novel *Maria Zef* met with critical acclaim and became basis for Italian telvision film in 1982.

Major works

La fortuna, Milan, 1913
La signorina Anna, Vicenza, 1932
Maria Zef, Milan, 1936, 1982; trans. B. Steinberg Kirschenbaum, Lincoln and London, 1989
Fine d'anno, Milan, 1936

Selected criticism

Santoro, Anna, *Il Novecento. Antologia di scrittrici italiane del primo ventennio*, Rome, 1997

Pickering-Iazzi, R., *Politics of the Visible. Writing Women, Culture, and Fascism*, Minneapolis, 1997

Bocelli, Arnaldo, 'Scrittori d'oggi: Paola Drigo, Maria Zef', *Nuova Antologia* (October 1937), 466–71

M. Barletta in *DBI* (x), pp. 52–3

Duranti, Francesca (Genoa 1935–   )

Novelist and translator (from German). Lives between Milan and her villa, La gattaiola, near Lucca. Has been awarded Bagutta (1984), Super Campiello (1989) and many other literary prizes.

Major works

La bambina, Milan, 1976, 1985; ed. F. M. Masini, Florence, 1986

La casa sul lago della luna, Milan, 1984, 1987; trans. S. Sartarelli, *The House on Moon Lake*, London, 1987

Lieto fine, Milan, 1987; trans. A. Cancogni, *Happy Ending*, London, 1991

Effetti personali, Milan, 1988, 1991

Ultima stesura, Milan, 1991

Sogni mancini, Milan, 1996; English version and intro. N. Di Ciolla McGowan, *Left-Handed Dreams*, Market Harborough, 2000

Selected criticism

Vinall, S., 'Francesca Duranti: Reflections and Inventions', in Z. Baranski and L. Pertile (eds.), *The New Italian Novel*, Edinburgh, 1993, pp. 99–120

Green, P., 'Writing as Movement: Francesca Duranti's *Ultima Stesura*', in *Novel Turns: Recent Narrative Writing from Western Europe. Antipodas Monograph Series*, Madrid–Auckland, NZ, forthcoming

Fallaci, Oriana (Florence 1930–   )

Journalist, essayist and novelist. Born into an anti-Fascist family, fought in Resistance as an adolescent. Has reported and written on controversial issues and famous political figures. Numerous prizes for *Un uomo* and *InsciAllah*.

Major works

Il sesso inutile: viaggio intorno alla donna, Milan, 1961; trans. P. Swinglehurst, *The Useless Sex,* London, 1964

Penelope alla guerra, Milan, 1962, 1994; trans. P. Swinglehurst, *Penelope at War* London, 1966

Niente e così sia, Milan, 1969; trans. I. Quigly, London, 1972; *Nothing and So Be It*, New York, 1972

Intervista con la storia, Milan, 1974; trans. J. Shepley, *Interview with History*, London, 1976

Lettera a un bambino mai nato, Milan, 1975, 1981, 1993; trans. J. Shepley, *Letter to a Child Never Born*, London, 1975; New York, 1976; rev. trans., London, 1982

Un uomo: romanzo, Milan, 1979; trans. W. Weaver, *A Man,* New York, 1980; London, 1981

InsciAllah, Milan, 1990; trans. J. Marcus, *InsciAllah,* New York, 1992; London, 1992

Selected criticism

Gatt-Rutter, J., *Oriana Fallaci: The Rhetoric of Freedom*, Oxford, 1996

Aricò, S., *Oriana Fallaci: The Woman and the Myth*, Carbondale and Edwardsville, 1998

S. L. Aricò in Aricò, pp. 170–82; V. Picchietti in Bondanella

Fedele, Cassandra (Venice *c.*1465–1558 Venice)

Humanist, writer of orations and letters. From a highly educated family, father encouraged studies in Latin and Greek. In 1487 was first woman to deliver a public speech at University of Padua. Regarded as a prodigy at Venetian state receptions. Corresponded with Poliziano, Lodovico il Moro and Alessandra Scala, who advised her not to marry if she wanted to pursue studies. Cassandra nevertheless married around 1497, after which her studies declined.

Major work

Divae Cassandrae Fidelis . . . pro Bertucio Lamberto Canonico . . . Oratio, Venice, 1488; *Epistolae et orationes posthumae*, crit. ed. Filippo Tomasini, Padua, 1636

Selected criticism

P. O. Kristeller, 'Learned Women of the European Past', in P. Labalme (ed.), *Beyond Their Sex* (New York–London, 1980), pp. 91–116

D. Robin in M. King and A. Rabil, *Her Immaculate Hand*, Binghampton, NY, 1983, pp. 69–77

F. Pignatti in *DBI* (XLV), pp. 566–8; G. M. Gianola in *Stanze*, pp. 15–26; D. Robin in Russell, pp. 119–27

Fieschi Adorno, Caterina (Genoa 1447–1510 Genoa)

Author of spiritual writings. Received sound religious and humanistic education at home. At sixteen married to Giulio Adorno for reasons of family politics. Went through a conversion after which, guided by visions and ecstasies, dedicated herself to charitable work among very poor, gathering together a group out of which the Confraternity of Divine Love was born. Canonised.

Major works

Libro de la vita mirabile & dottrina santa; de la beata Caterinetta da Genoa; nel quale si contiene una utile & catholica dimostratione & dechiaratione del purgatorio, Genoa, 1551

S. Caterina da Genova [I. *Teologica mistica di S. Caterina da Genova*; II. Critical edition of manuscripts of S. Caterina], ed. Umile Bonzi di Genoa, Genoa, 1961–2

Selected criticism

Hughes, S. and B. J. Groeschel, *Catherine of Genoa, Purgation and Purgatory: The Spiritual Dialogue*, New York–Toronto, 1979

Carpaneto da Langasco, C., *Sommersa nella fontana dell'amore. S. Caterina Fieschi Adorno. I. La vita*, Genoa, 1987

Fontana, P., *Celebrando Caterina. Santa Caterina Fieschi Adorno e il suo culto nella Genova Barocca*, Turin, 1999

S. Pezzella in *DBI* (XXII), pp. 343–5

Fonseca Pimentel, Eleonora (Rome 1752–1799 Naples)

Journalist and polymath. Of aristocratic family of Portuguese origin, lived in Rome and Naples. Wrote poetry, plays, essays on scientific, legal, and economic topics. Unhappily married to Neapolitan officer, from whom separated. Only child died aged eight months. Monarchist, favoured enlightened reforms in 1780s, became a Jacobin in 1790s, was arrested for alleged conspiracy. Took active part in formation of short-lived Neapolitan republic of 1799. Executed by hanging when the ousted monarchical regime was reinstated.

Major works

Il monitore napoletano, Naples, 1799; *Il monitore repubblicano del 1799*, ed. B. Croce, Bari,
    1943; *Il Monitore Napoletano 1799*, ed. M. Battaglini, Naples, 1974

Selected criticism

Croce, B., *La rivoluzione napoletana del 1799*, Bari, 1897
Schiattarella, F., *La marchesa giacobina. Eleonora Fonseca Pimentel*, Naples, 1973
Buttafuoco, A., 'Eleonora Fonseca Pimentel: una donna nella Rivoluzione', *Nuova
    DonnaWomanFemme* (1977), p. 3
Macciocchi, M., *Cara Eleonora. Passione e morte della Fonseca Pimentel nella rivoluzione
    napoletana*. Milan, 1993

C. Cassani in *DBI* (XLVIII), pp. 595–600

Fonte, Moderata (born Modesta da Pozzo) (Venice 1555–1592 Venice)

Lyric and narrative poet, prose writer. Born into upper-class, though non-noble
(*cittadino*) family; orphaned as infant. Elementary education in convent school;
encouraged to read further and to write by successive guardians, including biographer,
Gian Niccolo Doglioni. Married late (1583), to Filippo Zorzi, Venetian lawyer and civil
servant, with whom had four children. Died in childbirth aged thirty-seven.

Major works

Le feste, Venice, 1581
Tredici canti del Floridoro, Venice, 1581; ed. V. Finucci, Bologna, 1995
La passione di Christo, Venice, 1582
La resurretione di Giesù Christo, Venice, 1592
Il merito delle donne, Venice, 1600; crit. edn A. Chemello, Venice, 1988; trans. V. Cox, *The
    Worth of Women*, Chicago, 1997

Selected criticism

Chemello, A., 'La donna, il modello, l'immaginario. Moderata Fonte e Lucrezia
    Marinella', in M. Zancan (ed.), *Nel cerchio della luna. Figure di donna in alcuni testi del
    XVI secolo*, Venice, 1983, pp. 95–170
Malpezzi Price, P., 'A Woman's Discourse in the Italian Renaissance: Moderata Fonte's *Il
    merito delle donne*', *Annali d'Italianistica* 7 (1989), pp. 165–81
Collina, B., 'Moderata Fonte e *Il merito delle donne*', *Annali d'Italianistica* 7 (1989), pp.
    142–64
Cox, V., 'The Single Self. Feminist Thought and the Marriage Market in Early Modern
    Venice', *Renaissance Quarterly* 48 (1995), pp. 513–81

A. Chemello in *Stanze*, pp. 69–82; P. Malpezzi Price in Russell, pp. 128–37

Frabotta, Biancamaria (Rome 1946–   )

Literary critic, essayist, poet and novelist. Leading figure in the Roman feminist
movement in 1970s. Professor of modern Italian literature at University of Rome 'La
Sapienza'. Her work, *Donne in poesia*, presented women's poetry in a totally new light in
the late 1970s.

Major works

Femminismo e lotta di classe, Rome, 1973
La politica del femminismo 1973–1976, Rome, 1976
ed., *Donne in poesia: antologia della poesia femminile in Italia dal dopoguerra ad oggi*, Rome, 1976

Letteratura al femminile: itinerari di lettura a proposito di donne, storia, poesia e romanzo, Bari,
  1980
Velocità di fuga, Trento, 1989
Trittico dell'obbedienza, Palermo, 1996

Selected criticism
M. Gieri in Bondanella

Franceschi Ferrucci, Caterina (Narni 1803–1887 Narni)
Essayist. Wrote primarily on the subject of women's education, arguing for the need to
educate women while reasserting their principal role as wives and mothers. Her works
particularly appreciated after Unification when she was the only woman appointed to
the Accademia della Crusca.

Major works
Degli studi delle donne, Turin, 1854; rev. edn Florence, 1876
I primi quattro secoli della letteratura italiana dal secolo XIII al XVI. Lezioni, 2 vols., Turin, 1856;
  Florence, 1858
Ai giovani italiani. Ammaestramenti religiosi e morali, Florence, 1877

Selected criticism
Villani, C., *Stelle femminili. Dizionario bio-bibliografico*, Naples–Rome–Milan, 1915
Pastorini, G., *L'educazione della donna nel pensiero delle pedagogiste italiane del secolo XIX*,
  Pistoia, 1921
Porciani, I., *Le donne a scuola: l'educazione femminile nell'Italia dell'Ottocento: mostra
  documentaria e iconografica*, Florence, 1987

N. Danelon Vasoli in *DBI* (XLIX), pp. 610–13

Franco, Veronica (Venice 1546–1591 Venice)
Courtesan like her mother, practised her profession openly in Venice. Good
relationships with Venetian aristocracy (Martinengo and Venier families in particular)
and literary skills earned her a better social position. Loved Marco Venier, for whom
wrote many of her poems. Exchanged correspondence in rhyme with Maffio Venier who
had publicly insulted her in poems. Friend and pupil of Domenico Venier, master of a
whole generation of Venetian poets.

Major works
Lettere familiari a diversi, Venice, 1580
Lettere, ed. B. Croce, Naples, 1949
'Rime e lettere di Veronica Franco', *Giornale storico della letteratura italiana* (1986), pp.
  355–82
Selected Poems and Letters, trans. and ed. A. R. Jones and M. Rosenthal, Chicago, 1999
Rime di Gaspara Stampa e di Veronica Franco, ed. A. Salza, Bari, 1913

Selected criticism
Zorzi, A., *Cortigiana veneziana. Veronica Franco e i suoi poeti*, Milan, 1986
Rosenthal, M., *The Honest Courtesan: Veronica Franco, Citizens and Writers in Sixteenth-
  Century Venice*, Chicago, 1989
Doglio, M. L., *Lettera e donna. Scrittura epistolare al femminile tra Quattro e Cinquecento*,
  Rome, 1993

F. Calitti in *DBI* (L), pp. 209–13; Costa-Zalessow, pp. 107–16; A. Schiavon in *Stanze*, pp. 45–55; M. Migiel in Russell, pp. 138–44

Fuà Fusinato, Erminia (Rovigo 1831–1876 Rome)

Poet and teacher. Of Jewish background, gave up her religion to marry Arnaldo Fusinato. Established position in the political, social and cultural life of Rome. Her writing noted for its moralistic and pedagogical dimension.

Major works

Scritti educativi, Florence, 1873
Versi, Florence, 1874
Scritti letterari, ed. G. Ghivizzani, Milan, 1883
Ricordi e lettere ai figli, Milan, 1887

Selected criticism

L. Pes in *DBI* (L), pp. 653–5; Costa-Zalessow, pp. 230–3

Gambara, Veronica (Pratoalboino, Brescia 1485–1550 Correggio, Reggio Emilia)

Poet. Daughter of Count Giovan Francesco Gambara and Alda Pio dei Principi di Carpi. Married Gilberto X, prince of Correggio. Widowed 1518, looked after education of sons and continued to govern in place of husband. In 1535, a sonnet of hers published with Bembo's poetry and from then her poetry included in anthologies. Despite her fame, never published poems as single collection.

Major work

Rime, ed. A. Bullock, Florence, 1994

Selected criticism

Bozzetti, C., P. Gibellini and E. Sandal (eds.), *Veronica Gambara e la poesia del suo tempo nell'Italia settentrionale*, Florence, 1989

F. Pignatti in *DBI* (LII), pp. 68–71; Costa-Zalessow, pp. 57–62; R. Russell in Russell, pp. 145–53

Giaconi, Luisa (Florence 1870–1908 Fiesole)

Poet and painter. Earned living by copying famous paintings for tourists in Florence. Only volume of poetry published posthumously. Her poetry full of symbolism. Describes female unhappiness at turn of century.

Major work

Tebaide, Bologna, 1909

Selected criticism

Costa-Zalessow, pp. 263–7

Ginanni, Maria (Maria Crisi) (Naples 1892–1953 Florence)

Futurist poet, novelist, journalist. Briefly studied mathematics at University of Rome before becoming editor of Futurist journal *L'Italia Futurista*, which had own press co-directed by her. Married to Futurist painter and film-maker Arnaldo Ginna. Later married Ludovico Toeplitz (son of famous banker), with whom co-wrote poems *Le pietre di Venezia oltremare* (1930), dedicated to D'Annunzio.

Major works
Montagne trasparenti, Florence, 1917
Il poema dello spazio, Milan, 1919

Selected criticism
Verdone, M., *Cinema e letteratura del futurismo*, Rome, 1968
Salaris, C., *Le futuriste. Donne e letteratura d'avanguardia in Italia*, Milan, 1982

Ginzburg, Natalia Levi (Palermo 1916–1991 Rome)

Novelist, dramatist, essayist, translator. Grew up in Turin, daughter of a university professor. Married Russian scholar Leone Ginzburg, who died in 1943 after being tortured by Nazis. Although a mother of young children, she too became involved in anti-Fascist activities. *Lessico famigliare* (1963) recounts this period. After war worked for Einaudi publishing house. Her fiction focuses on disintegrating family life and is characterised by an ear for cadences of speech and a spare, ironic style.

Major works
Tutti i nostri ieri, Turin, 1952; trans. A. Davidson, *All Our Yesterdays*, Manchester, 1985
Le voci della sera, Turin, 1961; trans. D. M Low, *Voices in the Evening*, New York, 1963
Lessico famigliare, Turin, 1963; trans. D. M. Low, *Family Sayings,* rev. edn Manchester, 1984.
Ti ho sposato per allegria e altre commedie, Turin, 1968
Paese di mare e altre commedie, Milan, 1973
Opere raccolte e ordinate dall'autore, ed. C. Garboli, 2 vols., Milan, 1986–8
L'intervista: commedia in tre atti, Turin, 1989
Teatro, Turin, 1990

Selected criticism
Clementelli, E., *Invito alla lettura di Natalia Ginzburg*, Milan, 1972
Bullock, A., *Natalia Ginzburg: Human Relationships in a Changing World*, Oxford, 1990
Quarsiti, M. L., *Natalia Ginzburg: Bibliografia 1934–1992*, Florence, 1996

C. del Greco Lobner in Aricò, pp. 27–42; B. Merry and J. Docker in Russell, pp. 154–62; Wood, pp. 135–51

Giuliani, Veronica (Mercatello, Pesaro 1660–1727 Città di Castello Perugia)

Mystic. Received religious education from mother. Decided to enter a convent, against wishes of father, suitors and even some members of Church, who did not judge her to be suited for cloistered life. Entered the convent of Poor Clare Capuchin nuns (Città di Castello) in 1677 and stayed there until her death. Wrote 22,000 pages of diaries, poetry and letters. Canonised in 1870.

Major works
Un tesoro nascosto, ossia diario di Suora Veronica, Prato, 1895–1905; ed. D. Fiorucci, Città di Castello, Monastero delle Cappuccine, 1969–74, vol. IV; ed. L. Iriarte and A. De Felice, 1987 (2 edns); ed. M. Cittadini Fulvi and L. Iriarte, Assisi, 1989; ed. L. Iriarte, Assisi, 1991
Visioni, ed. M. Baldini, Florence, 1991

Selected criticism
Gatti, C., 'Gli scritti di Veronica Giuliani', *GSLI* 79 (1922), pp. 161–218
Pozzi, G. and C. Leonardi, *Scrittrici mistiche italiane*, Genoa, 1988

Forlani, A. and M. Savini (eds.), *Scrittrici d'Italia*, Rome, 1991

Courbat, M., 'Veronica Giuliani: scrittura e riscrittura', *Annali d'Italianistica* 13 (1995), pp. 333–49

Lollini, M., 'Scrittura obbediente e mistica tridentina in Veronica Giuliani', *Annali d'Italianistica* 13 (1995), pp. 351–69

Grasso, Silvana (Macchia di Giarre, Catania 1952–   )

Novelist and translator (from Greek). Teaches Latin and Greek at Liceo Classico, Gela, Sicily. Has won many literary awards and has been published in Germany, Holland and Greece.

Major works

Nebbie di ddraunàra [short stories], Milan, 1993
Il bastardo di Mautàna, Milan, 1994; Turin, 1997
Ninna nanna del lupo, Turin, 1995
L'albero di Giuda, Turin, 1997

Grisoni, Franca (Sirmione 1945–   )

Dialect poet who works as manicurist. Has contributed to revival of interest in dialect poetry. Received Viareggio poetry prize in 1997.

Major works

La böba, Genoa, 1986
El so che té se té, Florence, 1987
L'oter, Turin, 1988
De chí, Milan, 1997
La giardiniera, ed. F. Scataglini, Ancona, 1998

Guglielminetti, Amalia (Turin 1881–1941 Turin)

Sensual verse shows influence of Gabriele D'Annunzio. Relationship with poet Guido Gozzano drew attention to her own poetry.

Major works

Le vergini folli, Turin, 1907
Le seduzioni, Turin, 1909; Palermo, 1990 (intro. E. Sanguineti)
L'insonne, Milan, 1913
I serpenti di Medusa, Milan, 1934
Lettere d'amore di Guido Gozzano e Amalia Guglielminetti, ed. A. Asciamprener, Milan, 1951

Selected criticism

B. Turoff in Russell, pp. 163–70

Guidacci, Margherita (Florence 1912–1992 Rome)

Poet, translator and critic. Taught English Literature at Lumsa University, Rome. Poetry has strong religious dimension. Remained largely independent of dominant poetic schools of twentieth century.

Major works

La sabbia e l'angelo, Florence, 1946
Poesie, Milan, 1965
Neurosuite, Vicenza, 1970

Terra senza orologi, Milan, 1973
Il vuoto e le forme, Padua, 1977
L'altare di Isenheim, Milan, 1980
Inno alla gioia, Florence, 1983
La via Crucis dell'Umanità, Florence, 1984
Liber Fulguralis, Messina, 1986
Poesie per poeti, Milan, 1987
Il buio e lo splendore, Milan, 1989
Anelli del tempo (published posthumously), Florence, 1993

Selected criticism
R. Treitel and R. Feldman in Russell, pp. 171–8

Guiducci, Armanda (Naples 1923–1992 Milan)
Journalist, literary critic, anthropologist, poet and novelist. Marxist activist and feminist. Edited and contributed to many periodicals and newspapers and directed cultural programmes for Swiss television. Awarded literary prizes for poetry and literary criticism.

Major works
Poesie per un uomo, Milan, 1965
La mela e il serpente: autoanalisi di una donna, Milan, 1974, 1988
Due donne da buttare, Milan, 1976, 1980
La donna non è gente, Milan, 1977, 1980
All'ombra di Kali, Milan, 1979
A colpi di silenzio, Milan, 1982, rev. edn 1990
A testa in giù, Milan, 1984
Perdute nella storia: storia delle donne dal I al VI secolo d.c, Florence, 1989
Medioevo inquieto: storia delle donne dall'VIII al XV secolo d.c., Florence, 1990

Selected criticism
F. A. Bassanese in Aricò, pp. 152–69; F. A. Bassanese in Russell, pp. 179–87

Insana, Jolanda (Messina 1937–   )
Poet, literary critic, teacher, translator of Latin classics. Lives in Rome. Work noted for impatience with traditional language, and forging of new verse forms in an often strident tone.

Major works
Sciarra amara, Milan, 1977
Fendenti fonici, Milan, 1982
Il collettame, Milan, 1985
La clausura, Milan, 1987
Medicina carnale, Milan, 1994
L'occhio dormiente, Venice, 1997

Invernizio, Carolina (Voghera 1851–1916 Cuneo)
Novelist. As small child moved to Florence where father was tax inspector. In 1877, published first of many novels with Salani. Marriage to army officer, Marcello Quinterno, took her back to Turin (1896), where frequented Gozzano, Guglielminetti

and literary society of the time. Immense popularity spread overseas, particularly to Italian immigrants of Argentina.

Major works

Rina, o l'angelo delle Alpi, Florence, 1877
Il bacio d'una morta, Florence, 1886
L'orfana del ghetto, Florence, 1887
Amori maledetti, Florence, 1892
Storia d'una sartina, Florence, 1892
La vendetta d'una pazza, Florence, 1892
La sepolta viva, Turin, 1896
L'albergo del delitto, Florence, 1905
I drammi degli emigrati, Florence, 1916
Romanzi del peccato, della perdizione e del delitto, Milan, 1971
Nero per Signora, ed. Riccardo Reim, Rome, 1986
Ij delt d'na bela fia, 'L Birichin (September 1889 – February 1890).

Selected criticism

Eco, U., M. Federzoni, I. Pezzini and M. P. Pozzato, *Carolina Invernizio, Matilde Serao, Liala*, Florence, 1979
Davico Bonino, G., G. Ioli et al., *Carolina Invernizio. Il romanzo d'appendice*, Turin, 1983
Cantelmo, A., *Carolina Invernizio e il romanzo d'appendice*, Florence, 1992

Jarre, Marina (Riga (Latvia) 1925–   )

Novelist. Born of Jewish Latvian father (killed by the Germans in 1941) and Italian Waldensian mother, who moved to Italy in 1935 with her daughters, after leaving her husband. Fought in the Resistance. Lives in Turin.

Major works

Un leggero accento straniero, Rome, 1968; Turin, 1972
Negli occhi di una ragazza, Turin, 1971, 1985
Viaggio a Ninive, Turin, 1975
La principessa della luna vecchia, Turin, 1977, 1996
I padri lontani, Turin, 1987, 1995
Ascanio e Margherita, Turin, 1990
Un altro pezzo di mondo, Turin, 1997

Selected criticism

E. Gianini Belotti in Cutrufelli, pp. 53–9

Knering, Amanda (Bolzano 1922–   )

Journalist, novelist, poet and playwright. Graduate in philosophy and psychology, has also been an actress. Founded Roman 'Centro–Donna–Poesia' and started homonymous international prize. Still works as journalist and directs literary collection for publisher Fermenti. Lives in Almerimar, a fishermen's village in Andalusia, Spain. Her poetry has been translated into German and Greek. Has won many literary prizes.

Major works

Viaggiarsi dentro, Rome, 1983; Castel Maggiore, Bologna, 1999
Io, Rome, 1984

Memorie di un bracconiere, Rome, 1986
I Gruber: una saga sud-tirolese, Rome, 1988
La donna a due teste, Rome, 1990
Un omicidio necessario, Rome, 1991
Mia madre era una donna, Castel Maggiore, Bologna, 1996

La Spina, Silvana (Padua 1945–   )

Journalist and novelist. Sicilian father and mother from the Veneto. Divides her life between Catania and Milan. Has won a number of literary prizes.

Major works

Morte a Palermo, Milan, 1987
Scirocco e altri racconti, Milan, 1992
L'ultimo treno da Catania, Milan, 1992
Quando Marte è in Capricorno, Milan, 1994
Un inganno dei sensi malizioso, Milan, 1995
L'amante del paradiso, Milan, 1997
Penelope, Milan, 1998

Lagorio, Gina (Bra, Cuneo 1922–   )

Novelist, playwright, literary critic and journalist. Member of Chamber of Deputies, then of Senate, with left-wing Independent Group (1987–92). Lived in Savona for many years where taught in a high school. Now lives in Milan. Has received many literary awards, including Viareggio (1984) and Rapallo-Carige (1987).

Major works

Un ciclone chiamato Titti, Bologna, 1969
Approssimato per difetto, Bologna, 1971; Milan, 1976, 1981
La spiaggia del lupo, Milan, 1977, 1986, 1991
Fuori scena, Milan, 1979, 1990
Tosca dei gatti, Milan, 1983, 1988
Freddo al cuore e altri testi teatrali, Milan, 1989
Il silenzio, Milan, 1993
Inventario, Milan, 1997

Selected criticism

Gioanola, E., 'La divisione, la morte, l'amore: strutture profonde dei romanzi di Gina Lagorio', *Letteratura italiana contemporanea* 14 (1985), pp. 215–312

M. F. Pietralunga in Aricò, pp. 76–88; P. Blelloch in Russell, pp. 189–98

Lattanzi, Carolina (born Carolina Arienti) (Florence ?–1818 Milan)

Journalist and polemicist. Married Giuseppe Lattanzi. During Jacobin period lived in Mantua, where was admitted to *Accademia di Pubblica Istruzione* (Academy of Public Education) in May 1797 as member without voting rights. In the Academy's theatre, delivered oration on 'slavery of women'. In 1804, founded *Corriere delle Dame* in Milan.

Major works

Schiavitù delle donne, Mantua, 1797; ed. G. Zacché, Mantua, 1976
Corriere delle dame, Milan, 1804–18

Selected criticism
De Stefanis Ciccone, S., I. Bonomi and A. Masini, *La stampa periodica milanese della prima
   metà dell'Ottocento. Testi e concordanze*, Pisa, 1983

Liala (Amaliana Cambiasi Negretti Odescalchi) (Carate di Lario, Como 1897–1995 Varese)

Novelist. Started writing short stories for newspapers after finishing high school.
Shortly following marriage to a naval officer, fell in love with a pilot who died tragically
in 1926. This drama relived in first novels (*Signorsì*, 1931 and *Ombre di fiori sul mio cammino*,
written 1926, but only published 1981). Met D'Annunzio who suggested pen name Liala.
Uneventful life, spent mostly near Varese, in upper-middle-class comfort, devoting her
time to her writing (about seventy novels). A best-selling author snubbed by critics.

Major works
Signorsì, Milan, 1931
Dormire e non sognare, Milan, 1944
Lalla che torna, Milan, 1945
Vecchio smoking, Milan, 1952
Una carezza e le stade del mondo, Milan, 1957
Goodbye sirena, Milan, 1975
Opere di Liala, Milan, 1976–1984
Lo scrigno di Liala, Milan, 1984 ff
Frantumi di arcobaleno, Milan, 1985

Selected criticism
Eco, U., M. Federzoni, I. Pezzini and M. P. Pozzato, *Carolina Invernizio, Matilde Serao, Liala*,
   Florence, 1979
Pozzato, M. P., *Il romanzo rosa*, Milan, 1982
Arslan, A. and M. P. Pozzato, 'Il rosa', in A. Asor Rosa (ed.), *Letteratura italiana, Storia e
   geografia*, Turin, 1989, vol. III, pp. 1027–46
Roccella, E., *La letteratura rosa*, Rome, 1998

Limentani, Giacoma (Rome 1927–   )

Novelist, essayist, journalist and translator. Lives in Rome where leads study groups on
the Torah and the Midrash.

Major works
In contumacia, Milan, 1967
Gli uomini del libro: leggende ebraiche, Milan, 1975, 1979
Il grande seduto, Milan, 1979
L'ombra allo specchio, Milan, 1988
Dentro la D, Genoa, 1992
ed. with C. Pontecorvo, *Aiutare a pensare: itinerario di un ebreo* (essays in memory of M.
   Pontecorvo), Florence, 1996
Scrivere dopo per scrivere prima: riflessioni e scritti, Florence, 1997

Livi, Grazia (Florence 1932–   )

Novelist, short story writer, literary critic, journalist and translator. Started career as
journalist. After 1970 devoted herself entirely to literature, privileging short

narratives and a kind of narrated critical essay. Prize-winning collections of essays, *Da una stanza all'altra* and *Le lettere del mio nome* deal with women writers who influenced her.

Major works
Gli scapoli di Londra, Florence, 1959
La distanza e l'amore, Milan, 1978
L'approdo invisibile, Milan, 1980
Da una stanza all'altra, Milan, 1984, 1992
Le lettere del mio nome, Milan, 1991
Vincoli segreti, Milan, 1994
Donne senza cuore, Milan, 1996

Lombroso, Paola (Turin 1871–1954 Turin)
Essayist, author of children's books. Wrote articles on psychology – especially children's – for journals such as *Pensiero italiano*, *Nuova antologia*, *Critica sociale* and *La riforma sociale*. Contributed to creation of one of most important Italian children's weeklies of this century (*Il Corriere dei piccoli*) and engaged in the promotion of reading among schoolchildren in rural areas.

Major works
Saggi di psicologia del bambino, Turin, 1894
I segni rivelatori della personalità, Turin, 1902
La vita dei bambini, Turin, 1904
with M. Carrara, *Nella penombra della civiltà: da un'inchiesta sul pensiero del popolo*, Turin, 1906
Le fiabe di zia Mariù, Florence, 1912
Un reporter nel mondo degli uccelli, Florence, 1914

Selected criticism
Dolza, D., *Essere figlie di Lombroso. Due donne intellettuali tra '800 e '900*, Milan, 1990.

Lonzi, Carla (Florence 1932–1982 Milan)
Art historian, critic, philosopher and companion of sculptor Pietro Consagra. Founding member of feminist group 'Rivolta femminile'.

Major works
Scacco ragionato: poesie dal '58 al '63, Milan, 1968
Sputiamo su Hegel: La donna clitoridea e la donna vaginale e altri scritti, Milan, 1974
Taci, anzi parla: diario di una femminista, Milan, 1978
Armande sono io: scritti di rivolta femminile, Milan, 1992
Rapporti tra la scena e le arti figurative dalla fine dell' '800, ed. M. Bucci, Florence, 1995

Selected criticism
Livi, G., *Le lettere del mio nome*, Milan, 1991, 207–26

Lorena-Carignano, Giuseppina, Principessa di (Paris 1753–1797 Turin)
Novelist, essay writer, translator. Daughter of Luigi Carlo Count of Brionne. Aged fifteen left France to marry Amedeo Luigi di Savoia Carignano. In 1770, gave birth to Carlo Emanuele Ferdinando (future father of Carlo Alberto, king of Sardinia). Naturally reserved, was obliged to lead a public life that suited her poorly. Knew Vittorio Alfieri

(who composed a sonnet upon her death), Tommaso Valperga di Caluso and Parini. Died young of cancer.

Major works

Scelta di inediti di Giuseppina di Lorena-Carignano, ed. L. Ricaldone, Turin, 1980

'Réflexions sur le suicide', ed. L. Ricaldone in M. Cerruti (ed.), *'Il genio muliebre': percorsi di donne intellettuali fra Settecento e Novecento in Piemonte. Antologia*, Alessandria, 1993, pp. 3–21

'Tre lettere inedite di Giuseppina di Lorena-Carignano', ed. L. Ricaldone, *Studi Piemontesi* (November 1983), 428–32

Selected criticism

Gasperoni, G., *Giuseppina di Lorena, principessa di Carignano*, Turin, 1938

Cerruti, M., *La ragione felice e altri miti del Settecento*, Florence, 1973

Ferraris, A., 'Les nouveaux malheurs de l'amour. Appunti sugli scritti di Giuseppina di Lorena-Carignano (1753–1797)', in M. Cerruti (ed.), *'Il genio muliebre'. Percorsi di donne intellettuali fra Settecento e Novecento in Piemonte*, Alessandria, 1993, pp. 9–22

Ricaldone, L., *La scrittura nascosta*, Paris–Fiesole, 1996

Loy, Rosetta (Rome 1931–   )

Novelist. Piedmontese father and Roman mother. Lives in Rome. Has won many prizes, including Super Campiello, Viareggio and Rapallo-Carige prizes for *Le strade di polvere*.

Major works

La bicicletta, Turin, 1974, 1989

La porta dell'acqua, Turin, 1976

L'estate di Letuchè, Milan, 1982, 1989, 1993

All'insaputa della notte, Milan, 1984, 1990

Le strade di polvere, Turin, 1987, 1995; trans. William Weaver, *The Dust Roads of Monferrato*, London, 1990

Sogni d'inverno, Milan, 1992

Cioccolata da Hanselman, Milan, 1995

La parola ebreo, Turin, 1997

Selected criticism

Wood, S., 'Rosetta Loy: The Paradox of the Past', in Z. Baranski and L. Pertile (eds.), *The New Italian Novel*, Edinburgh, 1993, pp. 121–38

Palmaran, W., *Rosetta Loy*, Rome, 1994

Macinghi Strozzi, Alessandra (Florence 1407–1471 Florence)

Letter writer. Aged thirteen married Matteo Strozzi who was exiled by Medici in 1434. Widowed in 1435 and left on own to look after family of seven children. Her three sons exiled 1458–66.

Major works

Lettere di una gentildonna fiorentina del secolo xv ai figliuoli esuli, Florence, 1877, 1972

Lettere, ed. G. Papini, Lanciano, 1914

Tempo di affetti e di mercanti. Lettere ai figli esuli, ed. A. Bianchini, Milan, 1987

Selected criticism

Doglio, M. L., *Lettera e donna. Scrittura epistolare al femminile tra Quattro e Cinquecento*, Rome, 1993

Costa-Zalessow, pp. 39–43; M. Cocco in Russell, pp. 198–206

Manzini, Gianna (Pistoia 1896–1974 Rome)

Novelist, poet and essayist. After studying literature at Florence, joined group of experimental writers gathered around anti-Fascist journal *Solaria*. In 1933 moved to Rome where lived with critic Enrico Falqui. From the complex work-in-progress novel, *Lettera all'editore* (1945), until her death, wrote a number of semi-autobiographical narratives characterised by structural innovation and linguistic lyricism.

Major works
Tempo innamorato, Milan, 1928
Lettera all'editore, Florence, 1945
Forte come un leone, Milan, 1947
Ritratto in piedi, Milan, 1971
Sulla soglia, Milan, 1973
Delitto, Lungro di Cosenza, 1990

Selected criticism
Panareo, E., *Invito alla lettura di Gianna Manzini*, Milan, 1977
Fava Guzzetta, L., *Gianna Manzini*, Florence, 1978

Nozzoli, pp. 65–84; G. Miceli-Jeffries in Aricò, pp. 91–106; B. Ballaro in Russell, pp. 207–15

Maraini, Dacia (Florence 1936–   )

Novelist, playwright, poet, essayist. As a child lived for eight years in Japan, partly spent in a concentration camp. Leading figure in Italian feminist movement. Founded women's theatre collective La Maddalena in Rome (1973). Has written over sixty plays, almost all of which have been produced, but better known as novelist. Has received many literary prizes for her fiction.

Major works
La vacanza, Milan, 1962; Turin, 1998; trans. S. Hood, *The Holiday*, London 1966
L'età del malessere, Turin, 1963, 1996; trans. F. Frenaye, *The Age of Malaise*, New York, 1966
Memorie di una ladra, Milan, 1972, 1990; trans. N. Rootes, *Memories of a Female Thief*,
        London 1973
Donna in guerra, Turin, 1975; 1998; trans. N. Benetti and E. Spottiswoode, *Woman at War*,
        London, 1994
Dialogo di una prostituta col suo cliente, Padua, 1978
Lezioni d'amore e altre commedie, Milan, 1982
Isolina, la donna tagliata a pezzi, Milan, 1985, 1992; trans. S. Williams, *Isolina*, London, 1993
La lunga vita di Marianna Ucrìa, Milan, 1990; trans. D. Kitto and E. Spottiswoode, *The
        Silent Duchess*, London 1992
Bagheria, Milan, 1993; trans. D. Kitto and E. Spottiswoode, *Bagheria*, London, 1994
Voci, Milan, 1994; trans. D. Kitto and E. Spottiswoode, *Voices*, London 1997
Buio, Milan, 1999

Selected criticism
Mitchell, T., 'Scrittura femminile: Writing the Female in the Plays of Dacia Maraini',
        Theatre Journal 42.3 (1990), pp. 332–49
Sumeli-Weinberg, M. G., *Invito alla lettura di Dacia Maraini*, Pretoria, 1993
Merry, B., *Dacia Maraini and Her Place in Contemporary Italian Literature*, London, 1994

Gaglianone, P. (ed.), *Conversazione con Dacia Maraini. Il piacere di scrivere*, Rome, 1995
Blumenfeld, D., and A. Testaferri (eds.), *The Pleasure of Writing: Critical Essays on Dacia Maraini*, West Lafayette, IN, 2000

A. Tamburry in Aricò, pp. 138–51; C. Lazzaro-Weis in Russell, pp. 216–25; Wood, pp. 216–31; V. Picchietti in Bondanella

Maratti Zappi, Faustina (Rome 1680–1745 Rome)

Poet. Illegitimate daughter of painter Carlo Maratti, who married her mother after death of his wife. At a very young age was victim of attempted kidnapping. Many years later, illegitimate son of the kidnapper brought legal proceedings to be recognised as her son. Married Giovan Battista Felice Zappi, admired lawyer, poet and member of group of fourteen founders of Accademia dell'Arcadia. Of legendary beauty, frequented most important Roman salons and gained a considerable reputation for her writings.

Major works

Rime dell'avvocato Giovanbattista Felice Zappi e di Faustina Maratti Zappi sua consorte con l'aggiunta delle piu scelte di alcuni rimatori del presente secolo, Venice, 1723, 1729; Venice, Storti, 1736, 1748, 1752, 1770; Nice, 1781; Venice, Storti, 1790; Naples, 1818; Florence, 1819–20; Naples, 1833
Canzonieri di Alessandro Guidi e de' due Zappi, Venice, 1789

Selected criticism

Maier, B., *Faustina Maratti Zappi donna e rimatrice d'Arcadia*, Rome, 1954
Binni, W., 'Sviluppo della poesia arcadia nel primo Settecento', in *L'Arcadia e Metastasio*, Florence, 1963, pp. 129–37
Gronda, G. (ed.), *Poesia italiana del Settecento*, Milan, 1978
Allen, B. et al. (eds.), *The Defiant Muse. Italian Feminist Poems from the Middles Ages to the Present*, New York, 1986
Solmi, R. (ed.), *Poeti del Settecento*, Turin, 1989
Forlani, A., and M. Savini (eds.), *Scrittrici d'Italia*, Rome, 1991
Ricaldone, L., *La scrittura nascosta*, Paris–Fiesole, 1996

Costa-Zalessow, pp. 172–8; A. Franceschetti in Russell, pp. 226–33

Marchesa Colombi (Maria-Antonietta Torriani Torelli) (Novara 1840–1920 Milan? Turin?)

Novelist, short story writer, journalist, polemicist. Studied to become elementary school teacher then frequented *literati* in Milan. Married Eugenio Torelli-Viollier, founder of *Corriere della sera*, from whom eventually separated. Friend of Anna Maria Mozzoni, leader of Italian feminist movement, lectured alongside her and taught in an alternative secondary school for women.

Major works

In risaia, Milan, 1878; Naples, 1883; Milan, 1889, 1890; Abano Terme, 1990 (1878, ed. A. Arslan); Milan, 1992 (intro. R. Reim); Novara, 1994 (with crit. essays by C. Bermani and S. Benatti)
Un matrimonio in provincia, Milan, 1885; Turin, 1973 (intro. N. Ginzburg); Novara, 1993 (intro. G. Morandini)
Prima morire, Milan, 1881, 1887; Rome, 1988 (intro. G. Morandini)

Selected criticism

Kroha, L., 'The Marchesa Colombi's *Un matrimonio in provincia*: Style as Subversion', in A. Testaferri (ed.), *Donna: Women in Italian Culture*, Toronto, 1989, pp. 153–73

Pastore, A., 'Maria Antonietta Torriani Marchesa Colombi', *Otto/Novecento* 5 (1992), pp. 81–104

Pierobon, E., 'Pazzia, amore, morte: spunti scapigliati nell'opera della Marchesa Colombi', *Otto/Novecento* 1 (1992), pp. 147–63

Santoro, A., 'Il fatto è che ingrasso. Lettura di *Un matrimonio in provincia* della Marchesa Colombi', in S. Marino and A. Nunziante Cesaro (eds.), *Soggetto femminile e scienze umane*, Bologna, 1993, pp. 85–100

Marinella, Lucrezia (Venice 1571–1653 Venice)

Poet, polemicist. Most versatile, prolific, and learned woman writer of her generation. A lyric, narrative and epic poet, and brilliant polemicist who argued for women's moral and intellectual equality with men. Encouraged to study by father, Giovanni Marinelli, Venetian physician and writer, and owner of a vast library. Led reclusive life of private study. Married another physician and had two children.

Major works

Amore innamorato ed impazzato, Venice, 1598

La nobiltà et l'eccellenza delle donne, co' i difetti e mancamenti de gli uomini, Venice, 1600, 1601, 1620

The Nobility and Excellence of Women, ed. and trans. A. Dunhill, intro. L. Panizza, Chicago, 1999

La vita di Maria vergine imperatrice dell'universo. Descritta in prosa e in ottava rima, Venice, 1602; reprint, 1610, 1617

L'Arcadia felice, Venice, 1605; crit. edn F. Lavocat (Florence: Accademia toscana di scienze e lettere, 'La Colombaria', vol. 162, 1998)

De' gesti heroici e della vita meravigliosa della serafica Santa Caterina da Siena, Venice, 1624

L'Enrico, overo Bisantio acquistato, Venice, 1635

Selected criticism

Conti Oderisio, G., *Donna e società nel Seicento*, Rome, 1979

Chemello, A., 'La donna, il modello, l'immaginario: Moderata Fonte e Lucrezia Marinella', in M. Zancan (ed.), *Nel cerchio della luna: Figure di donne in alcuni testi di XVI secolo*, Venice, 1983, pp. 59–170

Chemello, A., 'The Rhetoric of Eulogy in Lucrezia Marinella's *Della nobiltà et l'eccellenza delle donne*', in L. Panizza, ed., *Women in Italian Renaissance*, Oxford, 2000, 463–77

Costa-Zalessow, pp. 139–45; A. Chemello in *Stanze*, pp. 95–108; P. Malpezzi Price in Russell, pp. 234–42

Mario, Jessie White (Portsmouth, England 1832–1906 Florence)

Essayist and journalist. English supporter of Italian unification and close friend of Mazzini and Garibaldi. Married Alberto Mario and lived permanently in Italy from 1864. Contributed to periodicals in England (*The Daily News*), Italy (*Nuova Antologia*) and United States (*The Nation*). Wrote important essays on the conditions of Southern Italy and on life and times of main democratic protagonists of Italian Risorgimento.

Major works

La miseria in Napoli, Florence, 1877
Garibaldi e i suoi tempi, Milan, 1882
Agostino Bertani e i suoi tempi, Florence, 1888
Della vita di Giuseppe Mazzini, Milan, n.d. (1886)

Selected criticism

Adams Daniels, E., *Jessie White Mario: Risorgimento Revolutionary*, Athens, OH, 1972

Masino, Paola (Pisa 1908–1989 Rome)

Novelist, short story writer, poet, librettist, design and fashion journalist, translator. Free spirit, friend of Pirandello, defied family and ran away to Paris to live with Massimo Bontempelli, thirty years her senior. Was his companion and collaborator from 1929 until his death in 1960. In 1945, co-founded and co-edited journal *Città*. Edited Bontempelli's complete works in 1961.

Major works

Monte Ignoso, Milan, 1931, 1994
Decadenza della morte, Rome, 1931
Periferia, Milan, 1933
Racconto grosso e altri, Milan, 1941
Memoria d'Irene, 1945
Nascita e morte della massaia, Milan, 1945, 1970; (intro. S. Giacomoni), 1982
Poesie, Milan, 1947
Colloqui di notte, ed. M. V. Vittori, Palermo, 1994
Io, Massimo e gli altri. Autobiografia di una figlia del secolo, ed. M. V. Vittori, Milan, 1995

Selected criticism

Petrignani, Sandra (ed.), *Le signore della scrittura*, Milan, 1984
Spagnoletti, G., *La letteratura italiana del nostro secolo*, Milan, 1985
Re, L., 'Fascist Theories of Woman and the Construction of Gender', in R. Pickering-Iazzi (ed.), *Mothers of Invention. Women, Italian Fascism, and Culture*, Minneapolis, MN, 1995
De Giovanni, N., *Carta di donna. Narratrici italiane del '900*, Turin, 1996

Matraini, Chiara (Lucca 1515–1604 Lucca)

Poet. Married Vincenzo Cantarini. Widowed in 1542, began to write. Published first book of poems in 1555. Intense frienship with judge Cesare Coccapani, to whom rest of her work probably dedicated.

Major work

Rime e Lettere, ed. G. Rabitti, Bologna, 1989

Selected criticism

Rabitti, G., 'Linee per il ritratto di Chiara Matraini', *Studi e Problemi di Critica Testuale* 22 (1981), pp. 141–65
Rabitti, G. (ed.), *Chiara Matraini, gentildonna lucchese. Atti della giornata di studi (18 aprile 1998)*, forthcoming

Costa-Zalessow, pp. 93–8; G. Rabitti in Russell, pp. 243–52

Menicanti, Daria (Piacenza 1914–1995 Milan)

Poet. Contemporary of Antonia Pozzi at Milan University. Married for some time to philosopher Giulio Preti, separated in 1951. He discouraged her from writing and she only published first collection late in life. Milan and animals figure largely in her poetry.

Major works
Città come, Milan, 1964
Un nero d'ombra, Milan, 1969
Poesie per un passante, Milan, 1978
Altri amici, Forlì, 1986
Ferragosto, Catania, 1986
Ultimo quarto, 1990

Merici, Angela (Desenzano *c.*1474–1540 Brescia)

Author of religious writings. Founder of Confraternity of St Ursula. Orphaned as young girl, lived with uncle in Salò until his death. Returned to Desenzano until 1516, and then moved to Brescia. Here met members of Brescian society involved in religious and charitable works, who became her fervent followers. Also accepted young girls without sufficient means to pay dowry required by monastery. In 1535, founded new type of religious confraternity, named after St Ursula, on model of consecrated virgins of early church.

Major works
Regola della nova compagnia di santa Orsola di Brescia, Brescia, 1569, 1582, 1620; Bologna, 1672; Brescia, 1673, 1795
Regola Ricordi Legati. Testo antico e testo moderno, ed. L. Mariani and E. Tarolli (intro. A. Faller), Brescia, 1975
Gli scritti di sant'Angela Merici, Regola Ricordi Testamento. Testi antichi, traslazione in italiano moderno, ed. L. Mariani and E. Tarolli, Brescia, 1996

Selected criticism
Ledochowska OSU, T., *Angèle Merici et la Compagnie de Ste Ursule à la lumière des documents. Une éducatrice et une apôtre de la Réforme Pré-Tridentine. II. L'évolution de la Compagnie primitive*, Rome–Milan, 1968
Mariani, L., E. Tarollia and M. Seynaeve, *Angela Merici. Contributo per una biografia*, Milan, 1986
Zarri, G., 'Ursula and Catherine. The Marriage of Virgins in the XVI Century', in E. A. Matter and J. Coakley (eds.), *Creative Women in Medieval and Early Modern Italy. A Religious and Artistic Renaissance*, Philadelphia, 1994

Merini, Alda (Milan 1931–   )

Poet and prose writer. Lives in Navigli area of Milan. Career interrupted for twenty years because of mental illness. Winner of Librex-Guggenheim 'Eugenio Montale' prize in 1993 and Viareggio in 1996.

Major works
La presenza di Orfeo, Milan, 1953, 1993 (includes her early collections from 1953 to 1962)
La Terra Santa, Milan, 1983, 1984
L'altra verità, Diario di una diversa, Milan, 1986, 1997
Testamento, ed. G. Raboni, Milan, 1988

Ipotenusa d'amore, Milan, 1992
Reato di vita, Milan, 1994
La pazza della porta accanto, Milan, 1995
La vita facile, Milan, 1996
Lettere a un racconto, prose brevi e lunghe, Milan, 1998
Fiore di poesia (1951–1997), ed. M. Corti, Turin, 1998

Messina, Maria (Palermo 1887–1944 Florence)

Novelist, short story writer, children's writer. Unhappy, isolated childhood, received only private tutoring. Began publishing in 1909. Corresponded for ten years with Giovanni Verga, who helped her gain access to the literary market. Work was very well received at the time but forgotten and only recently rediscovered by her compatriot Leonardo Sciascia.

Major works
Alla deriva, Milan, 1920
La casa nel vicolo, Milan, 1921; Palermo, 1982
Piccoli gorghi, Palermo, 1988, includes *Pettini fini* (1909), *Piccoli gorghi* (1911) and *Le briciole del destino* (1918)
L'amore negato, Milan, 1926; Palermo, 1993
Casa paterna, Palermo, 1981
Gente che passa, Palermo, 1989, includes *Ragazze siciliane* (1921) and *Il guinzaglio* (1921)

Selected criticism
Di Giovanna, M., *La fuga impossibile. Sulla narrativa di Maria Messina*, Naples, 1989
M. N. Lombardo in Russell, pp. 253–60

Morandini, Giuliana (Pavia di Udine 1938–   )

Novelist, playwright, poet, and literary and theatre critic. Has written extensive criticism on Svevo, other authors from Trieste, on women writers, and on theatre and cinema of Pasolini. Interested in psychoanalysis. Novels widely translated and awarded numerous prestigious prizes.

Major works
. . . E allora mi hanno rinchiusa. Testimonianze dal manicomio femminile, Milan, 1977, 1985
I cristalli di Vienna, Milan, 1978, 1989
ed., *La voce che è in lei. Antologia della narrativa femminile italiana tra '800 e '900*, Milan, 1980, 1997
Caffè specchi, Milan, 1983; trans. and intro. L. Quartermaine, *The Café of Mirrors*, Exeter, 1997
Angelo a Berlino, Milan, 1987
Da te lontano. Cultura triestina tra '700 e '900, Trieste, 1989
Sogno a Herrenberg, Milan, 1991
Giocando a dama con la luna, Milan, 1996

Selected criticism
Guagnini, E., 'Giuliana Morandini: Outer and Inner Frontiers', in Z. Baranski and L. Pertile (eds.), *The New Italian Novel*, Edinburgh, 1993, pp. 139–50
Quartermaine, L., 'Memorie di una frontiera. I cristalli di Vienna di Giuliana Morandini', in *Gli spazi della diversità. Rinnovamento del codice narrativo in Italia dal 1945 al 1992*, Rome, 1995, vol. II, pp. 167–78

Morante, Elsa (Rome 1912–1985 Rome)

Novelist, short story writer, poet and essayist. One of Italy's greatest twentieth-century writers. Began by writing fables for children, later collected as *Le straordinarie avventure di Cateri dalla trecciolina* (1959). Children continued to have privileged role in her writing. Lived almost all her life in Rome. In 1941 married Alberto Moravia; they separated twenty-one years later.

Major works

Menzogna e sortilegio, Turin, 1948; trans. A. Foulke, *The House of Lies,* New York, 1950
L'isola di Arturo, Turin, 1957; trans. W. Weaver, *Arturo's Island*, London, 1959
La Storia. Un romanzo Turin, 1974; trans. W. Weaver, *History. A Novel,* New York, 1977
Aracoeli; trans. W. Weaver, *Aracoeli,* New York, 1984
Opere, Milan, 1988

Selected criticism

Venturi, G., *Elsa Morante*, Florence, 1977
Ravanello, D., *Scrittura e follia nei romanzi di Elsa Morante*, Ravenna, 1980
Rosa, G., *Cattedrali di carta. Elsa Morante romanziere*. Milan 1995
Bardini, M., *Morante, Elsa. Italiana. Di professione, poeta*. Pisa 1999

R. Capozzi in Aricò, pp. 10–25; R. Capozzi in Russell, pp. 261–8; Wood, pp. 152–68

Mosconi Contarini, Elisabetta (Verona 1751–1807 Verona)

Letter-writer. Was at the centre of one of best-frequented salons of the Venetian Republic. Left one of richest collections of letters of eighteenth century (mostly to abbot Aurelio De' Giorgi Bertola, but also to daughters and friends including Ippolito Pindemonte, Alberto Fortis, Saverio Bettinelli, Giovanni Cristofano Amaduzzi, Silvia Curtoni Verza and Paolina Secco Suardo Grismondi).

Major works

A. Piromalli, *Aurelio Bertola nella letteratura del Settecento. Con testi e documenti inediti*, Florence, 1959
'Al mio caro ed incomparabile amico': lettere di Elisabetta Mosconi Contarini all'abate Aurelio De' Giorgi Bertola, ed. L. Ricaldone (with note by M. Cerruti), Padua, 1995

Selected criticism

Vannetti, C., *Opere*, Venice, 1826–31
De Blasi, J., *Le scrittrici italiane dalle origini al 1800*, Florence, 1930
Natali, G., *Il Settecento*, 2 vols., Milan, 1964

V. Lettere in *DBI* (XXVIII), pp. 151–3

Mozzoni, Anna Maria (born Marianna) (Milan 1837–1920 Rome)

Essayist and journalist. Most important Italian emancipationist of second half of nineteenth century and active supporter of democratic and socialist organisations. Contributed articles to several political journals, such as *La donna*, *La donna del popolo*, *La lega della democrazia*, *Critica sociale*, *Avanti!*. Author of tracts and pamphlets in which criticised gender bias in legislation of the new Italian state, and translator of John Stuart Mill's *The Subjection of Women*.

Major works

La donna e i suoi rapporti sociali, Milan, 1864
La donna in faccia al progetto del nuovo codice civile italiano, Milan, 1865

Del voto politico delle donne, Venice, 1877
La donna nella Famiglia, nella Città e nello Stato, Bologna, 1891
L'organizzazione dei lavoratori, Cremona, 1891
I socialisti e l'emancipazione delle donne, Alessandria, 1892

Selected criticism

Pieroni Bortolotti, F., *Alle origini del movimento femminile in Italia 1848–1892*, Turin, 1963
    Socialismo e questione femminile 1892–1922, Milan, 1974
Pieroni Bortolotti, F. (ed.), *La liberazione della donna*, Milan, 1975

Muraro, Luisa (Vicenza 1940–   )

Historian, philosopher, translator of Luce Irigaray and Virginia Woolf into Italian, founding member of Diotima. Regular contributor to left-wing newspaper *Il manifesto* and *Noi donne*.

Major works

La signora del gioco: episodi della caccia alle streghe, Milan, 1976
Giambattista Della Porta mago e scienziato, Milan, 1978
Maglia o uncinetto: Racconto linguistico-politico sulla inimicizia tra metafora e metonimia,
    Milan, 1981
Guglielma e Maifreda: storia di un'eresia femminista, Milan, 1985
L'ordine simbolico della madre, Rome, 1991
Lingua materna scienza divina: scritti sulla fisosofia mistica di Margherita Porete, Naples,
    1995

Neera (Anna Radius Zuccari) (Milan 1846–1918 Milan)

Novelist, short story writer, essayist, polemicist, journalist. Married an army officer in 1871 and bore one child. Prolific and widely translated. Enjoyed protection of both Luigi Capuana and Benedetto Croce. Avoided being associated with feminism or the literary high life. Wrote some poetry. In her work, favoured ideals of family, society and homeland popular at that time.

Major works

with Paolo Mantegazza, *Dizionario d'igiene per le famiglie*, Milan, 1881; ed. M. Corti, Milan,
    1985
Teresa, Milan, 1886, 1888, 1897, 1898, 1912, 1918, 1933; in *Neera*, ed. B. Croce, Milan, 1942;
    Turin, 1976 (intro. L. Baldacci); Lecco, 1995 (intro. A. Arslan)
L'indomani, Milan, 1890; Palermo, 1981
Il libro di mio figlio, Milan, 1891; ed. L. Baldacci, Bergamo, 1986
Poesie, Milan, 1898
Le idee di una donna, Milan, 1904; Florence, 1977 (with *Confessioni letterarie* (1911), intro. S.
    Sanvitale)
Crevalcore, Milan, 1907 (intros. G. Lagorio and A. Arslan), 1991
Crepuscoli di libertà, Milan, 1917; Reggio Emilia, 1977
Una giovinezza del secolo XIX, Milan, 1919; Milan, 1975
Poesie, Milan, 1919
Monastero e altri racconti, ed. by A. Arslan and A. Folli, Milan, 1987

Selected criticism

Capuana, L., 'Neera', in *Studi sulla letteratura contemporanea*, Catania, 1882, pp. 145–7
Croce, B. (ed.), 'Neera', in *Neera*, Milan, 1942, pp. 932–44

Finucci, V., 'Between Acquiescence and Madness: Neera's Teresa', *Stanford Italian Review* 7 (1987), pp. 217–39

Folli, A., 'Le arpe eolie. Lettura di Neera', *La rassegna della letteratura italiana* 1 (1987), pp. 98–120

Kroha, L., 'Neera. The Literary Career of a Woman of the Nineteenth Century', in *The Woman Writer in Late-Nineteenth Century Italy. Gender and the Formation of Literary Identity*, Lewiston and Lampeter, 1992, pp. 67–98

Corda, M. G., *Il profumo della memoria. Identità femminile e scrittura in Neera*, Florence, 1993

Costa-Zalessow, pp. 240–7; B. Merry in Russell, pp. 286–94; Wood, pp. 26–39

Negri, Ada (Lodi 1870–1945 Milan)

Poet, school teacher, journalist. Poetry noted for social awareness and way in which her lyrics closely parallel her life. Extremely popular in early part of century; association with Fascism diminished reputation in later years.

Major works

Fatalità, Milan, 1892

Tempeste, Milan, 1895

Maternità, Milan, 1904

Dal profondo, Milan, 1910

Esilio, Milan, 1914

Il libro di Mara, Milan, 1919; rev. edn Milan, 1934

I canti dell'isola, Milan, 1925

Vespertina, Milan, 1931

Il dono, Milan, 1936

Fons amoris, Milan, 1946

Selected criticism

B. Merry in Russell (1994), pp. 295–301.

Nizzoli Solla, Amalia (Marucchi) (Tuscany *c.*1806–1845?)

Born in Tuscany into Piedmontese family exiled during French republican occupation. In 1819, went with family to Egypt, where, aged fifteen, married Giuseppe Nizzoli. Stayed in Egypt until 1828. Was in Zante when wrote *Memorie*. The name Marucchi, often found in bibliographies, was her mother's. Died some time before 1849 (year in which her husband remarried).

Major work

Memorie sull'Egitto e specialmente sui costumi delle donne orientali e gli harem scritte durante il suo soggiorno in quel paese (1819–1828), Milan, 1841

Selected criticism

Amat di San Filippo, P., *Biografia dei viaggiatori italiani*, Rome, 1882

Cappuccio, C., *Memorialisti dell'Ottocento*, Milan–Naples, 1972

Scriboni, M., 'Il viaggio al femminile nell'Ottocento. La principessa di Belgioioso, Amalia Nizzoli e Carla Serena', *Annali d'Italianistica* (1996), pp. 304–25

Vanzan, A., *L'Egitto di Amalia Nizzoli. Lettura del diario di una viaggiatrice della prima metà dell'Ottocento*, Bologna, 1996

Costa-Zalessow, pp. 216–23

Nogarola, Isotta (Verona 1418–1466 Verona)

Humanist who, most unusually, remained single. Mother was instrumental in ensuring a classical education from private tutors for her and her sister, Ginevra. Corresponded with leading male humanists, including Guarino Veronese, and political figures. In 1438 was accused of incest and stopped writing except for a celebrated exchange, 1451–3, with Lodovico Foscarini over relative culpability of Adam and Eve.

Major work

'De pari aut impari Evae atque Adae peccato', in E. Abel (ed.), *Isottae Nogarolae opera quae extant omnia*, Vienna–Budapest, 1886, pp. 187–216; trans. in King and Rabil (eds.), *Her Immaculate Hand*, Binghampton, NY, 1983, pp. 57–69

Selected criticism

Jardine, L., 'Women Humanists: Education for What?', in A. Grafton and L. Jardine, *From Humanism to the Humanities*, London, 1986

King, M. L., 'The Religious Retreat of Isotta Nogarola (1418–1466)', *Signs* 3 (1978), pp. 807–22

M. L. King in P. Labalme (ed.), *Beyond Their Sex* (New York–London, 1980), pp. 66–90

P. O. Kristeller in P. Labalme (ed.), *Beyond Their Sex* (New York–London, 1980), pp. 91–116

G. Gardenal in *Stanze*, pp. 3–14; M. L. King in Russell, pp. 313–23

Ortese, Anna Maria (Rome 1914–1998 Milan)

Novelist, short story writer, journalist. Life was marked by poverty. Left school young and was self-educated. In 1937 published collection of semi-autobiographical tales, *Angelici dolori*. First came to critics' attention in 1953 with a collection of realist stories and travel writings, *Il mare non bagna Napoli*. These reveal glimpses of fantasy that will find fuller expression in works such as *L'iguana* (1965) and *Il cardillo addolorato* (1993).

Major works

Angelici dolori, Milan, 1937

Il mare non bagna Napoli, Turin, 1953; Florence, 1967, 1979; Milan, 1994; trans. F. Frenaye, *The Bay is Not Naples*, London, 1955

Silenzio a Milano, Bari, 1958; Milan, 1986, 1998

L'iguana, Florence, 1965; Milan, 1978, 1986; trans. H. Martin, *The Iguana*, London, 1990

Poveri e semplici, Florence, 1967; Milan, 1974

Il porto di Toledo. Ricordi della vita irreale, Milan, 1975, 1985, 1998

In sonno e in veglia, Milan, 1987, 1993

La lente scura: scritti di viaggio, ed. L. Clerici, Milan, 1991

Il cardillo addolorato, Milan, 1993; trans. Patrick Creagh, *The Lament of the Linnet*, London, 1993

Alonso e i visionari, Milan, 1996

Corpo celeste, Milan, 1997

La luna che trascorre, ed. G. Spagnoletti, Rome, 1998

Selected criticism

Borri, G., *Invito alla lettura di Anna Maria Ortese*, Milan, 1988

Wilson, R., 'Una realtà estranea: la narrativa di Anna Maria Ortese', *Italian Studies in Southern Africa* 3–4 (1990–1), pp. 100–8

Fofi, G., 'Anna Maria Ortese', in *Strade maestre. Ritratti di scrittori italiani*, Rome, 1996,
      pp. 201–12
Farnetti, M., *Anna Maria Ortese*, Milan, 1998

Wood, pp. 169–83; L. A. Salsini in Bondanella

Paolini Massimi, Petronilla (Tagliacozzo, L'Aquila 1663–1726 Rome)

Poet. Father killed and when still very young married Cavaliere Francesco Massimi,
keeper of the Castel Sant'Angelo, and relative of Pope Clement X. Disturbed by
spectacles of incarceration and persecution at Castel Sant'Angelo and life made
insufferable by arrogant, brutal husband. Separated from her three children as
punishment. Returned to monastery where had taken refuge after death of father. No
complete edition of her poetry exists.

Selected criticism

Thovez, E., 'Arcadi leopardiani', in *L'arco di Ulisse*, Naples, 1921, pp. 283–92
Croce, B., 'Fidalma Partenide ossia la marchesa Petronilla Paolini Massimi', in *La
      letteratura italiana del Settecento*, Bari, 1949, pp. 37–50
Binni, W., 'Sviluppo della poesia arcadia nel primo Settecento', in *L'Arcadia e il Metastasio*,
      Florence, 1963, pp. 125–9
Cardini, R., 'Alcuni inediti di Petronilla Paolini Massimi', *Rassegna della letteratura
      italiana* series 7 (1969), pp. 338–67
Gronda, G. (ed.), *Poesia italiana del Settecento*, Milan, 1978
Ricaldone, L., *La scrittura nascosta*, Paris–Fiesole, 1996
De Blasi, J., *Le scrittrici italiane dalle origini al 1800*, Florence, 1930
      Antologia delle scrittrici italiane dalle origini al 1800, Florence, 1930
Maier, B., *Lirici del Settecento*, Rome–Naples, 1959
B. Allen et al (eds.), *The Defiant Muse. Italian Feminist Poems from the Middle Ages to the
      Present*, New York, 1986

Costa-Zalessow, pp. 163–71

Petrignani, Sandra (Piacenza 1952–   )

Literary critic, journalist and novelist.

Major works

Le signore della scrittura: interviste, Milan, 1984; rev. edn 1996
Fantasia & fantastico, Milan, 1985
ed., *Una donna, un secolo*, Rome, 1986
Navigazioni di Circe, Rome–Naples, 1987
Il catalogo dei giocattoli, Rome–Naples, 1988; trans. R. Lombardo, *The Toy Catalogue*,
      London, 1990
Come cadono i fulmini, Milan, 1991
Come fratello e sorella, Milan, 1998

Selected criticism

Wood, pp. 261–6

Pozzi, Antonia (Milan 1912–1938 Milan)

Poet. Discovered after her death, poems were edited and published by her father. Other
editions followed and recent revival of interest generated by editors of her diaries and
poems, Alessandra Cenni and Onorina Dino.

Major works

Parole, Milan, 1939, 1943 (intro. E. Montale), 1945, 1964; ed. A. Cenni and O. Dino, 1989
La vita sognata e altre poesie inedite, ed. A. Cenni and O. Dino, Milan, 1986
Diari, ed. A. Cenni and O. Dino, Milan, 1988
L'età delle parole è finita, Lettere 1927–1938, ed. A. Cenni and O. Dino, Milan, 1989

Selected criticism

R. West in Russell, pp. 333–43

Pulci, Antonia (born Tanini) (Florence 1452–1501 Florence)

Playwright in fifteenth-century Florence. Married at eighteen to poet, merchant and later university administrator, Bernardo Pulci, a recipient of Medici patronage. The couple remained childless and after Bernardo's death early in 1488, she became an Augustinian tertiary, founding a lay order, the sisters of Santa Maria della Misericordia, in Florence in 1500.

Major works

La rapresentatione di Sancta Domitilla vergine, La rapresentatione di Sancta Guglielma, and *La rapresentatione di Sancto Francesco*, Florence: Miscomini, 1490–5; reprint (no date) with woodcut illustrations; various reprintings sixteenth and early seventeenth centuries; 'Guglielma', in A. D'Ancona (ed.), *Sacre rappresentazioni dei secoli IX, XV, e XVI*, Florence, 1872, 3 vols., III, pp. 129–234; in L. Banfi (ed.), *Sacre rappresentazioni del Quattrocento*, Turin, 1963, pp. 533–77; in G. Ponte (ed.), *Sacre rappresentazioni fiorentine del Quattrocento*, Milan, 1974, pp. 69–98; 'San Francesco', in P. Toschi (ed.), *L'antico dramma sacro italiano*, Florence, 1926
   Trans. of all three, and of attributed plays, J. Wyatt Cook and B. Collier Cook (eds.), *Antonia Pulci, Florentine Drama for Convent and Festival: Seven Sacred Plays*, annotated and trans. J. Wyatt Cook, Chicago and London, 1996

Selected criticism

Cardini, F., 'La figura di Francesco d'Assisi nella *Rappresentazione di Sancto Francesco* di Antonia Pulci', in *Il francescanesimo e il teatro medievale: atti del convegno nazionale di studi, San Miniato, 8–10 ottobre 1982*, Castelfiorentino, 1984, pp. 195–207
Newbigin, N., 'Plays, Printing and Publishing, 1485–1500: Florentine *sacre rappresentazioni*', *La Bibliofilia* 90 (1988), pp. 269–96
Ulysse, G., 'Un couple d'écrivains: les *sacre rappresentazioni* de Bernardo et Antonia Pulci', in *Les Femmes écrivains en Italie au Moyen Age et à la Renaissance*, Aix-en-Provence, 1994, pp. 177–96
Bryce, J., 'Adjusting the Canon for Later Fifteenth-Century Florence: The Case of Antonia Pulci', in C. Cairns (ed.), *The Renaissance Theatre: Texts, Performance, Design*: Ashgate, in preparation

Costa-Zalessow, pp. 49–53; Wilson (1991); B. Toscani in Russell, pp. 344–52

Rame, Franca (North Italy 1928–   )

Received dramatic training from father, who directed a troupe of travelling players. In early 1950s, met Dario Fo and entered long personal and professional partnership with him. With Fo produced and performed in mainstream theatre (1959–67) then founded new company Nuova Scena (1968 to 1970) collaborating with the Italian Communist Party. In early 1970s, broke with the Party and founded the theatrical collective La Comune. The couple became the best-known writers and performers in Italian theatre.

Major works

with D. Fo, *Tutta casa, letto e chiesa*, Verona, 1977

with D. Fo, *Female Parts*, London, 1981

with D. Fo, *Coppia aperta, quasi spalancata*, Turin, 1983, 1991

with D. Fo, *The Mother: A Dramatic Monologue*, London, 1984

with D. Fo, *Orgasmo Adulto Escapes From the Zoo*, New York, 1985

with D. Fo, *A Woman Alone and Other Plays*, London, 1991

with D. Fo, *Parliamo di donne: Il teatro di Franca Rame*, Milan, 1992

Selected criticism

Wood, S., 'Franca Rame's Feminist Stages', in J. Farrell and A. Scuderi (eds.), *Dario Fo: Theatre, Stage and Text*, Carbondale, 2000

Valeri, W., ed., *Franca Rame Herself*, West Lafayette, 2000

Ramondino, Fabrizia (Naples 1936–   )

Novelist. Lived in Naples until 1980 earthquake, but spent periods in Majorca (as a child), France (1948) and Germany (1954–7), as well as Milan and Rome. Had an intense period of political militancy in Naples during 1960s and 1970s before turning to writing. Her work has been awarded numerous prizes.

Major works

Althénopis, Turin, 1981, 1995; trans. M. Sullivan, *Althénopis*, Manchester, 1988

Storie di patio, Turin, 1983

Star di casa, Milan, 1991

In viaggio, Turin, 1995

L'isola riflessa, Turin, 1998

Selected criticism

Giorgio, A., 'A Feminist Family Romance: Mother, Daughter and Female Genealogy in Fabrizia Ramondino's *Althéonopis*', *The Italianist* 11 (1991), pp. 128–49

Giorgio, A., 'Enonciation and Enoncé in a Short Story by Fabrizia Ramondino: La signora di Son Batle', *ITS* 48 (1993), pp. 86–106

Giorgio, A., 'Moving Across Boundaries: Identity and Difference in the Work of Fabrizia Ramondino', *The Italianist* (1998).

Usher, J., 'Fabrizia Ramondino', in Z. Barański and L. Pertile (eds.), *The New Italian Novel*, Edinburgh, 1993, pp. 167–83

Rasy, Elisabetta (Rome 1947–   )

Literary critic, journalist, art critic and novelist. Founder of women's press, Edizioni delle donne (1975).

Major works

La lingua della nutrice. Percorsi e tracce dell'espressione femminile, Rome, 1978

Le donne e la letteratura. Scrittrici eroine e ispiratrici nel mondo delle lettere, Rome, 1984

La prima estasi, Milan, 1985

Il finale della battaglia, Milan, 1988

L'altra amante, Milan, 1990

Mezzi di trasporto, Milan, 1993

Ritratti di signora, Milan, 1995

Posillipo, Milan, 1997

Selected criticism

Tani, S., 'Elisabetta Rasy', in *Il romanzo di ritorno. Dal romanzo medio degli anni sessanta alla giovane narrativa degli anni ottanta*, Milan, 1990, pp. 355–9

Guidoni, C., 'Elisabetta Rasy: Un désir qui aurait pour toujours perdu son objet', in Centre Aixois de Recherches Italiennes (ed.), *Les femmes écrivains en Italie aux XIXe et XXe siècles*, Aix-en-Provence, 1993, pp. 239–50

M. Gieri in Bondanella (1996)

Ravera, Lidia (Turin 1951–   )

Novelist, essayist and journalist. Her first novel was a bestseller, translated into eight languages and made into a film and a musical.

Major works

with M. Lombardo Radice, *Porci con le ali. Dialogo sessuo-politico di due adolescenti*, Rome, 1976; Milan, 1985, 1996

Bambino mio, Milan, 1979

Bagna i fiori e aspettami, Milan, 1986, 1988

Voi grandi, Rome–Naples, 1990

In quale nascondiglio del cuore. Lettera a un figlio adolescente, Milan, 1993, 1995

I compiti per le vacanze, Milan, 1997

Renier Michiel, Giustina (Venice 1755–1832 Venice)

Scholar, critic and translator of Shakespeare. Daughter of Andrea Renier (son of Polo, penultimate doge) and Cecilia Manin (sister of Ludovico, last doge). Godfather was Marco Foscarini (also a doge). Married Marco Antonio Michiel in her twenties and moved with him to Rome, following the Venetian ambassador to the Pope. In August 1784 separated from Michiel and dedicated herself fully to her studies and her salon.

Major works

Origine delle feste veneziane, Venice, 1817–27; Milan, 1829 (6 vols.); ed. with intro. F. Pellegrini, Venice, 1916

La Regata: festa veneziana descritta da Giustina Renier Michiel, Venice, 1825

Lettere inedite della N.D. Giustina Renier Michiel e dell'abate Saverio Bettinelli, Venice, 1857

Selected criticism

Carrer, L., 'Giustina Renier Michiel', in *Vite e ritratti delle donne celebri d'ogni paese (Opera della Duchessa D'Abrantès continuata per cura di letterati italiani)*, Milan, 1835, vol. III, pp. 231–42

Malamani, V., 'Giustina Renier Michiel. I suoi amici e il suo tempo', *Nuovo Archivio Veneto* (1889), pp. 3–95

Vianello-Chiodo, M., 'Giustina Renier Miechiel e molte sue lettere inedite', *Ateneo Veneto* (1940), pp. 61–76

Bassi, E. and L. Urban Padoan, *Canova e gli Albrizzi. Tra ridotti e dimore di campagna del tempo*, Milan, 1989

Stanze, pp. 164–72

Robert, Enif (born Angelini) (Prato 1886–1976 Bologna)

Futurist writer and actress. Advocated women's reproductive freedom in opposition to Futurist ideas of compulsory motherhood. Her objections to Marinetti's misogyny appended to second edition of his *Come si seducono le donne* (1918). Starred in D'Annunzio's play *La Gioconda* with Eleonora Duse.

Major works

'Come si seducono le donne', *L'Italia Futurista* 2 (1917)
'Sensazioni chirurgiche. Parole in libertà', *L'Italia Futurista* 2 (1917)
'Malattia+infezione. Parole in libertà', *L'Italia Futurista* 2 (1917)
with F. T Marinetti, *Un ventre di donna: Romanzo chirurgico* (experimental novel, includes
    letters by F. T. Marinetti and E. Duse), Milan, 1919

Selected criticism

Verdone, M., *Prosa e critica futurista*, Milan, 1973
Salaris, C., *Le futuriste. Donne e letteratura d'avanguardia in Italia*, Milan, 1982
Re, L., 'Futurism and Feminism', *Annali d'Italianistica* 7 (1989), pp. 253–72
Blum, C., 'The Hero's War and the Heroine's Wounds: *Un ventre di donna*', in *The Other
    Modernism. F. T. Marinetti's Futurist Fiction of Power*, Berkeley, CA, 1996
Parati, G., 'Speaking Through Her Body: The Futurist Seduction of a Woman's Voice', in
    Public History, Private Stories: Italian Women's Autobiographies, Minneapolis, MI,
    1996.

Romano, Lalla (Demonte, Cuneo 1906–   )

Poet, novelist, essayist, critic, translator, artist, photographer. Poet until 1951 when published a narrative transcription of her dreams, *Le metamorfosi*. First novel *Maria* (1953) signalled start of series of autobiographical narratives which include *Tetto murato*, about life under German Occupation, *La penombra che abbiamo attraversato* (1964), about mother's death, and prize-winning *Le parole tra noi leggere* (1969), about a difficult relationship between mother and son.

Major work

Opere, ed. C. Segre, 2 vols., Milan, 1991, 1992

Selected criticism

Catelucci, A., *Invito alla lettura di Lalla Romano*, Milan, 1980
Piemontese, F. (ed.), *Autodizionario degli scrittori italiani*, Milan, 1989
Brizio, F., *La scrittura e la memoria: Lalla Romano*, Milan 1993

F. Brizio in Aricò, pp. 63–75

Rosà, Rosa (Edith von Haynau) (Vienna 1884–1978 Rome)

Futurist and feminist fiction writer, poet, artist. Studied art in Vienna. Settled in Rome after marriage to writer Ulrico Arnaldi (1908). Four children. During World War I joined 'Italia Futurista' group in Florence. Eclectic and prolific artist, specialised in ink drawings. Illustrated books written by Florentine Futurists. In 1950s, as Edyth Arnaldi, wrote books of archaeological fantasy and fiction.

Major works

'Le donne del posdomani', *L'Italia Futurista* 2 (1917)
'Donna+Amore+Bellezza. Le donne cambiano finalmente', *L'Italia Futurista* 2 (1917)
Una donna con tre anime, Milan, 1918; ed. with intro. C. Salaris, Milan, 1981 (includes some
    of Rosà's feminist articles)
Non c'è che te! Una donna con tre anime e altre novelle, Milan, 1919

Selected criticism

Vergine, L., 'Rosa Rosà' in *L'altra metà dell'avanguardia*, Milan, 1980

Salaris, C., *Le futuriste. Donne e letteratura d'avanguardia in Italia*, Milan, 1982

Re, L., 'Futurism and Feminism', *Annali d'Italianistica* 7 (1989), pp. 253–72

Re, L., 'Scrittura della metamorfosi e metamorfosi della scrittura: Rosa Rosà e il
   futurismo', in E. Genevois (ed.), *Les femmes écrivains en Italie (1870–1920): ordres et
   libertés*, Paris, 1994, pp. 311–27

Bentivoglio, M., and F. Zoccoli, *Women Artists of Italian Futurism. Almost Lost To History . . .*,
   New York, 1997

Katz, B., 'The Women of Futurism', *A Woman's Art Journal* 2 (1999), pp. 3–13

C. Della Coletta in Russell, pp. 353–9

Rosselli, Amelia (Paris 1930–1996 Rome)

Poet, writer, journalist. Daughter of Carlo Rosselli, who was assassinated in Paris in
1937. Lived in France, England and USA before settling in Italy in 1946. Poetry is noted
for use of Freudian lapsus and musical dimension. Many consider her the outstanding
Italian woman poet of the twentieth century.

Major works

La libellula, Milan, 1958; 1985 (also included *Serie ospedaliera*)

Variazioni belliche, Milan, 1964

Documento 1966–1973, Milan, 1976

Primi scritti (1952–1963), Parma, 1980

Antologia poetica, ed. G. Spagnoletti, Milan, 1987

Sonno-Sleep (1953–1966), Rome, 1989

Diario ottuso (1954–1968), Rome, 1990

Sleep – Poesie in inglese, Milan, 1992

Le poesie, ed. E. Tandello, Milan, 1997

Selected criticism

Attanasio, D., and E. Tandello (eds.), special issue of *Galleria* 48 (1997)

C. Della Coletta in Russell, pp. 360–7

Saluzzo Roero, Diodata (Turin 1774–1840 Turin)

Poet, playwright, short story writer. Father was celebrated scientist Giuseppe Angelo
Saluzzo and mother was Jeronima Cassotti di Casalgrasso. Unusually for women of her
time, was well educated in sciences as well as arts. In 1799 married Count Massimiliano
Roero di Revello but was widowed three years later and returned to paternal home. Very
secluded life, apart from a few journeys to Rome and Tuscany. Associated with many
academies, from Arcadia to the Science Academy of Turin.

Major works

Versi di Diodata Saluzzo fra gli Arcadi: Glaucilla Eurotea, Turin 1796; 2nd edn Turin, 1797

Poesie di Diodata Saluzzo torinese, Pisa, 1819

Ipazia, ovvero delle filosofie, Turin, 1827; 2nd edn Turin, 1830

Novelle, Milan, 1830; ed. L. Nay, Florence, 1989

Selected criticism

Badini Conflonieri, L., 'Sull'*Ipazia* di Diodata Saluzzo Roero: una variante e qualche
   considerazione', *Lettere Italiane* 2 (1983), pp. 189–99

Prosio, P. M., 'Agli albori del romanzo storico in Piemonte: le novelle di Diodata
     Saluzzo', in *Ludovico Di Breme e il programma dei romantici italiani. Atti del convegno di
     studi, 21–22 ottobre 1983*, Turin, 1985, pp. 169–82
Trivero, P., 'Diodata Saluzzo oltre *Le Rovine* (due tragedie Erminia e Tullia)', in *Ludovico
     Di Breme*, pp. 183–94
Ricaldone, L., 'Diodata Saluzzo e la sua attività nell'Accademia delle Scienze', in *I primi
     due secoli della Accademia delle Scienze di Torino. Atti del convegno 10–12 novembre 1983*,
     Turin, 1985, pp. 243–50
Trivero, P., 'Diodata e le altre, per una lettura delle Novelle', *Studi piemontesi* 1 (1986),
     pp. 27–43
Nay, L., 'Diodata Saluzzo: una femminista contra litteram', in M. Cerruti (ed.), *Il 'genio
     muliebre'. Percorsi di donne intellettuali fra Settecento e Novecento in Piemonte*,
     Alessandria, 1990, pp. 23–41
Tissoni, R., 'Considerazioni su Diodata Saluzzo (con un'appendice di lettere inedite ad
     Alessandro Manzoni)', in G. Ioli (ed.), *Piemonte e letteratura 1789–1870. Atti del
     convegno, San Salvatore Monferrato 15–17 ottobre 1981*, Turin: Regione Piemonte, no
     date, pp. 145–99

Costa-Zalessow, pp. 198–206; A. Franceschetti and G. Sanguinetti Katz in Russell,
     pp. 375–85

Sanvitale, Francesca (Milan 1928–   )
Novelist, literary critic, and translator (from French). Studied and lived in Florence
before moving to Rome where she now lives. Worked for RAI Due (Italian television) for
twenty-six years, writing plays and cultural programmes. Recipient of numerous
literary prizes.

Major works
Il cuore borghese, Florence, 1972; Milan, 1986
Madre e figlia, Turin, 1980; Milan, 1986; Turin, 1994
L'uomo del parco, Milan, 1984, 1987
La realtà è un dono, Milan, 1987
Verso Paola, Turin, 1991
Il figlio dell'impero, Turin, 1993, 1995
ed., *Le scrittrici dell'Ottocento* (anthology with intro. by Sanvitale), Rome, 1995
Separazioni, Turin, 1997

Selected criticism
A. Hallamore Caesar in Z. Barański and L. Pertile (eds.), *The New Italian Novel*,
     Edinburgh, 1993, pp. 184–99

P. Blelloch in Aricò, pp. 124–37

Sarfatti, Margherita (Venice 1883–1961 Cavallasca, Como)
Writer, critic. Highly influential figure in Italian cultural and artistic life in 1920s. Of
Jewish origin, originally a socialist, became Mussolini's mistress, confidante and
biographer. Instrumental in founding and promotion of prestigious Novecento group.
In 1930s ties with Mussolini weakened, definitively severed in 1934. Writing suppressed
due to anti-Semitic laws. Went into exile 1939, returned after war.

Major works

Dux, Milan, 1926; trans. London, 1925
Il palazzone, Milan, 1929
Storia della pittura moderna, Rome, 1930
America, ricerca della felicità, Milan, 1937

Selected criticism

Nozzoli, A., 'Margherita Sarfatti organizzatrice di cultura', in M. Addis Saba (ed.), *La corporazione delle donne. Ricerche e studi sui modelli femminili del ventennio*, Florence, 1988
De Grazia, V., *How Fascism Ruled Women. Italy, 1922–1945*, Berkeley, CA, 1992
Cannistraro, P. and B. Sullivan, *Il Duce's Other Woman*, New York, 1993

Sarrocchi, Margherita (Naples *c.* 1560–1618?)

Poet. Lived in Rome from at at least 1580s. Little known of personal life, other than husband's date of death (1613) and his family name (Birago). Praised by contemporaries as learned in all disciplines. Interest in science well testified. Correspondent of Galileo's, friend of prominent literary men such as Giambattista Marino.

Major work

La Scanderbeide, Rome, 1606 (incomplete edition); Rome, 1623 (complete edition); Naples, 1701

Selected criticism

Borzelli, A., *Note intorno a Margherita Sarrocchi*, Naples, 1935
Cox. V., 'Women as readers and writers of chivalric poetry', in G. Bedani et al. (eds.), *Sguardi sull'Italia*, Leeds, 1997, pp. 134–45

Costa-Zalessow, pp. 128–34

Secco Suardo Grismondi, Paolina (Lesbia Cidonia) (Bergamo 1746–1801 Bergamo)

Poet. Held important salon in Bergamo. In correspondence with main intellectuals of her day. Travelled in Italy, Netherlands, Germany, France. In Paris (1778) met leading French intellectuals. Published all her poetry herself or in occasional collections. Most letters remain unpublished.

Major works

L'epistolario, ossia scelta di lettere inedite famigliari curiose erudite storiche galanti ec.ec. di donne e d'uomini celebri morti o viventi nel secolo XVIII o nel MDCC, ed. A. Rubbi, Venice, 1795
Poesie della contessa Paolina Secco Suardo Grismondi tra le pastorelle arcadi Lesbia Cidonia, Bergamo, 1820, 1822
Quattro lettere inedite alla contessa Paolina Secco Suardo Grismondi (Lesbia Cidonia) in occasione delle nozze del conte Galeazzo Colleoni con la nobile signorina Margherita Antona Traversi, Naples, 1880

Selected criticism

Troiano, R., 'Paolina Grismondi. Note sulla scrittura femminile del Settecento (con un'appendice di documenti inediti)', in T. Iermano and T. Scappaticci (eds.), *Studi in onore di Antonio Piromalli*, Naples, 1994, vol. II, pp. 293–326
Tadini, F., *Lesbia Cidonia. Società, moda e cultura nella vita della contessa Paolina Secco Suardo Grismondi (Bergamo 1746–1801)*, Bergamo, 1995

Serao, Matilde (Patras, Greece 1856–1927 Naples)

Journalist, novelist, polemicist, short story writer. Daughter of Neapolitan expatriate journalist and Greek noblewoman. Italy's first high-profile woman journalist (ranging from the society column to investigative reports), founder of four major newspapers, very prolific novelist. Knew G. D'Annunzio and married E. Scarfoglio (from whom eventually separated).

Major works

Cuore infermo, Turin, 1881

Fantasia, Turin, 1883

La virtù di Checchina, Catania, 1884; Milan, 1920; ed. N. Ginzburg, Milan, 1974; in *Il romanzo della fanciulla*, ed. F. Bruni, Naples, 1985

Il ventre di Napoli, Milan, 1884, 1904; Naples, 1973,1994

La conquista di Roma, Florence, 1885

Addio amore!, Naples, 1890; Rome, 1977

Il paese di Cuccagna, Milan, 1891; Milan, 1977

Castigo, Turin, 1893; Florence, 1977

Suor Giovanna della Croce, Milan, 1901

Parla una donna. Diario femminile di guerra, Milan, 1916

Serao, ed. P. Pancrazi, Milan, 1946

Selected criticism

Banti, A, *Matilde Serao*, Turin, 1965

Infusino, G. (ed.), *Matilde Serao tra giornalismo e letteratura*, Naples, 1981

Fanning, U., 'Angel vs. Monster: Serao's Use of the Female Double', in Z. Barański and S. Vinall (eds.), *Women and Italy*, pp. 263–92

Kroha, L., 'Matilde Serao's *Fantasia*: an Author in Search of a Character', in Z. Barański and S. Vinall (eds.), *Women and Italy: Essays on Gender, Culture and History*, London, 1991, pp. 245–62.

Harrowitz, N. A., *Antisemitism, Misogyny and the Logic of Cultural Difference: Cesare Lombroso and Matilde Serao*, Lincoln and London, 1994

Costa-Zalessow, pp. 254–62; U. Fanning in Russell, pp. 386–94; Wood, pp. 40–57

Sereni, Clara (Rome 1946–   )

Novelist, journalist and translator (from French). Jewish family, Communist father, Emilio Sereni, and a Russian mother. Has been deputy mayor of Perugia since 1995.

Major works

Sigma Epsilon, Venice, 1974

Casalinghitudine, Turin, 1987

Il gioco dei regni, Florence, 1993

Eppure, Milan, 1995

ed., *Si può!*, Rome, 1996

Selected criticism

Gaglianone, P. (ed.), *Conversazione con Clara Sereni. Donne, scrittura e politica*, Rome, 1996

Chemello, A., 'La genealogia riconosciuta di Clara Sereni', in A. Chemello (ed.), *Parole scolpite. Profili di scrittrici degli anni Novanta*, Padua, 1998, pp. 103–19

Cicioni, M., and S. Walker, 'Picking Up the Pieces: Clara Sereni's Recipes for Survival', in

J. Gatt-Rutter (ed.), *Novel Turns: Recent Narrative Writing From Western Europe, Antipodas Monograph Series*, Madrid–Auckland, NZ, forthcoming

Spaziani, Maria Luisa (Turin 1924–)

Poet, critic, translator, dramatist. Former professor of French literature at Messina University, now lives in Rome. Dedicated to promotion of poetry, founded Montale International Poetry Centre in Rome in 1981.

Major works

Le acque del Sabato, Milan, 1954
Il gong, Milan, 1962
Utilità della memoria, Milan, 1966
L'occhio del ciclone, Milan, 1970
Transito con catene, Milan, 1977
Poesie, Milan, 1979
Geometria del disordine, Milan, 1981
La stella del libero arbitrio, Milan, 1986
Giovanna d'Arco, Milan, 1990
Donne in poesia, Venice, 1992
I fasti dell'ortica, Milan, 1996

Selected criticism

B. Zecchi in Russell, pp. 395–403

Stampa, Gaspara (Padua 1523–1554 Venice)

Received good literary and musical education and took active part in cultural life of Venice and Padua. Member of Accademia dei Dubbiosi (with name Anassilla). Friend of leading poets and prose writers Sperone Speroni, Benedetto Varchi and perhaps Trifon Gabriele. In 1548 fell in love with Count Collaltino di Collalto, who reciprocated for a while. During life published only three sonnets, but after death poems published by brother and sister Baldassare and Cassandra.

Major works

Rime di Gaspara Stampa, ed. G. Benzone and Cassandra Stampa, Venice, 1554
Rime di Madonna Gaspara Stampa con alcune altre di Collaltino e di Vinciguerra conti di Collalto, e di Baldassare Stampa, ed. L. Bergalli and A. Zeno, Venice, 1738
Rime di Gaspara Stampa e di Veronica Franco, ed. A. Salza, Bari, 1913
Rime, ed. R. Ceriello, Milan, 1954–76

Selected criticism

Bassanese, F., *Gaspara Stampa*, Boston, 1982
F. Warnke, 'Aphrodite's Priestess, Love's Martyr', in K. M. Wilson (ed.), *Women Writers of the Renaissance and Reformation*, Athens, 1987, pp. 3–21
Zancan, M., *Il doppio itinerario della letteratura femminile nella letteratura italiana*, Turin, 1998
Italian Poets of the Renaissance, ed. J. Tusiani, Long Island City, NY, 1971

Costa-Zalessow, pp. 85–92; M. Zancan in *Stanze*, pp. 35–44; F. Bassanese in Russell, pp. 404–13

Tamaro, Susanna (Trieste 1957–   )

Novelist and short story writer. Work has won many awards and has been translated into thirty-four languages. *Va' dove ti porta il cuore* an international bestseller and made into a film by Cristina Comencini (1996)

Major works

La testa fra le nuvole, Venice, 1989, 1994
Per voce sola, Venice, 1991, 1994; Milan, 1994; Venice, 1996; trans. S. Wood, *For Solo Voice*, Manchester, 1995
Va' dove ti porta il cuore, Milan, 1994; trans. A. Bardoni, *Follow Your Heart*, London, 1995
Anima Mundi, Milan, 1997

Selected criticism

Gaglianone, P. (ed.), *Conversazione con Susanna Tamaro. Il respiro quieto*, Rome, 1996
Rorato, L., 'Childhood Prisons. Denied Dreams vs. Denied Realities: The Ritualization of Pain in the Novels of Susanna Tamaro', *Romance Studies* 28 (Autumn 1996), pp. 61–78

Tarabotti, Arcangela (Baratotti/Barcitotti) (Venice 1604–1652 Venice)

Writer in prose of letters, satires, polemics and arguably first critique of patriarchy. Pressured by father to take religious vows in Benedictine Convent of Sant'Anna in 1620 because of a disability, and died there. Mainly self-taught, found some support from members of the libertine Accademia degli Incogniti, including its founder, nobleman and novelist G. F. Loredan.

Major works

La tirannia paterna, published posthumously as *La semplicità ingannata*, Leyden, 1654; trans. and ed. L. Panizza, *Paternal Tyranny*, Chicago, 2001
Lettere familiari e di complimento, Venice, 1650
L'Inferno monacale di Arcangela Tarabotti, ed. Francesca Medioli (from unpublished manuscript with notes and essays), Turin, 1990
Che le donne siano della spezie degli uomini (1651), ed. L. Panizza (crit. edn with essay and notes in English), London, 1994
Satira di Francesco Buoninsegi e Antisatira di Arcangela Tarabotti (1644), ed. Elissa Weaver, Rome, 1998

Selected criticism

Zanette, E., *Suor Arcangela, monaca del Seicento veneziano*, Venice, 1960
Conti Odirisio, G., *Donna e società nel Seicento*, Rome, 1979
De Bellis, D., 'Attacking Sumptuary Laws in Seicento Venice: Arcangela Tarabotti', in Panizza, ed., *Women in Italian Renaissance*, Oxford, 2000, pp. 227–42

Costa-Zalessow (1982), 153–62; M. Gambier in *Stanze* (1991), 117–25; E. Weaver in Russell, pp. 414–22

Tartufari, Clarice (born Gouzy) (Rome 1868–1933 Grosseto)

Poet, novelist, playwright. Spent childhood near Pesaro. Moved to Rome when married at very young age. Croce judged her work superior to Grazia Deledda's. In 1920s, her short fiction often published in daily press and in women's journals.

Major works

Il miracolo, Rome, 1909
Eterne leggi, Rome, 1911
All'uscita del labirinto, Bologna, 1914
Il Dio nero, Florence, 1921
Il mare e la vela, Florence, 1924
Il gomitolo d'oro, Milan, 1924
La nave degli eroi, Foligno, 1927
Imperatrice dei cinque labirinti, Rome, 1931
L'uomo senza volto, Rome, 1941
'A Life Story? (1925)', in R. Pickering-Iazzi (ed.), *Unspeakable Women. Selected Short Stories Written by Italian Women During Fascism*, New York, 1993, pp. 95–100

Selected criticism

Mondello, E., *La nuova italiana. La donna nella stampa e nella cultura del ventennio*, Rome, 1987
Pickering-Iazzi, R., 'The Poetics of Discovery: Female Storytelling and the Terza Pagina in Early Twentieth Century Literature', *Italiana* 1 (1988), pp. 291–306
Pickering-Iazzi, R., *Politics of the Visible. Writing Women, Culture, and Fascism*, Minneapolis, MI, 1997

Teotochi Albrizzi, Isabella (Corfu (Greece) 1760–1836 Venice)

Writer, critic. Aged sixteen, married Carlo Antonio Manin, moved to Venice where opened her first salon in 1782. Journeys and friendships contributed considerably to her learning and to her reputation as cultured and erudite. Circle included leading Italian poets and prose writers such as Pindemonte, Foscolo and Cesarotti. Divorced Manin, married Count Giuseppe Albrizzi in 1796.

Major works

Ritratti scritti da Isabella Teotochi Albrizzi, Brescia, 1807; Padua, 1808; Venice, 1816; Pisa, 1826, 1807; ed. and intro. Andrea Zanzotto, Milan, 1987; ed. G. Tellini, Palermo, 1992.
Opere di scultura e di plastica di Antonio Canova descritte da Isabella Albrizzi nata Teotochi, Florence, 1809; trans. *The Works of A. Canova in Sculpture and Modelling*, London, 1824–8
'Vita di Vittoria Colonna', in *Raccolta di Ritratti degl'Illustri Italiani*, Padua, 1812; in *Ritratti*, Venice,1816; in *Ritratti*, Pisa, 1826
'Ritratto di Giustina Renier Michiel', in *Strenna di Natale Vallardi*, Milan, 1833

Selected criticism

Carpani, G., *Lettere inedite a Isabella Teotochi Albrizzi (1805–1821)*, ed. R. Ciampini, Florence, 1973
Zaccaria, V., 'Lettere inedite di Ippolito Pindemonte a Isabella Teotochi Albrizzi', *Atti e Memorie dell'Accademia Patavina di Scienze, Lettere ed Arti* (1976–7), pp. 127–49
Pizzamiglio, G., 'Ugo Foscolo nel salotto di Isabella Teotochi Albrizzi', *Quaderni Veneti* 2 (1985), pp. 49–66
Palazzolo, M. J., *I salotti di cultura nell'Italia dell'Ottocento*, Milan, 1985
Gamba, C. M., 'I *Ritratti* di Isabella Teotochi Albrizzi', *Quaderni Veneti* 15 (1992), pp. 115–43

Giorgetti, C., *Ritratto di Isabella. Studi e documenti su Isabella Teotochi Albrizzi*, Florence, 1993

Pizzamiglio, G., 'Un epistolario neoclassico: Ippolito Pindemonte a Isabella Teotochi Albrizzi', in A. Chemello (ed.), *Seminario sull'epistolografia*, Milan, 1998

Stanze, pp. 174–83; Costa-Zalessow, pp. 207–10

Tornabuoni de' Medici, Lucrezia (Florence 1427–1482 Florence)

Religious poet, letter writer. From old family, married Piero di Cosimo de' Medici in 1444. Four children survived into adulthood: Lorenzo, Giuliano, Bianca and Nannina. Widowed in 1469, played important, supportive role to Lorenzo in his position as leading citizen of the Republic, shared in management of Medici client system, and promoted business enterprises.

Major works

Laudi, ed. F. Cionacci, Florence, 1680; ed. G. Volpi, Pistoia, 1900

Tre lettere di Lucrezia Tornabuoni a Piero de' Medici ed altre lettere di vari etc, ed. C. Guasti, Florence, 1859; crit. edn P. Salvadori, Florence, 1993 (all 49 of Tornabuoni's surviving letters and a selected 70 of 476 addressed to her)

'La Ystoria della devota Susanna', *Annali delle Università Toscane* 10 (1926), pp. 177–201

'Vita di Santo Giovanni Baptista and Ystoria di Iudith', in crit. edn F. Pezzarossa, *I poemetti sacri di Lucrezia Tornabuoni*, Florence, 1978

Selected criticism

Levantini-Pieroni, G., *Lucrezia Tornabuoni, donna di Piero di Cosimo de' Medici*, Florence, 1888

Martelli, M., 'Lucrezia Tornabuoni', in G. Ulysse (ed.), *Les femmes écrivains en Italie au Moyen Age et à la Renaissance*, Aix-en-Provence, 1994, pp. 51–86

Martelli, M., *Letteratura fiorentina del Quattrocento. Il filtro degli anni sessanta*, Florence, 1996

Costa-Zalessow, pp. 44–8; Wilson (1991); R. Russell in Russell, pp. 431–40

Trivulzio di Belgiojoso, Cristina (Milan 1808–1871 Milan)

Journalist. Travelled extensively in Italy, Europe and the Orient, mainly because of exile following participation revolutionary movements. Left an account of the fall of the Roman Republic (1849), and journey, during the following years until 1855, to Greece and then Asia Minor and Syria.

Major works

Un principe curdo, racconto turco-asiatico – Emina, Milan, 1857

Scènes de la vie turque, Paris, 1858

'Souvenirs dans l'exile', *Le National* (5 September–12 October 1850), appendix

Selected criticism

Giuli, P., 'Cristina di Belgioioso's Orient', *Nemla Italian Studies* 15 (1991), pp. 129–50

Scriboni, M., 'Se vi avessi avuto per compagna . . . Incontri tra donne nelle lettere e negli scritti dall'Oriente di Cristina Trivulzio di Belgioioso (1808–1871)', *Italian Culture* 12 (1994), pp. 163–74

Scriboni, M., 'Il viaggio al femminile nell'Ottocento. La principessa di Belgioioso, Amalia Nizzoli e Carla Serena', *Annali d'Italianistica* 14 (1996), pp. 304–25

Morandini, pp. 61–76

Varano, Battista (Camilla) (Camerino 1458–1524 Camerino)

Poor Clare, author of spiritual writings. Illegitimate daughter of Giulio Cesare Varano, lord of Camerino. Brought up in his court and received aristocratic education. In 1481, entered convent of Urbino and three years later founded new monastery of Poor Clares in Camerino, where she spent the rest of her life. Only the tragic murder of her family (on orders of Cesare Borgia), and tasks associated with setting up a new foundation took her away from Camerino. Beatified.

Major works

Le opere spirituali: Nuova edizione del quinto centenario della nascita secondo i più antichi codici e stampe e con aggiunta di alcuni inediti (contains all her known works), ed. by G. Boccanera (preface P. Bargellini), Jesi, 1958

I dolori mentali di Gesù nella sua passione, Venice, *c.*1488; Naples, 1490; Milan, 1515; Bologna, 1521; from 1593 numerous editions published with Scupoli's *Combattimento spirituale* (to whom long attributed)

Selected criticism

AA.VV. *Camilla Battista da Varano e il suo tempo. Atti del Convegno di Studi sul v centenario del monastero delle Clarisse di Camerino, Castello di Lanciano, Palazzo delle Clarisse di Camerino, 7–9 September 1984*, Camerino, 1987

Di Mattia Spirito, S., 'Una figura del francescanesimo femminile tra Quattrocento e Cinquecento: Camilla Battista da Varano (problemi e ricerche)', in *Cultura e società nell'Italia medievale. Studi per Paolo Brezzi*, 1988, vol. I, pp. 295–314

Gattucci, A., 'Le istruzioni al discepolo della beata Battista da Varano', *Collectanea francescana* 64 (1994), pp. 241–85

Vegri, Caterina (Bologna 1413–1463 Bologna)

Poor Clare, author of spiritual writings. Father was in service of the ruling d'Este family at Ferrara. Educated at court as lady-in-waiting. After 1426 entered lay community of women, but left later to found monastery of Poor Clares of Corpus Domini in Ferrara. In 1456, returned to Bologna where, with other sisters, founded new monastery of Corpus Domini and became its abbess. Writings (not always securely attributed to her) are in manuscript form in the monastery's archive. Canonised.

Major works

I dodici giardini, ed. G. Sgarbi, Bologna, 1996; ed. G. Aquini and M. M. Faberi, Bologna, 1999

Rosarium (uncertain attribution), Bologna, 1997

Le sette armi spirituali, Bologna: Baldassare Azzoguidi, *c.*1475, 1500, 1511, 1536, *c.*1550; Latin trans. G. A. Flaminio 1522; *Le armi necessarie alla battaglia spirituale* with *Vita della beata Caterina da Bologna*, Bologna, 1630; crit. edn C. Foletti, Padua, 1985

Selected criticism

Cardini, F., 'Santa Caterina da Bologna e il trattato Le sette armi spirituali', *Studi Francescani* 86 (1989), pp. 53–64

Zarri, G., 'Ecrits inédits de Catherine de Bologne et de ses soeurs', in G. Brunel-Lobrichon, D. Dinet, J. Gréal and D. Vorreux (eds.), *Sainte Claire d'Assise et sa posterité. Actes du colloque international organisé à l'occasion du VIII centenaire de la naissance sainte Claire, UNESCO (29 September – 1 October 1994)*, Paris, 1995, pp. 119–230

S. Spanò in *DBI* (XXII), pp. 381–3

Vernazza, Battista (Tommasina) (Genoa 1497–1587 Genoa)

Canoness of the Congregation of St John Lateran, author of spiritual texts. Prolific letter-writer. Entered monastery of S. Maria delle Grazie at age thirteen and took name Battista. Made solemn vows in 1511. Never left her monastery. Writings made up of sixteen treatises, published a year after death.

Major work

Le opere spirituali della reverenda et devotissima vergine di Christo donna Battista da Genova, 4 vols., Venice 1588–Verona 1602

Selected criticism

Solfaroli Camillocci, D., 'La monaca esemplare. Lettere spirituali di madre Battistina Vernazza (1497–1587)', in G. Zarri (ed.), *Per Lettera. La scrittura epistolare femminile tra archivio e tipografia secoli XV–XVII*, Rome, 1999, pp. 235–61

Vivanti, Annie (London 1868–1942 Turin)

Novelist, short story writer and poet. Father an exiled supporter of Garibaldi and mother the German writer Anna Lindau. Widely travelled; studied singing in Italy. Aged twenty-two, she took her poems to Carducci, who became her mentor. In 1902 married Irish patriot journalist John Chartres and settled in America. They returned to Italy in 1918. As a Jew she saw her books removed from circulation in Italy.

Major works

Lyrica, Milan, 1890
The Hunt for Happiness, London, 1896
The Devourers, London, 1910; Italian version by Vivanti, *I divoratori*, Milan, 1911
Circe, Milan, 1912; English version by Vivanti, *Marie Tarnowska*, London, 1915
Vae victis!, Milan, 1917
Naja tripudians, Milan, 1920; (intro. C. Garboli), 1970
Perdonate Eglantina!, Milan, 1926; ed. G. Anguissola, Milan, 1964

Selected criticism

Finotti, F., 'Naja tripudians: strutture e committenza del romanzo di consumo novecentesco', in A. Arslan (ed.), *Dame, droga e galline*, Milan, 1986, pp. 257–67
Molesini Spada, A., 'Idillio e tragedia: verifica di uno schema', in A. Arslan (ed.), *Dame, droga e galline*, pp. 241–56
Venturi, G., 'Serpenti e dismisura: la narrativa di Annie Vivanti da *Circe* a *Naja tripudians*', in E. Genevois, ed., *Les femmes écrivains en Italie (1870–1920): ordres et libertés*, Paris, 1994, pp. 292–309

Nozzoli, pp. 11–17; Morandini, pp. 308–19; Asor Rosa; B. Merry in Russell, pp. 441–6

Volpi, Marisa (Macerata 1931–   )

Short story writer. Lecturer in history of contemporary art at University of Rome and has written many essays on art. Short stories have won many awards, including Viareggio prize for her first collection.

Major works

Il maestro della betulla, Florence, 1986
Nonamore, Milan, 1988
Cavaliere senza destino, Florence, 1993

La casa di via Tolmino, Milan, 1993
Il condor, Florence, 1994
Congedi, Florence, 1995

Wertmüller, Lina (Rome 1928–)

Began career in early 1950s as producer of experimental plays, stage manager, set designer and puppeteer. At end of 1950s began writing for radio and television. Won international acclaim for films of 1970s starring Giancarlo Giannini. Continued to write and direct films; few distributed abroad in recent years. Films include *Questa volta parliamo di uomini* (1965), *Mimì metallurgico ferito nell'onore* (1972), *Pasqualino Settebellezze* (1975), *Un complicato intrigo di donne vicoli e delitti* (1985) and *Ninfa plebea* (1995).

Major work
The Screenplays of Lina Wertmüller (trans. S. Wagner), New York, 1977

Selected criticism
Ernest, F., and John R. May, *The Parables of Lina Wertmüller*, New York, 1977

Bibliography

Reference works and anthologies

Allen, Beverly, Muriel Kittel and Keala Jane Jewell, eds., *The Defiant Muse. Italian Feminist Poems from the Middle Ages to the Present. A Bilingual Anthology*, New York, 1986.

Arslan, Antonia, Adriana Chemello and Gilberto Pizzamiglio, eds., *Le stanze ritrovate. Antologia di scrittrici venete dal Quattrocento al Novecento*, Mirano–Venice, 1991.

Baldacci, L. ed., *Poeti minori dell'Ottocento*, Milan–Naples, 1958.

Bandini Buti, Maria ed., *Donne d'Italia. Poetesse e scrittrici*, in series *Dizionari biografici e bibliografici Tosi*, Almerico Ribera, ed., 2 vols., Rome, 1946.

Bono, Paola and Sandra Kemp, eds., *Italian Feminist Thought: a Reader*, Oxford, 1991.

Canonici Fachini, Ginevra, *Prospetto biografico delle donne italiane rinomate in letteratura dal secolo decimoquarto ai giorni nostri*, Venice, 1824.

Cerruti, M. ed., *Il 'Genio muliebre'. Percorsi di donne intellettuali fra Settecento e Novecento*, Alessandria, 1993.

Costa-Zalessow, Natalia, *Scrittrici italiane dal XIII al XX secolo. Testi e critica*, Ravenna, 1982.

De Blasi, Iolanda, *Le scrittrici italiane dalle origini al 1800*, Florence, 1930.

De Leo, Minna, *Autrici italiane. Catalogo ragionato dei libri di narrativa, poesia, saggistica 1945–1985*, Rome, 1987.

De Nicola, Francesco and Pier Antonio Zannoni, eds., *Scrittrici d' Italia*, Genoa, 1995.

Ferri, Pietro Leopoldo, *Biblioteca femminile italiana*, Padua, 1842.

Forlani, A. and M. Savini, eds., *Scrittrici d'Italia. Dalle eroine e dalle sante dei primi secoli fino alle donne dei nostri giorni*, Rome, 1991.

Frabotta, Biancamaria, *Donne in poesia. Antologia della poesia femminile in Italia dal dopoguerra ad oggi*, Rome, 1976.

Fusini, N. and N. Gramiglia, *La poesia femminista. Antologia di testi del Movimento*, Rome, 1974.

Giordano, A., *Letterate toscane del Settecento. Un regesto*, Florence, 1994.

Kadel, Andrew, ed., *Matrology. A Bibliography of Writings by Christian Women from the First to the Fifteenth Centuries*, New York, 1995.

Marotti, Maria Ornella, *Italian Women Writers from the Renaissance to the Present*, Philadelphia, PA, 1996.

Mazzuchelli, G. M., *Gli scrittori d'Italia*, Brescia, 1753–63.

Mengaldo, P. V., ed., *Poeti italiani del Novecento*, Milan, 1987.

Morandini, Giuliana, *La voce che è in lei. Antologia della narrativa femminile italiana tra '800 e '900*, Milan, 1980.

Negri, G., *Istoria degli scrittori fiorentini*, Ferrara, 1722, facsimile reprint, Bologna, 1973.

Pickering-Iazzi, Robin, *Unspeakable Women. Selected Short Stories Written by Italian Women during Fascism*, New York, 1993.

Pozzi Giovanni and Claudio Leonardi, eds., *Scrittrici mistiche italiane*, Genoa, 1988.

Russell, Rinaldina, ed., *Italian Women Writers. A Bio-Bibliographical Sourcebook*, Westport CT, 1994.

Santoro, Anna, *Guida al catalogo delle scrittrici italiane*, Naples, 1990.

   Il Novecento: antologia di scrittrici italiane del primo ventennio, Rome, 1997.

   Narratrici italiane dell'Ottocento, Naples, 1987.

Villani, Carlo, *Stelle femminili. Dizionario bio-bibliografico*, 2nd edn, Naples–Rome–Milan, 1915.

Wilson, Katharina, ed., *An Encyclopedia of Continental Women Writers*, 2 vols., New York, 1991.

   Medieval Women Writers, Athens, GA, 1984.

   Women Writers of the Renaissance and Reformation, Athens, GA, 1987.

Wilson, Katharina M. and Frank J. Warnke, eds., *Women Writers of the Seventeenth Century*, Athens, GA, 1989.

Wood, Sharon, *Italian Women Writing. An Anthology*, Manchester, 1993.

Primary texts (works by women authors asterisked in the chapters will be found in the Guide to Women Writers)

Alberti, Leon Battista, *The Albertis of Florence: L. B. Alberti's 'Della Famiglia'*, trans. Guido Guarino, Lewisburg NJ, 1971.

Ariosto, Ludovico, *Orlando furioso*, 2 vols., intro. Marcello Turchi, Milan, 1974, 1982. Trans. Guido Waldman, Oxford, 1983.

Boccaccio, Giovanni, *The Elegy of Lady Fiammetta*, trans. M. Causa-Steidler and T. Mauch, Chicago, 1990.

Bulifon, Antonio ed., *Rime di Lucrezia Marinella, Veronica Gambera, Isabella della Morra, Maria Selvaggia Borghini*, Naples, 1693.

Califronia, Rosa, *Breve difesa dei diritti delle donne*, Assisi, 1794.

Calvino, Italo, *Il sentiero dei nidi di ragno (1947)* Turin, 1964; trans. A. Colquhon, *The path to the nest of spiders*, preface by W. Weaver, Hopewell, NJ, 1993.

Carriera, Rosalba, *Diario degli anni MDCCXX e MDCCXXI*, Giovanni Vianelli, ed., Venice, 1793.

   Lettere, diari, frammenti, Bernardina Sani, ed., Florence, 1985.

Catalano, Michele, ed., *La leggenda della Beata Eustochia da Messina. Testo volgare del sec. XV*, Messina–Florence, 1950.

Chiari, Pietro, *Trattenimenti dello spirito umano sopra le cose del mondo passate presenti e possibili ad avvenire*, Brescia, 1781.

Darwin, Charles, *The Descent of Man*, London, 1871.

De Goncourt, Edmond, *Chérie*, Paris, 1883.

degli Arienti, Sabadino, *Gynevera de le clare donne*, C. Ricci and A. Bacchi della Lega, eds., Bologna, Commissione per i testi di lingua, 1887.

Del Sera, Beatrice, *Amor di virtù: commedia in cinque atti, 1548*, E. Weaver, ed., Ravenna, 1990.

di Breme, Ludovico, *Lettere*, P. Camporesi, ed., Turin, 1969.

Ebreo, Leone, *Dialoghi d'amore*, Bari, 1929; trans. F. Friedeberg-Sieley and J. H. Barnes, *The Philosophy of Love*, London, 1937.

Eliot, George, *The Mill on the Floss*, Leipzig, 1860.

Ficino, Marsilio, *Commentary on Plato's Symposium on Love,* trans. Sears Jayne, Dallas, 1985.

Flaubert, Gustave, *Madame Bovary*, Paris, 1857. Numerous translations.

Goldoni, Carlo, *Tutte le opere*, G. Ortolani, ed., 14 vols., Milan, 1936–56.

Gozzi, Gasparo, *Gasparo Gozzi. Scritti con giunta di inediti e rari*, N. Tommaseo, ed., Florence, 1849.

Gramsci, Antonio, *Quaderni del carcere (1975),* trans. J. Buttigieg, New York, 1992.

Ibsen, Henrik, *Et Dukkehjem (The Doll's House)*, 1879. Numerous translations.

Ingegneri, Angelo, *Della poesia rappresentativa, e del modo di rappresentare le favole sceniche*, Ferrara, 1598.

Leopardi, Paolina, *Lettere inedite di Paolina Leopardi*, Giampiero Ferretti, ed., Milan, 1979.

Manzoni, Alessandro, *I promessi sposi (1840–1842),* trans. B. Penman, *The Betrothed*, Harmondsworth, 1983.

Marino, Giambattista, *Adone*, Marzio Pieri, ed., Bari, 1975.

Mill, John Stuart, *The Subjection of Women*, 1869.

Piccolomini, Aeneas Sylvius, *Historia duobus amantibus*, in *L'exemplum nella novella latina del '400*, M. L. Doglio, ed., Turin, 1975.

Pirandello, Luigi, *Suo marito. Romanzo*, Florence, 1911.

Poliziano, Angelo, *Prose volgari inedite, poesie latine e greche edite e inedite*, I. Del Lungo, ed., Florence, 1867.

Speroni, Sperone, *Della dignità della donna*, in *Trattatisti del Cinquecento*, Mario Pozzi, ed., Milan–Naples, 1978.

Svevo, Italo, *La coscienza di Zeno (1923),* trans. B. de Zoete, *Confessions of Zeno*, New York, 1958.

    Una vita (1892), trans. A. Colquhoun, *A Life*, New York, 1963.

Tasso, Torquato, *Della virtù feminile e donnesca*, Maria Luisa Doglio, ed., Palermo, 1997.

    Discourses on the Heroic Poem, trans. M. Cavalcanti and I. Samuel, Oxford, 1973.

Verga, Giovanni, *I Malavoglia (1881),* trans. R. Rosenthal, *The House by the Medlar Tree*, Berkeley and Los Angeles, 1964.

Viganò, Renata, *L'Agnese va a morire*, 1949.

Zola, Emile, *Le Ventre de Paris (1873),* trans. D. Hughes and M.-J. Mason, *Savage Paris*, London, 1958.

Zonta, Giuseppe and Mario Pozzi, eds., *Trattati d'amore del Cinquecento*, Bari, 1975.

Studies

Antignani, Gerardo, *Domenica da Paradiso. Aspetti storici e momenti profetici*, Poggibonsi, 1995.

Aricò, Santo, ed., *Contemporary Women Writers in Italy*, Amherst, MA, 1990.

Arnaldi, G. and M. Pastore Stocchi, eds., *Storia della cultura veneta dalla Controriforma alla fine della Rebubblica*, Vicenza, 1985.

Arru, A. and M. T. Chialant, eds., *Il racconto delle donne. Voci, autobiografie, figurazioni*, Naples, 1990.

Arslan, Antonia, *Dame, droga e galline. Romanzo popolare e romanzo di consumo tra Ottocento e Novecento*, Milan, 1986.

    Dame, galline e regine. La scrittura femminile italiana fra Ottocento e Novecento, Milan, 1998.

    'Ideologia e autorappresentazione: Donne intellettuali fra Ottocento e Novecento', in *Svelamento. Sibilla Aleramo: una biografia intellettuale*, A. Buttafuoco and M. Zancan, eds., Milan, 1988, pp. 164–77.

'Luigi Capuana e Neera: corrispondenza inedita 1881–1885', in *Miscellanea di studi in onore di Vittore Branca*, Florence, 1983, vol. v, pp. 161–85.

Astaldi, Maria Luisa, *Nascita e vicende del romanzo italiano*, Milan, 1939.

Balbo, L. and M. P. May, 'Women's Condition: the Case of Postwar Italy', *International Journal of Sociology* 5 (1975/6), pp. 79–102.

Barański, Zygmunt and R. Lumley, eds., *Culture and Conflict in Postwar Italy*, Basingstoke, 1990.

Barański, Zygmunt and Lino Pertile, eds., *The New Italian Novel*, Edinburgh, 1993.

Barański, Zygmunt and Shirley W. Vinall, eds., *Women and Italy: Essays on Gender, Culture and History*, London, 1991.

Barzaghi, Antonio, *Donne o cortigiane?*, Verona, 1980.

Bassnett, Susan, *Feminist Experiences: the Women's Movement in Four Cultures*, London, 1986.

Bedani, Gino, Zygmunt Barański, Anna Laura Lepschy and Brian Richardson, eds., *Sguardi sull' Italia. Miscellanea dedicata a Francesco Villari dalla Society for Italian Studies*, Leeds (The Society for Italian Studies), 1997.

Bellocchi, U., ed., *Storia del giornalismo italiano*, 5 vols., Bologna, 1974–80.

Belloni, Antonio, *Gli Epigoni della Gerusalemme Liberata, con un'appendice bibliografica*, Padua, 1893.

Benson, Pamela Joseph, *The Invention of the Renaissance Woman: The Challenge of Female Independence in the Literature and Thought of Italy and England*, University Park, PA, 1992.

Berengo, Marino, *Intellettuali e librai nella Milano della restaurazione*, Turin, 1980.

Bernardi, Claudia, 'Pulp and Other Fictions: the Critical Debate on the New Italian Narrative of the Nineties', *Bulletin of the Society for Italian Studies* 30 (1997), pp. 4–11.

Besomi, Ottavio, Giulia Gianella, Alessandro Martini and Guido Pedrojetta, eds., *Forme e vicende per Giovanni Pozzi*, Padua, 1988.

Bettini, F, M. Lunetta and F. Muzzioli, *Letteratura degli anni ottanta*, Foggia, 1985.

Bianchi, D., 'Una cortigiana rimatrice del Seicento: Margherita Costa', *RCLI* 29 (1924), pp. 1–31, 187–203; and 30 (1925), pp. 158–212.

Bianchini, Angela, *Il romanzo d'appendice*, Turin, 1969.

    Voce donna, Milan, 1979.

Blelloch, Paola, *Quel mondo dei guanti e delle stoffe: profili di scrittrici italiane del '900*, Verona, 1987.

Boccia, Maria Luisa, 'Dentro e fuori le istituzioni. Le intellettuali tra professionalità e politica', *Memoria* 9 (1989).

Bochi, Giulia, *L'educazione femminile dall'Umanesimo alla Controriforma*, Bologna, 1961.

Bono, Paola, *Questioni di teoria femminista*, Milan, 1993.

Bono, Paola and Sandra Kemp, eds., *The Lonely Mirror. Italian Perspectives on Feminist Theory*, London, 1993.

Borghi, L., N. Livi Bacci and U. Treder, eds., *Viaggio e scrittura. Le straniere nell'Italia dell'Ottocento*, Florence, 1988.

Borzelli, A., *Laura Terracina, poetessa napoletana del Cinquecento*, Naples, 1924.

    Note intorno a Margherita Sarrocchi, Naples, 1935.

Bozzetti, C., P. Gibellini and E. Sandal, eds., *Veronica Gambara e la poesia del suo tempo nell'Italia settentrionale*, Florence, 1989.

Braidotti, Rosi, *Patterns of Dissonance: a Study of Women in Contemporary Philosophy*, London, 1991.

Brand, Peter and Lino Pertile, eds., *The Cambridge History of Italian Literature*, Cambridge, 1996, revised 1999.

Bridenthal, Renate, Claudia Koonz and Susan M. Stuard, eds., *Becoming Visible: Women in European History,* 2nd edn, Boston, 1987.

Bridgeman, Jane, ' "Pagare le pompe": Why Quattrocento Sumptuary Laws did not Work', in *Women in Italian Renaissance Culture and Society*, L. Panizza ed., Oxford (EHRC), 2000, pp. 209–26.

Brown, Alison, *Bartolomeo Scala (1430–1497) Chancellor of Florence*, Princeton, NJ, 1979.

Brunel-Lobrichon, D., D. Dinet, J. Gres and D. Vorreux, eds., *Sainte Claire d'Assise et sa posterité. Actes du Colloque international organisé a l'occasion du VIII centenaire de la naissance de sainte Claire*, Paris (UNESCO), 1995.

Brunetta, Gian Piero, *Storia del cinema italiano dal 1945 agli anni ottanta*, Rome, 1993.

Bullock, Alan, 'Vittoria Colonna: note e aggiunte alla edizione critica del 1982', *GSLI* 162 (1985), pp. 407–13.

Buttafuoco, Annarita, 'Italy: the Feminist Challenge', in *The Politics of Eurocommunism: Socialism in Transition*, C. Boggs and D. Plotke, eds., Montreal, 1980, pp. 197–219.

Caesar, M., 'Italian Fiction in the Nineteen-Eighties', in *Postmodernism and Contemporary Fiction*, E. J. Smith, ed., London, 1991.

Caesar, M. and P. Hainsworth, eds., *Writers and Society in Contemporary Italy*, Leamington Spa, 1984.

Caldwell, Lesley, 'Church, State and Family. The Women's Movement in Italy', in *Feminism and Materialism. Women and Modes of Production*, A. Kuhn and A. Wolpe, eds., London, 1978.

Camerino, Marinella, 'Donne nell'ingranaggio: la narrativa di Bruno Sperani', in *Les femmes écrivains en Italie (1870–1920): ordres et libertés*, E. Genevois, ed., Paris, 1994, pp. 75–89.

Cameron, Deborah, *The Feminist Critique of Language*, London, 1990.

Camilla Battista da Varano e il suo tempo: Atti del Convegno di Studi sul V centenario del monastero delle Clarisse di Camerino, Camerino, 1987.

Capuana, Luigi, 'Letteratura femminile' from *Nuova Antologia*, 1 January 1907, in *Luigi Capuana*, G. Finocchiaro Chimirri, ed., Catania, 1988.

Cardini, F., 'Santa Caterina da Bologna e il trattato "Le sette armi spirituali"', *Studi Francescani* 86 (1989), pp. 53–64.

Caretti, Laura, 'Capuana, Ibsen e la Duse', in *L'illusione della realtà: Studi su Luigi Capuana*, M. Picone and E. Rossetti, eds., Rome, 1990, pp. 199–200.

Castelli, Silvana, 'Miti, forme e modelli della nuova narrativa', in *La letteratura emarginata. I narratori giovani degli anni '70*, Walter Pedullà, Silvana Castelli and Stefano Giovanardi, eds., Rome, 1978, pp. 123–32.

Castronovo, V., G. Ricuperati and C. Capra, eds., *La stampa italiana dal Cinquecento all' Ottocento*, Bari, 1980.

Catalucci, A., *Invito alla lettura di Lalla Romano*, Milan, 1980.

Chemello, Adriana, 'The Art of Quotation in Marinella's *La nobiltà et l'eccellenza delle donne*', in *Women in Italian Renaissance Culture and Society*, L. Panizza ed., Oxford (EHRC), 2000, pp. 463–77.

'Il genere femminile tesse la sua tela: Moderata Fonte e Lucrezia Marinella', in *Miscellanea di studi*, Renata Cibin and Angiolina Ponziano, eds., Venice, 1993, pp. 85–107.

'La donna, il modello, l'immaginario', in *Nel cerchio della luna*, Marina Zancan, ed., Venice, 1983, pp. 59–170.

Chiavola Birnbaum, Lucia, *Liberazione della donna: Feminism in Italy*, Middletown, CT, 1989.

Cicioni, Mirna and N. Prunster, *Visions and Revisions: Women in Italian Culture*, Oxford, 1993.

Clough, Cecil, 'Daughters and Wives of the Montefeltro: Outstanding Bluestockings of the Quattrocento', *Renaissance Studies* 10.1 (1996), pp. 31–55.

Clubb, Louise George, *Italian Drama in the Age of Shakespeare*, New Haven, CT, and London, 1989.

Collina, Beatrice, 'Moderata Fonte e *Il merito delle donne*', *Annali d'Italianistica* 7 (1989), pp. 142–64.

Colombini, Giulia Molino, *Sull'educazione della donna*, Turin, 1869.

Conti Odorisio, Ginevra, *Donna e società nel Seicento*, Rome, 1979.

   Storia dell'idea femminista in Italia, Turin, 1980.

Corona, Daniela ed., *Donne e scrittura*, Palermo, 1990.

Cox, Virginia, 'The Single Self: Feminist Thought and the Marriage Market in Early Modern Venice', *Renaissance Quarterly* 48 (1995), pp. 513–81.

   'Women as Readers and Writers of Chivalric Poetry in Early Modern Italy', in *Sguardi sull' Italia*, G. Bedani et al., eds., Leeds, 1997, pp. 134–45.

Croce, Benedetto, 'Donne letterate del Seicento', in *Nuovi saggi sulla letteratura italiana del Seicento*, Bari, 1949, pp. 159–77.

   'La casa di una poetessa' (1901), in *Storie e leggende napoletane*, Bari, 1948.

   'La Sibilla alpina: Diodata Saluzzo Roero', in *Varietà di storia letteraria e civile*, Bari, 1935, pp. 233–42.

   Storia d'Italia dal 1871 al 1915, Bari, 1927.

Crocenzi, L., *Narratrici d'oggi*, Cremona, 1966.

Curzi, Candida, et al., eds., *Scrivere contro: esperienze, riflessioni e analisi delle giornaliste presentate al convegno 'Donne e informazione' [1977]*, Rome, 1977.

Cutrufelli, Maria Rosa, *Scritture, scrittrici. Invito alla lettura*, Palermo, 1995.

Cutrufelli, Maria Rosa, Rosaria Guacci and Marisa Rusconi, *Il pozzo segreto*, Florence, 1993.

De Clementi, A. and M. Stella, *Viaggi di donne*, Naples, 1995.

De Donato, Gigliola et al., eds., *La parabola della donna nella letteratura italiana dell'Ottocento*, Bari, 1983.

De Filippo, Titina, *Il teatro*, Naples, 1993.

De Giorgio, Michela, *Le italiane dall'Unità ad oggi*, Rome–Bari, 1992.

De Giovanni, Neria, *Artemide sulla soglia. Donne e letteratura in Italia*, Rome and Teramo, 1994.

   L'ora di Lilith. Su Grazia Deledda e la letteratura femminile del secondo Novecento, Rome, 1987.

De Giovanni, Neria and Maria Assunta Parsani, *Femminile a confronto su Alba De Céspedes, Fausta Cialente, Gianna Manzini*, Manduria, 1984.

   Femminile a confronto. Tre realtà della narrativa contemporanea: Alba de Céspedes, Fausta Cialente, Gianna Manzini, Bari–Roma, 1984.

De Grazia, Victoria, *How Fascism Ruled Women: Italy 1922–1945*, Berkeley, CA, 1992.

De Lauretis, Teresa, *Differenza e indifferenza sessuale*, Florence, 1989.

'The Essence of the Triangle, or, Taking the Risk of Essentialism Seriously: Feminist Theory in Italy, the US, and Britain', *Differences* 1.2 (1989), pp. 3–37.

'Figlie prodighe', *DonnaWomanFemme: Omelie di donne* 2–3 (1996), pp. 80– 90.

'The Practice of Sexual Difference and Feminist Thought in Italy: an Introductory Essay', Milan Women's Bookstore Collective, ed., Bloomington, IN, 1990.

De Majo, Romeo, *Donna e Rinascimento*, Milan, 1987.

De Marco, G., *Maddalena Campiglia. La figura e l'opera*, Vicenza, 1988.

De Michelis, Eurialo, *Grazia Deledda e il decadentismo*, Florence, 1938.

Del Grosso, Maria, *Donna nel Cinquecento. Tra letteratura e realtà*, Salerno, 1989.

Di Nola, Laura, ed., *Poesia femminista italiana*, Rome, 1978.

Dionisotti, Carlo, *Geografia e storia della letteratura italiana*, Turin, 1967.

Dobbs, D., 'Extra-Parliamentary Feminism and Social Change in Italy, 1971–1980', *International Journal of Women's Studies* 5.2 (1982), pp. 148–60.

Doglio, Maria Luisa, *Lettera e donna. Scrittura epistolare al femminile tra Quattro e Cinquecento*, Rome, 1993.

Duby, Georges and Michelle Perrot, eds., *A History of Women in the West*, 5 vols., Cambridge, MA, 1992–3.

Eco, Umberto, Maria Federzoni, Isabella Pezzini and Maria Pia Pozzato, *Carolina Invernizio, Matilde Serao, Liala*, Florence, 1979.

Esposito, V., *L'altro Novecento*, Foggia, 1997.

Ferguson, Margaret W., Maureen Quilligan and Nancy Vickers, eds., *Rewriting the Renaissance: The Discourses of Sexual Difference in Early Modern Europe*, Chicago, 1987.

Forgacs, David, ed., *Rethinking Italian Fascism. Capitalism, Populism and Culture*, London, 1986.

Forsas-Scott, Helena, *Textual Liberation. European Feminist Writing in the Twentieth Century*, London, 1991.

Frabotta, Biancamaria, *Letteratura al femminile*, Bari, 1980.

Fraisse, G. and M. Perrot, eds., *Emerging Feminism from Revolution to World War*, in series *A History of Women in the West*, G. Duby and M. Perrot, eds., 5 vols., vol. IV, Cambridge, MA, 1993.

Frati, Ludovico, *La donna italiana secondo i più recenti studi*, Turin, 1899.

Gatt-Rutter, John, *Oriana Fallaci. The Rhetoric of Freedom*, Oxford, 1996.

Gattucci, A., 'Le "istruzioni al discepolo" della beata Battista da Varano', *Collectanea francescana* 64 (1994), pp. 241–85.

Genevois, Emmanuelle, ed., *Les femmes écrivains en Italie (1870–1920): ordres et libertés*, Paris, 1994.

Getto, Giovanni, *Letteratura religiosa del Trecento*, Florence, 1967.

Gill, C., 'Women and the Production of Religious Literature in the Vernacular, 1300–1500', in *Creative Women in Medieval and Early Modern Italy. A Religious and Artistic Renaissance*, E. Ann Matter and John Coakley, eds., Philadelphia, PA, 1994, pp. 64–104.

Giorgetti, Cinzia, 'Il "petit tour" di Isabella Teotochi Albrizzi', *Studi Italiani* 8 (1992), pp. 117–73.

Graziosi, Marina, 'Women and Criminal Law: the Notion of Diminished Responsibility in Prospero Farinacci and other Renaissance Jurists', in *Women in Italian Renaissance Culture and Society*, L. Panizza, ed., Oxford (EHRC), 2000, pp. 166–181.

Grendler, Paul F., *Schooling in Renaissance Italy: Literacy and Learning, 1300–1600*, Baltimore, MD, 1989.

Guerci, Luciano, *La discussione sulla donna nell' Italia del Settecento. Aspetti e problemi*, Turin, 1987.

    La sposa obbediente. Donna e matrimonio nella discussione dell' Italia del Settecento, Turin, 1988.

Harrowitz, Nancy A., *Antisemitism, Misogyny and the Logic of Cultural Difference: Cesare Lombroso and Matilde Serao*, Lincoln, NE, and London, 1994.

Hellman, J. A., *Journeys among Women. Feminism in Five Italian Cities*, Oxford, 1987.

Holub, Renate, 'For the Record: the Non-Language of Italian Feminist Philosophy', *Romance Language Annual* 1 (1990), pp. 133–40.

    'The Politics of "Diotima"', *Differentia* 6 (1990), pp. 161–72.

    'Towards a New Rationality: Notes on Feminism and Current Discursive Practices in Italy', *Discourse* 4 (1981–2), pp. 89–107.

    'Weak Thought and Strong Ethics: the Postmodern and Feminist Theory in Italy', *Annali d'Italianistica* 9 (1991), pp. 124–41.

Illibato, Antonio, *La donna a Napoli nel Settecento: L'educazione femminile*, Naples, 1900.

Jardine, Lisa, 'Women Humanists: Education for What?', in *From Humanism to the Humanities: Education and the Liberal Arts in Fifteenth- and Sixteenth-Century Europe*, A. Grafton and L. Jardine, eds., London, 1986, pp. 29–57.

Jeffrey Howard, Judith, 'Patriot Mothers in the Post-Risorgimento: Women after the Italian Revolution', in *Women, War, and Revolution*, Carol R. Berkin and Clara Lovett, eds., New York, 1980, pp. 237–58.

Jordan, Constance, *Renaissance Feminism: Literary Texts and Political Models*, Ithaca, NY, 1990.

Kelly, Joan, 'Did Women Have a Renaissance?', in *Women, History and Theory*, Chicago, 1984.

    'Early Feminist Theory and the "Querelle des Femmes"', in *Women, History and Theory*, Chicago, 1984.

Kelso, Ruth, *Doctrine for the Lady of the Renaissance*, Urbana, IL, 1956, 1978.

Kemp, Sandra and Judith Squires, *Feminisms*, Oxford, 1997.

King, Margaret, *Women of the Renaissance*, Chicago, 1991.

King, Margaret and Albert Rabil Jr., eds., *Her Immaculate Hand. Selected Works by and about Women Humanists of Quattrocento Italy*, Binghamton, NY, 1983.

Kirkendale, Warren, 'L'opera in musica prima del Peri: le pastorali perdute di Laura Guidiccioni ed Emilio de' Cavalieri', in *Firenze e la Toscana de' Medici nell' Europa del '500*, Florence, 1982–3, vol. II, pp. 365–95.

Kirkham, Victoria, 'Laura Battiferra degli Ammannati's "First Book" of Poetry', *Rinascimento* (1996), pp. 1–40.

Klapisch-Zuber, Christiane, *La famiglia e le donne nel Rinascimento a Firenze*, Bari, 1988.

Klapisch-Zuber, Christiane, ed., *Silences of the Middle Ages*, in series *A History of Women in the West*, Georges Duby and Michelle Perrot, eds., 5 vols., vol. II, Cambridge, MA, 1992.

Koorn, Florence W. J., 'Women without Vows. The case of the Beguines and the Sisters of Common Life in the Northern Netherlands', in *Women and Men in Spiritual Culture, XIV–XVIII Centuries. A Meeting of South and North*, E. Schulte van Kessel, ed., The Hague, 1986, pp. 135–47.

Kraye, Jill, 'The Transformation of Platonism in the Renaissance', in *Platonism and the English Imagination*, Anna Baldwin and Sarah Hutton, eds., Cambridge, 1994, pp. 76–85.

Kristeller, Paul Oscar, 'Learned Women of Early Modern Italy: Humanists and University Scholars', in *Beyond Their Sex: Learned Women of the European Past*, P. Labalme, ed., New York–London, 1980, pp. 91–116.

Kroha, Lucienne, 'Scrittori, scrittrici e industria culturale: *Suo marito* di Luigi Pirandello', *Otto Novecento* 5 (1995), pp. 167–82.

    The Woman Writer in Late-Nineteenth Century Italy. Gender and the Formation of Literary Identity, Lewiston Queenston and Lampeter, 1992.

Labalme, Patricia, ed., *Beyond Their Sex: Learned Women of the European Past*, New York–London, 1980.

Labalme, Patricia, 'Venetian Women on Women: Three Early Modern Feminists', *Archivio Veneto* 117 (1981), pp. 81–109.

Langer, Ullrich, *Perfect Friendship: Studies in Literature and Philosophy*, Geneva, 1994.

Lazzaro-Weiss, Carol, *From the Margins to the Mainstream*, Philadelphia, PA, 1993.

Lenzi, Maria Ludovica, *Donne e Madonne: L'educazione femminile nel primo Rinascimento italiano*, Turin, 1982.

Leonardi, C., 'Caterina Vegri e l'obbedienza del diavolo', in *Forme e vicende per Giovanni Pozzi*, O. Besomi et al., eds., Padua, 1988, pp. 119–22.

Lilli, Laura and Chiara Valentini, *Care compagne. Il femminismo nel PCI e nelle organizzazioni di massa*, Rome, 1979.

Loffredo, Ferdinando, *Politica della famiglia*, Milan, 1938.

Lombroso, Cesare and Guglielmo Ferrero, *La donna delinquente, la prostituta e la donna normale*, 1893.

Lowe, Kate, 'History Writing from Within the Convent in Cinquecento Italy: the Nuns' Version', in *Women in Italian Renaissance Culture and Society*, L. Panizza, ed., Oxford (EHRC), 2000, pp. 105–21.

Lunetta, Mario, *Poesia italiana oggi*, Rome, 1992.

Luti, Giorgio, ed., *Narratori italiani del secondo Novecento*, Rome, 1985.

Macciocchi, Maria Antonietta, *Le donne e i loro padroni*, Milan, 1980.

Maclean, Ian, *The Renaissance Notion of Women: A Study in the Fortunes of Scholasticism and Medical Science in European Intellectual Life*, Cambridge, 1980.

MacNeil, A., 'The Divine Madness of Isabella Andreini', *Journal of the Royal Musical Association* 120 (1955), pp. 195–215.

Magli, Ida, *Matriarcato e potere delle donne*, Milan, 1978.

Magli, Patrizia, ed., *Le donne e i segni*, Ancona, 1985.

Magliani, Edoardo, *Storia letteraria delle donne italiane*, Naples, 1885.

Malpezzi Price, P., 'A Woman's Discourse in the Italian Renaissance: Moderata Fonte's *Il merito delle donne*', *Annali d'Italianistica* 7 (1989), pp. 165–81.

Manacorda, G., *Letteratura italiana d'oggi 1965–85*, Rome, 1987.

    Storia della letteratura italiana tra le due guerre 1919–1943, Rome, 1980.

Manieri, Rosaria M., *Donna e famiglia nella filosofia dell'Ottocento*, Lecce, 1975.

Mantese, G., 'Per un profilo storico della poetessa vicentina Maddalena Campiglia: aggiunte e rettifiche', *Archivio veneto* 81 (1967), pp. 89–123.

Marcuzzi, Cristina and Anna Rossi-Doria, *La ricerca delle donne. Studi femministi in Italia*, Turin, 1987.

Martelli, Mario, 'Lucrezia Tornabuoni', in *Les femmes écrivains en Italie au Moyen Age et à la Renaissance*, G. Ulysse, ed., Aix-en-Provence, 1994, pp. 51–86.

Masi, Ernesto, 'Il salotto di Isabella Albrizzi', in *Parrucche e sanculotti nel secolo XVII*, Milan, 1886.

Mattesini, L., 'Scrivere di sé: una rassegna critica sull'autobiografia femminile',
    Donnawomanfemme 2–3 (1993).

Meldini, Piero, *Sposa e madre esemplare. Ideologia e politica della donna e della famiglia durante
    il Fascismo*, Florence, 1975.

Merry, Bruce, *Women in Italian Literature. Four Studies Based on the Work of Grazia Deledda,
    Alba de Céspedes, Natalia Ginzburg, and Dacia Maraini*, Townsville, North
    Queensland, Australia, 1990.

Miceli Jeffries, Giovanna, ed., *Feminine Feminists: Cultural Practices in Italy*, Minneapolis,
    MN, 1994.

Migiel, Marilyn, 'Gender Studies and the Italian Renaissance', in *Interpreting the Italian
    Renaissance*, Antonio Toscano, ed., Stony Brook, NY, 1991.

Migiel, Marilyn and Juliana Schiesari, eds., *Refiguring Woman: Perspectives on Gender and
    the Italian Renaissance*, Ithaca–London, 1991.

Milan Women's Bookstore Collective, ed., *Sexual Difference: a Theory of Social-Symbolic
    Practice*, Bloomington, IN, 1990.

Mioni, Maria, *Una letterata veneziana del secolo XVIII: Luisa Bergalli*, Venice, 1908.

Moers, Ellen, *Literary Women*, London, 1977.

Moi, Toril, *Sexual/Textual Politics*, London, 1985.

Molino Colombini, Giulia, *Sull'educazione delle donne*, Turin, 1853.

Molmenti, P., *La storia di Venezia nella vita privata dalle origini alla caduta della Repubblica*,
    Bergamo, 1908.

Mondello, Elisabetta, *La nuova italiana: la donna nella stampa e nella cultura del ventennio*,
    Rome, 1987.

Montella, L., *Una poetessa del Rinascimento: Laura Terracina*, Salerno, 1993.

Morsolin, Bernardo, *Maddalena Campiglia, poetessa vicentina del secolo XVI. Episodio biografico*,
    Vicenza, 1882. Reprinted in *Atti dell'Accademia Olimpica* 17 (1982), pp. 5–76.

Mostaccio, S., 'Delle "visitationi spirituali" di una monaca. Le lettere di Tommasina
    Fieschi O. P.', in *Per lettera. La scrittura epistolare femminile tra archivio e tipografia
    secoli XV–XVII*, G. Zarri, ed., Rome, 1999, pp. 287–311.

Newbigin, Nerida, *Nuovo corpus di sacre rappresentazioni fiorentine del Quattrocento*, Bologna,
    1983.

Niccoli, Ottavia, ed., *Rinascimento al femminile*, Rome–Bari, 1991.

Nozzoli, Anna, '*La voce* e le donne', in *Les femmes écrivains en Italie (1870–1920): ordres et
    libertés*, E. Genevois, ed., vol. Paris, 1994, pp. 207–22.
    'Sul romanzo femminista degli anni settanta', *Donnawomanfemme* 5 (1977), pp. 55–74.
    Tabù e coscienza. La condizione femminile nella letteratura italiana del Novecento, Florence, 1978.

Olivieri, Mariarosa, *Tra libertà e solitudine. Saggi su letteratura e giornalismo femminile:
    Matilde Serao, Sibilla Aleramo, Clotilde Marghieri*, Rome, 1990.

Ossola, Carlo, *Dal 'cortegiano' all' 'uomo di mondo'*, Turin, 1987.

Pagels, Elaine, *Adam, Eve and the Serpent*, New York, 1988.

Palazzolo, M. I., *I salotti di cultura dell' Italia dell' Ottocento. Scene e modelli*, Milan, 1985.

Panizza, Letizia ed., *Women in Italian Renaissance Culture and Society*, in series *Legenda*,
    Oxford, European Humanities Research Centre, 2000.

Parati, Graziella, *Public History, Private Stories. Italian Women's Autobiography*, Minneapolis,
    MN, 1996.

Passerini, Luisa, *Storia e soggettività: Le fonti orali, la memoria*, Scandicci, 1988.
    Storie di donne e femministe, Turin, 1991.
    Torino operaio e fascismo, Bari, 1984.

Passerini, Luisa, ed., *Storia orale: vita quotidiana e cultura materiale delle classi subalterne*, Turin, 1978.

Petrignani, Sandra, *Firmato donna. Una donna, un secolo*, Rome, 1986.

Petrignani, Sandra, ed., *Le signore della scrittura (Interviste)*, Milan, 1984.

Pickering-Iazzi, Robin ed., *Mothers of Invention: Women, Italian Fascism, and Culture*, Minneapolis, MN, 1995.

Pickering-Iazzi, Robin, *Politics of the Visible: Writing Women, Culture and Fascism*, Minneapolis, MN, 1997.

Piéjus, F., 'La première anthologie de poèmes féminins', in *Le pouvoir et la plume*, Paris, 1982, pp. 193–213.

Pieri, Marzia, *La scena boschereccia nel Rinascimento italiano*, Padua, 1983.

Pieroni Bortolotti, Franca, *Alle origini del movimento femminile in Italia, 1848–1892*, Turin, 1963; 1986.

Porciani, Ilaria, ed., *Le donne a scuola. L'educazione femminile nell'Italia dell'Ottocento*, Florence, 1987.

Pozzato, Maria Pia, *Il romanzo rosa*, Milan, 1982.

Prosperi, Adriano, *Tribunali della coscienza. Inquisitori, confessori, missionari*, Turin, 1996.

Pullini, Giorgio, *Il romanzo italiano del dopoguerra (1940–1960)*, Padua, 1965.

Quintavalle, Maria Pia, ed., *Donne in poesia*, Udine, 1988.

Quondam, Amedeo, ed., *Le 'carte messaggiere'. Retorica e modelli di comunicazione epistolare: per un indice dei libri di lettere del Cinquecento*, Rome, 1981.

Rabil, Albert Jr., *Laura Cereta: Quattrocento Humanist*, Binghamton, NY, 1981.

Rasy, Elisabetta, *Le donne e la letteratura. Scrittrici, eroine e ispiratrici nel mondo delle lettere*, Rome, 1984.

   Ritratti di signora. Tre storie di fine secolo, Milan, 1995.

Re, Lucia, *La futurista: Benedetta Cappa Marinetti (exhibition catalogue)*, Philadelphia, PA, 1998.

Ricaldone, Luisa, *La scrittura nascosta. Donne di lettere e loro immagini tra Arcadia e Restaurazione*, Paris–Fiesole, 1996.

Robin, Diana, 'Humanism and Feminism in Laura Cereta's Public Letters', in *Women in Italian Renaissance Culture and Society*, L. Panizza, ed., Oxford (EHRC), 2000, pp. 368–84.

Roccella, Eugenia, *La letteratura rosa*, Rome, 1998.

Romano, Massimo, *Mitologia romantica e letteratura popolare. Struttura e sociologia nel romanzo d'appendice*, Ravenna, 1977.

Rose, Mary Beth, ed., *Women in the Middle Ages and the Renaissance: Literary and Historical Perspectives*, Syracuse , NY, 1986.

Rossanda, Rossana, *Anche per me: donna, persona, memoria dal 1973 al 1986*, Milan, 1987.
   Le altre: conversazioni sulle parole della politica, Milan, 1989.

Rossi, G., *Salotti letterari in Toscana*, Florence, 1992.

Salaris, Claudia, *Le futuriste: donne e letteratura d'avanguardia in Italia (1909–1944)*, Milan, 1982.

Salza, A., 'Madonna Gasparina Stampa secondo nuove indagini', *GSLI* 62 (1913), pp. 1–101.

Santoro, Anna, *Caterina Franceschi Ferrucci e le lezioni di letteratura italiana*, Naples, 1984.
   La crisi dell'intellettuale nella narrativa dell'ultimo Ottocento, Naples, 1976.

Scaraffia, L. and G. Zarri, eds., *Donna e fede. Santità e vita religiosa in Italia*, Rome–Bari, 1994.

Schio, M. and F. Taviani, *Il segreto della Commedia dell'Arte. La memoria delle compagnie italiane del* XVI, XVII *and* XVIII *secolo*, Florence, 1982.

Scriboni, M., 'Il viaggio al femminile nell' Ottocento. La principessa di Belgiojoso, Amalia Nizzoli e Carla Serena', *Annali d' Italianistica* 14 (1996), pp. 304–25.

Seidel Menchi, Silvana, Anne Jacobson Schutte and Thomas Kuehn, eds., *Tempi e spazi di vita femminile tra medioevo ed età moderna*, Bologna, 1999.

Servadio, Gaia, *La donna nel Rinascimento*, Milan, 1986.

Smarr, J. Levarie 'The Uses of Conversation: Moderata Fonte and Edmund Tilney', *Comparative Literary Studies* 31.1 (1995), pp. 1–25.

'A Dialogue of Dialogues: Tullia d'Aragona and Sperone Speroni', *MLN* 113 (1998) pp. 204–212.

Sovente, Michele, *La donna nella letteratura italiana*, Fossano, 1979.

Spagnoletti, G., *Storia della letteratura italiana del Novecento*, Rome, 1994.

Tassistro, Carlotta, *Luisa Bergalli Gozzi, la vita e l'opera sua nel tempo*, Rome, 1920.

Testaferri, Ada, ed., *Donna. Women in Italian Literature*, Toronto, 1989.

Todd, Janet, *Feminist Literary History*, Oxford, 1988.

Tomalin, Margaret, *The Fortunes of the Warrior Woman in Renaissance Literature*, Ravenna, 1982.

Troiano, R., 'Paolina Grismondi. Note sulla scrittura femminile del Settecento (con un'appendice di documenti inediti)', in *Studi in onore di Antonio Piromalli*, T. Iermano and T. Scappaticci, eds., Naples, 1994.

Turchini, Angelo, *Sotto l'occhio del padre. Società confessionale e istruzione primaria nello Stato di Milano*, Bologna, 1996.

Tylus, J., 'Natural Woman: Isabella Andreini and the First Italian Actresses', *Italian Culture* 13 (1995), pp. 75–85.

Ulysse, Georges ed., *Les femmes écrivains en Italie au Moyen Age et à la Renaissance*, Aix- en Provence, 1994.

Valerio, Adriana, *Domenica da Paradiso. Profezia e politica in una mistica del Rinascimento*, Spoleto, 1992.

Ventrone, Paola, 'Per una morfologia della sacra rappresentazione fiorentina', in *Teatro e cultura della rappresentazione. Lo spettacolo in Italia nel Quattrocento*, Raimondo Guarino, ed., Bologna, 1988, pp. 195–225.

Villari, Pasquale, *Lettere meridionali*, 1878.

Violi, Patrizia, *L'infinito singolare. Considerazioni sulla differenza sessuale nel linguaggio*, Milan, 1987.

Vovelle, M., ed., *L'uomo dell' Illuminismo*, Rome–Bari, 1992.

Walker, John, '*Ginevra de' Benci* by Leonardo da Vinci', in *National Gallery of Art: Report and Studies in the History of Art, 1967*, Washington DC, 1968.

Wanrooij, Bruno, *Storia del pudore. La questione sessuale in Italia 1860–1940*, Venice, 1990.

Weininger, Otto, *Sex and Character*, London, 1903.

Wend, Petra, *The Female Voice: Lyrical Expression in the Writings of Five Italian Renaissance Poets*, Frankfurt am Main, 1995.

West, Rebecca and Dino S. Cervigni, eds., *Annali d'Italianistica. Women's Voices in Italian Literature (Special Issue)*, 7 (1989).

Wood, Sharon, *Italian Women's Writing 1860–1994*, London, 1995.

Zaccaria, Giuseppe, ed., *Il romanzo d'appendice*, Turin, 1977.

Zambon, Patrizia, *Letteratura e stampa nel secondo Ottocento*, Alessandria, 1993.

Zancan, Marina, 'Gaspara Stampa. La differenza: questioni di scrittura e di lettura', in *Studi in onore di Vittorio Zaccaria*, M. Pecoraro ed., Milan, 1987, pp. 263–73.

Il doppio itinerario della scrittura. La donna nella tradizione letteraria italiana, Turin, 1998.

Zancan, Marina, ed., *Nel cerchio della luna: Figure di donne in alcuni testi del XVI secolo*, Venice, 1983.

Zanette, Emilio, *Suor Angelica monaca del Seicento veneziano*, Venice, 1960.

Zannoni, Pier Antonio, *Narratrici liguri del Novecento*, Genoa, 1985.

Zanotti, Francesco Maria, *Delle lettere familiari d'alcuni biografi del nostro secolo*, Venice, 1764.

Zappulla Muscarà, Sarah, ed., *Letteratura siciliana al femminile: donne scrittrici e donne personaggio*, Catania-Roma, 1984.

Zarri, Gabriella, *Le sante vive. Cultura e religiosità femminile della prima età moderna*, Turin, 1990.

'Ecrits inédits de Cathérine de Bologne et de ses soeurs', in *Sainte Claire d'Assise et sa posterité*, Brunel-Lobrichon G. et al., eds., Paris, 1995, pp. 119–230.

'Ursula and Catherine. The Marriage of Virgins in the XVIth Century', in *Creative Women in Medieval and Early Modern Italy. A Religious and Artistic Renaissance*, E. Ann Matter and John Coakley, eds., Philadelphia, PA, 1994.

Zarri, Gabriella, ed., *Donna disciplina creanza cristiana tra XV e XVII secolo. Studi e testi a stampa*, Rome, 1996.

Il monachesimo femminile in Italia dall' alto medioevo al secolo XVII, Verona, 1997.

Per lettera. La scrittura epistolare femminile tra archivio e tipografia secoli XV–XVII, Rome, 1999.

Zemon Davis, Natalie and Arlette Farge, eds., *Renaissance and Enlightenment Paradoxes*, in series *A History of Women in the West*, Georges Duby and Michelle Perrot, eds., 5 vols., vol. III, Cambridge, MA, 1993.

Zonta, Giuseppe, 'La *Partenia* di Barbara Torelli-Benedetti', *RBLI* 14 (1906), pp. 206–10.

Index

Note: page numbers in **bold type** indicate entries in the bibliographical guide.

Lightning Source UK Ltd.
Milton Keynes UK
177584UK00001B/76/P